The 1857 Indian Uprising and the Politics of Commemoration

The Cawnpore Well, Lucknow Residency, and Delhi Ridge were sacred places within the British imagination of India. Sanctified by the colonial administration in commemoration of victory over the 'Sepoy Mutiny' of 1857, they were read as emblems of empire, which embodied the central tenets of sacrifice, fortitude, and military prowess that underpinned Britain's imperial project. Since independence, however, these sites have been rededicated in honour of the 'First War of Independence' and are thus sacred to the memory of those who revolted against colonial rule, rather than those who saved it. *The 1857 Indian Uprising and the Politics of Commemoration* tells the story of these and other commemorative landscapes and uses them as prisms through which to view over 150 years of Indian history. Based on extensive archival research from India and Britain, Sebastian Raj Pender traces the ways in which commemoration responded to the demands of successive historical moments by shaping the events of 1857 from the perspective of the present. By telling the history of India through the transformation of mnemonic space, this study shows that remembering the past is always a political act.

SEBASTIAN RAJ PENDER is a research associate at Balliol College, University of Oxford.

The 1857 Indian Uprising and the Politics of Commemoration

Sebastian Raj Pender

University of Oxford

CAMBRIDGE
UNIVERSITY PRESS

University Printing House, Cambridge CB2 8BS, United Kingdom

One Liberty Plaza, 20th Floor, New York, NY 10006, USA

477 Williamstown Road, Port Melbourne, VIC 3207, Australia

314–321, 3rd Floor, Plot 3, Splendor Forum, Jasola District Centre,
New Delhi – 110025, India

103 Penang Road, #05–06/07, Visioncrest Commercial, Singapore 238467

Cambridge University Press is part of the University of Cambridge.

It furthers the University's mission by disseminating knowledge in the pursuit of
education, learning, and research at the highest international levels of excellence.

www.cambridge.org
Information on this title: www.cambridge.org/9781316511336
DOI: 10.1017/9781009052276

First published 2022

A catalogue record for this publication is available from the British Library.

Library of Congress Cataloging-in-Publication Data
Names: Pender, Sebastian Raj, 1982– author.
Title: The 1857 Indian uprising and the politics of commemoration /
Sebastian Raj Pender, University of Oxford.
Description: Cambridge ; New York, NY : Cambridge University Press, 2022. |
Includes bibliographical references and index.
Identifiers: LCCN 2021059615 | ISBN 9781316511336 (hardback) |
ISBN 9781009052276 (ebook)
Subjects: LCSH: India – History – Sepoy Rebellion, 1857–1858 – Anniversaries,
etc. | Lucknow (India) – History – Siege, 1857 – Anniversaries, etc. |
War memorials – India – History. | Collective memory – India – History – 21st
century. | Great Britain – Colonies – Public opinion – History. | India – Politics
and government – 1765–1947 – Public opinion. | Public opinion – India. |
BISAC: HISTORY / Asia / India & South Asia
Classification: LCC DS478 .P365 2022 | DDC 954.03/17–dc23/eng/20211208
LC record available at https://lccn.loc.gov/2021059615

ISBN 978-1-316-51133-6 Hardback

This book is dedicated to Janet, who never stopped reading, Ranjit, who never stopped believing, Tatsiana, who never stopped loving, and Florence, who never stopped paying!

Contents

Figures

Acknowledgements

My fascination with the history of India was born over the course of one remarkable summer when I was around fifteen years old. I had grown up listening to the stories of Madan Singh, my paternal grandfather, describing his time serving in the Royal Indian Navy (RIN) during the Second World War and better still his account of the RIN 'Mutiny' of 1946, in which he had played a notable part. But it was during that long summer holiday that I rigged up an old ADAT audio recorder and spent several weeks documenting his remarkable life. My task was made much easier by having such a willing subject! My grandfather would spend many hours writing and arranging his notes in the evening so that he would be ready to help organise his interrogator's haphazard questions into a coherent narrative the following day. The result was a long series of often comical, but sometimes tragic, personal anecdotes of events that occurred in India, the United States, the United Kingdom, Russia, the Middle East, and Africa, all seamlessly blended into an overarching story of the end of empire, and the complex and bloody process of decolonisation.

My interest in the 'Mutiny' of 1857 is a direct consequence of these and subsequent conversations, but it was whilst studying in Aberystwyth under Professor Jenny Edkins that I first began to formulate the idea for the current book. This outline was further developed during my graduate studies at Oxford under Professor Nandini Gooptu, although I didn't have the time or resources to fully develop my thoughts until I arrived at Cambridge. Supervised by Dr Shruti Kapila, I wrote a thesis which is the foundation of this book. During my time as a PhD student, I accumulated many debts of gratitude to senior academics who took the time to read and comment on my work, especially Professor Sir Christopher Bayly and Dr David Washbrook. In addition, I am enormously grateful to Dr Rosie Llewellyn-Jones, who was kind enough to discuss my work with me, and to provide me with a wealth of additional information and ideas for this project. I am likewise grateful to Dr Mary Ann Steggles, who was kind enough to offer advice and help me locate relevant information. I am also enormously grateful to my examiners, Dr Jon Wilson and Professor Kim Wagner, whose enthusiasm for and critical engagement with my thesis helped it develop significantly. I am especially grateful to Kim, who has continued to be a source of support and help ever since. I would especially like to thank him for reading draft after draft of the introduction and for giving me invaluable advice which proved instrumental in how I framed the study.

Since completing my PhD, I have been fortunate to work with a great number of senior colleagues in London, Delhi, and Oxford who have greatly supported my work. I would especially like to thank Dame Helen Ghosh, Dr Indra Sengupta, Professor Sudhir Hazareesingh, and Professor Martin Conway, who in different ways have been most generous with their help. I am also enormously grateful to everyone I have worked with at Cambridge University Press, especially Santosh Laxmi Kota, Rachel Blaifeder, and Lucy Rhymer, for all their help and support. I am also deeply indebted to the two anonymous reviewers whose comments and suggestions have been invaluable in improving and finalising this text.

A particularly rewarding and interesting part of this project was my work on Sir Joseph Noel Paton's *In Memoriam*. I am incredibly grateful to Lord Andrew Lloyd Webber for giving me access to the painting and allowing me to analyse it as well as to Sarah Miller for all her logistical help. I am most grateful to Simon Gillespie, who oversaw the technical analysis of the painting, and David Parmiter for photographing it. I am especially indebted to Galina Maksimova and Dmitry Repin, who painted a reproduction of *In Memoriam* as it would have looked when first exhibited. Another challenging but ultimately fruitful period of research was completed during my last field trip to India for this book in 2017–18 as a Max Weber Foundation Postdoctoral Fellow at The M. S. Merian – R. Tagore International Centre of Advanced Studies: Metamorphosis of the Political (ICAS:MP). I would like to thank Dr Elvira Graner, Dr Laila Abu-Er-Rub, and Mr Himanshu Chawla for all their support as well as Dr Mareen Heying, Dr Zarin Ahmad, and Dr Emilija Zabiliute for many interesting and informative conversations. I am immensely grateful to my old friend Dr Jan-Jonathan Bock, for advice on research methodology. During my fieldwork, many different individuals connected with the commemoration of the 1857 Indian uprising allowed me to interview them, or gave me access to commemoration ceremonies that they were involved in organising. I would especially like to thank Pravin Rajwanshi, Vinod Kumar Rawat, Rajendra Pratap Pandey, Rajeshwari Devi, M. P. Singh, Amaresh Misra, and Deepak and Sufi Kabir for all their help. I also owe a tremendous debt of gratitude to Prateek Hira and Pankaj Singh of Tornos, who guided me around various sites associated with 1857 and helped me locate the descendants of various individuals associated with the uprising. Pankaj also acted as my interpreter at many of the different events I attended and astounded me with his knowledge of the uprising and his ability to talk to, and make friends with, anyone!

I would also like to thank the kind and helpful staff at the Centre for South Asian Studies, the University of Cambridge; the British Library; the Bodleian

Library; the National Archives of India; the Imperial War Museum; the Lidell Hart Military Archives, Kings College London; the Manuscripts and Special Collections Room, Nottingham University; the National Archives, Kew; Rhodes House Library, Oxford; the Royal Engineers Museum, Gillingham; the Staffordshire Regiment Museum; the Templer Study Centre at the National Army Museum; and the Royal Green Jackets Museum. Whilst I am grateful to all those working at these institutions, I am especially indebted to Jill Shepherd of Wellington College for helping me locate a number of intriguing letters relating to the last flag to fly from the Residency, and to Ivor Edgar for all of his invaluable help in ferreting out every last document contained in the archives of the Royal School, Dungannon, pertaining to the transfer of Nicholson's monument from Delhi to the school grounds. I am also grateful to several funding bodies and institutions which have supported my work at different points, including the Bruckmann Trust, Peterhouse Travel Bursary, Peterhouse Fund, the Max Weber Foundation, ICAS:MP, and the School of Advanced Studies at the University of London. I am also grateful to Carmen, Gigi, and all my students at Peak Courses.

   My greatest debt is, however, to my friends and family who have put up with so very much whilst I have been writing this book and have contributed even more! I am especially grateful to Catriona Toms, Swanny, Arturas Ratkus, Ilya Berkovich, Sohan Dasgupta, Tadas Jucikas, Levi Baljer, and everyone at CUABC and KNG whose friendship has meant a great deal. I would have certainly perished on numerous occasions in India had it not been for my uncle Guru, aunty Annu, and cousin Zora Dhillon. I am especially grateful for the friendship of Zora and the many high jinks we have enjoyed together over the years. I am likewise grateful for the encouragement of my uncle and aunt Vijay and Amrita Singh, my paternal grandmother Pritam Kaur, who always ensured that I was supplied with homemade aloo paratha when I was able to visit her in Chandigarh, and my sister Jasmine Pender, who probably did write that line. Finally, my greatest thanks are to my mother Janet, who never stopped reading, my father Ranjit, who never stopped believing, my wife Tatsiana, who never stopped loving, and my grandmother Florence Morris, who never stopped paying! This book could not have been completed without each of you.

Abbreviations

ASI	Archaeological Survey of India
BJP	Bharatiya Janata Party
BMGS	British Monuments and Graves Section of the High Commission
BSP	Bahujan Samaj Party
CRO	Commonwealth Relations Office
EIC	East India Company
IOR	India Office Records
IWM	Imperial War Museum, London
LDTA	Lucknow Diocesan Trust Association
MLN	Maharani Lakshmibai Nyas
NAI	National Archives of India, Delhi
OBC	Other Backward Class
OIOC	Oriental and India Office Collection, the British Library, London
RSS	Rashtriya Swayamsevak Sangh
SP	Samajwadi Party
SPG	Society for the Propagation of the Gospel
TNA	The National Archives, Kew, London
UKHCI	United Kingdom High Commission in India
UP	Uttar Pradesh
USPG	United Society for the Propagation of the Gospel

Introduction
Meaning, Memory, and Monument

For as long as England endures, pilgrims from the mother-land will journey
to the Memorial Garden that encloses the Well of Cawnpore
                                                    – Edwin Hodder, 1882.[1]

We wandered about the grounds of the battered, shell-shattered, bullet stud-
ded Residency ... how proud we felt that night that we were British!
                                                    – John Foster Fraser, 1899.[2]

A very living interest, and all that pathos and romance which belong to a
deed of great heroism, are associated with the Ridge at Delhi
                                                    – Sir Fredrick Treves, 1905.[3]

The Cawnpore Well, Lucknow Residency, and Delhi Ridge were sacred places within the British imagination of India. Sanctified by the colonial administration in commemoration of victory over the 'Sepoy Mutiny of 1857', they were read as emblems of empire which embodied the central tenets of sacrifice, fortitude, and military prowess that underpinned Britain's imperial project in the late nineteenth century.[4] So central were these locations to British conceptions of India that Brigadier H. Bullock, head of the Graves and Monuments Section of the British High Commission, could still note their overwhelming significance as late as 1948. Writing specifically about the Cawnpore Well, Bullock claimed that it was still seen as 'hallowed ground' and was 'one of the few things in India that every Briton has heard of'.[5] Whilst these sites acted as nodal points within colonial discourse, they have gradually been incorporated into India's national story. The Lucknow Residency, for example, was designated a site of national importance in a ceremony marking the twenty-fifth anniversary of Indian Independence in 1972, during which the Residency

---

[1] Hodder, *Cities of the World*, p. 199.   [2] Fraser, *Round the World on a Wheel*, pp. 215–217.
[3] Treves, *The Other Side of the Lantern*, p. 100.
[4] To avoid unnecessary confusion, this book retains the original place names as they are spelled in the primary sources.
[5] Brigadier H. Bullock, Minute Sheet, 18 November 1948, Minute Sheet, File 11/1b Historical Monuments in India: Mutiny Memorial Well at Cawnpore, fol. 43, OIOC, IOR/R/4/84, p. 43.

was 'declared to be saturated with the blood of the Indian Martyrs, who had thus laid the First Foundation of the Freedom Fight, discounting the erstwhile belief that it was reminiscent of British Glory'.[6] Rededicated in honour of what is now officially known in India as the First War of Independence, and thus sacred to the memory of those who revolted against colonial rule, rather than those who saved it, the Cawnpore Well, Lucknow Residency, and Delhi Ridge are today proud signifiers of Indian nationalism.[7]

This book tells the story of these commemorative landscapes alongside other practices of memorialisation dedicated to the events of 1857 and, in so doing, uses them as prisms though which to view over 150 years of Indian history. Employing a methodology that sees memory as an inherently contingent and contested process rooted within the broader sociopolitical terrain, this book traces the ways in which commemoration responded to the demands of successive historical moments by shaping the events of 1857 from the perspective of the ever-changing present. From post-mutiny reconciliation, to the development of late-Victorian popular imperialism, and from the politics of post-war decolonisation, through to the rise of identity politics in post-colonial India, commemoration has consistently reflected and refracted the hopes and fears, aspirations and exigencies that defined the period. Accordingly, as the following chapters explore, the shifting practices of commemoration demanded by each of these historical contexts enables us to better understand a range of questions pertaining to identity, legitimacy, and power as successive generations (re)produce and (re)package the past for mass consumption in the constantly evolving present.

Whilst the last thirty years has seen commemoration become a focal point for studies examining a broad range of subjects including Europe's world wars, the holocaust, and the former Soviet Union, the memory building projects developed in colonial settings have been understudied.[8] This is a deficiency within the literature which is made all the more surprising when one considers that commemoration played a crucial role within the imperial project. An important component of empire's ideological apparatus, commemoration

---

[6] B. N. Chaubey to the Director General ASI, 17 August 1972, 'Improvements of Lucknow residency premises suggestion by B. N. Chaubey', NAI, ASI/HQ/Monuments/26/97/72-M.

[7] The nomenclature applied to the events of 1857 by different people at different times reflects divergent interpretations of the nature and causes of the conflict. In a very real sense, those commemorating the Sepoy Mutiny of 1857 and those commemorating the First War of Independence are memorialising fundamentally different events and their respective discussions require different terminology. This book therefore employs the most appropriate language in any given context.

[8] Though this area remains understudied, a number of important texts should be noted including the collected essays published in Geppert and Muller (eds.), *Sites of Imperial Memory*; Schwarz, *Memories of Empire*; Rothermund (ed.), *Memories of Post-Imperial Nations*; Evershed, *Ghosts of the Somme*. For studies focusing on the legacy of empire in South Asia, memory of partition has become an important subject. See for example, Pandey, *Remembering Partition*; Saint, *Witnessing Partition*.

ceremonies, and public monuments were routinely deployed by European colonial powers working alongside an informal network of elite actors to propagate an official memory of empire. Developed for consumption by coloniser, as much as for the colonised, these programmes of commemoration constructed a licensed and self-aggrandising narrative of empire's past that, at any one time, both justified its existence in the present and legitimised its continued expansion in the future.

This ideological function of colonial commemoration is apparent from even the very earliest practices of memorialisation to be conducted by the British in India. Constructed in the immediate aftermath of Robert Clive's victory at the Battle of Plassey and marking, therefore, a crucial juncture in the history of Britain's relationship with India, the first colonial monument to be built by the British on the subcontinent was explicitly concerned with justifying Britain's shift from trading power to territorial power. Taking the form of an obelisk, the monument commemorated the deaths of 123 innocent British prisoners who died in the notorious 'Black Hole of Calcutta', before going on to celebrate the fact that this 'Horrid Act of Violence' was avenged by 'his Majesty's Arms, under the conduct of Vice Admiral Watson and Coll. Clive'.[9] So construed, the Battle of Plassey is not remembered as it might well have been as a victory of conquest which was waged by the East India Company (EIC) against a legitimate local ruler with the intention of re-establishing lucrative markets and bolstering profits, but the conflict is instead justified and framed as a reaction to the cruel and merciless crimes of a tyrannical despot.[10]

This monument, marking the foundation of British superiority in India, was soon joined over the course of the following decades by additional statues dedicated to those who consolidated and extended British power in India. Accordingly, from the start of the nineteenth century onwards, monuments dedicated to men such as Warren Hastings, Lord Cornwallis, and Lord Mornington, the Marquis of Wellesley, began to become increasingly common sights in cities such as Madras, Calcutta, and Bombay.[11] Portrayed as great leaders who had succeeded in cementing British control of India, these monuments not only celebrated such men for their victories and successes in the name of Britain but also underscored the moral good they brought to India. Helping depict empire as a righteous, and sometimes even divinely ordained, mission that set out to rescue the grateful inhabitants of Asia,

[9] Inscription on monument. For more on this monument, see Coutu, *Persuasion and Propaganda*. For an analogous case of colonial commemoration, see Brown, 'Inscribing Colonial Monumentality', pp. 91–113.

[10] For more on this monument and analysis of the (re)narration of the events it commemorates, see Chatterjee, *The Black Hole of Empire*.

[11] For more on this period of commemoration in India, see Coutu, *Persuasion and Propaganda*, Chapter 9: 'India: Empire Building as a Moral Imperative', pp. 270–321.

Africa, and the New World from the enthrals of a primitive and timeless barbarism, such statues conformed to empire's metanarrative which, from the early sixteenth century onwards, helped legitimise the colonial endeavour. Among the monuments constructed by the British in India over the course of the first half of the nineteenth century, it is perhaps that dedicated to Lord Bentinck which most clearly embodies this. Portraying a governor-general who, as the memorial inscription tells its readers, 'infused into oriental despotism the spirit of British freedom, who never forgot that the end of government is the welfare of the governed, who abolished cruel rites, who effaced humiliating distinctions, who allowed liberty to the expression of public opinion', Lord Bentinck is depicted as a ruler who generously laboured on behalf of India in an attempt to replace barbarism and superstition with the values and ethos of Europe.[12]

The first half of the nineteenth century therefore saw a range of memorials constructed in prominent public spaces dedicated to notable events and individuals considered worthy of public memory, but it was from the mid-nineteenth century onwards that the construction of colonial monuments reached its zenith in India. The popularity of monumentalisation in India during this period may well be attributed to a number of local and specific causes, not least the assumption of power by the Crown in 1858, but it also reflects broader trends in how nations were choosing to perpetuate the memory of significant events and individuals. The 1850s are often seen as the start of 'statuemania' in Britain, a European-wide phenomenon that also found resonance in North America, and which developed in the second half of the nineteenth century and lasted at least until the outbreak of the Great War.[13] Within the British context, the popularity of public monumentalisation might be attributed to the widespread desire to commemorate the death, and celebrate the life, of Prime Minister Sir Robert Peel.[14] Following the great statesman's untimely death in 1851, after falling from his horse at Hyde Park Corner, a great cross-section of Britain's middle classes came together to mourn the death of a man whose life they saw as synonymous with their own rise to power and affluence in the first half of the century.[15] With monuments dedicated to the memory of Peel becoming especially profuse over the following decades in manufacturing and commercial centres across Britain, the commemorative statue became an increasingly popular form of public memorialisation utilised to mark any

---

[12] Additional details of this monument can be found in Steggles, *Statues of the Raj*, pp. 46–48; Coutu, *Persuasion and Propaganda*, pp. 313–15; Groseclose, *British Sculpture and the Company Raj*, pp. 120–21.

[13] For a useful overview of 'Statuemania' across Europe and North America, see Curtis, *Sculpture 1900–1945*, Chapter 2, 'The Tradition of the Monument', pp. 37–73.

[14] Read, 'The British Contribution to Statuemania in the nineteenth century', pp. 370–77.

[15] Ibid.

number of prominent individuals and events over this period.[16] Nor was this trend isolated to Britain. With the monument ideal spreading to British territories throughout the empire, an increasing number of monuments were commissioned for Britain's colonial territories including India.[17]

Although this period of colonial commemoration remains an area but little studied, Mary Ann Steggles has been at the forefront of attempts to catalogue such monuments. Focusing on British monumentalisation in India, Steggles has shown the extent to which cities such as Calcutta had a rich strain of memorials generously erected throughout their cityscapes, making these colonial commemorative landscapes some of the most underappreciated examples of nineteenth-century public art anywhere in the world. Whilst many of the monuments erected by the British were designed and built by local artisans, a thriving trade developed between Anglo-Indian and European artists, who were commissioned to produce some of the grandest and most significant memorials constructed in the subcontinent. This trade brought statues and memorials designed by well-known sculptors including Baron Carlo Marochetti, Sir Thomas Brock, and Matthew Noble to urban India's many vistas, *maidans*, and public parks.[18] Though successive generations of colonial administrators continued to prove popular subjects for the artists who worked on these commissions, from the mid-nineteenth century onwards, two additional motifs grew in significance.

The first of these was the British monarch. Developing in tandem with Queen Victoria emerging as the figurehead of a vast empire in the years which followed her elevation to Empress of India in 1877, statues of the imperial monarch became an extremely common sight in cities across the subcontinent. From Rawalpindi in the north to Bengaluru in the south and from Rajkot in the east to Kolkata in the west, dozens of monuments dedicated to Queen Victoria were erected in India over the course of her lifetime, as well as during the years that followed.[19] Alongside the various pageants and ceremonies which were hosted by successive Viceroys to celebrate Jubilees, coronations, and Royal visits, monuments dedicated to Queen Victoria and her successors embodied the veneration of the British monarchy that developed from the late nineteenth century onwards.[20] Acting as a unifying symbol, the imperial monarch made it possible to imagine Britain's Indian empire as a regimented and consolidated

---

[16] For useful discussions on the politics of commemoration in Britain during the latter nineteenth century, see the collection of essays in Pickering and Tyrrell (eds.), *Contested Sites*.

[17] Steggles and Barnes, *British Sculpture in India*.

[18] Ibid.

[19] For details of the many statues of Queen Victoria which were sculpted in Britain and erected in India, see Steggles, *Statues of the Raj*, pp. 178–214.

[20] For more on the relationship between monachism and empire, see MacKenzie, *Propaganda and Empire*. See also Cannadine, *Ornamentalism*.

system into which princely rulers were integrated through their allegiance to the Crown. In this respect, it was those monuments that were financed in part or in whole by Indian princes which proved the most significant. An act of reverence and deference to the British monarch, such statues stood as enduring symbols of native loyalty to the established order.

Just as the emergence of statues dedicated to members of the Royal family marked the widespread veneration of the British monarchy that developed in the late nineteenth century, monuments constructed to honour the lives and deeds of imperial soldier heroes captured the growth of popular militarism which spread throughout the empire during approximately the same period.[21] Idealised symbols of masculinity which were represented so as to embody all the attributes of the late nineteenth-century soldier hero, such monuments were erected to honour the glorious deeds of valiant British soldiers or else immortalise the contributions of whole regiments who took part in one or another of the various colonial 'small wars' that characterised the age.[22] Though there was certainly no shortage of military engagements to commemorate on the subcontinent, and still more British soldier heroes whose legacies seemed to demand memorialisation, the Indian Mutiny of 1857 stands out for the unprecedented outpouring of commemorative attention it received. The subject of enormous commemoration ceremonies and the inspiration for numerous statues and large-scale public monuments, the mutiny of 1857 became a cultural lodestone in the late Victorian era and continued to grip British attention in India until the very last days of the Raj.

Though the mutiny of 1857 would quickly emerge as the most commemorated military conflict of the era, it started out as little more than a skirmish in the garrison town of Meerut, before rapidly growing into the most serious armed challenge faced by the British empire in the nineteenth century.[23] Spreading quickly to neighbouring stations before engulfing much of north India, the mutiny brought violence to many of the region's most important towns and cities before the colonial superpower succeeded in crushing the rebellion with military resources brought to bear from across the empire, enabling the British administration to formally declare an end to hostilities in mid-1858.[24] Even before the conflict was over, the mutiny became the subject of considerable attention for writers approaching the subject from a range of

---

[21] For more on Britain's changing attitude towards the military from the mid-nineteenth century onwards, as well as its relationship with imperialism, see the collection of essays brought together in MacKenzie, *Popular Imperialism and the Military, 1850–1950*.

[22] Ibid. See also Dawson, *Soldier Heroes*.

[23] One of the best accounts of how the mutiny developed in Meerut can be found in Palmer, *The Mutiny Outbreak at Meerut in 1857*. See also Wagner, *The Great Fear of 1857*.

[24] Though hostilities were formerly brought to an end in mid-1858, the final embers of rebellion would not be extinguished until early 1859.

perspectives.[25] In addition to ubiquitous narrative histories which continue to be written to the present day, those analysing the causes and nature of the uprising number among the most abundant.[26] Focusing on a diverse range of issues including the professional grievances of sepoys, real and imagined religious violations committed by the EIC, and the political and social changes of the previous decades, this body of literature has helped us understand the dynamics of the uprising in interesting and informative ways.[27] If the causes and nature of the uprising have attracted interest from scholars concerned with imperial historiography, then the same has been true for the mutiny's impact on colonial rule. Focusing on post-mutiny trajectories of British rule, this body of literature has investigated the numerous ways in which the mutiny influenced the emerging shape of colonial policies in India in particular and the empire in general.[28]

Though the causes, nature, and material implications of the uprising remain important subjects for historians, the last forty years have seen the emergence of scholarship concerned with the mutiny's impact on British imperial culture. As this body of work has highlighted, the mutiny became an almost obsessively rehearsed story and a central component of colonial identity. Focusing on the written word and analysing how the mutiny was recorded in Britain's literary imagination, scholars working in this area have analysed an enormous number of texts often written by some of the most prominent authors of Victorian England. Poets including Lord Tennyson and Christina Rossetti, historians such as Sir George Trevelyan and Charles Ball, authors from Rudyard Kipling to Charles Dickens, and popular novelists such as George Alfred Henty and Meadows Taylor each contributed to a vast archive that has become the focus for studies interested in Britain's literary imagination of 1857.[29] Though far from identical in nature, the theoretical frameworks adopted by these studies have overwhelmingly been shaped by post-colonial theory and therefore profess a debt of gratitude to the methodological approach

---

[25] For an excellent study of British debate on the causes and nature of the mutiny during the conflict itself, see Malik, *1857: War of Independence or Clash of Civilisations?*

[26] For a good recent narrative history, see David, *The Indian Mutiny.*

[27] For recent contributions to this debate, see David, *The Bengal Army and the Outbreak of the Indian Mutiny*; Wagner, *The Great Fear of 1857*; Chakravarty, 'Mutiny, War, or Small War? Revisiting an Old Debate', pp. 135–46, (London: SAGE, 2014).

[28] Classic statements on the impact of 1857 on colonial policy in India can be found in Metcalf, *The Aftermath of Revolt*; Hutchins, *The Illusion of Permanence.* For an inciteful recent analysis of how 1857 had a broader transformative effect on colonial policy throughout the empire, see Bender, *The 1857 Uprising and the British Empire.*

[29] Trevelyan, *Cawnpore*; Ball, *The History of the Indian Mutiny*; Tennyson, *The Defence of Lucknow*; Rossetti, 'In the Round Tower at Jhansi, June 8, 1857', p. 160; Kipling, 'The Undertakers', pp. 234–55; Dickens and Collins, 'The Perils of Certain English Prisoners', pp. 237–327; Taylor, *Seeta*; Henty, *In Times of Peril.*

pioneered by Edward Said in his ground-breaking text, *Orientalism*.[30] Heavily influenced by post-structuralist theory and especially the power/knowledge nexus developed in the work of Michael Foucault, Said set out to show that the west's hegemonic discursive construction of the east was an essential technology of colonial expansion.[31] Writing in this vein, a slew of studies produced by literary theorists including Patrick Brantlinger, Gautam Chakravarty, and Grace Moore have interrogated Britain's literary archive to better understand how Britain's literary representation of the conflict contributed to colonial discourse and thus helped support European imperialism in the decades that followed.[32]

This vast and voluminous literary outpouring occasioned by 1857 was nevertheless matched by an unprecedented period of colonial commemoration. Focusing on monuments dedicated to 1857, as well as commemoration ceremonies held to mark anniversaries of the uprising, this study engages with a different, though no less significant, repository of meaning and memory that both helped shape and reflect how the mutiny was remembered in the decades that followed. Indeed, the cultural significance of 1857 is readily seen if one focuses on the practices of commemoration dedicated to the mutiny. In addition to the many small and localised commemorative acts performed on a largely ad hoc basis in conflict zones across India by both soldiers and civilians in the mutiny's immediate aftermath, the first plans for large-scale commemoration and monumentalisation began to be discussed long before the conflict was even over.[33] This early desire to memorialise the mutiny did not subside with British victory, rather the number and the complexity of proposals to commemorate the mutiny grew exponentially over the following decades leading to the construction of mnemonic landscapes in areas most closely associated with the conflict. Among these, however, it was the Cawnpore Well, Lucknow Residency, and Delhi Ridge, which succeeded in transcending their local environs to become three of the best known, and most instantly recognisable sites, and sights, of empire. When James Ricalton came to compile *India Through the Stereoscope: A Journey through Hindustan*, some fifty years after the mutiny, the author

---

[30] Said, *Orientalism*.

[31] See Foucault, *Discipline and Punish. The Birth of the Prison,* Alan Sheridan (Trans.) (London: Penguin, 1991).

[32] Brantlinger, *Rule of Darkness*, see Chapter 7, 'The Well at Cawnpore: Literary Representations of the Indian Mutiny of 1857', pp. 199–224; Chakravarty, *The Indian Mutiny and the British Imagination*; Moore, *Dickens and Empire*. For a very different approach to the subject, see Herbert, *War of No Pity*.

[33] Among the first organisations to consider how the conflict should be commemorated was the Society for the Propagation of the Gospel which began discussing the subject in October 1857. Minutes of the Standing Committee of the SPG for 29 October 1857, 'Minutes of the Standing Committee, 1857-9', Papers of the United Society for the Propagation of the Gospel, p. 56, USPG/Standing Committee Minutes 1857-9/26. For more on this proposal, along with other early discussions on large-scale commemoration, see Chapter 2 of this book.

no doubt thought it only natural that he should include these mutiny monuments among the 100 most important sites in India.[34] If such sources provided remote access to these commemorative landscapes for the many, the monuments became popular destinations for the more wealthy or adventurous who wanted to personally bear witness to them. Travelling to South Asia in order to fulfil work commitments or visiting the subcontinent purely for leisure, thousands of individuals considered visits to these sacred sites to be among the most important components of their travel itinerary within India.[35]

Visitors to these sites did more than passively experience them, rather these sacred spaces were (re)developed by successive generations impelled by the need to negotiate the past in light of the constantly evolving present and accordingly, the last British memorial dedicated to the conflict was not unveiled until 1938.[36] Even then, it is likely that monumentalisation could have continued into the 1940s had the government not decided that further commemoration should be discouraged owing to the politically precarious condition of India.[37] Nor did commemorative attention cease with formal Indian Independence in 1947. In keeping with a broader discourse on 1857 which awards it the distinction of being the prime mover within a linear nationalist narrative of the Indian Independence Movement, sites of colonial memory such as the Cawnpore Well, Lucknow Residency, and Delhi Ridge have been transformed into nationalist monuments celebrating the 'First War of Independence'. Remembered as a heroic, if unsuccessful story of resistance to colonial rule which is as replete with iconic national heroes as it is with episodes of brutal and indiscriminate retributive colonial violence, 1857 stands as a powerful element within the official history of the modern nation state's own foundation. The subject of countless new monuments constructed by a range of actors in prominent locations across north India, as

---

[34] Ricalton, *India through the Stereoscope*.

[35] Bernard Cohn helped coin the phrase 'Mutiny Pilgrimage' to describe the visits made by British tourists to these sites. Cohn, 'Representing Authority in Victorian India', pp. 165–211. See also Goswami, '"Englishness" on the Imperial Circuit', pp. 54–84. For more on the Mutiny Pilgrimage, see Chapter 3 of this book.

[36] There were, in fact, two monuments dedicated to 1857 erected in 1938. The last of these was unveiled on 1 December 1938 at Badli-ki-serai, a few miles outside of Delhi. Anon, 'Form and Order of the Unveiling and Dedication of the Memorial to the Gordon Highlanders at Badli-ki-serai near Delhi on Thursday, December 1st, 1938', 'Correspondence as Colonel of the Gordon Highlanders 1912-49', Papers of Gen. Sir. Ian Standish Monteith Hamilton, Lidell Hart Military Archives, Kings College London, HAMILTON-10-31.

[37] The unveiling of the monument resulted in a motion of adjournment being tabled in the Central Legislative Assembly by Sri Prakasa and Radhabai Subbarayan to 'censure and condemn' the Government of India for their involvement in its construction. See Extracts from Central Legislative Assembly Debates, 2 December 1938, Vol. III, 1938, published in Chatterji and Gopal (eds.), *Towards Freedom*, pp. 995–1001. For the British response to this and other suggestions to commemorate 1857 at this time, see 'Extract from Lord Zetland to Lord Lithgow, 6 December 1938', p. 14, Films Offensive to Indian Public Opinion Pts. XIII-XIX, OIOC, IOR/L/PJ/8/128 Coll. 105/A. For more on this, see Chapter 5 in this book.

well as regular commemoration ceremonies held at the national, regional, and local levels, the memory of 1857 is still alive and salient today.[38]

In comparison to the burgeoning literature on Britain's literary imagination of the mutiny, commemoration has been the subject of only piecemeal investigation by separate scholars.[39] Though significant in helping us understand elements of memorialisation, these fragmentary vignettes fail to situate the seemingly isolated memorial activities they focus on within a broader programme of commemoration. This book, therefore, offers the first systematic and comprehensive study of the subject from the immediate aftermath of the conflict up to the present day. In charting the commemoration of 1857 over this period, this book shows how a sustained focus on memorialisation helps us understand broader questions relating to Indian history. By viewing commemoration as a ship sailing upon the sociopolitical ocean of the past 160 years, this book tells us as much about the ship as the ocean, when charting its course over this period. Accordingly, the commemoration of 1857 is a lens though which a wide range of issues and sociopolitical developments which occurred over this period may be evaluated and better understood. By telling the history of India through the transformation of mnemonic space, this study reminds us that remembering the past is always a political act. Specifically, this book emphasises the extent to which the events of 1857 are in a perpetual state of becoming, as the past is negotiated by successive generations living within the ever-changing present. Before further interrogating the practices of commemoration deployed to memorialise the events of 1857, it is first necessary to outline the methodological framework utilised to understand this process, and, in so doing, it is necessary to make clear exactly what is meant here by the twin notions of 'remembering' and 'forgetting', as well as how these concepts relate to practices of 'commemoration'.

Meaning, Memory, and Monument: Commemoration and Collective Memory

Within popular western thought, and no less within much of the psychological literature on memory, remembering and forgetting are generally seen

---

[38] See Chapter 7 of this book for more on commemoration in India today.

[39] The most wide-ranging attempt to study the commemoration of 1857 can be found in Jones, *The Great Uprising in India 1857–58*, Chapter 7, 'Mutiny Memorials', pp. 180–206. For other studies which consider elements of commemoration, see Chakrabarty, 'Remembering 1857', pp. 1692–95; Tickell, *Terrorism, Insurgency and Indian-English Literature, 1830–1947*; Hannam, 'Contested Representations of War and Heritage at the Residency, Lucknow, India', pp. 199–212; Heathorn, 'Angel of Empire'; Bates and Carter, 'An Uneasy Commemoration: 1957, the British in India and the "Sepoy Mutiny"', pp. 113–35; Nagai, 'The Writing on the wall', pp. 84–96.

as fundamentally opposed phenomenon that are, at least in some respects, analogous to success and failure. In this regard, forgetting is seen as a personal failure or deficiency that one must attempt to prevent, and others must be vigilant against. Thus, even when convinced of the sincerity of a given witness, a hypothetical jury recognises that the testimony presented may not be entirely accurate owing to the inherent imperfection of memory. In this regard, shifts in sequential ordering, rhetorical emphasis, or points of fact within a witness's account over time may be seen to point towards unreliability, as may inconsistency between a witness's testimony and independent material evidence. Similarly, discrepancies between accounts provided by two or more honest witnesses would generally be seen to indicate a failure of memory. Seen in this way, forgetting appears to be a purely negative phenomenon in which otherwise significant memories are lost to a given individual, impairing their ability to faithfully recall past events and experiences. If forgetting is typically considered a deficiency, then, on the other hand, we must also acknowledge that it is a desirable necessity. Cases of hyperthymestic syndrome, in which individuals display an almost involuntary ability to remember every single excruciating detail of their lives, are considered more a burden than a blessing and certainly the exception and not the rule.[40] Like Jorge Luis Borges's 'Funes the Memorious', individuals suffering from such a condition typically experience it as a great curse which is not only mentally exhausting but also an impediment to actual cognitive reasoning.[41]

If the fallibility of our memories is generally a fact that goes unquestioned, then the cause and nature of this is rather more open to debate. In so evaluating this question, we generally encounter two diametrically opposed perspectives. Whilst some suggest that the dynamics between remembering and forgetting centre on the *availability* of memories, others point towards *accessibility* as the central problematic. The first position suggests that due to decay, displacement, or some other factor or variable, certain memories are irrevocably and irretrievably lost to a remembering individual, whilst the second perspective argues that all conscious experiences leave an indelible imprint on the mind, and any difficulty encountered in accessing these is therefore a failure of retrieval rather than encoding.[42] These two dominant perspectives on memory within psychology thus share two basic assumptions. First, memory is stored and retrieved from within the individual's brain. Second, memory and

---

[40] See, for example, Parker, Cahill, and McGaugh, 'A Case of Unusual Autobiographical Remembering', pp. 35–49.

[41] Borges, 'Funes the Memorious', pp. 87–95.

[42] Cf. Habib and Nyberg, 'Neural Correlates of Availability and Accessibility in Memory', pp. 1720–26; Tulving and Pearlstone, 'Availability versus Accessibility of information in memory words', pp. 381–91; Loftus and Loftus, 'On the Permanence of Stored Information in the Human Brain', pp. 409–20.

forgetting are locked within a purely negative opposition. If such assumptions are embedded within many academic accounts of memory and tally with a common-sense approach to the subject in the west, then it is argued here that, if we want to more fully understand the British imagination and memory of the mutiny, both of these fundamental assumptions must be seriously questioned.

With the impact of studies such as Pierre Nora's *Les Lieux de Memoire*, James Young's *The Texture of Memory*, and Paul Connerton's *How Societies Remember*, the assumption still prevalent within psychological approaches to memory that the individual is the appropriate level for analysis has been comprehensively problematised.[43] Though in many respects divergent in their approaches, such studies share a common appreciation for the social dimension of memory. In this respect at least, these perspectives owe a great debt to the methodological approach first explored in detail by Maurice Halbwachs.[44] A former student of both Henri Bergson and Emile Durkheim, Halbwachs's thought was decisively shaped by the latter resulting in him adopting a broadly functionalist approach to the study of social institutions.[45] Accordingly, Halbwachs's founding texts on what he called 'collective memory' instituted a movement away from popular psychological conceptualisations of memory, towards an approach better informed by sociological concerns. Rather than treat memory as an individual's capacity to recall past events, the approach taken by Halbwachs recognises the inherently social aspects of memory formation. Thus, within this account, memory is not individually preserved and sporadically accessed by an isolated subject, but rather 'reconstructed on the basis of the present' through collective frameworks, without which an individual has no access to the past.[46]

Such an approach to collective memory helps us better understand how the past is moulded by the present but, it may be argued, such an emphasis fails to explain how the past helps construct the present.[47] This is a central question posed by Kim A. Wagner in his study on what he calls the 'Mutiny-Motif'.[48] As Wagner shows, colonial memory of the mutiny

---

[43] Nora (ed.), *Realms of Memory*; Nora, *Rethinking France*; Young, *Texture of Memory*; Connerton, *How Societies Remember*.

[44] For a collection of Halbwachs's founding texts translated into English, see Halbwachs, *On Collective Memory*.

[45] In some respects, Halbwachs's work could be read as a detailed exposition and extension to Durkheim's social approach to memory at the same time as it is a rejection of Bergson's subjective approach. See Bergson, *Matter and Memory*; Durkheim, *The Elementary forms of the Religious Life*.

[46] Halbwachs, 'The Social Frameworks of Memory', p. 40.

[47] Although the approach taken here diverges from that developed by Barry Schwartz, I have found his discussion on the topic especially useful in considering my own approach. See Schwartz, 'Social change and collective Memory', pp. 221–36.

[48] Wagner, 'Treading upon Fires', pp. 159–97.

played an important role in shaping how later events were understood and in particular helped otherwise innocuous occurrences, or small-scale disturbances, take on the form of incipient rebellions, animating frenzied panics in response.[49] In this respect, Wagner relies upon a more traditional view of memory which sees it as an always already existing system of knowledge which is itself immune from the exigencies of the present, but may shape and direct how the present itself is understood. And yet such an approach to memory is not so irreconcilable with Halbwachs's work as may first appear. Rather a synthesis is possible, which sees each approach provide an important corrective to the other. Rather than giving the past primacy over the present or the present primacy over the past, the framework utilised in this study sees past and present existing within a mutually constitutive relationship in which each helps define the other within an interdependent and dynamic relationship.

The adoption of such a framework will further help address another tension within the literature on memory. Whilst the 'presentist' framework developed by Halbwachs emphasises the malleability of memory, other theorists have emphasised its continuity and resistance to change. In this respect, the work of Michael Schudson and Barry Schwartz has been particularly influential.[50] Addressing the mnemonic legacies of the Watergate scandal and the life of Abraham Lincoln, respectively, each author has shown how memory is produced in the present whilst, at the same time, noting that change is contingent on previous memory formations embodied in the form of, for example, books, poems, and plays. By conceptualising past and present within a mutually constitutive framework, it becomes easier to understand how each pole limits and enables the other. By refusing to give either pole primacy, it is clear that the present is, in part, a reflection of the past meaning that its impact on memory is partially a stabilising one. This, of course, holds equally true when seen from the opposite perspective. Understood thus, it is useful to consider Schwartz's point that the past is not so much replaced by novel formations, as it is perpetually being built upon. Therefore, if given enough time, it may be possible to mould collective memory into any number of novel forms which bear little or no resemblance to how they were once conceived although this is a slow and contingent process. Further, we might add, this process almost always leaves a scar, a trace, or better yet, a stain of the forgotten which persists at the margins of memory from where it may yet return.[51]

---

[49] Ibid.
[50] See Schwartz, *Abraham Lincoln and the Forge of National Memory*; Schudson, *Watergate in American Memory*.
[51] This is reminiscent of, but clearly distinct from, Sigmund Freud's work on memory. See Freud, 'A note upon the mystic writing pad'. It is also influenced by Assmann, 'Canon and Archive', pp. 97–109.

Applying this corrective to the work of Halbwachs, and returning to his socially grounded theory of memory, it is important to note that even in this pioneering approach to collective memory he was keen to stress that what was being studied was not a homogenous social phenomenon. In this respect, he presents memory as a greatly fractured and heterogeneous enterprise, in which memory is not tied to an overarching society or culture, but rather to distinct social groupings such as the family – what Yael Zerubavel has termed "'remembrance environments", lying somewhere between the strictly personal and the absolutely universal'.[52] What lies at the heart of Halbwachs's work is the conception of collective memories, in which any given individual belongs to innumerable social groups with their own collective frameworks for the reconstruction of the past. Then again, it is precisely here that collective memory taken at the national level is significant. Despite the plethora of social groups, each with distinct social frameworks of memory, broader identity positions connected with the nation have historically presented important mnemonic structures in which individuals remember their position within the nation. Thus, whilst memory across a nation is fractured by a plethora of sub- and supra-national collective memories, this is not to dispense with national memory, and certainly not to suggest that it too is divided. Despite the ubiquity of remembrance environments cutting across a nation, collective memory taken at the national level is an essential component of the construction of what Benedict Anderson has called the national imagined community.[53]

So viewed, this approach to collective memory not only shifts the level of analysis from the individual to the social, but it also requires a rather different understanding of the relationship between remembering and forgetting. Far from seeing these two forces as antagonistic elements within a struggle for memory, such an approach must recognise their inherently cooperative relationship. Forgetting is not simply the inability to remember, it is also the possibility to (re)remember. Certain memories inhibit, disrupt, or disturb the formation of new conceptions of the past and thus their 'loss' is not simply a negative act but is also productive of new memories by opening up mnemonic spaces previously hindered, congested, or barred by otherwise existing memories. It is in this respect that we may suggest that memory is a result of a dialectic of remembering and forgetting, in which the past is in a perpetual state of becoming as it is forever remade in the specific historical context of the present.

Never is the fluidity of memory more apparent than when close attention is paid to formal acts of commemoration which promise to talk about the past but inadvertently tell us more about the present. Conceived, designed, organised,

---

[52] Zerubavel, *Recovered Roots*, p. 81.   [53] Anderson, *Imagined Communities*.

and implemented within a specific historical context, commemoration invariably reflects contemporary ideological, political, and aesthetic ideals. In this respect, events and individuals once allowed to fall into obscurity may suddenly become the subject of large-scale memorial attention as they become imbued with significance owing to contemporary concerns. Alternatively, once celebrated figures may be rendered irrelevant in the present, or even become reviled as their legacies are evaluated with reference to subsequent historical developments, and in the light of modern attitudes and contemporary ideas.

To view commemoration as an inert process which reflects but does not effect change would be, however, to adopt an overly naïve approach to the subject which fails to appreciate the role of power within mnemonic articulations. Like clay on a potter's wheel, rather than an artefact found on an archaeological dig, the past is moulded through practices of commemoration to serve specific purposes or to satisfy contemporary needs. Accordingly, commemoration is a powerful tool in the hands of modern nation states and large institutions, which routinely utilise commemoration to further their own social agenda and achieve specific political objectives. Arguably, few works have done more to understand the power of commemoration than Eric Hobsbawm and Terence Ranger's notion of *The Invention of Tradition*.[54] This pioneering collection of essays demonstrates the extent to which dominant groups within society are able to mould memory according to their own interests and needs – a compelling argument that has informed a host of studies which have set out to expose specific historical processes of memory production tied to elite-led commemoration and manipulation.[55]

Nonetheless, though of undeniable importance in better understanding the operation of power within the dialectics of memory, to adopt such a top-down approach does not seem to adequately account for the construction and contestation of memory. If official articulations are studied to the exclusion of alternative conceptions of the past, then one is left with little more than ideology, or what might be called 'official memory', which may bear more or less resemblance to how the past is actually collectively remembered within the lived realities of target groups at specific historical moments.[56] In so doing, studies which conflate official memory and collective memory tend to overstate the

---

[54] Hobsbawm and Ranger (eds.), *The Invention of Tradition*.

[55] The diversity of the field is impressive. Though all critical of the 'Invention of Tradition' thesis, and sometimes, like Zerubavel, invoking the notion of 'counter-memories' which challenge dominant conceptions of the past, the following are excellent investigations into the power of state sponsored memory. Zerubavel, *Recovered Roots*; Podeh, *The Politics of National Celebrations in the Arab Middle East*; Fujitani, *Splendid Monarchy*.

[56] The notion of 'official memory' is closely associated with John Bodnar, who used the term to distinguish between how the state remembered events, and divergent 'vernacular memories', associated with specific groups. Bodnar, *Remaking America*.

power of dominant groups to construct shared ideals and beliefs by fashioning a shared past propagated by public commemoration.

This is certainly a limitation for studies that set out to understand collective memory through elite-led commemoration, but it is no less of a problem for many studies that reject a top-down approach, to focus on collective memory from the bottom-up. Such studies frequently demonstrate that what we have called official memory does not accord with how the past is remembered by specific, and generally marginalised, groups.[57] Thus, official memory as an instrument of power is shown to stand in stark contrast to how groups mobilised around class, sex, race, or any other identity position, remember the past. Often invoking Michel Foucault's insistence that power always stands in relation to resistance, many of these studies conclude that collective memory is an important space of contest in practices of domination, and thus, their study can be revealing of how power relations structure the social.[58] Nevertheless, whilst such studies are invaluable in revealing the contested nature of memory, they do not go substantially beyond Halbwachs's formula which, as we have noted, readily acknowledged the plurality of collective memory and their limitation seems closely analogous to those studies which focus purely on elite manipulation. By focusing on conflict, rather than consensus, these studies seem to either undermine the existence of collective memory taken at the national level or else, as appears to be the case, they take official memory to be dominant memory which is then shown to be contested. However, in doing so, they therefore acknowledge the ability for elites to speak for the nation and against subordinated groups.

Thus seen, both approaches to collective memory seem to share similar assumptions and whilst providing useful studies of commemoration, ultimately conflate official memory and collective memory, regardless of whether they emphasise contest or consensus. For this reason, this study develops a methodological framework that prioritises the study of official memory embodied in elite commemoration, along with a better understanding of how these acts of commemoration are incorporated into national frameworks of collective memory.[59] Seen in this way, what we are calling collective memory lies in the complex points of contact between competing memories, and commemoration provides a space in which this process is played out and might, therefore,

---

[57] See, for example, Bodnar, *Remaking America*; Centre for Contemporary Cultural Studies, *Making Histories: Studies in History-Writing and Politics*; Baker, *What Reconstruction Meant*.

[58] For Foucault's clearest exposition of power/resistance perhaps, see Foucault, *Discipline and Punish*. For Foucault's discussion of popular memory and counter-memory, see Foucault, 'Film in Popular Memory', 1989.

[59] In different ways, this can be seen as a central concern for Confino, 'Collective Memory and Cultural History', pp. 1386–403; Kansteiner, 'Finding Meaning in Memory', pp. 179–97; Schwartz and Schuman, 'History, Commemoration, and Belief', pp. 183–203.

be better understood. If collective memory is to be fully appreciated, it must be viewed as a product of this complex process of translation, negation, and conflict and not as a blanket mnemonic framework imposed by the state or any other elite group whose interest in directing and manipulating memory rarely transitions into how the past is collectively remembered. Seen in this way, the identity between how the past is framed in state-led memorialisation and how the past is actually remembered should be a matter of careful and detailed research, rather than an often unstated assumption.

This is not to depreciate those studies which choose to focus solely on ideology embodied in practices of commemoration and in better understanding the construction and contestation of official memory in relation to 1857, such a position is essential to this study. However, we will also go beyond the politics of memory, by trying to better ascertain the relationship between official memory and collective memory within the context of 1857. Such an enterprise is, however, inherently problematic. Whilst archives are piled high with accounts of construction and contestation in relation to commemoration, useful accounts of consensus are harder to locate. In this respect, we might say that in assessing the relationship between a monument and collective memory, we must look further than the accounts of those who built it, or even the accounts of those who, for example, threw tar over it. Collective memory more often resides in the quotidian experiences of those who sit quietly in the shadow of the monument, reflecting on the subject of commemoration. Such accounts are harder to locate and often simply don't exist. Then again, where such accounts are available, their utilisation can help us to reassess commemoration and rethink the relationship between official and collective memory. Whilst it can be taken as a given that elite groups attempt to mould memory into a usable form that supports their aspirations within specific historical moments, collective memory can and does remain immune from elite manipulation. A failure to fully appreciate this may produce interesting and informative studies concerning how elite groups attempt to co-opt the past and utilise it in the present, but they rarely succeed in uncovering collective memory, which does not automatically accord with the wishes, intentions, and inducements of those with the power to lead commemoration.

1 'Remember Cawnpore!'

British Counter-insurgency and the Memory of Massacre

On 1 May 1858, the ninetieth Royal Academy Summer Exhibition opened its doors to the public. Competing for the attention of viewers, from diverse positions of prominence within the Academy's Trafalgar Square gallery, were over one thousand works of art. Of varying quality and contrasting styles, the paintings incorporated such assorted subjects as the hustle and bustle of William Powell Frith's *The Derby Day* to the calm and tranquillity of Edward William Cooke's *Sunset on the Lagune*. Though many of these artworks elicited discussion among the thronging crowds who passed through the Royal Academy of Arts, one painting stood out above all others for the level of debate and dispute that it engendered among art critics and the viewing public alike.[1]

An example of the dominant Pre-Raphaelite style of the exhibition, and painted with the care and attention for which Sir Joseph Noel Paton was already becoming known, *In Memoriam* proved to be of unusual significance owing more to its choice of subject than its style or execution. As described by *The Royal Academy Review*, *In Memoriam* depicted a

group of English ladies and children ... assembled in one of the houses of Cawnpore, some in agonies of terror, others bearing themselves with the most courageous resignation, but all about to be barbarously massacred by the advancing Sepoys, who are seen passing the window, and bursting in at the door, with blood-thirsty exultation. You know at once, by the tiger eyes, and diabolical expression of the foremost mutineer, that there is no escape.[2]

Following nearly one year of violence, during which Britain's drawing rooms, public houses, and classrooms became accustomed to daily discussion centred on the unfolding events of the Indian Mutiny, the subject of Paton's painting would have been instantly recognised by all those who inspected his commemorative composition.[3] Indeed, of the many events to

---

[1] Of the various guides and reviews concerning the exhibition, the most comprehensive is The Council of Four, *The Royal Academy Review: A Guide to the Exhibition of the Royal Academy of Arts 1858.*

[2] Ibid, p. 26.

[3] For a detailed study of how the mutiny was represented in debate and in the popular press during the mutiny, see Malik, *1857: War of Independence or Clash of Civilisations?*

grab public attention, the subject of Paton's painting was among the most notorious. Following a desperate though short-lived siege in Cawnpore, the British garrison had surrendered on a promise of safe passage across the River Ganges en route to the relative safety of Allahabad. However, in what the British press considered a treacherous massacre, the fleeing party was attacked before they could escape. The surviving women and children were first incarcerated within a small building known locally as Bibighar and were subsequently brutally murdered before British forces could reach them.[4]

With the Cawnpore Massacre still so fresh in the public's memory, many found Paton's commemorative composition too distressing to confront. Therefore, even though John Ruskin seemed to consider the choice of subject matter and mode of presentation fitting, the public's reaction to the painting was described by *The Critic* as one of 'admiration mixed with repulsion' – admiration of the painting's execution, but repulsion at the subject matter.[5] As *The Times* reported, 'few love to pause on a representation, however powerful, of an incident at once so real, so ghastly, and so recent as the Indian massacres of women and children', an opinion shared by *The Royal Academy Review*, which stated that the painting would have 'attracted more attention and favourable notice had the subject been less revolting'.[6] Confronted by this wide-scale criticism of the subject and ever conscious of the commodification value of his work, achieved primarily through the sale of mass-produced engravings, Paton took the remarkable decision of making a significant alteration to his commemorative composition.[7] Accordingly, by the time *In Memoriam* was exhibited in February of the following year as part of the Exhibition of the Royal Scottish Academy, Paton had replaced the 'tiger eyed' sepoys with the distinctive figures of highland soldiers by painting over parts

---

[4] The most detailed account of the 'Cawnpore Massacre' can be found in Ward, *Our Bones Are Scattered*.

[5] Ruskin, *Notes on Some of the Principal Pictures Exhibited in the Rooms of the Royal Academy, the Old and New Societies of Painters in Watercolours, the Society of British Artists, and the French Exhibition*, pp. 14–15; Anon, 'Talk of the Studios', p. 208.

[6] Anon, 'Exhibition of the Royal Academy', p. 9; The Council of Four, *The Royal Academy Review*, p. 26.

[7] Paton's decision to alter the painting when confronted by wide-scale criticism was most likely a commercial one, owing to the fact that the vast majority of Paton's income was generated from the sale of reproductions. Accordingly, he displayed a keen interest in making his works suitable for this medium. In this regard, he was not only interested in ensuring that his subjects were carefully selected to ensure mass appeal, but he was also susceptible to technical suggestions to ensure that his paintings were suitable for reproduction. In regard to the latter, he worked closely with his brother-in-law, noted photographer David Octavius Hill, to make his later paintings particularly suitable for photographic reproduction in the late nineteenth century. See Story, *The Life and Work of Sir Joseph Noel Paton*.

of the original canvas and thus transferred the imagined space of the painting from Cawnpore to Lucknow.[8]

Located just forty miles away from Cawnpore on the opposite bank of the Ganges, Lucknow had witnessed an armed uprising at the same time as Cawnpore was engulfed in violence. Ultimately, the Lucknow garrison defended its position for eighty-seven days, all the time keeping the Union Flag flying from the highest point of the compound, until reinforcements commanded by Generals Henry Havelock and James Outram arrived to assist. The siege was finally broken by an extensive army commanded by the newly appointed commander-in-chief, Sir Colin Campbell, who succeeded in rescuing the beleaguered garrison after nearly six months of combat.[9] If Cawnpore, therefore, proved to be a troubling and destabilising depiction of the uprising that undermined previously solidified discourses of racial superiority, imperial strength, and even national security, Lucknow may legitimately be seen as its counter-weight. Though the siege of Cawnpore represented a signal failure on behalf of the British empire to maintain the security of its colonial possessions, enacted through the impotence of the British soldiers stationed at Cawnpore to protect even their own mothers, wives, and children, the siege of Lucknow was seen as a suturing signifier which reaffirmed many of the exact values undermined by the Cawnpore Massacre.

Here, on a single canvas, two of the most powerful, though conflicting, representations of the Indian Mutiny in the British imagination are explored. Whilst the military disaster that culminated in the 'Cawnpore Massacre' represents the fragility and vulnerability of Britain's imperial project, the Relief of Lucknow symbolises British gallantry, martial victory, and the ultimate stability of empire. Whilst news of the fate of the Cawnpore garrison dominated how the British public and popular press imagined the uprising in the latter months of 1857, by the start of the following year, there was a clear shift away from the troubling, humiliating, and

---

[8] Heather Streets has argued that Paton's choice of Highland soldiers to represent the triumphant arrival of British forces is far from incidental and rather represented a broader appreciation of the unrivalled martial prowess of Highland soldiers, which itself owed much to the mutiny. See Streets, *Martial Races*, pp. 61–62. See also Mukharji, 'Jessie's Dream at Lucknow', pp. 77–113, p. 88.

[9] For a useful history of the mutiny in Awadh that sets the events in Lucknow and the Residency within context, see Mukherjee, *Awadh in Revolt, 1857–58*. There are many published diaries and first-hand accounts of the siege, each of which is invaluable in and of itself. If one wanted to read a first-hand account that gives a broad narrative of the siege, a good choice would be Gubbins, *An Account of the Mutinies in Oudh and the Siege of the Lucknow Residency*. However, the experiences of Gubbins were not universal. For a fascinating study of six separate diaries kept by women during the siege, which show the disparate conditions endured depending on sex, race, class, and resources, see Blunt, 'Spatial Stories under Siege', pp. 720–38.

Figure 1.1 Sir Joseph Noel Paton, *In Memoriam*. c. 1858, oil on panel, 123 cm × 96.5 cm, private collection. Photo by David Parmiter.

destabilising narration of the mutiny in Cawnpore in favour of an emphasis on the heroic struggle and victory exemplified by Lucknow. In this respect, Paton's decision to alter his commemorative painting was part of a broader process in which the meaning and memory of the mutiny was rewritten and reformulated in the immediate aftermath of the conflict. Eschewing a focus on British impotence to prevent the bloody and traumatic slaughter of the women and children held prisoner in Cawnpore and instead moving towards a celebration of British success in relieving the Residency, the painting appears to be an excellent example of how Britain's memory was reconfigured from early 1858 onwards.[10]

This chapter focuses on the construction and reconstruction of the mutiny in the British imagination and charts how this shift in representation exemplified by Paton's painting developed over the course of the conflict itself. As will be argued in subsequent chapters, however, the apparently triumphant representation of the conflict that began to develop from 1858 onwards was only ever superficial in nature. Eagerly consumed, if never really believed, such an imagining of 1857 could sometimes belie, but never efface, the terrifying memories of violence and bloodshed that animated them. In beginning to formulate this argument, this chapter will reread Paton's *In Memoriam*. By viewing the painting as a palimpsest, it is apparent that Paton's final version of it remains stained by the acute fear that characterised the original work: the very fear that the revised painting was consciously designed to obscure. By viewing the modified canvas as an unsuccessful attempt to efface the residue of colonial anxiety that continued to linger in the wake of the mutiny, *In Memoriam* comes to serve as an invaluable allegory for how the mutiny would be publicly commemorated and collectively remembered by the British over the following decades.

Initial Reports of Mutiny and the British Imagination

Though the causes of the mutiny continue to be a widely debated topic, it is incontrovertible that the introduction of greased cartridges for use with the newly issued Enfield rifle was the immediate source of the disturbances which grew into an armed uprising engulfing much of North India.[11] Up until the 1850s, variations of the Land Pattern Musket, commonly known as 'Brown Bess', remained the weapon of choice for the armies of both the British and the East India Company and thus served in conflicts across Europe and throughout the British Empire for over 100 years. Despite the weapon's longevity, the limited effective range of the rifle was highlighted during the

---

[10] Moore, *Dickens and Empire*. Focusing on the written word rather than pictorial representation, Gautam Chakravarty makes a similar argument in Chakravarty, *The Indian Mutiny and the British Imagination*.

[11] Though it is necessary to recount the major events of 1857–58 that would become the focus of commemoration in the years which followed, this chapter does not intend to engage with or resolve the myriad points of contention which exist within the literature. Nor does this chapter intend to set out an objective account of events against which subsequent memory formations may be judged and ranked according to their 'accuracy'.

1840s in a number of colonial conflicts, including the First Anglo-Afghan War at the start of the decade and the Anglo-Sikh wars at its conclusion. The Enfield rifle, which boasted an effective range of one thousand yards, ten times that of the Brown Bess, appeared to offer the solution and, following its use during the Crimean War, emerged as a fully battle-tested replacement for the iconic Brown Bess.[12]

Whilst the British soldiers who returned from the Crimea generally found the Enfield rifle to be one of the few pieces of standard-issue kit which proved itself in the field, the weapon was immediately unpopular in the sub-continent owing to rumours that the cartridges were coated in pig and cow fat, coupled with the necessity for the soldier to bite open the cartridge to access the gun powder or even suck the cartridge to increase lubrication prior to firing.[13] This practice was in contravention of the dietary prohibitions followed by both Hindus and Muslims, making the gun entirely unsuitable for large sections of the army who, from the moment of the Enfield's introduction at the start of 1857, began to make their feelings known to their officers both individually and collectively through acts of protest and insubordination which ranged from the voicing of individual concerns to acts of collective violence.[14] The most notable among these early disturbances occurred in the garrison town of Barrackpore, where one Sepoy named Mangal Pandey openly encouraged his fellow soldiers to refuse the greased cartridges and attempted to incite a general revolt against the British before attacking and injuring his sergeant-major and a lieutenant-adjutant. Sepoys who witnessed the scuffle were implored by each party to intervene on their respective side, but in the main the onlookers remained passive observers.[15] Finally, after a desperate struggle, Mangal Pandey turned his rifle on himself in an attempt to commit suicide but failed to deliver an immediately lethal shot. The badly injured and incapacitated sepoy was arrested and subsequently executed on 8 April 1857 in the presence of a large number of British and Indian soldiers assembled for the occasion. With the intention of emphasising the message which those who witnessed the macabre spectacle should take away with them, Major-General J. B. Hearsey ordered that the native troops present should approach the gallows subsequent to the execution, before announcing

---

[12] Smithurst, *The Pattern 1853 Enfield Rifle*. See also Reynolds, *The Lee-Enfield Rifle*.

[13] Adjunct General's Office Horse Guards, *Instruction of Musketry 1856*.

[14] The best accounts of these early events and their relationship to the later uprising can be found in Wagner, *The Great Fear of 1857*; Palmer, *Mutiny Outbreak at Meerut*.

[15] Major-General J. B. Hearsey, C. B., Commanding the Presidency Division, to Colonel R. J. H. Birch, C. B., Secretary to the Government of India, in the Military Department, dated Barrackpore, 9 April 1857, Forrest (ed.), *Selections from the Letters, Despatches, and Other State Papers, Preserved in The Military Department of the Government of India, 1857–58*, pp. 109–13.

that 'they had now witnessed the punishment for mutiny' and that he 'bid them to take warning by it'.[16]

News of this event in Barrackpore spread quickly across India, as did reports of similar incidents at Berhampore, Lucknow, and Ambala, where protest and resistance to the new rifle caused further trouble to develop. With unrest and ill-discipline seemingly running throughout the army, commanding officers of native regiments began to view their own men as a potential source of danger and, as a consequence, many sought to take steps to prevent or mitigate against a potential mutiny occurring within the ranks of the soldiers under their command. One such officer was Colonel George Carmichael Smyth, the commanding officer of the 3rd Bengal Light Cavalry which, following service during the First Anglo-Sikh War, had returned to Meerut from the Punjab in 1854. Meerut, situated at an important junction on the Grand Trunk Road around forty miles away from the ancient Mughal capital of Delhi, was home to one of the largest and most important cantonments in India. Separated into distinct living quarters, it was home to three British and three native regiments and thus boasted one of the highest ratios of British to native soldiers anywhere in India. Whilst this parity made Meerut an unlikely location for open mutiny, it perhaps also resulted in increased complacency among the British officers based there, who acted with a greater sense of impunity than those living in stations with a higher numerical discrepancy.

This was exemplified by the actions of Colonel Smyth who, on 24 April, decided to confront reports of dissatisfaction, disturbances, and agitation among the native troops by assembling ninety trusted members of his regiment in an open and public forum and giving them each a direct order to load the newly issued rifle. The result was disastrous, with only five of the soldiers acquiescing, leaving the divisional commander, General Hewitt, with little alternative but to pursue the conviction of the remaining eighty-five on a count of mutiny.[17] The men were duly convicted, with seventy-four sepoys sentenced to ten and the remainder to five years' imprisonment. As recorded by the joint-magistrate of Meerut, Francis Spencer Wigram, their punishment was given maximum publicity, presumably to

[16] Major-General J. B. Hearsey, C. B., Commanding the Presidency Division, to Colonel R. J. H. Birch, C. B., Secretary to the Government of India, in the Military Department, dated Barrackpore, 8 April 1857, Forrest, *Selections*, p. 107. Like much of 1857, the meaning, intentions, and impact of Mangal Pandey's actions in Barrackpore are the subject of considerable debate. For a concise evaluation, see Mukherjee, *Mangal Pandey*. For a record of the interrogation of Mangal Pandey, see Captain G. C. Hatch, Deputy Judge Advocate-General, to Colonel R. J. H. Birch, C. B., Secretary to the Government of India, in the Military Department, No. 131, dated Calcutta, 9 April 1857, Forrest, *Selections*, Vol. I, pp. 107–08.
[17] Memorandum from Colonel K. Young, Judge Advocate-General of the Army to Colonel C. Chester, Adjunct-General of the Army, No. 389, dated Head-Quarters, Shimla, 29 April 1857, Forrest (ed.), *Selections from the Letters, Despatches, and Other State Papers, Preserved in The Military Department of the Government of India*, 1857–58, pp. 237–40.

act as a deterrent, and also carried additional aspects of humiliation when their 'sentence was read to them at a general parade, before all the troops here stationed.... They were ironed and marched straight to our gaol, there to be confined until we could find means of distributing them to the different large Indian gaols'.[18]

Hewitt's punishment of those sepoys who disobeyed Smyth did not prove popular among the other native soldiers stationed in Meerut, who publicly and privately protested against their imprisonment until an open state of mutiny developed within the cantonment on 10 May. Ultimately, this disorder saw members of the 3rd Light Cavalry breaking into the local jail, freeing the incarcerated members of their regiment being held there, along with around 720 other prisoners convicted of a range of offences.[19] Joined by the two native infantry units also stationed in Meerut, and with their numbers further bolstered by a broad spectrum of the local population, the rebels now turned on the British community, killing several officers and their families and further destroying the houses and property of many more over the course of a frantic few hours in which the pre-existing order was inverted in a most sudden outburst of violence. The apparent freedom with which the mutinous sepoys operated was greatly aided by the initial indecision shown by the senior officers commanding at Meerut and further exasperated by their later adoption of purely defensive tactics which enabled the bulk of the mutineers to leave the city bound for Delhi with almost complete impunity.[20]

The mutineers, many on horseback others on foot, covered the short distance separating them from Delhi in a single night and began arriving in the ancient Mughal capital during the early hours of 11 May.[21] Their first objective on reaching the walled city was to contact Bahadur Shah II, nominally the twentieth Mughal Emperor, but in reality, a man whose position was entirely dependent upon the East India Company. Shown little respect by the British, and devoid of any tangible political power, Bahadur Shah could at least enjoy the comforts which a most generous pension could provide and the autonomy to live as he chose within the imposing confines of the Red Fort.[22] Despite

---

[18] Wigram, *Mutiny at Meerut, 1857–58*, p. 6.

[19] The 3rd Light Cavalry's decision to attack the jail may have been motivated by more than simply a desire to release their comrades. In total, forty-one jails were attacked during the mutiny, often as the first overt sign of rebellion in an area. Following Clare Anderson, it may be argued that the colonial jail was seen by the indigenous population as a potent symbol of British power in India, making it a natural target for attack. For a detailed analysis of the role of the prison building as a focus for mutinous soldiers, both in Meerut and elsewhere, see Anderson, *Indian Uprising of 1857–58*.

[20] For an objective assessment of how commanding officers responded to the uprising, see Palmer, *Mutiny Outbreak at Meerut*, pp. 106–18.

[21] The best account of the mutiny in Delhi can be found in Dalrymple, *The Last Mughal*.

[22] For the role of Bahadur Shah II in the early nineteenth-century Delhi, see Spear, *Twilight of the Mughals*.

the emperor's advanced age and physical frailty, he provided an important, if somewhat reluctant rallying point for the mutineers who were drawn to him as a symbol of a bygone age. Despite the rebels' enthusiasm, Bahadur Shah remained apprehensive about joining the rebellion, and it was not until the numerical superiority of the rebels left the ailing emperor with little feasible alternative that he accepted his position at the head of the mutiny.[23]

With eyewitness reports of the sudden and unexpected arrival of the rebels at Delhi finally reaching the British lines, orders were given to prevent the mutineers from gaining access to the walled city by closing and barricading all of the gates. To help strengthen their position, arrangements for guns to be placed on the walls and to guard the most vulnerable positions were made, and the British began to prepare for a potential siege. Unlike Meerut which, as we have seen, boasted a strong British military presence, Delhi was not stationed by any British regiments and was instead home to just three native infantry regiments commanded by British officers. With the sepoys' loyalty in doubt, a more forward defence was considered unwise; rather, Brigadier Harry Graves, the senior British officer, preferred to await relief from reinforcements which he wrongly assumed were in pursuit of the mutineers from Meerut. With no sign of the much anticipated relief force reaching Delhi and with more mutineers continuing to arrive as the morning wore on, a report of a large gathering of rebels at the Kashmiri Gate was received by Brigadier Graves, who promptly sent Colonel John Ripley to lead the 54th Native Infantry Regiment to help strengthen the position. This decision, however, proved a disaster with the 54th sympathising with the mutineers and joining their ranks after helping to murder their own officers. As the number of rebels pouring into Delhi began to swell, the 38th and the 74th Native Infantry Regiments were quick to also side with the mutineers whose numbers were further augmented by a large crowd drawn from the civilian inhabitants of the city. This unruly and uncoordinated mob turned its attention on the British inhabitants of Delhi, who found themselves trapped within the city walls and were thus afforded little chance of escape unless they could find passage to the relative safety of the British lines below the Delhi Ridge.[24]

In the ensuing bloody scenes, men, women, and children were openly murdered and their bodies left where they fell. Shops and houses were pillaged, and any valuables were seized by the crowd, who then set ablaze whatever remained

[23] The extent to which Bahadur Shah II was unwilling to assume a position at the head of the rebellion is a matter of some disagreement among scholars, which often hinges on broader debates over whether the mutiny was the result of a conspiracy. Cf. Hussain, *Bahadur Shah Zafar and the War of 1857 in Delhi*; Dalrymple, *The Last Mughal*, see especially pp. 171–74 and pp. 439–45; Wagner, *The Great Fear of 1857*, see especially Chapters 13 and 15.
[24] As Dalrymple emphasises, the violence was aimed at Indian Christians as much as at British Christians. Dalrymple, *The Last Mughal*, pp. 207–13.

behind. By the early afternoon, those looking eastwards from the British lines were alarmed to see thick clouds of black smoke rising from the walled city and moving towards them. Many of the survivors of the initial outburst of violence who were fortunate enough to find their way towards the Ridge began to take shelter within the confines of the Flagstaff Tower, which was hurriedly being secured on the orders of Brigadier Graves. Under the protection of a small and dishevelled, though still loyal company of the 38th Light Infantry, and with the tenuous security offered by a growing number of armed officers with two light field guns at their disposal, conditions remained desperate. With no sign of the expected relief force from Meerut, and with conditions ever deteriorating, the survivors were left with little choice but to beat a hasty and disorganised retreat. Some on horseback, others crowded into carriages, and the least fortunate on foot, the surviving British population fled the city, leaving it in the hands of the mutineers with the startled octogenarian emperor at their head.[25]

Initial Reaction in Britain

Pierre Nora distinguishes between two types of 'event' which may come to occupy a central position within a nation's memory – 'foundational' and 'spectacular'. The former being 'events that may have seemed relatively minor and gone almost unnoticed at the time but upon which posterity has conferred the grandeur of a new beginning ... then there are events ... that are immediately invested with symbolic significance and treated, even as they are unfolding, as if they were being commemorated in advance'.[26] It is with the latter of these that the 'Sepoy Mutiny' appears most naturally identified. Within a remarkably short period of time, popular 'mutiny novels', blending fact with fiction, became part of the staple diet of British school children eager for adventure.[27] Graphic 'personal accounts' were consumed by a British public hungry for the authentic experience of 'far India', and a range of poems and plays explored the event and helped shape a collective memory of the mutiny for all those who came into contact with them.[28] However, the initial response in Britain to reports of disturbances was rather different. Characterised by a critical engagement with a great range of British institutions which were held accountable for the disaffection,

---

[25] For an astounding collection of documents that paint a vivid picture of daily life in rebel held Delhi, see Farooqui (ed.), *Besieged*.

[26] Nora, *Realms of Memory*, pp. 17–18.

[27] According to Patrick Brantlinger, there were at least eighty novels dealing with the mutiny published before the start of the Great War. Brantlinger, *Rule of Darkness*, pp. 199–224.

[28] Among the most read personal accounts of the mutiny were Forbes-Mitchell, *Reminiscences of the Great Mutiny, 1857–59*; Sherer, *Havelock's March on Cawnpore 1857*. Among the earliest plays to deal with the mutiny was Boucicault, 'Jessie Brown, or, the Relief of Lucknow', pp. 101–32. The most famous poets to write about the mutiny were Lord Tennyson and Christina Rossetti. Tennyson, *The Defence of Lucknow*; Rossetti, 'In the Round Tower at Jhansi, June 8, 1857'.

the unfolding events in India were thought to be the product of British administrative failings. Following in the immediate aftermath of the Crimean War, it seems certain that this initially critical response to news of the mutiny was significantly framed by the British experience of the recently concluded conflict.

Whilst the prospect of war with Russia had been greeted with unabashed national enthusiasm in the winter of 1853, this changed as reports of supply-line blockages, failing equipment and bumbling senior military figures turned enthusiasm to disappointment, frustration, and even national shame in what was perceived to be a deeply embarrassing episode carried out on the global stage.[29] Though such a representation of the unfolding events is perceivable within a broad range of the cultural production over the course of the conflict, it was *The Times* that most fundamentally guided public opinion on the war.[30] Helping *The Times* dictate how the war was understood on the home front were two developments in news media, one technological and the other editorial, which combined during the conflict to alter how the British public conceptualised armed conflict. The electric telegraph had first been used by the British press to report the birth of Queen Victoria's fourth child, Alfred Ernest Albert, in 1844, and now was to revolutionise the way in which the British press was able to report on the Crimean War, and to change how armed conflict itself was conceptualised within Britain by speeding up communication between the war zone and the British metropole.[31] It was, however, the editorial innovation which saw the birth of the modern war correspondent embedded with the troops, in the form of Irish journalist William Howard Russell, that brought the 'reality' of war to the British breakfast table in a way never before thought possible.[32]

Whilst Russell's reports on the early phases of the conflict primarily sought to convey a 'bird's eye view' of proceedings in the form of a relatively traditional grand battle narrative which focused on the fight and underlined the gallant and the brave, this was to change as the British Army was forced to contend with the harsh winter of 1854–55. Confronted by a bitter Russian winter for which the British army was ill-prepared, Russell turned his attention to the plight of the common soldier who was being forced to contend with many deprivations as a result of a lack of equipment suitable for the conditions.[33] With the limitations and failings of the army further brought into focus for

[29] Markovits, *The Crimean War in the British Imagination*.
[30] This point was well expressed in the official history of *The Times* when it stated that 'nothing is more notable in the history of *The Times* than the part it played in the Crimean War. It was not only the chief recorder of the events of that war: it can be counted among the protagonists'. The Times, *The History of the Times*, p. 132.
[31] Markovits, *The Crimean War in the British Imagination*.
[32] Ibid. For William Howard Russell's writing during the war, see Bentley (eds.), *Russell's Despatches from the Crimea, 1854–56*.
[33] The causes of Britain's military failures are the subject of debate. Cf. Woodham-Smith, *The Reason Why*; Luvaas, *The Education of an Army*; Strachan, *Wellington's Legacy*.

Russell through the direct and immediately evident comparison of the British army with its allies, *The Times* began a campaign at home to raise awareness of the state of the army.[34] Eschewing the traditional focus on the deeds of gallant officers, Russell's reports at this time succeeded in exposing levels of military mismanagement and incompetence never before imagined and held them responsible for the intense suffering of ordinary soldiers.[35] The response in Britain was both immediate and overwhelming, with public opinion swiftly swinging away from the collective confidence with which the war was greeted and towards an intensely critical engagement with both the military hierarchy and the government, both of which were seen to be responsible for the unfolding disaster in the Crimea.[36]

The Crimean War was brought to a final, though unconvincing and unsatisfactory conclusion with the treaty of Paris, signed around a year before the first reports of military disturbances in India reached British shores. Accordingly, the British response to news of the mutiny in India seems to have been greatly shaped by the critical discourse that still emanated from the multiple failings in Russia. As a result, many British commentators and correspondents writing for British newspapers seem to have sympathised with the Indian sepoy in much the same way they had with the common soldier during the war with Russia, and thus the mutiny was portrayed as something between a justifiable protest in response to legitimate grievances and an unfortunate result of administrative errors. *The Times*, in particular, was ever ready to apportion blame on what Charles Dickens famously termed 'The Circumlocution Office' in his serial novel, *Little Dorrit*, and the mutiny at first appeared to the general public as yet another example of organisational and managerial failure.[37]

An interesting example of this can be seen in a letter written by Major-General H. T. Tucker and addressed to the editor of *The Times*, which stated that whilst 'many causes have combined' to lead to the present situation, there is none which has proven more significant than 'the glaring error of greasing cartridges … with tallow…. It appears truly wonderful that it should not have occurred to any of the authorities in Calcutta charged with the issuing of these cartridges that tallow … would seriously outrage the feelings and prejudices of all the native troops'.[38] A number of days later, in a second letter, he went

---

[34] Markovits, *The Crimean War in the British Imagination.*   [35] Ibid.

[36] The traditional focus on written sources in evaluating how the Crimean War was understood by contemporary audiences has recently been expanded to consider other mediums. See, for example, Keller, *The Ultimate Spectacle*; Lalumia, 'Realism and Anti-Aristocratic Sentiment in Victorian Depictions of the Crimean War', pp. 25–51; Williams (ed.), *Hearing the Crimean War.*

[37] Dickens, *Little Dorrit.*

[38] Major-General H. T. Tucker, Letter to editor, *The Times*, 24 June 1857, p. 5.

on to add that the blame for the mutiny rested 'primarily with certain Calcutta functionaries' responsible for the issuing of the aforementioned cartridges, asking his reader if it is 'strange, or anything but simple human nature, that the Hindoo soldier should feel outraged and incensed at this act, which so compromises and lowers him in the estimation of the native community.... Why, the least prejudiced may well be excused for suspecting in such a procedure an organized design against caste'.[39]

Major-General Tucker's sympathetic attitude towards the 'Hindoo soldier' was far from an isolated example, rather it was indicative of the general feeling pervading the country at this time, and indeed, whilst the sepoy was almost universally portrayed as more sinned against than sinning, the only real debate concerned whether the true blame for the mutiny should be attributed to bureaucratic failings or military incompetency.[40] A well-aimed example of the latter may be found in a lengthy article published in *The Times* on 10 June 1857, just days after the first reports of the mutiny reached Britain. So striking is the article in light of the popular perception which would grip the nation just a couple of short months later that it deserves to be considered at some length. Drawing attention to the passive and submissive nature of the native sepoy, the article juxtaposes the character of the 'Hindoo' with the shortcomings of the British officer on whom the 'disorder' is blamed, an assertion which would become very popular over the following weeks as speculation into the causes of the mutiny became widespread.

The article draws attention to the intrinsic 'gentleness of the Hindoo character', with whom 'experience ... shows that a long succession of follies, violences, wrongs, and neglects can ... be committed without bearing their legitimate fruit'. Given the native population's 'wonderful pliancy of temper', the cause of the mutiny must be sought elsewhere, and an appropriate target is immediately identified in the 'British Officers' stationed in India:

We all know what young British Officers can be in their own country; we can imagine what they may become with ... many opportunities of mischief; we know from sufficient sources what the Hindoos are themselves. We have only to put these things together.... If a master neglects his school it is sure to fall into disorganisation; if the head of a mercantile business becomes slack ... it soon goes to wrack and ruin.... There must be some very positive fault, some gross misrule, to produce the deplorable events said to have taken place.

Here, what the Association for Administrative Reform, which was established in response to the managerial failings of the Crimean War, called 'an essential similarity between commercial enterprise and public administration' is provocatively expressed with this equation between private business

---

[39] Major-General H. T. Tucker, Letter to editor, *The Times*, 29 June 1857, p. 10.
[40] Malik, *1857: War of Independence or Clash of Civilisations?*

and the army which clearly apportions blame to the military's inability to function as an efficient organisation, a sentiment made explicit when the author concludes by taking issue with the punishments meted out to native regiments which had mutinied.[41] The article suggests that the company should punish the true guilty party, and thus, 'let it put all the European officers on half pay, seeing that their neglect is the chief cause of these misfortunes', a proportionate and just punitive measure which would universally 'be hailed as a triumph of justice'.[42]

As should therefore be apparent, this initial discourse on the mutiny, which emerged in response to early reports of disaffection and the first signs of violence, depicted the mutinous sepoy as a largely innocent victim of British failings. In this respect, the sepoy was equated with the common British soldier who fought against Russia earlier in the decade, and whose suffering, as a result of incompetent officers and administrative inefficiency, had so outraged the British public. Overtly sympathetic to the demands made by the Indian sepoys, and clearly critical of the British hierarchy, this initial response to news of the mutiny stands in stark distinction to the popular imagination of the conflict which would develop over the course of the following months.

A Tale of Two Cities: Lucknow and Cawnpore

Whilst commentators and politicians in Britain continued to dissect the causes of the mutiny, violence spread quickly across north India. With news of the fall of Delhi reaching neighbouring towns, the rebellion grew swiftly and, as Rudrangshu Mukherjee has argued, the ripples of disorder ran down the River Ganges with each outbreak occurring just long enough apart to account for the relay of information from one station to another and then outwards along the great trunk roads until great portions of north India became engulfed in violence.[43] Whilst the conflict ranged across a vast and varied number of locations and terrains from the isolated hill station of Muree in the north-west of the Himalayas to the rolling planes which surrounded the coastal town of Karachee, within the British imagination, the conflict became synonymous with the urban warfare which engulfed many of north India's most important cities. The focus on this brand of fighting helped build a picture of the mutiny in which civilians in general, and women and children in particular, were important aspects of the ontology, and their vulnerability played an important ideological function within the narration of the conflict. Whilst the reconquest of Delhi was undoubtedly the single most significant strategic objective for the

---

[41] Seale, *The Quest for National Efficiency*, p. 17. See also Anderson, 'The Administrative Reform Association of 1855', pp. 231–42.
[42] Anon, *The Times*, 10 June 1857, p. 9.   [43] Mukherjee, *Awadh in Revolt, 1857–58*.

reconquering British forces, it was the tale of two other cities that most captivated popular attention, and their disparate fates proved greatly significant in the forging of a shared imagination and collective memory of the mutiny. Located on opposite sides of the River Ganges but separated by less than fifty miles, the British populations of Cawnpore and Lucknow each found themselves besieged by numerically superior forces which, during the first days of June 1857, surrounded their hastily made and improvised fortifications, heavily bombarding their respective positions and cutting off all supply lines to the outside world.

Lucknow, famously described by William Howard Russell as one of the most beautiful cities on earth, became the capital of Awadh in 1775 during the reign of Asaf-ud-Daula.[44] Though the city was already an affluent town by the sixteenth century, its designation as the capital saw it rapidly grow into one of the most wealthy and significant cities in India, gaining a reputation beyond its prosperity to also include a distinctive sociocultural environment rich in poetry, art, and literature.[45] Whilst the Nawabs of Awadh long defended their independence, the East India Company managed to obtain significant influence in the province over the course of the late eighteenth and early nineteenth centuries, which included signing a treaty giving them direct control of a significant proportion of the region including Cawnpore, a small and seemingly insignificant town on the banks of the River Ganges. Owing to the town's proximity to the affluent city of Lucknow, matched by its convenient location for transportation, the town immediately started to grow with many traders choosing the location as a convenient site to conduct business. The rapid growth of the city, both in terms of prosperity and size, was matched by an equally rapid military expansion until, by the middle of the nineteenth century, Cawnpore had become one of the most important military stations in North India and a centre for business and commerce for the civilian population.[46]

Though Awadh was effectively under British control throughout the first half of the nineteenth century, it was officially annexed in 1856 leading to the province falling under formal British control for the first time.[47] This measure was an ostensive reaction to the follies of the Royal Court, which were argued to have a negative impact on the population of the province, but was also motivated by a desire to increase revenues and establish better and more efficient

---

[44] Russell, *My Diary in India, in the Year 1858–59*, p. 257.
[45] See Fisher, *A Clash of Cultures*. Graff (ed.), *Lucknow*, contains several relevant chapters on the development of Lucknow; Sharar and Sharar, *Lucknow*.
[46] For the development of Cawnpore from a small town into an important industrial city, see Yalland, *Traders and Nabobs*.
[47] For a useful discussion on the annexation of Awadh, with specific reference to the mutiny, see Mukherjee, *Awadh in Revolt*, see especially Chapter 2, 'Annexation and the Summary Settlement of 1856–57', pp. 32–63.

administrative control of the region. Though adamantly supported by some British administrators, the sagacity of annexation was questioned by others who argued that the measure was unworthy of a just government or simply inexpedient and likely to effect disaffection among the Indian population. The sapience of the latter view was soon justified, and it became clear that the population of the province openly mourned the demise of their former rulers and resented the formal British presence within their territory.[48] Following a year of quiet hostility punctuated by regular acts of open disobedience, sabotage, and vandalism, conditions in Lucknow rapidly deteriorated prompting the chief commissioner of Awadh, Sir Henry Lawrence, to begin preparing entrenchments in anticipation of an uprising in the province. Located on an elevated plateau to the south of the Gomti River, the entrenchments extended over a thirty-three-acre compound which surrounded the British Residency, a stately three-storey structure which was described by Martin Gubbins, the financial commissioner of Awadh, as an 'imposing pile of building'.[49] Originally built in the late eighteenth century to serve as the official seat of the British Resident General, the buildings within the compound were now fortified and stocked with provisions to mitigate against the implications of a prolonged siege in the city.

Colonel Hugh Wheeler, the commanding officer in Cawnpore, was equally mindful of the growing threat of insurrection and accordingly made his own preparations for a potential rebellion in the town.[50] A diminutive sixty-seven-year-old man who had spent nearly fifty years of his life living in India, the colonel represented an older generation of British officer who was more assimilated in the local culture than had become the habit for British officers arriving in India from the 1830s onwards. Believing in the fidelity of his troops and trusting in local power broker, Nana Sahib, to assist in dampening any rebellion among the civil population of Cawnpore, Wheeler remained confident that his station could avoid being caught up in the violence spreading outwards from Delhi. In the event of an uprising, Wheeler selected two large barrack buildings as a last refuge. Neither built substantially, and one with a thatched roof, the location offered an unlikely spot for a last stand.[51] Located

---

[48] Ibid.   [49] Gubbins, *An Account of the Mutinies in Oudh*, p. 183.

[50] As early as 19 May, Colonel Hugh Wheeler was instructed by Calcutta to 'make all preparations for the accommodation of a European force and to let it be known that you are doing it'. Telegram from the Secretary to the Government of India, in the Military Department, to the Officer Commanding at Cawnpore, dated Calcutta, 19 May 1857, Forrest, *Selections*, pp. 107–08. For an excellent account of the mutiny in Cawnpore, see Ward, *Our Bones Are Scattered*.

[51] Though subsequent historians have criticised Wheeler's choice of location for the entrenchments, the spot was also criticised by many of those forced to take shelter within them. See Shepherd, *A Personal Narrative of the Outbreak and Massacre at Cawnpore during the Sepoy Mutiny of 1857*, 4th edn., p. 7.

on the main Allahabad road and out of the native city, Wheeler suspected that in the unlikely event of a rebellion, the mutinying troops would leave the city for Delhi in much the same way as had happened in Meerut and consequentially did not see the utility in fortifying or stocking the location with supplies or ammunition. The only measure taken by Wheeler to protect the building from possible attack was the erection of a thin, four-foot mud wall around its perimeter.[52]

With both Lucknow and Cawnpore on the verge of rebellion, it was the former which was engulfed in violence first. On the evening of 30 May, the cantonments were set ablaze and a number of British officers killed before a large body of mutineers attacked the British lines before retreating to a position outside the city. With conflicting reports regarding the enemy's strength and position, Sir Henry Lawrence was persuaded to lead a pre-emptive strike against the enemy. Known as the Battle of Chinhut, the engagement quickly became a rout. With the entire British population, together with many loyal Indian soldiers and civilians, now confined to the Residency the siege of Lucknow had begun. Further strengthening the position by demolishing surrounding buildings which could act as cover to an approaching enemy and building additional earthworks around the area, Lawrence prepared for further attacks which soon came, cutting off the Residency from the outside world and pinning down the British party in a perilous position.

With conditions in Cawnpore also rapidly deteriorating, the British population of the city took shelter within the scanty protection afforded by their entrenchments when a small skirmish around the city's treasury and magazine indicated the start of insurrection. Initially, the mutinying force seemed to conform to Wheeler's expectation by appearing to leave Cawnpore en route to their comrades in Delhi; however, their return two days later dispelled the beleaguered party of its hope that it would be able to wait out the conflict. Under the command of Nana Sahib, who now threw in his lot with the rebellion, the mutinying soldiers attacked Wheeler's entrenchments on the morning of 6 June. Confined to a precarious and poorly fortified position, running low on rations and with precious little protection from enemy fire, illness, and the beating sun, the surviving British party was nearing annihilation when Nana Sahib sent Wheeler an ultimatum, offering him the opportunity to surrender in return for safe passage out of the city. Capitulating to the rebels, the surviving members of the garrison were escorted to Satichaura Ghat where, as previously agreed, they were presented with dozens of boats ready to bear them across the river. In what the British press subsequently described as a treacherous ambush, the majority of the party were killed as they boarded these boats

[52] See Ward, *Our Bones Are Scattered*, pp. 112–18.

with the surviving women and children taken prisoner and incarcerated in a building locally known as Bibighar. Following over two weeks' imprisonment, during which British forces commanded by General Henry Havelock won a series of engagements bringing them to within reach of Cawnpore, the rebels decided to eliminate the last living witnesses to events in the city.[53] Hacking the women and children to death before stripping their dead bodies of clothing and depositing their bloody, dismembered corpses into a nearby well, Nana Sahib and the great majority of the rebel force quit Cawnpore and took refuge in a number of nearby towns and cities.[54]

'Remember Cawnpore!': Cawnpore and Counter-insurgency

Although the exact motives that animated the 'Cawnpore Massacre' remain opaque, its impact on counter-insurgency and the British imagination of the conflict is clear. Though the military response to the mutiny had, from the very earliest stages, employed oppressive and brutal tactics designed to put down the revolt, it is possible to identify a degree of distinction between the initial military response and the bloody vengeance that was waged in the wake of the massacre. Just as importantly, it is possible to chart a significant shift in how the conflict was imagined in Britain. As noted previously, Britain's initial engagement with the mutiny was highly critical of British officers and administrators, who were seen to collectively shoulder responsibility for the developing troubles in India. At the same time, early reports elicited sympathy for the disaffected sepoys, who were depicted as innocent victims of British misadministration. However, with reports of rebel violence filtering back to the metropole, this initial response rapidly dissolved in the flood of outrage and public animosity that welled up the moment news of the 'Cawnpore Massacre' reached British shores. Indeed, reports of the bloody and brutal murder of innocent and helpless women and children were productive of an intense imperial crisis during which a blend of fear and hatred helped produce popular support for British troops, who were actively encouraged in their utilisation of savage methods to avenge those women and children who had already perished, whilst also battling to defend or rescue those who remained imperilled in other active theatres. At the same time, all sympathy for the rebels' cause

[53] Probably unbeknown to the rebels, a small number of the victims of the Satichura Ghat Massacre had survived. There were also a few survivors who were either imprisoned or living in secret in Cawnpore. For the account of one such survivor, see Shepherd, *A Personal Narrative*.

[54] For contrasting though useful analyses of the massacres in Cawnpore, see Mukherjee, *Spectre of Violence*; Mukherjee, 'Satan Let Loose upon the Earth', pp. 92–116; English, 'The Kanpur Massacres in India in the Revolt of 1857', pp. 169–78. For a popular Victorian account of the Cawnpore Massacre, see Trevelyan, *Cawnpore*.

quickly dissipated. Rather than equating the causes of disaffection articulated by the sepoys with the suffering of the common soldier in the Crimea, the mutineers were reimagined as depraved demons against whom no act of war was too extreme or merciless if it could help bring an end to what was now understood to be a barbaric uprising.

The connection between British counter-insurgency and the desire for revenge in the wake of the Cawnpore Massacre is exemplified by the emergence of the popular battle cry, 'Remember Cawnpore!', which could be heard screamed by inflamed British soldiers as they charged into combat across northern India. In this way, British soldiers seized on the memory of massacre as an inducement to give no quarter to the rebels as they continued to wrestle for control of towns and cities seized by mutiny. Thus, as recalled by one soldier who served with the Volunteer Cavalry under Havelock in Cawnpore and subsequently formed part of the General's attempts to reach Lucknow, '"Cawnpore, my lads, remember Cawnpore," was the battle-cry: and woe to the black skin that came under our swords'.[55] For those rebels unfortunate enough to be captured by British forces, death came with additional levels of sadism aimed at both the mortal body and the eternal soul. This was especially true for any Indian captured in or around Cawnpore and, often arbitrarily, accused of any degree of complicity in the mutiny. In this vein, Major Bingham describes the execution of a deputy collector accused of complicity with the mutineers: 'We stuffed pork, beef and everything which could possibly break his caste down his throat ... I only wonder he lived to be hung, which I had the pleasure of witnessing'.[56] The disposal of the body carried like designs, thus, as reported by Lance Corporal Tracey, 'any person that is hanged is to remain so until eaten by the dogs and birds of prey', making the burial rituals necessary for reincarnation impossible, an eternal punishment also achieved by the burial of Hindus and cremation of Muslims.[57]

If the punitive punishments of rebels in and around Cawnpore were excessive, then the same was true across northern India. Whilst accounts of summary execution by hanging, beating, and bayonetting proliferated in contemporary accounts, the most spectacular were undoubtedly those in which the accused was blown from cannon mouth. According to one witness, such punishments were 'a horrid sight' which resulted in a 'shower of human fragments of heads, or arms, or legs', with the devastation to the mortal body of the condemned preventing reincarnation.[58] Such a sight was undoubtedly shocking to all those

---

[55] A Volunteer, *My Journal or What I did and saw between the 9th June and 25th November 1857 with an account of General Havelock's March from Allahabad to Lucknow.*
[56] Major Bingham, quoted in Hibbert, *The Great Mutiny*, p. 210.
[57] David Tracey, Lance Corporal Her Majesty's 84th, to a comrade in Dum Dum, quoted in the *Morning Post*, Friday, 2 October 1857, p. 6.
[58] Anon, 'A Few Words from the Khyber', p. 609.

who witnessed it but none more so than those closest to the scene. According to another witness of such an execution, the artillerymen responsible for firing the cannons 'had neglected putting up backboards to their guns so that, horrible to relate, at each discharge the recoil threw back pieces of burning flesh, bespattering the men and covering them with blood and calcined remains'.[59] Performed in front of large crowds of British and Indian spectators compelled by the military authorities to bear witness to the bloody scenes, these gruesome executions were clearly designed as not only a punishment to the condemned men but also a warning to all those who watched on.

Whilst reports of blowing prisoners from guns would most certainly have been roundly condemned in Britain if reported in the popular press in early 1857, such measures were greeted with considerable glee owing, according to Thomas Macaulay, to the fact that the:

...cruelties of the sepoys have inflamed the nation to a degree unprecedented in my memory ... there is one terrible cry for revenge. The account of that dreadful military execution at Peshawar – forty men blown all at once from the mouths of cannons, their heads, legs, arms flying in all directions – was read with delight by people who three weeks ago were against all capital punishment.[60]

Seen in this way, the memory of 'Cawnpore' was not only directly implicated in the ruthless measures utilised to suppress the uprising, but remembering Cawnpore also performed an important ideological service 'at home', where it helped legitimise and justify the inhuman violence which characterised British counter-insurgency. Though the reports of the Cawnpore Massacre itself may well have been sufficient to generate such a response, it was the widespread insinuation that the women suffered 'dishonor' before death which helped heighten the moral outrage to fever pitch. Indeed, such accusations of rape were not limited to Cawnpore, rather reports of systematic and often organised sexual violence were prevalent in many of the cities gripped by mutiny. To take one gruesome though almost certainly apocryphal account published in *The Times* at the height of the mutiny:

They took forty-eight females, most of them girls of from ten to fourteen ... violated them; and kept them for the base purpose of the heads of the insurrection for a whole week. At the end of that time they made them strip themselves, and gave them up to the lowest of the people, to be abused in broad daylight in the streets of Delhi. They then commenced the work of torturing them to death, cutting off their breasts, fingers and noses, and leaving them to die ... I do not believe that the world ever witnessed more hellish torments than have been inflicted on our poor fellow-countrywomen.[61]

---

[59] Griffiths, *A Narrative of the Siege of Delhi with an Account of the Mutiny at Ferzepore in 1857.*
[60] Thomas Macauley, quoted in Dawson, *Soldier Heroes*, p. 93.
[61] This account, purporting to come from a clergyman, was published as a letter to the editor of *The Times*, 25 August 1857, p. 6.

As has been discussed by a number of writers, the emergence of rape within the discourse on the mutiny was far from inevitable, rather it was a response to a specific moment of crisis within the history of the empire.[62] Indeed, such an argument is made all the more convincing when viewed alongside the paucity of actual substantiated evidence that proved or even indicated incidence of rape on anything like the levels which were reported in the popular press. Indeed, if one takes Cawnpore as the most prevalent example of widespread alleged sexual violence, official reports and depictions of the mutiny in Cawnpore consistently denied that the allegations had any veracity.[63] Similarly, if one takes the first-hand accounts written by survivors of the mutiny, including those who were taken captive by rebels, it is hard to find anything beyond rumour and suspicion to substantiate the popular belief that British prisoners suffered rape before death. This is certainly not to claim that rape did not occur, but to point out that its positioning at the centre of the mutiny was not a simple reflection of overwhelming evidence but was contingent on a number of other factors.

In explaining the emergence of rape as a trope within the discourse on the mutiny, Jenny Sharpe and Nancy Paxman have pointed towards its ideological impact.[64] With the mutiny posing a significant threat to British control of India, these writers have argued that gendered violence and accusations of sexual abuse helped support British power by positioning British women at the heart of what the mutiny meant. By construing the colonial crisis as a struggle to protect 'English ladies' from depraved Indian rebels, the threat posed to British women provided a powerful ideological justification for brutal counter-insurgency practiced in the name of protecting the sanctity of British femininity.[65] Further, this discursive construction of the mutiny helped lionise the British soldiers tasked with suppressing the rebellion. By casting them within a binary opposition with the cruel and treacherous other, British soldiers were constructed as chivalrous and courageous protectors and avengers of imperilled British women as they fought to crush the rebellion.[66] At the same time as supporting British claims of racial superiority, this same discourse helped support dominant constructions of gender. With British women portrayed as passive, if sacred objects, which required protection by their countrymen, British masculinity was threatened through a portrayal of the failure to protect the women and children in Cawnpore. Seen in this way, British masculinity could reassert itself through the bloody and vindictive acts of revenge practiced in response.

---

[62] Sharpe, *Allegories of Empire*. See also Lothspeich, 'Unspeakable Outrages and Unbearable Defilements', pp. 1–19.

[63] See Mukherjee, *Spectre of Violence*, pp. 156–59.

[64] Sharpe, *Allegories of Empire*. See also Lothspeich, 'Unspeakable Outrages'.

[65] Ibid. See also Paxman, 'Mobilizing Chivalry', pp. 5–30.

[66] Blunt, 'Embodying War', pp. 403–28.

With widespread reports of rape and massacre permeating the popular press and transforming the dominant discursive representation of the mutiny over the course of the late summer, events in India were the cause of a truly unprecedented level of public fear, fascination, and outrage. To a population which habitually paid little attention to Indian concerns, the mutiny now seemed to bring the subcontinent into public and private spaces with a truly terrifying and destabilising effect. Evidenced in the stream of incendiary newspaper articles, the fraught parliamentary debates conducted in the House of Commons and the House of Lords, and the first literary responses to the conflict that began to emerge before the end of the year, the mutiny quickly assumed its position as a national trauma perceived in specifically racial terms. Accordingly, news of signal victories over the following months was the cause of considerable solace in Britain, as much as in India, and the recapture of Delhi coupled with the Relief of Lucknow in late 1857 were heartily celebrated as essential triumphs which laid the foundations for British victory in the coming year.

Commemoration, Celebration, and Trepidation: Lucknow and Delhi

As we have seen previously, the preparations for a potential siege had been rather more robust in Lucknow than had been the case in Cawnpore and accordingly the former garrison had been rather better equipped to survive a lengthy siege when, on 30 May, several regiments of native infantry mutinied and attacked the civil lines before retreating to a position outside the city. With Lucknow in a state of open revolt, Lawrence concentrated his garrison within the Residency, which soon sheltered nearly 2,000 people of whom half were non-combatants including an overwhelming number of women and children.[67] Dramatically outnumbered by their well-provisioned enemy, the Residency was soon besieged by the rebels who, from the start of July, began to press their advantage. Laying siege to the compound and bringing several artillery pieces into range, the rebels poured volley after volley of shot and shell into the enclosed buildings resulting in death and serious injury becoming part of the daily experience of the beleaguered garrison.[68] Following news of Wheeler's

---

[67] The exact strength of the garrison is contested, and the figure given here is conservative. For details of the strength of the garrison as recorded by Martin Gubbins, see Gubbins, *An Account of the Mutinies in Oudh*, pp. 446–47.

[68] Attempts to understand the lived reality of the beleaguered garrison must take into account the disparate experience based on class, race, and gender. Blunt, 'Spatial Stories under Siege'. As Rosie Llewellyn Jones has pointed out, this is not easy owing to a lack of material written by people other than British military and civilian officers and their wives. As for life outside the Residency, even less information is available. Jones, *The Great Uprising*, Chapter 3, 'The Great Wall of Lucknow', pp. 96–128.

capitulation in Cawnpore and the subsequent massacres in the city, the siege of the Residency attained an almost sacred aura within the British imagination of the mutiny. Accordingly, a great deal of emphasis was placed on the need to relieve the beleaguered garrison which was finally reached by a relief force commanded by Generals Havelock and Outram on 25 September. Though it had initially been hoped that this relief force would be able to settle the city, or at least effect an evacuation of all those trapped within the Residency, it was soon resolved that this would not be possible owing to the numerical strength of the rebels coupled with the severe losses inflicted on the relief force as they fought their way to the Residency through the narrow winding streets of Lucknow. Nonetheless, the reinforcements helped man the various posts which had been depleted of able-bodied defenders over the previous months, and thus, their timely arrival helped secure the compound more effectively than had thus far been the case, even if it did little to discourage the besieging rebels.[69]

With the arrival of the relief force in Lucknow proving to be a key moment during the siege in Awadh, news that Delhi had been recaptured was celebrated by many as signalling the long awaited turning point in the conflict. After its capture by rebel forces in May, the following weeks and months saw Delhi become the focal point for rebels located in other centres of disaffection and a steady stream of mutineers entering the city made the recapture of Delhi an increasingly important strategic objective for the British forces tasked with suppressing the rebellion. Whilst British forces succeeded in recapturing the tactically significant Ridge in early June, with a view to launching further operations, it was decided that it would be impossible to immediately push on into the city and the British force contented themselves with attempting to establish a position overlooking the city from where they could shell many of the principal buildings of Delhi. Despite constructing an elaborate series of entrenchments on the Ridge their position remained exposed, and from the moment they set up camp they faced repeated sorties from the rebels who attempted to uproot the besieging force and drive them from the city.[70]

The attacks were ferocious with heavy casualties on both sides, but the British succeeded in holding their position until the arrival of Brigadier John Nicholson at the head of a flying column of over 4,000 men turned the conflict decisively in their favour. With British confidence already bolstered by the arrival of Nicholson, the subsequent arrival of a siege train in early September convinced many that the time was now ripe to make a concerted assault on the city. Under the charge of Lieutenant, later General Sir Alexander Taylor, and at a large cost of life, four siege batteries were established within range of the

---

[69] Mukherjee, *Awadh in Revolt*, p. 88.
[70] For a fascinating first-hand account of life on the Ridge, see Reid, *Centenary of the Siege of Delhi, 1857–1957.*

city walls and soon commenced a fierce bombardment. On the morning of 14 September, two columns entered Delhi through the breaches created by the siege batteries whilst a third column was tasked with entering the city through the Kashmiri Gate which, though badly damaged, would first have to be blown in by a small detachment of engineers. Following a great deal of desperate and often close quarter combat, the city was finally settled on 21 September.[71] With Delhi once again under British control, much of the rebellion's lifeblood was sapped and with the tide of the rebellion beginning to turn, Sir Colin Campbell, the newly appointed commander-in-chief, decided that it was now possible to launch a second attempt to relieve Lucknow. Personally leading the force into Awadh, Campbell was able to reach the Residency despite great resistance and, in late November, finally effected a full evacuation.

Though fierce conflict continued well into the new year with Lucknow not settled until March and a significant rebel army, led by Tantia Tope and Rani Lakshmibai, not suffering a conclusive defeat until June, the string of British victories in late 1857 was seen by military and political authorities to have dealt a mortal blow to the wider rebellion.[72] Similarly, many commentators writing in both India and Britain announced that the victories heralded the ultimate suppression of the uprising, bringing much needed relief, solace, and comfort to a reading public which had become accustomed to encountering newspapers filled with anxious speculation punctuated by reports of horrifying murder and sexual violence. Whilst it would have undoubtedly been possible for these commentators to take this opportunity to highlight the numerous errors made by British officers whilst fighting to suppress the mutiny, or to even return to the sharply critical discourse which had characterised Britain's initial response to the revolt, such sources of negativity were elided by the jubilance which now characterised the national mood, resulting in an almost unadulterated outpouring of celebration and triumphalism.[73] This period of unabashed euphoria saw the British soldiers responsible for defeating the mutiny credited with saving the empire and, perhaps even more importantly, defending and avenging British femininity resulting in them becoming a source of considerable national and racial pride.

---

[71] Dalrymple, *The Last Mughal*, pp. 347–49.

[72] Even then many remaining rebels attempted to rally under Tope leading to further guerrilla warfare in central India until the rebel leader was betrayed, captured, and executed by the British the following year effectively drawing a curtain on the uprising.

[73] The proximity of the mutiny to the Crimean War has been identified as an important component in how the British army was understood in the mid-nineteenth century. Whilst, as discussed earlier in the chapter, the British public were outraged by the multiple military failings of the Crimean War, the euphoric celebration of British victory over the mutiny helped temper, and even reverse, the profound sense of popular dissatisfaction with the army, and the associated calls for urgent military reform. See Hoppen, *The Mid-Victorian Generation, 1846–86*, p. 197; Burroughs, 'An unreformed Army?', pp. 161–87, p. 184. For more on the celebration of mutiny heroes in the wake of British victory, see Dawson, *Soldier Heroes*.

Represented as courageous and chivalrous heroes, *The London Review* captured something of the popular sentiment when it eulogised the army's efforts, writing:

They charged against fearful odds, crying, 'Remember the Ladies, Remember the Babies;' and now the ladies of England ought to remember them.... Let gold be gathered by our ladies, not one atom being accepted but what has been worn by a British lady; (some precious trinket would surely be cast into the collection warm from the person of England's Queen;) let all be melted, refined to the purest standard, made into the finest golden hair, and then let a braid be fixed, by a lady's hand, on the breast of every one.[74]

As melodramatic as this description is, it is far from remarkable when viewed within the context of equally laudatory depictions which appeared in the popular press around this time. If the superlatives utilised to describe British mutiny heroes in the immediate wake of the mutiny seem striking, they appear even more surprising when compared to the anxious and deeply critical response which first characterised the British reaction to the mutiny considered previously. Amounting to an abrupt shift away from the negativity and anxiety which gripped British representations of the conflict throughout the summer of 1857, this emergent discourse helped transform the mutiny from a colonial catastrophe into a glorious imperial victory within British memory over the course of the years to come. In this respect, the story of Sir Joseph Noel Paton's *In Memoriam* outlined at the start of this chapter might be seen as an allegory for a broader process in which, as Grace Moore has argued, the meaning and memory of the mutiny was rewritten and reformulated in the immediate aftermath of the mutiny.[75] Eschewing a focus on British impotence to prevent the bloody and traumatic slaughter of the women and children held prisoner in Cawnpore and instead moving towards a celebration of British success in relieving the Residency, Moore has argued that the painting 'may be viewed as a superb motif for the revisionist process'.[76] With the replacement of the Cawnpore Massacre by the Relief of Lucknow, 'key elements of the insurrection were ... removed from the painting in an attempt to turn an unpalatable catastrophe into triumph'.[77]

Whilst the celebratory discourse which emerged in the first month of 1858 and came to characterise Paton's painting is most naturally read as an assertion of imperial strength and colonial confidence, the following chapters of this book will argue that such a superficial understanding fails to adequately explain the unprecedented period of commemoration demanded by 1857. As will be argued, colonial commemoration must be read alongside the intense

---

[74] Anon, 'Crisis of the Sepoy Rebellion', pp. 530–70, pp. 557–58.
[75] Moore, *Dickens and Empire*. Maya Jasanoff makes a similar point in Jasanoff, 'Secret Signals in Lotus Flowers' p. 27:14, 21 July 2005.
[76] Moore, *Dickens and Empire,* p. 145.   [77] Ibid, pp. 145–46.

fear of further insurrection in the mould of the mutiny which coloured the colonial experience until the very last days of the British Raj. Viewed against this anxious backdrop formed by a perpetual fear of insurrection imagined through the prism of the remembered mutiny, commemoration is best read as a largely conscious and always active attempt to variously conciliate, reassure, and embolden a colonial community wracked by a pronounced sense of its own vulnerability. Designed to reassure and embolden the colonial community at times of intense fear, commemoration was less an assertion of imperial strength so much as it was an expression of colonial insecurity, vulnerability, and anxiety which could only ever succeed in belying, and sometimes concealing, but never finally effacing the anxieties it was deployed against.

In beginning to more fully explore this process, it is useful to reread *In Memoriam*. Although the abundance of contemporary reviews of the painting leaves no doubt that it originally depicted the 'Cawnpore Massacre' rather than the 'Relief of Lucknow', the lack of any photographical or pictorial record of the original painting has left art historians to speculate about exactly what changes Paton made to the original composition, and how it would have originally looked.[78] The use of X-ray analysis begins to address these questions by, in the first instance, clearly demonstrating that the changes were limited to the doorway and window. Such investigation is, however, otherwise disappointing, though not entirely futile. Paton painted using thin layers of paint which he was in the habit of scraping off the panel before making alterations limiting what X-ray analysis can tell us about the original painting. It is, however, possible to locate several significant inconsistencies and deviations using this analytical technique, which are otherwise invisible to the naked eye and which begin to fill in some of these details. It is when X-ray is combined with a range of other techniques including the use of raking light and ultraviolet light that a clearer picture of the original painting begins to emerge. Further, when the results of these analytical techniques are combined with the descriptions of the original painting which are contained in contemporary reviews, it becomes possible to recreate the original painting with a reasonably high degree of certainty revealing how the painting would have originally appeared to all those who filed through the Royal Academy of Arts in 1858 (Figure 1.2).[79]

[78] Sir Joseph Noel Paton's *In Memoriam* has drawn considerable interest from a range of writers. See, for example, Procida, *Married to the Empire*, pp. 111–35; Allen, 'The Indian Mutiny and British Painting', pp. 152–58. See also Harrington, *British Artists and War*; Thomas, *Pictorial Victorians*, see Chapter 5, 'A Tale of Two Stories', pp. 125–44.

[79] There are several sketches made by Sir Joseph Noel Paton which are also useful in this regard and which, when taken together, might indicate the evolution of how Paton envisaged his original composition. See 'Study for the painting "In Memoriam"', Scottish National Gallery of Modern Art, D 4252/70 B; 'Two Heads. Study for the painting "In Memoriam"', Scottish National Gallery of Modern Art, D 4252 D; 'Study of a sepoy for the painting "In Memoriam"', The British Museum, 2003,0429.8.

Figure 1.2 This painting, which shows how *In Memoriam* would have looked when first exhibited, was commissioned by the author and painted by Galina Maximova and Dmitry Repin of the Moscow State Academic Art Institute named after V. I. Surikov, based on research conducted by the author and an analysis of the painting conducted by Simon Gillespie, which was generously funded by Peterhouse, Cambridge, through the Greta Burkill Fund.

As the aforementioned reproduction of the original painting shows, Paton chose to depict the approaching Indian threat dressed in *dhoti kurta*, rather than in military uniform. Indeed, though many mutinous sepoys retained their uniforms, summer temperatures soon persuaded many more to opt for white *dhoti kurta* as a more comfortable alternative.[80] If one considers the drawings made by Captain George Atkinson of rebel soldiers, for example, one can see many similarities between how Paton depicted mutinous sepoys and how they were represented by an eyewitness to the conflict.[81] Though Paton's historically accurate depiction of mutinous sepoys is interesting, it is when one compares the painting in its original form to how it looks today that a number of apparently incongruous details emerge. Whilst the amended painting portrays the triumphant moment that Highland soldiers reached a group of besieged women and children hiding within one of the rooms of the Lucknow Residency, the bible clutching captives are not greeting their kilted saviours with the jubilation one might have expected. Though the 'tiger-eyed sepoys' have been replaced with Highlanders, the fear and dread written on the captives' faces as they await certain death remains as clearly visible today as it was for those who encountered the unaltered painting in 1858. Indeed, this effect was not entirely lost on those who viewed the painting when it was exhibited in its altered form in Scotland. Discussing Paton's decision to replace the terrifying presence of the sepoys with the reassuring image of the highland soldier, one reviewer writing for *The Stirling Observer* expressed the opinion that 'in order to preserve the unity of the piece, the expressions of the ladies ought to have been changed from despair and agony to joy and pleasure. As it is the effect is quite lost. You look on a beautiful work of art, highly finished, but without meaning, and even *contradictory*'.[82]

When read as a palimpsest, therefore, Paton's final composition emerges as an ambivalent representation of the mutiny which both captures a strong desire to celebrate British victory at the same moment as it betrays residual fears stemming from memories of 1857. It is in this respect that the painting is an allegory for British memory. As the following chapters will show, whilst a host of ideological tools were utilised in an attempt to transform the mutiny into a triumphant imperial victory, memories of horror, doubt, and fear continued to stain Britain's canvas of memory in the same way that they stained Paton's commemorative canvas.

---

[80] Mollo, *The Indian Army*, p. 101.
[81] It is impossible to know exactly how much Paton knew about the events he was depicting and to what extent his depictions of mutinous soldiers was a matter of luck or judgement.
[82] Anon, 'Art: A Hurried Visit to the Royal Scottish Academy', p. 4.

2　'Forget Cawnpore!'
Commemorating the Mutiny, 1857–1877

As was shown in Chapter 1, the incursion of 'Cawnpore' into British discourse on the mutiny had an immediate and dramatic impact on how the conflict was understood. Whilst the initial response to news of the mutiny was a largely critical engagement with the British institutions deemed responsible for the ensuing problems in India, news and rumours of the bloody massacre and the systematic rape of female victims transformed the conflict into a desperate struggle for existence within the popular British imagination at 'home' as much as abroad. If this representation of the mutiny played an important ideological role during the conflict, in the years that followed it led to increased anxieties over Anglo-Indian security. Twelve months of bloody warfare, characterised by extreme brutality and punitive retribution, took their toll on Indian society and the British community in India. With memories of the horrors of warfare still fresh, post-mutiny India saw the two groups view each other with a habitual anxiety that led to each one becoming increasingly insular. Such an effect can be observed across India, even in regions untouched by the uprising, but it was in the centres of violence most associated with the mutiny that the greatest influence was apparent. With displaced populations returning to cities torn apart by violence, the steady flow of returning victims, perpetrators, and witnesses of the many horrors that had occurred brought with them a legacy of inter-communal resentment, anxiety, and suspicion which led to an increasingly fractured population along racial lines.[1]

Living within this fraught post-mutiny climate, the British, for their part, reminisced about the halcyon days that preceded the mutiny with a mixture of romantic nostalgia for a more innocent time and incredulous reproaching of the naivety which had allowed them to enter into a state of false security. However, with the mutiny seen as both a sobering break with the past and an ominous portent of future insurrection, the British vowed never to be caught off guard again, and accordingly physically withdrew from the native population, preferring instead to maintain a greater degree of separation than ever before. Living within towns and cities characterised by increasing segregation,

---

[1]　See Metcalf, *Aftermath of Revolt*, Chapter VIII, 'The Legacy of the Mutiny', pp. 289–327.

the small colonial community developed a siege mentality in response to their increasingly isolated position within British India. Plagued by an acute sense of vulnerability in response to what now appeared to be a tenuous and imperilled position on the subcontinent, British memory of the mutiny proved a source of considerable anxiety and a wellspring of contemporary fears.

The centrality of anxiety to the imperial project is an important corrective to the story of empire. Whilst the figure of the brash, arrogant, and self-assured colonial official has become deep-rooted in our cultural memory of empire, the impact of colonial anxieties, habitual fears, and large-scale panics is only now provoking the academic interest it deserves. In many ways, this research topic is well expressed by Gregor Thum and Maurus Reinkowski's conception of the 'helpless imperialist'.[2] As the essays contained in their edited volume *Helpless Imperialists* demonstrate, anxieties concerning a range of issues were important components of the imperial experience, which together resulted in a pronounced sense of fragility and insecurity on the part of the colonisers. Among the most recurring of these anxieties were disease, racial degeneration, and sexual transgression, but the prevalence of colonial anxieties concerning armed rebellion suggests that this was very often the most destabilising and terror inducing.[3]

With specific reference to India, the possibility of armed insurrection posed a consistent threat to British control of the subcontinent; however, it was in the years that followed the mutiny that these anxieties became most pronounced. Throughout the period under consideration, it is possible to discern a growing fear of a 'second mutiny', which, it was widely felt, would explode with as little warning as the first but with quite possibly even greater ferocity. In this respect, Neil Charlesworth has argued that, following 1857, the British administration became obsessed with 'mutiny-spotting', in which potentially dangerous situations were identified and forestalled before they developed.[4] However, rather than 'mutiny-spotting', this was more often a matter of what we might call 'mutiny-making'. As Kim Wagner has argued, British memory of the mutiny helped structure contemporary events which occurred over the course of the period under consideration, resulting in a disproportionate response. Looking specifically at the 'Wahabi Movement' of 1863 and the 'Kooka Uprising' of 1872, Wagner shows how British memory of the mutiny structured how these contemporary events were imagined and experienced, resulting in frenzied responses to what were in reality only limited threats.[5] In this respect, the words of the colonial administrator Sir Malcolm Darling are revealing. Assessing

[2] Thum and Reinkowski (eds.), *Helpless Imperialists*.

[3] For more on the prevalence and impact of anxiety on empire, see Fischer-Tiné (ed.), *Anxieties, Fear and Panic in Colonial Settings*; Peckham (ed.), *Empires of Panic*; Condos, *The Insecurity State*; Wagner, *Amritsar 1919*.

[4] Charlesworth, 'The Myth of the Deccan Riots of 1875', pp. 401–21, p. 417.

[5] Wagner, 'Treading upon Fires'.

the impact of the mutiny on how the British administration governed India and responded to potential threats in the decades that followed the uprising, Darling described the lingering memories of the conflict as 'a kind of phantom standing behind official chairs'.[6]

If this perpetual anxiety could make itself known in these moments of colonial panic, then it also coloured the lived reality of the colonial community and could, accordingly, frame even the most quotidian of experiences. This elevated sense of fear stemming from memories of 1857 is well captured in an account written by Lord Robert Baden-Powell, describing one of the first nights he spent in India at the start of his military career. Conceding that two decades had elapsed since the mutiny, but admitting that 'our knowledge of India was chiefly derived from reading accounts of that episode', Powell records how his party could not escape an overwhelming fear 'of having our throats cut at any moment, and therefore we slept with our pistols handy, when, as a matter of fact, we were as safe as if we had been in a hotel in London'.[7]

This legacy of fear and its implications for the colonial project is becoming an important focus for the literature on post-mutiny India, but rather less attention has been paid to how the British administration responded to these fears and attempted to contain their potentially debilitating results.[8] If 'working through' the traumatic memories of the mutiny offered one solution, then a second option was to domesticate the mutiny by transforming it into something less divisive and problematic than it was currently considered to be. Of these two options, it was the latter that was adopted and primarily achieved through large-scale acts of commemoration and memorialisation that aimed at negotiating the available memories of the mutiny to arrive at a conciliatory representation of the event. Through a detailed analysis of the practices of memorialisation conducted in Delhi, Lucknow, and Cawnpore, this chapter argues that commemoration was a response to this colonial culture of fear, which sought to forget the multiple horrors of the uprising whilst remembering the fidelity of those native sepoys who remained loyal and fought valiantly alongside British soldiers in an attempt to suppress the uprising. In this respect, commemoration helped silence the fear, doubt, and uncertainty that plagued the Anglo-Indian community by recasting the mutiny narrative as a seminal example of native loyalty and fidelity as opposed to treachery and dishonesty.

In addition to ameliorating the anxiety felt by the colonial community, this commemorative narrative also helped consolidate the army in the wake of the

---

[6] Darling, *Apprentice to Power*, p. 116.
[7] Baden-Powell, *Indian Memories*, pp. 14–15. Quoted in Schwarz, *Memories of Empire*, p. 234.
[8] Whilst the mutiny's legacy of fear has become an important topic for scholars studying post-mutiny India, Jill Bender has shown that this effect was not limited to India but had implications across the empire: Bender, *The 1857 Uprising and the British Empire*.

mutiny. Rather than remembering the mutiny with censure of the native army, this official memory transformed the revolt into a moment of pride and affirmation that could be celebrated by Indian sepoys and British soldiers alike. Consequently, commemoration provided an opportunity for the entire Indian army to derive communal pride in a harmonious collective memory of an event which might otherwise prove divisive. This argument finds support in the work of Heather Streets on the construction and deployment of martial race theory. In her work on this subject, Streets has pointed to the mutiny as a decisive moment in Britain's relationship with, and imagination of, Punjabi Sikhs, Nepalese Gurkhas, and Scottish Highlanders.[9] Portrayed as unsurpassably brave, fierce, and, above all, loyal, Streets has argued that the mutiny helped affirm many of these characteristics that would help establish these groups as the foremost representatives of late-century conceptions of masculinity.[10] As this chapter shows, this popular memory of the mutiny, which helped lionise these groups, was part of a broader process in which the British administration attempted to produce a conciliatory and 'usable' memory of the mutiny to help re-establish a suitable colonial relationship between the two estranged communities in post-mutiny India. Nevertheless, just as we argued in Chapter 1 that Sir Joseph Noel Paton's final commemorative composition remained stained by the fear that his changes were designed to conceal, so too does this chapter argue that the first phase of commemoration, which unfolded over the course of the two decades that followed the mutiny, was riddled with deep-seated anxieties connected to perceived imperial vulnerability and the likelihood of further armed insurrection against colonial rule.

Commemoration and Reconciliation: Remembering to Forget

The reassertion of British control in India over the decades that followed the mutiny was as much a product of conciliation as it was of military might. Significantly, Viceroy Charles Canning may be seen to have recognised this even at the height of the revolt. Whilst Charles Dickens probably spoke for many when he claimed that if he were the commander-in-chief in India, he would issue a proclamation informing all Indians that he intended to 'exterminate the Race upon whom the stain of the late cruelties rested', Canning clearly recognised that a lasting peace could only be achieved if a reconciliation between the Indian and British communities could be brokered.[11] Earning himself the derisive moniker 'Clemency Canning' for attempting to limit the all-pervasive desire for revenge that permeated the avenging army and realised

---

[9] Streets, *Martial Races.*   [10] Ibid.
[11] Charles Dickens to Angela Burdett Coutts, 4 October 1857, in Storey and Tillotson (eds.), *The Letters of Charles Dickens*, p. 459.

itself in bloody bouts of extreme retribution, Canning adopted a conciliatory approach towards the rebels from a remarkably early stage.[12]

If Canning seems to have championed peace through reconciliation, then the directors of the East India Company (EIC) adopted a similar position following the reconquest of Lucknow. With the city once again in British hands but with the rebels continuing to offer resistance in the countryside, reconciliation appeared to offer a more prudent solution to bringing the uprising to a successful conclusion than the prospect of protracted guerrilla warfare in Awadh. Indeed, it was these sentiments that animated the Secret Committee of the Court of Directors to write to Canning recommending that, following the capture of Lucknow, the remaining rebels be treated with the utmost leniency and clemency other than when their conduct during the rebellion absolutely prohibited such a policy.[13] Though there were still evocative calls for stern punishments from many quarters in the years that followed the mutiny, this conciliatory attitude came to characterise Britain's post-mutiny policies and was accordingly enshrined in the Royal proclamation of 1858 that replaced the company's rule with that of the crown. Aimed at helping secure the country in the wake of the mutiny, Canning's post-conflict policies turned away from the desire for social reform that had driven British governance in the first half of the nineteenth century, and helped inaugurate a period of conservative rule in which the government sought to support the Indian aristocracy, who were now considered the natural leaders of the people, alongside an official commitment to uphold traditional Indian practices and social norms, with the intention of re-establishing amicable colonial relations.[14] These policies proved largely successful over the twenty years that followed the mutiny and led to the coronation of Queen Victoria as the 'Empress of India' in 1877.[15]

---

[12] Metcalf, *Aftermath of Revolt*, pp. 293–96. For an interesting and engaging biography on Canning, see Maclagan, *Clemency Canning'*.

[13] 'The Secret Committee of the Court of Directors of the East India Company to the Governor-general of India in Council', 24 March 1858, quoted in Ball, *The History of the Indian Mutiny*, pp. 480–81. Interestingly, Canning seems to have at first been less prepared to pursue peace through reconciliation in Awadh. For discussion on the infamous Awadh proclamation of March 1858, and the politics of conciliation, see Metcalf, *Aftermath of Revolt*, Chapter 4, 'The Restoration of the Aristocracy', pp. 134–73; Trivedi, *Law and Order in Upper India*, Chapter 3, 'The Pacification and Restoration of Law and Order, 1858–9', pp. 64–107; Chand, *The Administration of Avadh, 1858–1877*, pp. 26–31.

[14] The classic statement on this can be found in Metcalf, *Aftermath of Revolt*. See also Hutchins, *The Illusion of Permanence*. For an alternative perspective on the apparent end of Britain's commitment to reform after 1857, see Klein, 'Materialism, Mutiny and Modernization in British India', pp. 545–80; For a contrast between the commitment to non-intervention into traditional Indian society at the highest levels of government and a continued commitment to reform Indian society at the local level, see Oldenburg, *The Making of Colonial Lucknow, 1856–1877*.

[15] For a very relevant discussion on this and other durbars in the post-mutiny period, see Cohn, 'Representing Authority'.

Nevertheless, Canning was not only interested in conciliating the Indian aristocracy, he was also deeply concerned about negating the lasting legacy of resentment, fear, and hatred in the British community. Whilst he had hoped that his support for the Indian aristocracy would have a beneficial effect on the British community by producing what he thought would be an amply visible class of amenable and dignified gentlemen, he was quickly disabused of this earnest hope.[16] Moreover, throughout his tenure as Viceroy, Canning grew ever more concerned about British attitudes towards Indians, which he saw as threatening harmonious and stable rule. If the various policies that contributed to post-mutiny imperial rule have been carefully scrutinised, the interdependent practices of memorialisation that helped construct a conciliatory collective memory of the mutiny have been altogether less considered. Aimed primarily at the British community, these commemorative acts are best understood as a crucial component of the governmental policies of the period, enabling the broader policies of reconciliation to be achieved. This fact was readily grasped by the directors of the EIC who wrote to Canning in March 1858 championing a conciliatory policy in bringing the mutiny to a final close and noting that whilst it may be impossible to 'forget the insanity which, during the last ten months, has pervaded the army and a large portion of the people, we should at the same time remember the previous fidelity of a hundred years' and so 'reestablish, if we can, that confidence which was so long the foundation of our power'.[17] This desire for post-conflict reconciliation achieved by forgetting the mutiny and remembering a largely invented tradition of Indian 'fidelity' to British rule is far from unique. Rather, it is an adoption and an adaptation of a common practice dating back at least as far as ancient Greece, in which divisive memories of past conflicts are actively forgotten in an attempt to facilitate a return to a functioning present.[18] Termed 'prescriptive forgetting' by Paul Connerton, this form of forgetting is especially common in the wake of communal violence, in which it is thought that a shared future, free from further conflict, relies heavily on the re-establishment of amicable relations – even if these are ultimately underpinned by a politically and militarily oppressive regime.[19]

---

[16] Gopal, *British Policy in India, 1858–1905*, see Chapter 1, 'The Aftermath of Revolt, 1857–1869', pp. 1–63. See specifically p. 57.

[17] 'The Secret Committee of the Court of Directors of the East India Company to the Governor-general of India in Council', 24 March 1858, quoted in Ball, *The History of the Indian Mutiny*, pp. 480–81.

[18] Andrew Wolpert has given an excellent account of the complex role played by remembering and forgetting in Athens following the reassertion of democracy after the defeat of the 'Thirty Tyrants'. As Wolpert shows, an indefinite period of civil war may have been prevented by a period of reconciliation that concentrated on strategies of remembering and forgetting in the period that followed conflict. Wolpert, *Remembering Defeat*.

[19] Connerton, 'Seven Types of Forgetting', pp. 59–71.

Though such programmes of forgetting have a long lineage, their ultimate utility is open to debate. As Connerton himself recognises, silence is not the same as forgetting, and, in fact, we might add, the work involved in actively silencing certain thoughts, feelings, and memories guarantees that 'prescriptive forgetting' rarely, if ever, results in a community succeeding in actually forgetting whatever debilitating memories are mutually silenced. Rather than fading from possible recollection, these memories are more likely to fester and smoulder at the margins of social interaction from where they continue to affect and effect attitudes and behaviour long after they have been 'forgotten'.[20] Seen in this way, practices of what Aleida Assmann has called 'remembering to forget' may be more successful in realising reconciliation than is the case with 'prescriptive forgetting'.[21] Rather than simply enveloping an awkward or uncomfortable event in silence, such a mnemonic technique also involves practices of remembering. Instead of prohibiting the recollection of a divisive memory, this form of remembering/forgetting involves the production of a conciliatory, or at least less destabilising, memory that helps effect reconciliation by establishing a fresh beginning that is untainted by an awkward past. This mnemonic policy exactly characterises the trajectory of ostensive attempts by the British administration to commemorate and memorialise the mutiny of 1857 over the first two decades of its history. If the Directors of the EIC proposed an attempt to forget the mutiny in favour of remembering a history of Indian fidelity, then Canning took this process further by first silencing the many tales of horror that dominated British attention in late 1857 and then attempting to (re)remember the mutiny as itself an exemplary illustration of Indian fidelity.

Remembering and Forgetting Cawnpore: Negotiating the Horrors

In beginning to consider the conciliatory memory of the mutiny installed within centres of violence, it is useful to start by focusing on Cawnpore. As explored in Chapter 1, Cawnpore was the scene of some of the most horrifying acts of violence committed by both parties during the mutiny. However, if it was important for the British to 'Remember Cawnpore' during the conflict, then over the following years it became necessary to forget the bloody horrors that had been witnessed within the city. In exploring this process, it is useful to focus on the different ways in which the mutiny in Cawnpore was commemorated over the period under consideration. In so doing, we will begin by tracing early mnemonic acts performed on an ad hoc basis by both British and

---

[20] For a broader, but directly relevant discussion on the differences between silence and forgetting, see Zerubavel, *The Elephant in the Room*.
[21] Assman, 'From Collective Violence to a Common Future', pp. 8–23.

Indian actors during the mutiny, before comparing these to the formal acts of commemoration performed by the British administration, and other interested parties, in the two decades that followed the conflict. As we will see, whilst early acts of commemoration suspended memory within the moment of horror, and thus promoted further violence by encouraging feelings of revenge, those enacted later were consciously designed to bring closure to the traumatic event by moving the space of memory beyond the moment of violence and bloodshed to a place of acceptance or even collective amnesia.[22]

Bibighar and Bloodshed

As we explored in Chapter 1, the 'Cawnpore Massacre', in which around 200 imprisoned women and children were slaughtered in a small building known locally as Bibighar, quickly became the source of considerable outrage in Britain and India alike. Motivating and justifying an escalation in the violence and brutality of the conflict, the massacre was deployed as a potent signifier within the discursive construction of the ongoing conflict. Whilst many individuals in Britain, including Sir Joseph Noel Paton, thought it necessary to commemorate the massacre through such mediums as prose, poetry, and painting, the soldiers and civilians who discovered the bloody murders during their reoccupation of the city likewise attempted to commemorate the event in their own ways.

Although there were undoubtedly many ways in which this might have been approached and achieved, the great majority focused their attention on Bibighar. Described by Captain Mowbray Thomson, one of the few survivors of the ill-fated siege in Cawnpore, to have 'comprised two principal rooms, each about twenty feet long', Bibighar would have appeared to be a small and rather anonymous building to the British soldiers who reoccupied the city.[23] However, once told about the massacre that had been perpetrated within the little house, many hurried to the location to, at first, search for survivors and later simply to bear witness to what was clearly a traumatic scene. As later recorded by one of the first officers to find the building, 'the clotted gore lay ankle deep on the polluted floor, and also long tresses of silken hair, fragments of female wearing-apparel, hats, boots … and toys were scattered about in terrible confusion'.[24] Whilst many soldiers were paralysed by the horror at the site of Bibighar, still others followed the thick trail of blood that led out from the house to the well, in which the dead bodies had ultimately been deposited. According to another witness, when staring down into the well, 'a map of naked arms, legs and gashed trunks was visible', with the lifeless body

---

[22] Alex Tickell has also emphasized the practices of reconciliation at the heart of commemoration in Cawnpore. See Tickell, *Terrorism, Insurgency, and Indian-English Literature, 1830–1947*.

[23] Thomson, *The Story of Cawnpore*, p. 211.

[24] North, *Journal of an English Officer in India*, p. 76.

of a young boy lying on the top.[25] Although one may have expected the grizzly site to be quickly sanitised, the decision was instead taken that, beyond roughly filling in the well, the site should be kept in the exact condition in which it had first been found.[26] Thus when, some four months later, in early November, Rev. Thomas Moore arrived in Cawnpore to assume his duties as chaplain, one of the first places he sought to visit was Bibighar which he found

in much the same condition as when the troops entered it, when they took Cawnpore.... The mats were black with clotted blood – the women's hair had been collected by handfuls ... the walls were bespattered with blood, the marks of bloody fingers where the fiends had wiped them after the slaughter, were in several places visible.[27]

If the blood stains told a horrifying story of indiscriminate violence, then the walls further narrated the meaning of Bibighar to its visitors by connecting the traumatic scene with a powerful inducement to vengeance. Written in charcoal, ink, or simply scratched into the plaster, the walls bore the frantic pleas of their inhabitants: 'Avenge us', 'Countrymen, revenge it', or most commonly, 'Remember Cawnpore!'. Whilst these messages purportedly came from the women and children whose blood stained the walls, in reality, they were written by the thousands of soldiers who visited Bibighar during 1857.[28] By sewing the bloody scene into a narrative of revenge, the massacre was given meaning for all those who passed through the building in late 1857. A similar effect was achieved through the act of taking mementoes, an activity which was itself often accompanied by promises of revenge. An officer carrying a strip of dress is reported to have said, 'I shall carry this with me in my holsters ... the sight of it, and the recollection of this house, will be sufficient to incite me to revenge'.[29] Captain Garnet-Wolseley reported that he took the

[25] John Walter Sherer to Cecil Beadon, 17 July 1857, 'Contemporary Mutiny letter from I. W. Sherer [sic] Esq., Bengal Civil Service to Cecil Bradon [sic] Esq., B.C.S describing the Mutiny and the massacre at Cawnpore etc.', Reid Papers, Box 2, No. 19B, fol. 13, Centre of South Asian Studies Archive, University of Cambridge. N.B. Contrary to the catalogue, the letter is not on Microfilm. 'Deposition of Lalla Bhudree Nath, Commissariat Gomastha, Cawnpore' in Forrest (ed.), *Selections from the Letters, Despatches and Other State Papers Preserved in the Military Department of the Government of India, 1857–58*, Appendix CXXXVi.
[26] Sherer, *Daily Life during the Mutiny*, pp. 80–81.
[27] Rev. Thomas Moore to his mother, 15 January 1858, 'Thirteen Letters or journal-letters from Rev. Thomas Moore and Dora Moore to his mother, and to his brother Tony Moore. With typed transcriptions', Letters of Rev. Thomas Moore and his wife Dorothy Moore from India, fol. 69, OIOC, Mss EUR F630/2.
[28] Shepherd makes it clear in his own narrative that when he first visited Bibighar, there was no writing on the walls. Rev. Moore discussed the subject with many people and came to the same conclusion. William Howard Russell apparently concurred after meeting Moore. Shepherd, *A Personal Narrative*; Moore to his mother, 15 January 1858, Letters of Rev. Thomas Moore and his wife Dorothy Moore from India, fol. 69, OIOC, Mss EUR F630/2; Russell, *My Diary in India*, Vol. 1, p. 191.
[29] Anon., 'From Our Own Correspondent', p. 5.

'vow most soldiers take there – of vengeance', swearing that he would not take 'drop for drop, but barrels and barrels of the filth which flows in these niggers' veins for every drop of blood which marked the floors and walls of that fearful house'.[30] This process even came to be formalised, as Private Metcalfe of the 32nd Regiment of Foot noted when writing about his own visit to the site, during which he concurred with members of the Highland Regiment, kneeling down and taking 'the Highland vow', which stated that 'for every one of our poor creatures who were thus slain, 100 of the enemy should bite the dust'.[31]

These promises of revenge that were inscribed on the walls and sworn by the soldiers who visited the building were themselves enacted within the memorial space of Bibighar when, a little over two weeks after the city's reoccupation, command of the city passed to Brigadier James Neill. Claiming that 'one cannot control one's feelings' after entering the little house, Neill passed his infamous 'strange law', which stipulated that the 'house in which ... [the women and children] were butchered, and which is stained with their blood, will not be washed or cleaned by their countrymen', rather:

every stain of that innocent blood shall be cleared up and wiped out, previous to their execution, by such of the miscreants as may be hereafter apprehended.... Each miscreant, after sentence of death is pronounced upon him, will be taken down to the house in question, under a guard, and will be forced into cleaning up a small portion of the blood-stains; the task will be made as revolting to his feelings as possible, and the Provost-Marshall will use the lash in forcing any one objecting to complete his task. After properly cleaning up his portion, the culprit is to be immediately hanged, and for this purpose a gallows will be erected close at hand.[32]

Neill's regulations were scrupulously followed and the gallows was immediately erected and pressed into service by British troops who no doubt agreed with the opinion expressed by Arthur Moffatt Lang, who wrote that the sight of the gallows was 'the only pleasant thing in the compound on which to rest the eye'.[33] Played out in front of large crowds of soldiers and sailors eager to participate in these rituals of revenge, the unfortunate individuals were taken into the little house and, as explained by Rev. Moore to his mother:

beaten till they licked up some of the clotted blood – this of course they were always unwilling to do as they then lost caste, and so were according to their creed sure to be damned and therefore many cruel scenes have been witnessed – eyes cut out, and the men half killed before they would submit – the soldiers often assisting in the torture and

---

[30] The future Field Marshal Garnet-Wolseley, quoted in Hibbert, *The Great Mutiny*, p. 212.

[31] Metcalfe, quoted in Hibbert, *The Great Mutiny*, p. 212. Hibbert's reference is incorrect. The correct reference for this should be Metcalfe, *The Chronicle of Private Henry Metcalfe*, p. 68.

[32] Brigadier-General James Neill, quoted in Kaye, *A History of the Sepoy War in India, 1857–1858*, p. 399.

[33] Arthur Lang, *Lahore to Lucknow*, p. 121.

gloating over the agonies of the brutes – many disgusting scenes occurred even after they had complied with the demands of the whip ....[34]

These increasingly formalised and even ritualised mnemonic practices that imbued Bibighar with meaning and memory were clearly therefore a part of the discursive construction of the mutiny discussed in Chapter 1. By maintaining Bibighar in the exact same condition in which it had been found immediately after the massacre, the moment of memory is suspended within the traumatic moment of murder. Further, by converting the small building into a shrine of sorts dedicated to righteous revenge, these early mnemonic acts are productive of a shared memory of the Cawnpore Massacre which is intimately bound up with the perpetuation of violence. Interestingly, it may be argued that Bibighar was utilised in a remarkably similar way when, in late November, the city once again briefly passed into rebel hands whilst the British forces in the city found themselves besieged. Though the 'second siege of Cawnpore' lasted just a matter of days, whilst the city was once again briefly under rebel control, the meaning and memory of Bibighar underwent a remarkable reversal.

Located around 400 yards away from the newly built entrenchments in which the British forces were confined, Bibighar was quickly occupied by the mutineers and utilised as cover for the rebels' guns, which kept up a fierce bombardment of the British position throughout the siege.[35] Further, fugitive British soldiers who had been unable to reach the entrenchments before the city fell, or who were otherwise captured, were rounded up by Tantia Tope's forces, including two members of the 64th (2nd Staffordshire) Regiment of Foot, who were captured after an engagement with the rebels. Defectors to the British entrenchment brought with them tales of how these two soldiers were 'ill-treated in every way possible' before being hanged from Neill's gallows, which still stood outside Bibighar.[36] Such was the notoriety and infamy of the little house that it is hard to believe that the rebel soldiers did not fully appreciate the significance of this act. However, most remarkably of all, the rebels also took it upon themselves to clean the interior of the building. Rev.

---

[34] Rev. Thomas Moore to his mother, 15 January 1858, Letters of Rev. Thomas Moore and his wife Dorothy Moore from India, fol. 69, OIOC, Mss EUR F630/2.

[35] Rev. Thomas Moore, 'Copy of description sent with the sketches of the Cawnpore Massacre & the memorial raised by the 32nd' 16 December 1857', 'Letters from Dora Moore to Mrs. Moore', Letters of Rev. Thomas Moore and his wife Dorothy Moore from India, fol. 76, Mss EUR F630/3. Though written sometime later using his own letters to his wife as a guide, see also 'Account by the Rev. Thomas Moore, chaplain to the forces at Cawnpore, of events at Cawnpore, Lucknow, etc.', p. 46, British Library, Add MS 37151.

[36] Oliver to Wife, 4 December 1857, printed in Major-General John Ryder Oliver, 'Campaigning in Oude etc.', c.1859, John Ryder Oliver Papers, p. 29, OIOC, Mss Eur A66. Arthur Moffatt Lang, who was camped with Campbell's forces just outside Cawnpore on their return from Lucknow, noted in his journal that they received reports of a fugitive member of the 64th being hanged from Neill's gallows. Lang, *Lahore to Lucknow*, p. 147.

Moore, who, the moment the siege was broken, went to check on the condition of Bibighar, was amazed to discover that 'the whole of the floors were thoroughly cleaned and the walls white-washed' by the mutineers. What 'may have been their object in performing this rather dangerous work under fire from the entrenchment we cannot fathom', he admitted, 'except it be that they wished to prove their disapprobation of the bloody murder'.[37] A second plausible theory is offered by Lieutenant Ashton Warner, who wrote to his brother to tell him that upon his arrival from Lucknow with Campbell's forces, 'I went to see that place at Cawnpore where our poor women and children were massacred, when the enemy were in possession of the place the other day, they had the place white-washed, to prevent our inflicting the punishment upon any more sepoys of sweeping and clearing the house'.[38]

These explanations for the rebels' activity are indeed plausible; however, a third possibility exists. If the execution of British soldiers from Neill's gallows was indeed a self-conscious subversion of the memorial space, then it is entirely possible that the rebels decided to completely invert Neill's strange law by first having the British soldiers clean the room before they were hanged from the same gallows which had been used to dispatch countless rebels over the preceding four months. Seen in this way, Bibighar was converted into a space of memory dedicated to the hundreds of often innocent and sometimes completely random victims of colonial violence who were brutally tortured and savagely massacred by British troops over the previous few months. If the little house was the scene of the alleged sexual defilement and murder of British women, then for the rebels it was the scene of religious defilement and murder of Indians. Whichever way the building was read, it was implicated in the profound desire for revenge that in both cases was conducted within its four walls, and thus Bibighar was a symbol of continued violence and struggle throughout 1857.

---

[37] Rev. Thomas Moore, 'Copy of description sent with the sketches of the Cawnpore Massacre & the memorial raised by the 32nd' 16 December 1857', 'Letters from Dora Moore to Mrs. Moore', Letters of Rev. Thomas Moore and his wife Dorothy Moore from India, fol. 76, Mss EUR F630/3. See also 'Account by the Rev. Thomas Moore, chaplain to the forces at Cawnpore, of events at Cawnpore, Lucknow, etc.', p. 46, British Library, Add MS 37151.

[38] Ashton C. Warner to Richard Warner, 16 December 1857. 'Letters of Major Ashton Cromwell Warner in India to and from his family', Journals of Captain Richard Warner and letters of his son, Major Ashton Cromwell Warner, to and from friends and family, fol. 43, Mss Eur F580/4. Please note that my reading of Warner's letter is different to the accepted understanding. All other accounts of the massacre which mention the fate of Bibighar follow Christopher Hibbert in claiming that the British painted and cleaned the little house in 'early 1858'. This Hibbert bases on the above quoted letter written by Lieutenant Ashton Warner. However, upon inspection, the letter is dated 16 December 1857. With the correct date, and read together with Rev. Moore's letter (which was only acquired by the British Library in 2011), I would suggest that the most natural reading of Warner's letter sees it agree with Moore. Therefore, it seems clear to me that the rebels painted and cleaned the little house, in Warner's opinion, to prevent the British from 'inflicting the punishment upon any more sepoys of sweeping and clearing the house'. Hibbert, *The Great Mutiny*, n. 47, p. 415.

The Angel of the Resurrection

If these early attempts to commemorate the mutiny were closely connected to the perpetuation of violence which thus helped sustain conflict and even justify some of the most brutal and horrifying acts of revenge, then, from at least mid-1858 onwards, these same memories of horror and bloodshed became antithetical to colonial rule. Accordingly, it is possible to chart a significant shift in how the massacre was commemorated over this period. Just as Sir Joseph Noel Paton was compelled to make significant alterations to his commemorative canvas, so too was the colonial administration impelled to promote a very different meaning and memory of the Cawnpore Massacre than that which predominated throughout 1857. In beginning to investigate this shift in commemoration, it is useful to turn our attention away from the ad hoc practices of memorialisation considered previously and rather focus on prescribed plans to memorialise the mutiny.

The earliest formal proposal to commemorate the mutiny which generated serious discussion came from the Society for the Propagation of the Gospel (SPG), a large and influential Anglican missionary organisation whose well-established mission in Cawnpore was all but destroyed during the hostilities.[39] The SPG was in fact already involved in the erection of a high-profile public memorial in Constantinople to commemorate the British soldiers who died during the Crimean War and were inclined to believe that a plan to build a Memorial Missionary Church in Cawnpore would be greeted with similar enthusiasm and financial support.[40] Accordingly, the Standing Committee of the SPG resolved in October 1857 to raise funds for the construction of a memorial church in Cawnpore which, whilst serving as a monument to the dead women and children, would also be a place of Christian worship 'for all who in the present or future generations may be moved by the Holy Spirit to turn from dumb idols to serve the living God'.[41]

---

[39] The exact fate of every missionary is contested. Cf. The Society for the Propagation of the Gospel, *The Story of the Cawnpore Mission*; Thomson, *The Story of Cawnpore*, p. 105; Dr William Kay, the principal of Calcutta's Bishop's College, to Rev. Hawkins, 22 August 1857, 'Copies of Letters Received', Papers of the United Society for the Propagation of the Gospel, p. 186, Rhodes House Library, Oxford University, USPG/Calcutta/14.

[40] For information on the Crimean Memorial Church, see 'Crimean War 1854–6', Papers of the United Society for the Propagation of the Gospel, Files 1–5, Rhodes House Library, University of Oxford, USPG/C/CRIMEA/3.

[41] Minutes of the Standing Committee of the SPG for 29 October 1857, 'Minutes of the Standing Committee, 1857–9', Papers of the United Society for the Propagation of the Gospel, p. 56, USPG/Standing Committee Minutes 1857–9/26. The SPG was not alone in their desire to memorialise the massacre and a similar committee was initially convened by the Earl of Shaftesbury who, upon hearing of the SPG's plans, conceded to not pursue his own proposals but to simply support those of the SPG. Shaftesbury to Hawkins, 11 November 1857, Copies of Letters Received (HOME), 'Papers of the United Society for the Propagation of the Gospel', p. 158, Rhodes House Library, University of Oxford, USPG/CLR/Home/219.

Part of a broader discourse that saw the mutiny as a divine judgement on Britain's apparent failure to better spread Christianity in India, the SPG's plans achieved support in England but encountered significant opposition in India where social and religious reform was seen as an important causal factor leading to the mutiny.[42] Though the SPG's plans to construct a memorial missionary church on the site of the 'bloody well', into which the women and children who died during the Cawnpore Massacre had been thrown, were formally rejected on military grounds, official and popular antipathy towards the mnemonic project seems to have been part of the increasingly conservative policies and attitudes towards Indian society that developed in the wake of the mutiny.[43] In fact, Canning was strongly opposed to the memorial plans and even when the SPG shifted its attention from the well to 'Wheeler's entrenchments', where no military argument could reasonably be made against the construction of a mission church, Canning continued to oppose the plans and ultimately prohibited them outright.[44] Following a great deal of protracted discussion, the SPG contributed the funds that it raised for a Memorial Missionary Church to a government-backed scheme that saw All Souls' Memorial Church, intended primarily for British soldiers stationed in the city, constructed on the site of 'Wheeler's entrenchment'.[45]

---

[42] For discussion on this discourse that saw the mutiny as a divine retribution, see Stanley, 'Christian Responses to the Indian Mutiny of 1857', pp. 277–91; Randall, 'Autumn 1857: The Making of the Indian "Mutiny"', pp. 3–17; Van der Veer, *Imperial Encounters*, Chapter 4, 'Moral Muscle', pp. 83–105; Major, 'Spiritual Battlefields', Bates and Major (eds.), *Mutiny at the Margins*, pp. 50–74.

[43] For details on the military reasons given, see Kay to Hawkins, 19 March 1858, 'Copies of Letters Received', Papers of the United Society for the Propagation of the Gospel, p. 204, Rhodes House Library, University of Oxford, USPG/CLR/Calcutta/14. Thomas Metcalf sees the debates over the Cawnpore Memorial church to signify how, in the wake of the mutiny, Christianity became a signifier of difference. See Metcalf, *The New Cambridge History of India,* III.4, *Ideologies of the Raj,* p. 48. See also Metcalf, *Aftermath of Revolt,* Chapter 3, 'Education and Social Reform', pp. 92–133. For a somewhat different discussion, that focuses on pre-mutiny attitudes towards religion, but concludes with an interesting discussion on continuities between EIC and Crown rule in connection to religion, see Carson, *The East India Company and Religion, 1698–1858.*

[44] Canning to Inglis, 3 February 1860, 'Miscellaneous letters from the Governor-General to persons in India, 1860', The Indian Papers of the Rt. Hon. Charles John Earl Canning, fol. 4, Centre for South Asian Studies Archive, University of Cambridge, Reel 28. If the plan faced official antipathy, then it found no more support from the British community in Cawnpore or in India more generally. See 'Proceedings of a General meeting held at Cawnpore on Monday the 22nd day of August 1859 for the purpose of deciding on the steps to be taken for erecting a memorial of those who fell at Cawnpore 1857', Collections to Public Works Dispatches to India: Nos. 1–4, Col. 83, p. 56, OIOC, IOR/L/PWD/3/336.

[45] For details on these discussions and the associated fate of Christ Church in Cawnpore, see Rev. Fellows, Chaplain of Cawnpore, to Pratt, Archdeacon of Calcutta, 9 February 1859, Collections to Public Works Dispatches to India: Nos. 1–4, Col. 83, pp. 6–8, OIOC, IOR/L/PWD/3/336 ; see also 'Extract from the Proceedings of the Hon'ble the Lieutenant Governor of the N.W Provinces in the Public Works Department under date the 18th March

With construction beginning to coincide with the fifth anniversary of the reoccupation of Cawnpore, the church was not completed and consecrated until 1876, owing to a scarcity of building materials.[46]

If Canning's opposition to the SPG's plans to commemorate the mutiny in Cawnpore can be seen as part of his broader post-conflict policies, then the same can be said for his involvement in what would become one of the most iconic images of the empire. From as early as August 1857, Lord Canning's wife, Lady Charlotte Canning, had expressed a strong desire to build a monument over the well into which the victims of the 'Cawnpore Massacre' had been thrown. Lady Canning was not alone in her fervent desire to see the event commemorated, and the years which immediately followed the mutiny saw considerable local and international pressures exerted on Major-General Sir John Inglis, the commanding officer in Cawnpore, leading to the noted mutiny hero further raising the issue with Canning.[47] With a suitable mnemonic project in mind, Canning instructed that a significant portion of land around the well should be marked out and fenced off whilst he solicited suitable designs from sculptors in England.[48]

1859', Pratt to Bayley, 21 February 1859, Collections to Public Works Dispatches to India: Nos. 1–4, Col. 83, p. 5, OIOC, IOR/L/PWD/3/336. Of the total private contributions, a little over 30 per cent came from the SPG with the remainder raised in India by the Cawnpore Memorial Committee. For a breakdown of private contributions, see 'Report of Proceedings in the Public Works Department 1861–62', p. 26, OIOC, IOR/V/24/3277. For details on a number of smaller memorials around the church dedicated to those who died and commissioned by Canning, see Cecil Beadon to G.E.W Couper, 8 November 1859, Collections to Public Works Dispatches to India: Nos. 1–4, Col. 83, p. 46, OIOC, IOR/L/PWD/3/336; Secy. to govt. of India, P.W. Dept. with G. G. to Secy. to Govt of N.W.P., in the P.W.D. 25 January 1861. 'Report of Proceedings in the Public Works Department during the official year 1860–61' Appendix H. P. XXXV, Administration Reports of the Government of India 1860–61, Part I, OIOC, IOR/V/10/14; Blunt, List of Inscriptions on Christian Tombs, p. 131.

[46] For the laying of the foundation stone, see Thornhill to Secy. to Govt. of N.W.P, in the P.W. Dept., 5 August 1862, Collections to Public Works Despatches to India, Desp. 8 Jan. (No. 1) 1863, Col. 9, p. 3, OIOC, IOR/L/PWD/3/344; Will. F. Johnson to Father Kerr, 3 August 1862 in Tull (ed.), Affectionately Rachel, pp. 143–44. For consecration, see Bishop Milman to Frances M. Milman, 10 December 1876, quoted in Milman (ed.), Memoir of the Rt. Rev. Robert Milman, with a Selection from His Correspondence and Journals, p. 352.

[47] Journal letter of Lady Canning, 3 August 1857, quoted in Augustus Hare, The Story of Two Noble Lives Being Memorials of Charlotte, Countess Canning, and Louisa, Marchioness of Watereford, p. 258; Inglis to Canning, 26 August 1859, Collections to Public Works Dispatches to India: Nos. 1–4, Col. 83, p. 55, OIOC, IOR/L/PWD/3/336. In fact, there seems to have been considerable pressure in Cawnpore for a monument. See also Rev. J. Moore to John Henry Pratt, 9 February 1859, Collections to Public Works Dispatches to India: Nos. 1–4, Col. 83, p. 5, OIOC, IOR/L/PWD/3/336.

[48] Henry Yule to Sir George Couper, 27 June 1859, Collections to Public Works Dispatches to India: Nos. 1–4, Col. 83, p. 29, OIOC, IOR/L/PWD/3/336. The work was entrusted to Cuthbert Bensley Thornhill, Commissioner of the Allahabad Division, due to his own painful association with the mutiny and massacre. See Ward, Our Bones Are Scattered, for the fate of his family members during the conflict.

With the gardens beginning to take shape, Lord and Lady Canning turned their attention to the form the central monument should take. With a view to obtaining a suitable design, Canning approached his close personal friend Lord Granville on the subject, writing, 'I have a commission for you about a monument over the well at Cawnpore into which the massacred women and children were thrown ... it will require the discreetest taste and judgment in deciding whom to employ'.[49] Given Canning's emphasis on the need for the 'discreetest taste and judgement', he would show alarm when he received a letter from Charlotte's sister, Lady Waterford, who, after meeting with Granville, wrote to Canning to champion a possible design for the monument consisting in 'a women clinging to a cross, with the bodies of murdered children near her'.[50] Waterford was most likely describing a sketch for the monument prepared by noted sculptor, Thomas Woolner. Though favoured by Waterford, the model was not to the apparent liking of all and, after viewing the sketch, James Anthony Froude, historian and close personal friend of Woolner, wrote to the artist noting that 'the figure appeared to me intensely expressive but expressive of unthinkable agony. The child appeared as if it had just dropped from the hands. Did you mean that?' (Figure 2.1).[51]

Froude's concerns about the intense expression of agony were shared by Canning who, in a subsequent letter to Granville, expressed his unease writing that 'this is the sort of design I had wished to avoid', adding that 'it would be a very painful record to some English families, and a very exasperating one to our fellow countrymen - soldiers for instance. Nor do I think it desirable to put before the natives for all time to come so literal a picture of the horrors of 1857'.[52] Canning continues:

It was very much with the view of steering clear of anything of the sort that I asked for something ethereal - ghostly; something in which the figures should not represent flesh and blood, but angels or guardian spirits.... The crisis of murder and terror is not the moment to be perpetuated, nor is the first great agony of grief; but rather the after-condition of sober mournfulness sustained and cheered by hopefulness.... To convey the story of the massacre is quite a secondary object - if indeed, it be an object at all.[53]

Canning and Froude's reading of Woolner's monument seems most natural, and both perceived it as an attempt to further highlight the horrors of the massacre by freezing the space of memory within the moment of terror and bloodshed. However, as is apparent in the dialogue between Canning and Granville, it is precisely this representation of the massacre that the Viceroy wished to erase.

---

[49] Canning to Granville, 3 March 1861, quoted in Lord Fitzmaurice, *The Life of Granville George Leveson Gower Second Earl Granville 1815–1891*, p. 395.
[50] Canning to Granville, 17 June 1861, quoted in Fitzmaurice, *The Life of Granville*, p. 396.
[51] Froude to Woolner, 2 July 1861, quoted in Woolner (ed), *Thomas Woolner Sculptor and Poet, His Life in Letters Written*, p. 204.
[52] Canning to Granville, 17 June 1861, quoted in Fitzmaurice, *The Life of Granville*, p. 396.
[53] Ibid.

Figure 2.1 Photograph showing Woolner's design for the Cawnpore monument. Printed in Amy Woolner (ed.), *Thomas Woolner Sculptor and Poet*, p. 85.

Canning was not concerned with remembering the massacre as such, rather he wished to suture the psychological wound inflicted by the violence of the mutiny by encouraging a policy of forgetting and thus erasing, or at least silencing, a significant impediment to the reassertion of a productive and stable present which was no longer haunted by the ghosts that surrounded the well.

If Woolner's monument was thus antithetical to the mnemonic policies being pursued by Canning, then another equally incompatible, though clearly distinct, memory appears not to have even been countenanced. If the site might have been marked by a monument depicting the bloody massacre of British women and children, then it could have also been marked by a memorial propagating a memory of brutal revenge and thus reclaim the space of British trauma, by replacing it with a memory of violent and ruthless retribution. In any case, the absence of such a suggestion may well be indicative that it was generally accepted that such a memory was not suitable and would have almost certainly been blocked by Canning on similar grounds as animated his rejection of Woolner's design.

Figure 2.2 Left: The Memorial Well of Cawnpore. Right: The Angel of the Well. Photos by Samuel Bourne, 1865–66.

Granville promptly responded to Canning's concerns by informing him that the design suggested was just one of many proposals produced by a range of sculptors, but that the 'sketch which we prefer is a new sort of Britannia ... a handsome pathetic woman with a wreath of cypress on her head, clasping a large plain cross'.[54] The final commission was given to Baron Carlo Marochetti who ultimately used a design prepared by Lady Canning to execute the statue. The intention of the monument is well captured by Lady Emily Bayley who was a personal friend of Lady Canning and whose husband, Sir Edward Clive Bayley, had been involved in early discussions on the monument. According to Lady Bayley, Lady Canning was of the opinion that 'the thought and hope of the Resurrection is the only thought [that] can calm the sorrow or give any comfort' to those affected by the massacre, and therefore, her design took the form of 'The Angel of the Resurrection'.[55] This ostensive attempt to produce a 'comforting' memory of the mutiny was faithfully recreated by Marochetti, and further enclosed within 'an octagonal gothic screen and platform encircling the closed well' designed by the Cannings' close personal friend, Henry Yule.[56] By early 1861, the garden

[54] Granville to Canning, 10 July 1861, quoted in Fitzmaurice, *The Life of Granville*, pp. 397–98.

[55] Lady Bayley's comments were written by her on a photograph of the monument contained in a commemorative album made after Lady Canning's death. 'Memorial Volume of photographs, news-cuttings, letters and souvenirs, relating to Charlotte Elizabeth Canning', Charlotte Elizabeth Canning Papers, fol. 29, Mss Eur D661.

[56] Ibid. Marochetti's work faithfully recreated Lady Canning's design with the exception of the addition of a second palm. Commenting on the alteration, Bayley wrote that 'The original drawing had only one and was more graceful'. For details of the octagonal screen, see Secretary to Government of India in the PWD with Governor General to Secretary to Government of N.W.P., in the P.W.D., 9 January 1861, Appendix to Report of Proceedings in the Public Works Department during the official year 1860–61, Administration Reports of the

was beginning to take shape and assembly of Yule's stone screen and the plinth for Marochetti's statue had begun under the authority of Thornhill.[57] With work continuing apace over the following three years, the Cawnpore monument was complete with the exception of the expected 'Angel of the Resurrection' which was to adorn the enclosed well itself and thus the official consecration ceremony was performed by the bishop of Calcutta, Rev. George Cotton, during a tour of the region in 1863.[58]

Replacing the horrors of the mutiny enacted within Bibighar with carefully cultivated gardens and mournful architecture which eschew any direct reference to the traumatic scenes which had been witnessed on the site, it is clear that the practices of commemoration deployed by Canning and the British administration were a coordinated attempt to move beyond the moment of horror to a space of forgiving or even forgetting. A response to the pronounced sense of fear and loathing which gripped the Anglo-Indian community in the wake of the mutiny, these practices of commemoration were designed to both conciliate and reassure the British population of India by containing the deep-seated desire for revenge, and fear of further insurrection, which might otherwise continue to be intrinsically connected to popular inducements to 'Remember Cawnpore!'.

Horror in Lucknow

If the commemoration of the massacres considered previously were thus an incitement to 'Forget Cawnpore!', then this appears to have been a generally adopted policy under the period of commemoration presided over with such care by Canning. Thus to consider briefly one more instance of remembering/forgetting the horrors of the mutiny, one may shift attention to another great theatre of violence during the conflict: Lucknow. If Lucknow quickly became most famous for the siege of the Residency, then it was also possible to remember the gruesome deaths of those British civilians who did not find shelter

Government of India 1860–61, Part I, IOR/V/10/14. As Canning would later record in a letter to his sister, Yule and Charlotte spent a great deal of time discussing the monument in common with other subjects, and 'they generally agreed. He knew her tastes well...' See Canning to The Marchioness of Clanricarde, 19 November 1861, quoted in Hare, *Two Noble Lives* Vol. 3, p. 168.

[57] 'Report on the Administration of the North-Western Provinces for the year 1860–61', Section VII, Public Works, pp. 69–70, Administration Reports of the Government of India, IOR/V/10/15.

[58] For a description of the event and Bishop Cotton's assessment of it, see Bishop Cotton to Sophia Anne Cotton, 16 January 1863, quoted in Cotton (ed.), *Memoir of George Edward Lynch Cotton, D.D., Bishop of Calcutta, and Metropolitan: With Selections from His Journals and Correspondence*, p. 283. For a more detailed programme of the event, see 'The Office for the consecration of the Memorial Well and adjacent graves at Cawnpore', Papers of Robert Bensley Thornhill and family, Mss Eur B298/9.

there, but were instead captured and often held prisoner in the city. In this respect, the tale of three British men who had been held captive by the rebels in Awadh before being executed in November 1857, during Campbell's approach to the Residency, garnered particular interest. Sir Mountstuart Jackson, Captain Patrick Orr and Sergeant Major Morton had escaped from Sitapur, located around fifty miles from Lucknow, and had been given refuge in nearby Mitauli. However, as the balance of power within the area seemed to decisively move in favour of the mutineers, the party was soon transported to Lucknow where they were held captive by the rebels. Following over four months' imprisonment, the three prisoners were finally killed during Campbell's successful relief of the Residency and their bodies buried in a hastily prepared communal grave by the rebels.[59]

As we have already seen in the case of Cawnpore, the attachment between memory and place was particularly strong in the practices of memorialisation employed to mark the mutiny and its events, and accordingly, there was an overriding desire to locate the exact location of their grave. To this end, Captain George Hutchinson of the Bengal Engineers, who had been made military secretary to the Chief Commissioner of Awadh when Sir Robert Montgomery replaced Outram in this capacity in April 1858, was given the task of attempting to locate their burial site. Hutchinson, who had been based in Awadh on his return to India from furlough in May 1856 and served in the Residency throughout the siege, knew the city extremely well and with the help of a 'Madrassee' named Lorgeress, attempted to trace the exact place where the three men had been buried.[60] As Lorgeress later explained in his deposition, he was a camp follower who entered the city as part of the first relief of the Residency before being captured by the rebels. Working as a prisoner, Lorgeress was assigned several menial tasks, including the burial of the small British party.[61] With the help of the 'Madrassee' and a number of Indian carpenters who professed to be familiar with the line of fortifications erected by the mutineers, Hutchinson attempted to locate the grave. Despite his best endeavours, however, the final resting place eluded him owing to the fact that, as Lorgeress pointed out, the 'ground [had] been so altered since, that I cannot recognize the place where they were buried'.[62]

[59] For a narrative of these events written by Captain Alexander Orr, together with a number of relevant letters, see Hutchinson, *Narrative of the Mutinies in Oude*, pp. 134–76.
[60] George Hutchinson, 'Memo', printed in Hutchinson, *Narrative of the Mutinies*, p. 250. For more on Hutchinson, see Morris, *George Hutchinson*.
[61] 'Deposition of Lorgeress, Madrasee, a Christian native of Belaree, born and bred a camp follower', in Hutchinson, *Narrative of the Mutinies*, p. 248. See also 'Mutiny Papers, Oude, Information Regarding the death of Sir M. Jackson, Captain A. Orr and Sergeant Major Morton', 'Collections to India Political Dispatches, Vol 1', OIOC, IOR/L/PS/6/459, Coll. 4.
[62] Ibid.

Despite the exact location of burial proving elusive, there was, as Canning informed Lord Stanley, the secretary of State for India, 'sufficient data' for Hutchinson to arrive at 'an approximation to the place of sepulchre' within what appears to be an optimistic estimate of 'fifty yards of their last resting place'.[63] As we explored in the case of Cawnpore earlier, Canning's efforts to memorialise the horrors of the mutiny amounted to a coordinated attempt to 'remember in order to forget' and to remove the traumatic associations of the events that now destabilised all attempts to reinstate a productive colonial relationship on which to pursue the imperial project. The case of memorialisation of horror in Lucknow was no different and whilst Canning felt certain that it 'is right that the British Government should thus evince the importance which it attached to the lives of its servants', he further observed that 'memorials of crime and of suffering' should never be installed if they risked further exacerbating the antipathy which currently existed between the British and native populations.[64] Hutchinson seems to have shared Canning's attitude on the matter and accordingly wholeheartedly approved of the former's assertion that it was of utmost importance that the monument not 'perpetuate the ill feelings between the white man and the black'.[65]

Animated by this desire for reconciliation, Hutchinson recommended a simple inscription for the monument that eschewed any detail of the events commemorated. Rather than an attempt to narrate what public opinion chastised as the treacherous betrayal of Jackson's party or record the circumstances of their deaths, Hutchinson suggested a vague inscription consisting in 'the names of the fallen ... with the date as near as can be given, and this simple remark – "Victims of 1857"'.[66] Plans were also prepared for a second monument to be dedicated to a related party of British captives including Mountstuart Jackson's sister, Georgina Jackson, who were separated from the rest of their group before being executed. However, this second rather larger monument was never completed. Instead, the decision was taken to combine the two memorials into a single edifice with a face dedicated to each group of 'victims' (Figure 2.3).

As this section has made clear, the British administration carefully attempted to eschew any reference to the memories of the multiple horrors committed during the mutiny. Rather, official practices of commemoration carefully negotiated these destabilising memories of treachery, savagery and vengeance in an

[63] 'Erection of two monuments at Lucknow in memory of Sir Mountstuart Jackson and other European and native victims of the Mutiny', Collections to India Political Despatches, Vol. 5, 1858, OIOC, IOR/L/PS/6/463, Coll. 36/18.

[64] Ibid.   [65] Ibid.

[66] George Hutchinson, 'Memo', printed in Hutchinson, *Narrative of the Mutinies*, p. 252. For approval, see Letter 24, 8 April 1859, 'Political Letters to India dated 31st August (at 36) 1859', Copies of Political Letters and Despatches to India, Vol 1, Oct 1858–Aug 1861, 31 August 1859, No. 24, p. 203, OIOC, IOR/L/PS/6/455.

Figure 2.3 Erection of two monuments at Lucknow in memory of Sir Mountstuart Jackson and other European and native victims of the Mutiny. Collections to India Political Despatches, Vol. 5, 1858, pp. 253–54, OIOC, IOR/L/PS/6/463, Coll. 36/18.

attempt to help the populations of cities affected by the mutiny 'remember to forget'. Understood in this way, British commemoration of the multiple horrors of the mutiny was a response to inter-communal resentment and the strength of British fear and loathing which predominated within the colonial community. By attempting to move Britain's space of memory away from the moment of horror exemplified by the early ad hoc practices of memorialisation which imbued Bibighar with meaning and memory, and focus on what Canning called an 'after-condition of sober mournfulness sustained and cheered by hopefulness', commemoration was clearly an attempt to help mollify and reassure the colonial community by constructing a less anxious memory of the horrors of the mutiny than that which dominated in 1857.[67]

Remembering British Heroes and Celebrating Native Loyalty

The previous section of this chapter explored how official memory responded to the multiple horrors of the mutiny. Though important in understanding the trajectory of official memory, such an account does not sufficiently explore the mnemonic policies pursued by the British administration over this period. To more fully interrogate the formation of official memory within the cities most affected by the uprising, it is also necessary to consider the celebration of

[67] Canning to Granville, 17 June 1861, quoted in Fitzmaurice, *The Life of Granville*, p. 396.

heroes and how this element of official memory helped broker reconciliation. In so doing, it is useful to begin by considering the construction of the Mutiny Monument that was built on the Delhi Ridge in the 1860s and which power- fully demonstrates the interplay between remembering and forgetting that was so central to the construction of this memory. As we have seen in the previous chapter, both the British and the rebel forces treated the conquest of Delhi as the single most important strategic objective of the conflict and, accordingly, the alternate victories in the city represented significant turning points in the course of the mutiny as each side found themselves in the ascendency.[68] With this in mind, commemorating the mutiny in Delhi presented a choice between celebrating victory and commemorating defeat as it would be as possible for British memory to focus on the fall of Delhi on 11 May 1857, as it would be for it to concentrate on the reconquest of the city some four months later.

In this regard, it is possible to chart a careful negotiation of available and accessible memories in which the question asked by those engaged in com- memorating the mutiny in Delhi is clearly not what *can* be remembered, but what *should* be remembered. The politics of this process are quite apparent when one considers the nature of this choice. If focusing on the fall of Delhi, then one would most naturally be forced to confront the traumatising image of thousands of sepoys, once seen as the very backbone of British India, arriving at the city in a state of open mutiny. One would have to remember the misplaced confidence of Colonel John Ripley who was ordered to lead the 54th Native Infantry regiment to the Kashmiri Gate to help strengthen the position against the mutineers. One would have to linger on the terrifying moment when his sol- diers made common cause with the mutineers outside the city walls and turned on their own officers whilst helping the rebels open the gate. Finally, such a memory would have to confront the image of sepoys joining with a broad cross- section of the population and engaging in an orgy of violence during which British civilians were murdered in broad daylight on the streets of Delhi.

As we have seen in the previous chapter, such a representation of the mutiny dominated the British imagination throughout the latter half of 1857 helping motivate and legitimise the brutal British response that was deemed necessary for the reestablishment of British supremacy in the subcontinent. However, with the mutiny suppressed and the British administration now attempting to re-establish peace and authority in India, such a memory could only hinder the broader policies of reconciliation being implemented by the government. However, if Delhi could conceivably be a site of horror, treachery, doubt, and uncertainty, then it could also be a space of honour, heroism, and loyalty. If, rather than concentrating on the fall of Delhi, memory focused on its recon- quest, then one was asked to embrace the heroic narrative of a four-month

---

[68] For an insightful exploration of the mutiny in Delhi, see Dalrymple, *The Last Mughal*.

struggle during which a small though determined force consisting primarily of British soldiers, Punjabi sepoys, and Nepalese Gurkhas worked hand in hand to stubbornly hold their precarious position on the Ridge and repel the deadly daily sorties made by the numerically superior rebel force.[69] One would be welcomed to remember heroes such as General Nicholson, who was seen to embody the essential values of the Victorian soldier hero and finally, of course, one could conclude such a memory with the daring and eventually triumphant storming of the city in which a mixture of British and Indian soldiers succeeded in breaching the city walls and ultimately conquering the city.

With such divergent and conflicting memories available, commemorating the mutiny in Delhi necessarily involved a careful negotiation of the events that occurred in the city. Accordingly, the group of British officers who came together at the end of 1858 with the intention of memorialising the conflict carefully considered what the monument should commemorate, before finally resolving on a dedication that embraced both 'the mutiny and massacre at and near Delhi in 1857, and the dangers and triumphs of the siege'.[70] Whilst the memorial committee were thus determined to memorialise both the fall and the reconquest of the city, the central government held a rather different opinion and, when approached on the subject sometime later, agreed to provide financial backing for the project on the proviso that the monument be built solely in 'commemoration of the siege and in honour of those who fell in that operation'.[71] Thus, the monument was to eschew any reference to the massacres of 11 May and the ultimate loss of the city; instead, the monument was to solely focus on the heroic endeavours of those British and Indian soldiers who succeeded in retaking the city and not the trauma of those who lost it.[72]

Ultimately, the building work was completed in the early 1870s with the installation of a number of inscribed tablets.[73] These tablets recorded the

---

[69] For a remarkable first-hand account of the Gurkhas contribution to the siege, and the close friendship that they developed with the 60th Rifles, see Reid, *Centenary of the Siege of Delhi*.

[70] Major F. C. Maisey, Honorary Secretary, Delhi Memorial Fund, to Secy to Govt of India, P.W.Dept., with G.G., Proceedings of the PWD, January 1864, Ecclesiastical Part A. No. 4, OIOC, IOR/P/191/4.

[71] India Proceedings, August 1869, Public Works Department, Civil works Buildings, Part B, No. 22, OIOC, IOR/P/435/9.

[72] For debates on the design's aesthetic merits and budget, see Note by ECSW [Major E.C.S. Williams] NAI, Public Works Department Proceedings, April 1868, No. 14A. India Proceedings, PWD, CWB, November 1864 Part B, No. 2–3, OIOC, IOR/P/191/7; Punjab Proceedings, PWD, CWB, September, Part A, No. 37, OIOC, IOR/P/239/41; Punjab Proceedings, PWD, CWB, February, Part B, No. 106–7, OIOC, IOR/P/239/42.

[73] The original architect of the monument was a young and inexperienced engineer named Edward James Martin, who had only arrived in India from England in 1859 after securing employment with the Public Works Department as an assistant executive engineer. *The Dublin Builder* claimed that there had been over 180 entries to the competition. This extraordinary number appears to be erroneous with Maisey recording a total of six applicants. Anon *The Dublin Builder*, 15 November 1861, p. 689. For details of the myriad financial problems

casualty roles of both British and native soldiers along with a list of regiments involved in the siege and even a chronological list of military actions fought between 30 May and 20 September in and around the city. With the fall of Delhi on 11 May overlooked, the monument's amnesia presents the conflict as an unambiguous victory and almost a simple conquest rather than counterinsurgency. These same tablets further make the monument's dedication clear, informing their reader in English, Urdu, and Hindi that the monument was 'In Memory of the Officers and soldiers British and Native of the Delhi Field force who were killed in action or died of wounds or disease between the 30th May & 20th September 1857. This Monument has been erected by the comrades who lament their loss and by the Government they served so well'. The inscription makes no reference to the identity of the 'enemy', rather the inscription seems to present a conflict fought by British soldiers and Indian sepoys in union against an enemy whose very identity seems to have been forgotten by the monument. Further, the fact that this was a monument not only commemorating Indian soldiers who remained loyal but also a monument to be consumed by an Indian as well as by a British audience is made clear by the multilingual inscriptions. One can almost imagine the government's wish that the British and Indian communities might meet one another around the column and together share in a unifying memory of shared sacrifice and endeavour. Whilst the monument marks difference through the physical separation of audience according to language and the separate listings of Indian and British casualties on the monument, it is ultimately best read as a unifying symbol that not only 'cleanses' the conflict of horror but also almost cleanses it of an enemy. What both Indian and British visitors to the site of memory *should* now collectively remember is that Indian and British soldiers fought together and won a famous victory.[74]

If the construction of the Delhi Mutiny Monument thus involved practices of forgetting as much as it required practices of remembering, then the same was

that the memorial committee had, along with the various design changes which were made, culminating in the protracted period of construction and a number of strange anomalies in the design, see E. Martin, Executive Engineer, 'Report on the expense of constructing the Delhi Memorial Monument', 28 August 1867, NAI, Public Works Department Proceedings, April 1868, No. 13A. India Proceedings, August 1869, Public Works Department, Civil works Buildings, Part B, No. 22, OIOC, IOR/P/435/9. Note by ECSW, NAI, Public Works Department Proceedings, April 1868, No. 14A. India Proceedings, PWD, CWB, November 1864 Part B, No. 2–3, OIOC, IOR/P/191/7; Punjab Proceedings, PWD, CWB, September, Part A, No. 37, OIOC, IOR/P/239/41; Punjab Proceedings, PWD, CWB, February, Part B, No. 106–7, OIOC, IOR/P/239/42. Major F. C. Maisey, Honorary Secretary, Delhi Memorial Fund, to Secy. to Govt. of India, P.W. Dept., with G.G., Proceedings of the PWD, January 1864, Ecclesiastical Part A. No. 4, OIOC, IOR/P/191/4.

[74] For a useful guide to the technical specifications of the monument that includes a number of diagrams as well as an overview of the financial problems written by the architect, see Martin, 'Delhi Memorial Monument', pp. 199–208.

Figure 2.4 The Delhi Mutiny Monument. Photograph by the author, 2012.

no less true for the other major monument to be established in the city. With the Kashmiri Gate baring deep gorges and damage as a result of the mutiny in the city, the decision was taken to not repair the badly damaged structure, rather it was to be kept in the exact condition in which it was left following the conflict.[75] However, here again the question remains open as to what the gate was intended to convey and what one was expected to remember whilst observing it. The Kashmiri Gate had, after all, witnessed two of the most dramatic events of the mutiny in Delhi, and from a British perspective, it could be a mnemonic marker of defeat and betrayal as much as it could be seen as an emblem of victory and triumph.

However, once again, the dedication to the monument makes clear what should be remembered whilst standing and staring at the shot-pitted building.[76]

---

[75] As Mrinalini Rajagopalan has argued, the use of photography was central to the process by which the Kashmiri Gate came to be seen as an important site of memory. See Rajagopalan, 'From Colonial Memorial to National Monument: The Case of the Kashmiri Gate, Delhi', pp. 73–101.

[76] The small memorial giving a dedication to the Kashmiri Gate was established at the behest of Lord Napier when commander-in-chief of India, India Proceedings 1876–7, Public Works: Military Works, March, 137–8 Part B, OIOC, IOR/P/977.

These were not the holes that had been left by bullets fired by the mutineers as they stormed the city in May; these were the marks left by British forces that stormed the same gate four months later. In particular, the monument was dedicated to the bravery and courage of a small party tasked with blowing in the gate during the reconquest of the city. Whilst the assault column led by Colonel Campbell of the 52nd Light Infantry lay down out of range of the rebels' guns, a small demolition party, consisting of eight sappers led by two officers and accompanied by a bugler, approached the gates with the intention of blowing them in. In the face of heavy fire, the party succeeded in first nailing several powder bags to the gates before lighting the charge and forcing an entry to the city. In the process, eight of the eleven strong parties were killed and four would later receive the Victoria Cross including the bugler, Robert Hawthorne who, throwing himself into the ditch before hearing the ensuing explosion, sounded the advance which saw the city stormed by the onrushing assault column.[77]

As we have seen previously, official memory of the Mutiny in Delhi involved a careful negotiation of memory. Eschewing a focus on divisive memories of treachery, massacre, and bloodshed, official commemoration was careful to construct a memory of victory won by British and Indian soldiers fighting side by side. If this memory of the mutiny in Delhi came to characterise British commemoration, then a remarkably similar process can be observed in Lucknow. As we have already seen in the previous section of this chapter, incidence of murder and bloodshed was carefully remembered in such a way as to facilitate amnesia. This was also true in the case of the defence of the Residency which, from an extremely early date during the mutiny itself, was seen as an archetypal example of bravery, sacrifice, endurance, and ultimate victory. Significantly, however, just as we have seen in the case of Delhi, this glorious episode was presented as a shared victory won by British and Indian troops.

The first movement towards commemorating the defence of the Residency was formalised by Charles Wingfield, the chief commissioner of Awadh.[78] Hosting a number of meetings to solicit the views of the British population of Lucknow on how the conflict should be commemorated, it was ultimately resolved to build a suitable monument 'on or near the site of the Residency', dedicated to all those who died defending the building up to its first relief.[79] Though this time frame may appear almost arbitrary, it emphasised the mnemonic focus of the monument. Rather than commemorate the mutiny in Awadh

---

[77] Dalrymple, *The Last Mughal*, pp. 347–49.

[78] Anon, 'The Lucknow Memorial' in Hilton, *The Tourists Guide to Lucknow*, Appendix B, Extract from the *Express*, pp. vi–xi.

[79] Ibid.

as a whole, the memorial was ostensibly dedicated to the heroic defence of the Residency during what was seen as the most trying and perilous period. With the appointment of a small committee based in Lucknow and consisting of a number of senior ranking British military officers, subscriptions were gradually collected and eventually surpassed what was required to construct a suitable structure. Accordingly, the Memorial Committee announced a design competition with the winning entry declared in late 1861.[80] Considering a range of memorial structures submitted by several different individuals, the committee selected an imposing design prepared by George Gilbert Scott who is best known for his gothic revival architecture in England. The design had originally been considered for the Cawnpore Memorial, but Marochetti's statue had ultimately been preferred.[81]

Despite the Memorial Committee being eager to begin work on construction, broader security concerns mired their progress. Closely following Brigadier General Sir Robert Napier's plans, Lucknow was to be secured through a range of measures including the construction of three new forts in the city, including one on the site of the former Residency.[82] However, whilst two of these forts were rapidly completed, the Residency location remained undeveloped owing to a lack of resources leading to some speculation on its necessity.[83] With debate and discussion on the subject continuing into 1864 and with the shattered buildings in much the same condition as when the city was retaken, Wingfield, for one, was extremely critical of what he saw as an impediment to the development of Lucknow, describing the ruins as nothing but 'a disfigurement' to the landscape which should be cleared as soon as possible.[84] Seeing no aesthetic value in the compound, Wingfield instead favoured converting it into residential housing as 'there is great want of house accommodation at Lucknow, and many persons are most anxious to build on the site of the old Residency ... if the site is made available on building leases'.[85] Ultimately, the military decided that the

---

[80] Ibid.

[81] George Gilbert Scott also designed the monument outside Westminster Abbey in commemoration of the members of Westminster School who had died during the Crimean War and the Indian Mutiny.

[82] See Brigadier General Sir R. Napier, 'Memorandum on the Military Occupation of the City of Lucknow', Professional Papers of the Royal Engineers 9 (1860), Paper v, pp. 17–38, p. 17, Royal Engineer's Museum and Library Collection. For further details on the post-conflict reconstruction of Lucknow, see Oldenburg, *The Making of Colonial Lucknow*.

[83] See Lieut. Col. Henry Yule to Secretary to Government of India, Military Dept, 21 November 1861, India Proceedings, Public Works Department, Military Works, March 1864, No. 81, p. 112, OIOC, IOR/P/191/5. See also Major Crommelin, 'Memorandum on the Military Works that have been executed at Lucknow, in Pursuance of Brigadier General Sir R. Napier's Scheme for the Occupation and Defense of the City'. Paper v. Professional Papers of the Royal Engineers 9 (1860), pp. 17–38, p. 17. Royal Engineer's Museum and Library Collection.

[84] C. Wingfield, 'Memo', India Proceedings, Public Works Department, Military Works, March 1864, No. 84, p. 115, IOR/P/191/5.

[85] Ibid.

Residency fort was not necessary but were eager to retain the location in case future developments necessitated the construction of a fort.[86]

With the site not in immediate demand from the military but with a prohibition on building on the site, interest refocused on a plan first suggested by Canning during a visit to Awadh in 1861, after which he expressed a bold opinion on the future of the site arguing that, should the land not be needed for defensive purposes, then all ramparts and earthworks should be neatly and decently levelled, and as 'the Residency itself cannot be restored:

> The best course will be to remove loose timbers and other portions threatening to fall, to keep the brick-work free from peepul trees, and to grow some good creepers judiciously over the remains, so that this interesting ruin shall be preserved and rendered as sightly as possible. Thus it will harmonize well with the monument for which so admirable a site has been selected near the building.[87]

As we have seen throughout this chapter, Canning was acutely concerned with how the mutiny should be memorialised; however, his suggestion for the future of the Residency is undoubtedly his most innovative. The practice of preserving ruins as monuments became fashionable during the twentieth century with structures such as the Hiroshima Peace Memorial capturing public attention; however, Canning's proposal for the Residency is perhaps the first of its kind. Of greatest interest is the disjunction between Canning's suggestion for the Residency and the scheme of memorialisation he employed to mark the horrors of the mutiny in Cawnpore and Lucknow. As we explored previously, Canning instituted a process of commemoration that is perhaps best recognised as an attempt to forget. If Canning was positive on the need to move beyond the moment of horror, then his suggestion for the Residency is the inverse. By maintaining the buildings in their shot torn and ruined condition, Canning suspends memory within the moment of heroic endeavour, endurance, and sacrifice rather than moving memory to a space beyond the event.

Canning's suggestion proved popular, and accordingly, all defensive works were removed whilst the buildings were reinforced and preserved.[88] In addition, the ground was heavily remodelled and in time made increasingly ornate with a wide selection of flowers, shrubs, and trees planted throughout and with special care and attention paid to the graveyard which was finally consecrated

---

[86] See 'Extract from the proceedings of His Excellency the Governor General of India in Council in the Military Department', 1 March 1864, India Proceedings, Public Works Department, Military Works, March 1864, No. 86, p. 117, OIOC, IOR/P/191/5.

[87] Lieut. Col. H. Yule, R. E., Secy. to Govt. of India, P.W. Dept., to Chief Commissioner of Oudh, 21 November 1861, India Proceedings, Public Works Department, Military Works, March 1864, No. 80, p. 112, IOR/P/191/5.

[88] 'Extract from the proceedings of His Excellency the Governor General of India in Council in the Military Department', 1 March 1864, India Proceedings, Public Works Department, Military Works, March 1864, No. 86, p. 117, IOR/P/191/5.

in December 1864, and meticulously landscaped and replanted by a dedicated team of gardeners.[89] In time, the Residency would become famous for being the only site within the empire to fly the Union Jack both during the day and night; however, it is not clear when this practice began.[90] With the ruined Residency now secured as a memorial, a large ceremony could swiftly be planned and promoted by the Memorial Committee to mark the laying of the foundation stone for the monument dedicated to the dead European defenders.[91] With the foundation stone laid, construction work began immediately and the monument, bearing the inscription 'In memory of Major Genl Sir Henry Lawrence KCB and the brave men who fell in defence of the Residency AD 1857', was complete by the time Henry Lawrence's brother, John Lawrence, arrived in Lucknow as governor-general to host a durbar within the city in November 1867; the tenth anniversary of the end of the siege (Figure 2.5).[92]

Though Lawrence's Cross was of undoubted significance to the commemorative landscape of the Residency, perhaps the single most important addition to the site of memory was the monument dedicated to the native defenders which was constructed at the behest of Thomas George Baring, 1st Earl of Northbrook, who had been appointed Viceroy in 1872. Erected near to the Baillie Guard Gate and dedicated to the 'native officers and sepoys ... who died near this spot nobly performing their duty', this second monument was

---

[89] Llewellyn-Jones, *Engaging Scoundrels: True Tales of Old Lucknow*, p. 171. The grave monuments appeared gradually as part of an ad hoc process following the reconquest of Lucknow despite the fact that it was obvious to numerous people that many of the bodies had been dug-up, presumably in search of hidden treasure. Lieutenant Ashton Warner, for example, noted with some disgust that it was obvious to him that 'the niggers have destroyed' the Residency buildings a great deal since the Relief of Lucknow and more worryingly they had 'desecrated some of the graves'
  Ashton C. Warner to Aunt Betsey, 21 March 1858. 'Letters of Major Ashton Cromwell Warner in India to and from his family', Journals of Captain Richard Warner and letters of his son, Major Ashton Cromwell Warner, to and from friends and family, fol. 68 Mss Eur F580/4.

[90] Contrary to popular belief, pictorial and written evidence suggests that this was most likely an invented tradition within the early twentieth century; possibly to coincide with the visit of the Prince of Wales in 1905. Certainly, this practice would be more in keeping with the second phase of commemoration to be discussed in Chapter 3.

[91] For details of the ceremony arranged for the laying of the foundation stone, see 'Laying the Foundation of the Lucknow Memorial', pp. 255–56, p. 256; Anon, 'The Lucknow Memorial'.

[92] Visitors to the Residency today will find Lawrence's Cross is no longer set on this mound. The mound proved extremely unpopular and had not been part of the landscape in 1857 soliciting regular calls for its removal including that of the Commissioner of Lucknow, Leslie Porter, in 1903. This opinion was supported by the Lieutenant-Governor of the United Provinces, Sir J. D. LaTouche and the Viceroy, Lord Curzon, resulting in its removal in the early twentieth century. See LaTouche to Curzon, 26 April 1903, No. 122, p. 112d, 'Correspondence with People in India, Jan 1903 – Jun 1903', Papers of Marquess Curzon of Kedleston, MSS EUR F111/207. Curzon to LaTouche 11 May 1903, No. 81, pp. 64–65, 'Correspondence with People in India, Jan 1903 – Jun 1903', Papers of Marquess Curzon of Kedleston, MSS EUR F111/207.

Figure 2.5 The Residency and 'Lawrence's Cross'. Photograph by John
Sache, 1872.

specifically dedicated to the Indian soldiers who helped defend the position
throughout the siege.[93] Construction work was entrusted to Llewelyn and Co.
which had operated in Calcutta under various owners since 1806 and was also
responsible for the construction of the Mutiny Memorial located in the Jhansi
Cantonment Cemetery commemorating the victims of the so-called Jhansi
Mutiny Massacre.

If the construction of George Gilbert Scott's monument required a significant and widely reported ceremony, then the laying of the foundation stone
for Northbrook's monument proved infinitely grander and was reported with
interest throughout the empire. Presided over by the Prince of Wales, later
King Edward VII, as part of his Royal Tour of India in 1875–76, the event
naturally garnered significant interest and discussion. Indeed, according to
George Wheeler, a journalist who travelled with the Prince throughout the
tour, the occasion was the 'most impressive ceremony in which the Prince took
part in India'.[94] At the suggestion of the commander-in-chief, Lord Napier of

[93] Inscription on monument, author's notes.   [94] Wheeler, *India in 1875–6*, p. 227.

Magdala, the presence of the 16th (The Lucknow) Bengal Infantry formed an important component of this ceremony.[95] Formed out of the remnants of the 13th, 48th, and 71st Bengal Native Infantry Regiments, the 16th Bengal Infantry provided an important connection to the heroes commemorated.[96] It was, however, the apparently impromptu decision taken by the Prince to meet each of the surviving Indian veterans which proved to be the most evocative aspect of the ceremony. According to Couper, who reported on the ceremony to Northbrook in the latter's absence, 'It was rather a touching spectacle, as some of the poor old fellows were stone blind, and others were so decrepit that they had some difficulty in coming forward'.[97]

Upon its completion, this monument joined an already existing memorial 'erected in memory of the devoted gallantry and fidelity of the Native Officers and Sepoys of the Hon'ble Company's 13th Bengal Native Infantry who fell during the defence of Lucknow'. Naming the native officers and listing the numbers of other ranks who died defending the Residency, this memorial further helped underscore what should be remembered by all those who visited the compound. If British bravery, courage, and fortitude were a central focus of commemoration, then Indian loyalty was perhaps the single most important element. Just as the monument built on the Delhi Ridge is dedicated to the British and Indian soldiers who lay siege to the city, so too does the Residency remember that it was defended by British and Indian troops fighting side by side. Loyalty not treachery – that is what *should* be remembered in the decades that followed the mutiny.

Reconciliation and the Stain of the Forgotten

The announcement that Queen Victoria was to become the Empress of India in 1877 was seen by many commentators as the end of a remarkable process during which India was successfully reincorporated into the empire following the bloody uprising of 1857. Achieved in large measure by a prolonged period of careful administration that attempted to appease the Indian

---

[95] Napier to Northbrook, 31 December 1875, 'Correspondence with persons in India 1874–5' Papers of the Earl of Northbrook as Viceroy of India, p. 500, Mss Eur C144/17.

[96] Indeed, in recognition of the regiment's participation in the defence of Lucknow, the regiment had been permitted to adopt the 'design of a "turreted gateway"', 'in recognition of the good service rendered by the sepoys who formed the nucleus of the corps in the defence of the Baillie Guard Gate during the siege of the Residency'. Military Despatch of the Government of India, 14 December 1871, 'Regimental Colors & Appointments, Honorary Distinctions & Titles 1871, 16th (Lucknow) Bengal Infantry Grant of Design of "Turreted Gateway" for colours'. IOR/L/MIL/7/10672.

[97] Couper to Northbrook, 11 January 1876, 'Correspondence with persons in India 1876–7' Papers of the Earl of Northbrook as Viceroy of India, p. 13, Mss Eur C144/18. Russell gives a more detailed and melodramatic description of this event, see Russell, *The Prince of Wales' Tour*, p. 395.

population and reinstall a sense of British authority in the subcontinent, the twenty years which separated the mutiny from the Delhi Durbar appeared to see much of the rancour and residual animosity, harboured by the British and the Indian communities in the immediate aftermath of the mutiny, dissipate. As this chapter has shown, commemoration was an important part of this official policy in India, which therefore played a significant role in helping re-establish British control of the subcontinent by shaping the events of 1857 into a useable form. Indeed, the Royal Tour of India taken by the Prince of Wales, which was briefly discussed previously, both demonstrates the central role of commemoration in the conciliatory policies pursued by the British Administration in India, whilst also underscoring their broader success.

Landing in Bombay in November 1875, the Prince was able to travel the country, spending his time visiting numerous cities where he participated in a wide array of ceremonies including a number of grand and lavish durbars and carefully coordinated and choreographed levees at which the Prince of Wales was brought into contact with a diverse selection of the colonial elite as well as countless numbers of the most powerful and significant members of the Indian population. Among the many cities and locations selected for the Prince to visit, those associated with the mutiny were among the most conspicuous. Visiting Lucknow, Cawnpore, and Delhi over the course of twelve days, the royal party visited all of the principal mutiny monuments and, as shown earlier in connection with Lucknow, these mnemonic spaces witnessed many of the most important events conducted in each of the locations. These ceremonies, along with the others presided over by the Prince, were carefully constructed to emphasise an ideology of British military strength and political control which was presented in such a way as to portray it as not only accepted by indigenous Indians but also actively desired by native rulers and the great mass of the population. These expressions of military power set against explicit Indian consent and loyalty during the Royal Tour had a decisive impact upon how the colonial relationship was imagined in England as much as in India. Indeed, the apparent harmony that had replaced the poisonous relationship that had existed between the British administration and the Indian population twenty years earlier proved to be a decisive factor in the decision to crown Queen Victoria as Empress of India.[98]

If the conservative policies that were pursued in India helped secure the subcontinent in the two decades that followed the mutiny, then the mnemonic policies considered in this chapter also played an important role in re-building British India. As we have seen, the official memory of the mutiny, which was

[98] See Cohn, 'Representing Authority'.

deployed over this period, was an active and often self-conscious attempt to suture the physiological wound left by a year of bloody and traumatic warfare. Accordingly, official memory attempted to transform the revolt into a celebration of native loyalty and fidelity to the British Raj which both helped consolidate the army and reconcile the British and Indian communities in the months and years which followed the cessation of open violence. Eschewing a focus on the bloody massacres which had occupied British attention throughout the latter half of 1857, the mutiny was now represented as a glorious victory won by British soldiers and Indian sepoys fighting side by side against an enemy whose very identity is almost forgotten or at least obscured within these mnemonic practices.

However, for all the official celebration of native loyalty and inter-communal cordiality twenty years on from the uprising, there still existed a powerful undercurrent of resentment, anger, and anxiety which stemmed from residual memories of bloodshed and massacre during the conflict. Indeed, the habitual fear that developed in the wake of 1857 and which was discussed at the start of this chapter was not a short-lived phenomenon, rather it proved to be a pervasive aura that continued to engulf the Anglo-Indian community long after the uprising had been suppressed. Indeed, throughout the two decades that elapsed between the Mutiny and the elevation of Queen Victoria to Empress of India, it is possible to identify a series of panics predicated on that perennial colonial spectre, 'The Second Mutiny'. Rather than seeing these as aberrations they are rather moments at which the shadow cast by the carefully constructed official memory of 1857 come into focus. Perhaps the earliest of these occurred within just months of the 'first mutiny' being decisively suppressed. Based on extremely flimsy evidence primarily obtained from a house search in Lahore, the supposed conspiracy was said to extend across an extensive network of Sikhs and centre on an ageing Sikh colonel who was accused of actively fomenting another mutiny. Apparently planned for 1863, reports of the nascent uprising made it into British newspapers in mid-1859 where it was reported that the Sikhs intended to rise, 'exterminate the children of Christ, keep English women in their houses, and restore the supreme power of the Khalsa'.[99] Whatever the validity of these rumours, the intelligence was immediately acted upon resulting in the pre-emptive arrest and imprisonment of several supposed ringleaders, causing the colonial administration to be congratulated by the British press on forestalling another violent outburst against colonial rule.[100]

If the prevalence of such rumours betrays something of the habitual fear that clouded the colonial experience after 1857, then this legacy of anxiety

[99] Anon, *John Bull*, 2 May 1859, p. 4.   [100] Ibid.

is perhaps best exemplified over this period by the remarkable panic which developed in response to a series of small-scale skirmishes between members of the Sikh Kuka sect and local Muslims in the Punjab. Following a small raid on several Muslim villages in early 1872 which resulted in the capture of sixty-eight Kuka aggressors, L. Cowan, the British deputy commissioner, became convinced that he was now confronted by an incipient rebellion which must be suppressed by whatever means were necessary to ensure that it would not develop into a large-scale rebellion in the mould of the mutiny.[101] Imagining that there were hundreds of armed Kukas preparing for attack, but lacking the troops to directly confront the threat, the deputy commissioner decided that the only course of action available to him was to present his shadowy enemy with a devastating display of colonial violence sufficient to dissuade any would-be rebels from their plans. Turning to the mutiny as a guide, he executed each of the sixty-eight Kuka prisoners by having them blown from guns. The selection of execution method, along with Cowan's discursive construction of an imagined rebellion as well as his own role in helping forestall an incipient insurrection betrays, as Kim A. Wagner has argued, the extent to which the mutiny helped colour the colonial experience after 1857.[102]

If this persistent sense of fear and loathing is best read as the 'dark shadow' cast by these exultant displays of loyalty and trust considered previously, then it can also be identified in the form of fissures running throughout these practices of commemoration. Just as the previous chapter argued that Sir Joseph Noel Paton's commemorative composition remained stained by the very fear that it was designed to belie, so too were these large-scale acts of commemoration coloured by the pervasive colonial anxieties and intense desires for revenge. This fact becomes abundantly clear if we consider a quite different response to the commemorative landscapes considered previously, which was apparent when, just months after the Prince of Wales had visited Cawnpore as part of his Royal Tour in 1876, another group of visitors travelled to the city with the intention of baring witness to the memorial environment.[103] Among these visitors was Private McGrath, a young soldier serving with the 22nd Regiment of Foot, who travelled with the rest of his regiment to the city from where they were stationed a little over 100 miles north of Cawnpore in the garrison town of Shahjahanpur. The various mutiny monuments apparently had a great impact on many members of the regiment but 'The Angel of the

---

[101] For the most comprehensive study of this event, see Condos, *The Insecurity State*, Chapter 3, 'Law, the Punjab School, and the Kooka Outbreak of 1972', pp. 103–39.

[102] Wagner, 'Treading upon Fires'; Wagner, 'Calculated to Strike Terror', pp. 185–225; Wagner, *Amritsar 1919*.

[103] Anon, 'Extraordinary Murders by a European Soldier', p. 4.

Resurrection' had the longest lasting and ultimately most troubling impact on McGrath. Arriving at the monument with a small group, McGrath circled the Angel with several other members of his regiment whilst Lieutenant Deering, another member of the same regiment, felt compelled to kneel down and copy out the inscription engraved on the rim of the well. Whilst all those present were affected by their shared experience of the monument, it had no greater impact on any present than it did on McGrath who, as he would later admit under interrogation, returned to Shahjahanpur harbouring a newfound hatred for the native population.[104]

Wrestling with his emotions following this troubling and emotive experience of remembering the mutiny within the Memorial Gardens, McGrath was ultimately unable to suppress an overwhelming sense of fear and loathing that slowly bubbled to the surface. Leaving the barracks before the morning parade on 7 April 1876 and carrying with him his rifle and two pouches of ammunition, McGrath walked purposely into the native town in search of a victim on whom he could exercise vengeance. With Cawnpore dominating his thoughts, McGrath went on a terrifying murder spree that ultimately saw the young private kill three Indians chosen, it would appear, quite at random.[105] With reports of the shootings quickly reaching the cantonment and with McGrath's absence from morning parade already noted, the soldier was immediately apprehended when he reappeared at the cantonment. Questioned about his earlier whereabouts and the fact that his gun had evidently been recently discharged, McGrath at first denied any wrongdoing but, at length, told Lieutenant Deering that he was prepared to confide in him. Informing the officer that ever since visiting the Cawnpore Well he had developed a strong hatred towards every Indian and 'could never bear the sight of these natives', he admitted that he had 'been out this morning and shot three', before ominously adding under his breath 'a dozen more'.[106]

Though McGrath's pathological reaction to the Angel of the Resurrection might be considered a perverse aberration born of any number of psychological problems, I believe that it points towards something far more endemic that lay at the heart of what it meant to remember the mutiny. The fear and loathing that overcame the private was an essential component of remembering the mutiny in 1876, just as it had been at the height of the conflict and throughout the intervening decades. The stain of the forgotten still coloured Private McGrath's canvas of memory every bit as much as it did that of the Anglo-Indian community, as was evidenced in their feverish and panicked responses to even the smallest disturbance or sign of unrest. Living in a country in which the ghosts of mutineers still ran down every thoroughfare, and menaced every

---

[104] Ibid.   [105] Ibid.   [106] Ibid.

English lady, these mnemonic shadows were given human form. Whether in the form of the sixty-eight imprisoned Kukas who were blown from cannons in an attempt to exorcise the spectre of revolt in 1872 or in the three Indians chosen, so it would appear, quite at random by Private McGrath in 1876, the British imagination created mutineers everywhere around them and then feverishly attempted to destroy them.

3   Negotiating Fear
Celebration, Commemoration, and the 'Mutiny Pilgrimage'

Chapter 2 interrogated the practices of commemoration employed to memorialise the mutiny of 1857 over the first two decades that followed the uprising. Instituted by Lord Canning and developed further by subsequent viceroys, these acts of commemoration were a response to the overwhelming legacy of colonial anxiety that haunted the Anglo-Indian community in the wake of 1857. Responsible for a habitual sense of vulnerability that frequently developed into a desperate panic predicated on fears of a 'second mutiny', this colonial anxiety – stemming from British memories of 1857 – proved a significant impediment to the reassertion of a productive colonial relationship in this period. Accordingly, commemoration was an active and largely conscious attempt to manage, contain, and even transform the pernicious legacy of the mutiny by constructing a representation that eschewed anxiety-provoking recollections of violence and bloodshed whilst celebrating British courage and, above all, Indian loyalty as essential components of a glorious imperial victory. However, in Chapter 2, despite the administration's best efforts to convert the uprising into a reassuring narrative of native fidelity, colonial anxieties connected to memories of the mutiny continued to exist and help define Anglo-India's lived reality in the post-mutiny period.

This chapter will continue to interrogate British memorialisation by turning attention to what may legitimately be considered the second phase of commemoration. Conducted during the 'high-noon of empire', and most closely associated with Viceroy Lord Curzon, this stage of commemoration shifted the mnemonic focus to the exploits of British mutiny heroes. Ostensibly a celebration of British martial prowess, and a proud assertion of colonial confidence, this official memory of the 1857 uprising was embedded within a broad range of commemorative activities over this period. However, this chapter argues that, as was the case in the first two decades that followed the cessation of violence, these practices of commemoration utilised by the British administration developed in response to the intensity of colonial anxiety concerning the possibility of further armed insurrection in the mould of 1857. In this respect, Thomas Metcalf's assessment of this period is revealing, when he notes that 'as anxiety mounted, the British turned for reassurance to a ringing show of self-confidence'.[1] Metcalf's perceptive account of how the British responded to the sociopolitical climate of the period seems to be an apt description of the mnemonic practices employed to memorialise the mutiny. Seen in this way, the sudden re-emergence of commemoration in the 1890s and the early twentieth century should alert us to the growing sense of colonial apprehension in late Victorian India connected to the increasing Indian threat to British supremacy. Therefore, as will be shown, this celebratory memory of 1857 continued to be riven by intense anxieties that refused to be completely silenced by the excessive displays of confidence.

In developing this argument, this chapter will call into question those studies that have sought to show how the mutiny attained an almost sacred aura within British conceptions of empire in the late Victorian era. Among the most engaging studies to develop such an argument is Gautam Chakravarty's important work *The Indian Mutiny and the British Imagination*.[2] According to Chakravarty's careful readings of numerous texts written in this period, the mutiny was shaped by the jingoistic and imperialistic sentiments that gradually rose to prominence in the 1870s before reaching their apogee in the 1890s, following the Berlin Conference of 1884 and the start of the so-called scramble for Africa. In this respect, Chakravarty shows how the mutiny was imagined as an archetypal colonial small war that demonstrated the martial qualities of an inherently imperial race at the height of its confidence.[3]

In many ways, Chakravarty's work on the mutiny concurs with the scholarship on late-century commemoration and what it meant to remember the mutiny within these spaces of memory. Contending that the uprising was remembered by the British as 'a heroic myth embodying and expressing their central values which explained their rule in India to themselves', Bernard Cohn argues that visitors who travelled to mutiny monuments remembered and celebrated British 'sacrifice, duty, fortitude', and, above all, 'ultimate triumph over those Indians who had threatened properly constituted authority and order'.[4] More recently, Cohn's engagement with the Mutiny Tour has been significantly extended and developed by Manu Goswami.[5] Through careful readings of a range of texts, consisting primarily of travelogues and guide books published in the late nineteenth century and up to the end of 1905, Goswami argues that the Mutiny Tour was a greatly regimented practice that helped reinforce an already well-established 'official mutiny script'.[6] Presenting the mutiny

---

[1] Metcalf, *The New Cambridge History of India*, p. 167.
[2] Chakravarty, *The Indian Mutiny and the British Imagination*.   [3] Ibid.
[4] Cohn, 'Representing Authority', p. 179.
[5] Goswami, 'Mutiny Tours in Colonial South Asia'.   [6] Ibid, p. 56.

as a triumphant example of English martial prowess demonstrated by heroic soldier-saints who embodied all the essential qualities of an idealised conception of masculinity, Goswami argues that this official memory of the mutiny played a crucial role in the formation of what it meant to be English in the late nineteenth century.[7]

Examining broadly the same set of published and unpublished tour diaries consulted by Goswami and asking what it meant to remember the mutiny when coming into contact with these commemorative sites, this chapter draws a significantly different conclusion to that proposed by those studies considered above. If, as Goswami and Cohn suggest, the Mutiny Tour exuded a strident colonial confidence, then this chapter will argue that this superficial façade was riven by an abject fear of rebellion. Memories of the mutiny as a heroic conflict that helped construct the English soldier hero and sustain and support the aggressive imperial policies of the era were a fraught response to the uncertainty and precariousness of the contemporary political situation within India. Indeed, if the late Victorian era exuded a strident colonial confidence, then it was also gripped by growing British apprehensions over the rise of Indian nationalism and increasing Indian resistance to imperial rule. Focusing on a range of issues, including racism, colonial economic exploitation, and social and cultural intrusion, an array of sub-nationalist and nationalist voices rose in opposition to the British Raj in the late nineteenth century. Among these critical voices, it was those that emanated from within the Indian National Congress which proved to be among the most significant.

Formed in 1885, the Congress developed over the following two decades into a platform that became synonymous with a brand of moderate middle-class Indian nationalism espoused by prominent spokespeople such as Gopal Krishna Gokhale. Though supportive of Western political institutions, the Congress developed significant critiques of colonial rule which initially, at least, centred on the racist sentiments which had risen to prominence in response to the 1883 Ilbert Bill, which proposed that Indian judges should have the ability to try Europeans in certain criminal cases, and a nuanced economic critique of colonialism that highlighted the drain of wealth from India to Britain. Developing alongside this strain of moderate Indian nationalism was a rather more reactionary and extremist critique of colonialism. Indeed, just as the belligerent spirit of new imperialism reached its apogee in the 1890s, this brand of more extreme Indian nationalism made itself known through a range

---

[7] Ibid. With the Mutiny Tour helping establish and cement the values that formed the core of this idealised English subject, Goswami argues that expositions of national identity have failed to acknowledge the extent to which 'Englishness' was not a category that was produced in the metropole before radiating outwards to the periphery – rather it was shaped in large measure beyond English borders and then transported back to the imperial centre.

of movements, including the anti-colonial protests that accompanied the 1891 Age of Consent Act, inter-communal violence and anti-British feeling arising from the Cow Protection Movement, and, most significantly, agitations arising as a result of the measures introduced by the British administration to tackle the plague that spread from Bombay to Pune in late 1896–97.[8] With the maturation of Indian nationalism accelerating in the last years of the nineteenth century, the appointment of Lord Curzon as Viceroy in 1899 occurred at a critical juncture in the history of the British Raj. Though India under Curzon witnessed such excessive and, at points, vulgar displays of imperial control, confidence, and affluence such as the Coronation Durbar of 1903, it was also a period during which this increasingly assertive and sometimes openly belligerent and radical brand of Indian nationalism made itself known. Though Curzon, upon his arrival in India, hoped that Indian nationalist aspirations would naturally wither in the face of an efficient imperial administration, he also directed considerable attention towards monitoring and directly combatting the growth of Indian nationalism.[9] Accordingly, his amendments to the Calcutta Corporation in 1899, the Universities Act in 1904, and, most controversially of all, his partition of Bengal in 1905 each carried designs of combatting the rise of Indian nationalism.[10] However, far from checking its growth, these measures only succeeded in stoking the flames of protest and discontentment which, as a result, burned brighter than ever before.[11]

With the rise of Indian nationalism convincing many British commentators that India was on the brink of rebellion, fear of armed insurrection in the mould of 1857 began to pervade the Anglo-Indian community, which once again became readily excited to the state of panic at often the most insubstantial intelligence.[12] With these debilitating anxieties colouring daily interactions with the Indian population and otherwise proving an impediment to the efficient functioning of the colonial state, commemoration re-emerged in an excessively triumphant form. Like a prize fighter celebrating former victories on the eve of a title defence, the British constructed for themselves a jubilant and ostensibly self-confident representation of the mutiny designed to reassure and embolden present generations at a moment of imperial crisis. Though successful in masking the intense feelings of vulnerability and anxiety that animated these displays of exultant confidence, commemoration once again failed to efface the deep-seated fears of rebellion which are discernible in the form of fissures running through these mnemonic activities.

---

[8] For more on these issues, see Engles, 'The Age of Consent Act of 1891', pp. 107–31; Robb, 'The Challenge of Gau Mata', pp. 285–319; Catanach, 'Poona Politicians and the Plague', pp. 1–18.
[9] Gilmour, *Curzon: Imperial Statesman*.
[10] See Sarkar, *The Swadeshi Movement in Bengal 1903–1908*.   [11] Ibid.
[12] An excellent example of this is the 'mud-daubing incident' of 1894, which is discussed at length in Wagner, 'Treading upon Fires'.

In exploring the second phase of commemoration, this chapter will be divided into two principal sections. The first will consider the resurgence of commemoration in the 1890s and early 1900s that witnessed the construction of new mutiny monuments in the three major mnemonic landscapes associated with the mutiny, as discussed in Chapter 2. The second will reconsider the mutiny pilgrimages made by a diverse selection of British travellers over the same period and to the same locations. As we will see, the superficial triumphalism of these commemorative practices was an active and often conscious response to contemporary anxieties that could only ever succeed in occasionally silencing, but never effacing, the fears of rebellion that animated them.

Commemoration, Celebration, and Reassurance

As noted in the previous section, the late Victorian era witnessed a second phase of commemoration in India. If the first was primarily aimed at containing the tremendous fear and loathing that was induced by a year of bloody warfare, then the second appears to have extended this memory by producing an ever more strident and bombastic memory of the mutiny as an exemplary colonial small war. However, this memory of the mutiny was largely a response to the intensity of colonial anxieties that developed over the period. Seen thus, this excessively triumphant projection of imperial celebration developed as an often active attempt to conceal its own motivating factor.

To take the mnemonic development of the Residency first, one of the most important additions to the thirty-three-acre site was the establishment of a museum. The lineage of this idea can be traced back to the 1870s and to the construction of a small room to house a scale model of the Residency built by the chaplain of Lucknow, Reverend Thomas Moore.[13] This rather modest room was transformed into a dedicated museum thanks, in large measure, to the efforts and support given to the project by the viceroy, Lord Curzon, who sanctioned the conversion of the room to fulfil its new function and personally donated a number of items to start the collection.[14] Celebrating the bravery and fortitude

---

[13] Thomas Moore, whilst in Cawnpore in late 1857, demonstrated an acute interest in the defence and relief of the Residency, reflected in a number of detailed drawings and plans that he made of the military activities around the city. Thomas Moore, 'Plan of the three advances on Lucknow, also showing residency siege for 87 days, disaster at Chinhut on 30th June and defence of Alum-Bagh from 23rd September to 16 March'. Maps and plans, accompanying diary. Add. MS 37152 B. For the history of the model, see Moore, *Guide to the Model of the Residency, Lucknow: Deposited in the Museum by the Rev. T. Moore.*

[14] Lord Curzon to Sir J. D. LaTouche, 15 April 1905, 'Correspondence with people in India Jan 1905–Jun 1905', Papers of the Marquess Curzon of Kedleston, No. 105, p. 84, OIOC Mss. Eur. F111/210. See also LaTouche to Curzon, 6 May 1905, enclosing Mr L. A. S Porter to H. G. S Taylor, 3 May 1905, 'Correspondence with people in India Jan 1905–Jun 1905', Papers of the Marquees Curzon of Kedleston, No. 191, pp. 240–41, OIOC Mss. Eur. F111/210.

required to defend the building in 1857, this museum helped propagate a memory of endurance, duty, and ultimate victory. This celebration of the defenders was further emphasised over this period by a number of monuments built within the compound. Among the most conspicuous of these was a memorial dedicated to Colonel Robert Hope Moncrieff who had been awarded the Victoria Cross for helping defend the Baillie Guard Gate during the siege. Raised 'by some of his surviving comrades and other friends in token of their appreciation of his sterling worth as a man, and of the splendid gallantry and chivalrous devotion which he displayed as a soldier in command of this post', the monument remembers Moncrieff as the archetypal late century hero.[15] Similarly, a monument dedicated to Major-General Sir John Inglis was also constructed within the Residency compound, followed by a memorial dedicated to the 32nd Regiment of Foot. Fashioned from granite quarried at Bosaham in Cornwall and erected in 1899 by the regiment themselves following their return to the city after their involvement in the Tirah campaign of 1897, the inconveniently positioned obelisk designed by Howard Ince marked a regiment distinguished by the award of four Victoria Crosses won by members of the regiment during the siege.[16]

If the Lucknow Residency was thus imbued with a memory of bravery, courage, and victory over this period, then the commemorative landscape of the Delhi Ridge was likewise developed by a number of monuments, including an obelisk unveiled by Curzon in 1902 and dedicated to the role played by the telegraph during the mutiny.[17] The most important additions to the Delhi Ridge, however, came in the form of statues dedicated to two of the most well-known British mutiny heroes. The first of these was built in honour of Brigadier-General John Nicholson. Born and raised in Northern Ireland, Nicholson departed for India to join the Bengal Infantry in 1839 at just sixteen years of age. He saw active duty in the First Anglo-Afghan War, during which he was involved in some of the fiercest fighting, and quickly earned a reputation for self-confidence, endurance, and extreme bravery, bordering on personal recklessness.[18] Over the following years, Nicholson cemented this reputation whilst seeing more active duty and

---

[15] Blunt, *List of Inscriptions on Christian Tombs*, pp. 222–23.

[16] Interestingly, the inconvenient location of the monument was apparently the result of the van that transported the monument breaking down. With no chance of restarting the van and with the unveiling ceremony due to start, the decision was taken to simply unload the monument and locate it where it stood. See Curzon to Latouche, 'Correspondence with people in India Jan 1905–Jun 1905', Papers of the Marquess Curzon of Kedleston, No. 97, pp. 72–73, Mss. Eur. F111/210.

[17] Curzon, 'Mutiny Telegraph Memorial, Delhi', pp. 476–80, p. 479, Papers of the Marquess Curzon of Kedleston, Mss. Eur. F111/560. For more details on the monument and especially for technical details of the unveiling, see A. E. Orr, 'Note on the arrangements for unveiling the Telegraph Mutiny Memorial at Delhi, 19 April 1902', Punjab Public Works Department Papers 1889–1928, OIOC, IOR/V/25/700/83 No. 53.

[18] Trotter, *The Life of John Nicholson, Soldier and Administrator; Based on Private and Hitherto Unpublished Documents*.

gained the admiration of Henry Lawrence who, following the annexation of the Punjab in 1849, appointed him Deputy Commissioner of Rawalpindi and later of Bannu. Over these periods, Nicholson made it his duty to pacify the regions. Sporting a long, jet-black beard and standing at over six feet tall, Nicholson cut an imposing and intimidating figure as he led irregular cavalry into combat against truculent and warlike tribesmen in the province. During this period, Nicholson meted out what he believed to be a brand of severe yet fair justice and, as a result, became a feared and revered figure among the tribes and apparently even inspired a religious following from Hindu devotees who, much to Nicholson's distress, worshipped the pious Ulster protestant.[19]

Remembered as a natural leader and devout Christian imbued with extreme courage and a pronounced sense of justice, Nicholson could have obtained a place among the pantheon of soldier-saints without playing a central part in the suppression of the mutiny; however, it was for his exploits at Delhi that he was chiefly remembered. Leading a flying column of over 4,000 men to the Delhi Ridge, Nicholson played a crucial role in helping storm the city on 14 September 1857 during which he received a fatal wound that would eventually lead to his death a little over a week later. Nicholson's exploits during the siege culminating with his death in the hour of victory coalesced, as Lionel Trotter's 1897 biography indicates, to help make Nicholson a beacon of late Victorian masculinity.[20]

With this in mind, a monument dedicated to the soldier hero had been conceived by Lord Curzon whilst acting as Viceroy, with Lord Roberts and Sir Henry Norman helping him to arrange for the collection of funds.[21] The statue itself was completed by the celebrated sculptor Thomas Brock, but preparations were somewhat impeded in that it proved impossible to procure any pictorial evidence capable of giving a more detailed impression of Nicholson's appearance.[22] Due to this, Brock elected to base his depiction of Nicholson on an earlier bust prepared by John Henry Foley and completed at a time when Brock was himself Foley's assistant. The statue further benefitted from visits to Brock's studio by Lord Roberts, Sir Henry Norman, and Sir Seymour Blane, who had each known Nicholson personally and were thus able to advise him on the statue's likeness. In addition, it proved possible to procure the very sword and coat worn by Nicholson on 14 September, thus giving the statue a greater authenticity.[23] The design and location of the monument underscored

[19] Ibid.
[20] Ibid. By the time the monument was unveiled in 1906, Trotter's biography of Nicholson was in its 9th edition in as many years of print, attesting to the fame of the mutiny hero over this period.
[21] Earl Minto, Unveiling of the Nicholson Statue at Delhi, 6 April 1906, 'Speeches made by Lord Minto, 1905–10', The Indian Papers of the 4th Earl of Minto, Ms.12686, pp. 52–54, Centre for South Asian Studies Archive, University of Cambridge, Reel 35.
[22] Ibid.   [23] Ibid.

its meaning and memory. Located near Kashmiri Gate at a spot, as recorded
by Roberts, that was the last place where he saw Nicholson before he received
his fatal wound – the mutiny hero was depicted 'turning towards the Gate
about to lead the final assault'.[24]

Just as he was in life, Nicholson was soon joined in commemoration by
a similar monument dedicated to Sir Alexander Taylor. Though Nicholson
did not respect many of his fellow officers tasked with retaking Delhi, he
did hold Taylor in high regard, reportedly announcing, as he lay dying, that
'If I live through this, I shall let the world know who took Delhi; Alex
Taylor did it'.[25] Unlike Nicholson, Taylor did survive the conflict and went
on to have a successful career, eventually serving as the principal of the
Royal Indian Engineering College at Cooper's Hill before his death.[26]
With Lord Roberts acting as Chairman and General Sir Frederick Richard
Maunsell serving as Vice-Chairman, the committee collected funds and
unveiled Taylor's monument, designed by Charles Hartwell, close to that of
Nicholson a few years after the latter was built. Generally dedicated to individual soldier heroes and built within the Residency compound or on the
Delhi Ridge, these monuments clearly conform to the celebratory memory
of the mutiny that is argued to have dominated late Victorian conceptions
of the conflict. However, a closer look at these monuments often reveals the
anxieties that seem to have animated them. In so doing, it is instructive to
consider the inauguration ceremonies that accompanied the unveiling of
these monuments.

Indeed, we may well first look to the Delhi Telegraph Monument. As noted
above, this monument was constructed in 1902 just inside the Kashmiri Gate
and outside the former Telegraph Office. Whilst it may naturally be read as
a monument to British technological superiority, a closer look at the inauguration ceremony reveals a series of anxieties over the then security of
British India running throughout and seemingly animating the ceremony.
In so considering the monument, it is useful to pay close attention to the
speech made by Curzon, where the Viceroy goes into some detail on his
own attitude towards remembering the mutiny. Curzon considers if it would
not be better that incidences such as the mutiny be 'wrapped in oblivion',
before taking the opposite view.[27] Arguing that they serve as valuable lessons for the present generation, Curzon goes on to tell his audience that this
is especially true when it is remembered that 'it was not the white men on
one side and the Indians on the other'. Going on to praise the monument
constructed at the Residency to celebrate the loyal native defenders, Curzon

[24] Ibid.
[25] See Taylor, *General Sir Alex Taylor G. C. B., R. E.*, pp. 324–25.   [26] Ibid.
[27] Curzon, 'Mutiny Telegraph Memorial, Delhi', pp. 476–80, Papers of the Marquess Curzon of
Kedleston, Mss. Eur. F111/560.

gives his opinion that they 'merited equal honour with the white men who fell'. However, the true thrust of his speech becomes clear when he goes on to praise the 'more than 300 natives of India' who contributed to the present monument, arguing that their doing so assured him that, 'should the occasion ever arise, I doubt not that many of them, at the risk of life, would be ready to follow the same example' as was given by the 'European Telegraphic Staff of May 1857'.[28]

The introduction of a future revolt requiring the same exertion as had been required during the mutiny betrays the pronounced sense of anxiety that ran through Curzon's speech and suggests the animating force behind the present act of commemoration. The Telegraph Monument was an inducement of loyalty to Indian members of the Telegraph Office, as well as the Indian population as a whole. Seeing it as a simple celebration of British technological superiority and colonial confidence is thus undermined. More significantly, it was an anxious appeal for support in the face of growing fears of a 'second mutiny'. We can see a not entirely different process at work if we consider the statue built in honour of Nicholson a few years later and installed not far away. As we have seen earlier, this monument was also sanctioned by Curzon, although its inauguration was conducted after the Viceroy left office to be replaced by Lord Minto at the end of 1905. Presiding over the unveiling of the monument in his first months in office, Minto seems to have utilised the occasion in a not dissimilar way to how Curzon used the Telegraph Monument. With the partition of Bengal recently completed, and with significant unrest developing in several Indian centres as a result, the Anglo-Indian community and the British population at home were evincing considerable fear of another mutiny. One such example was published in the pages of *The Spectator*, warning that 'a condition of unrest has been created in the Indian Army to which no parallel can be found since the days of the Mutiny'.[29]

It was in direct response to this growing anxiety that Minto designed the unveiling ceremony for Foley's monument. Writing to Sir Arthur Godley, the Under Secretary of State for India, Minto told him that

[i]t will be a very impressive ceremony. We are arranging that as many [Indian] Mutiny veterans as we can manage shall be present, and it is pleasant to remember the part the loyal portion of the Native Army played all through the horrors of the Mutiny, so that now-a-days British and Indian troops can well share together the honour paid to the memory of John Nicholson.[30]

---

[28] Ibid.   [29] Anon, 'The Problem of the Indian Army', pp. 5–6, p. 5.

[30] Minto to Sir Arthur Godley, 22 March 1906, 'Printed copies of correspondence with the Secretary of State for India, Nov 1905–June 1906', The Indian Papers of the 4th Earl of Minto, Ms.12735, No. 31, Centre for South Asian Studies Archive, University of Cambridge, Reel 38.

This was evocatively represented during the ceremony itself by the presence of two Punjabi regiments, in the form of the 35th Sikhs and the 18th Tiwana Lancers, parading alongside the 1st Royal Irish Rifles.[31] Minto's understanding of what it should mean to remember Nicholson in 1906 was further emphasised by the Viceroy's speech. Replying to General Sir Beauchamp Duff who spoke first on behalf of the Nicholson Memorial committee, Minto informed all who were present that

British and Indian troops stand here together as they have stood side by side on many a hard-fought field to do honour to the memory not only of a British Officer of the Indian Army, the John Nicholson of his British comrades, but to the memory of the beloved and worshipped Nikalsain Sahib, the revered leader of Pathan and Punjabi warriors. It is the statue of a great and chivalrous soldier, of a high-minded and straightforward man, that I have been asked to unveil a man whose memory may be reverently cherished by soldiers and civilians of whatever race and of whatever creed.[32]

Minto was very satisfied with the ceremony and only regretted that his speech did not get a wider audience through British newspapers, as

the opportunity had seemed to be a good one to say something of the historic relations between Indian and British troops, and I had hoped that just now when so much has been said as to the unsatisfactory feeling in the Indian Army that some good might be done by a public recognition of the comradeship-in-arms which has so long existed between British and Indian soldiers.[33]

Once again, it is plain to see that Nicholson's monument was used by Minto as a direct response to the growing anxiety, and thus once again this monument seems to be better read as an expression of imperial anxiety rather than as an assertion of colonial confidence. Both an inducement to the Indian soldiery to remain loyal to the present generation of British military officers and a reassuring reminder of past loyalty to the anxious Anglo-Indian community, the monument was a response to growing fears of insurrection.

---

[31] The 1st Royal Irish Rifles could trace its lineage to the 83rd Regiment of foot, which was formed in Dublin in 1793 and saw service in the mutiny.

[32] Unveiling of the Nicholson Statue at Delhi, 6 April 1906, 'Speeches made by Lord Minto, 1905–10', The Indian Papers of the 4th Earl of Minto, Ms.12686, pp. 52–54, Centre for South Asian Studies Archive, University of Cambridge, Reel 35.

[33] Minto to Morley, 2 May 1906, 'Printed copies of correspondence with the Secretary of State for India, Nov 1905–June 1906', The Indian Papers of the 4th Earl of Minto, Ms.12735, No. 39, Centre for South Asian Studies Archive, University of Cambridge, Reel 38. For more on the ceremony, see Minto to Sir Arthur Godley, 25 April 1906, 'Printed copies of correspondence with the Secretary of State for India, Nov 1905–June 1906', The Indian Papers of the 4th Earl of Minto, Ms.12735, No. 38, Centre for South Asian Studies Archive, University of Cambridge, Reel 38; Minto to John Morley, 9 April 1906, 'Printed copies of correspondence with the Secretary of State for India, Nov 1905–June 1906', The Indian Papers of the 4th Earl of Minto, Ms.12735, No. 35, Centre for South Asian Studies Archive, University of Cambridge, Reel 38.

The Mutiny Tour

Developing in tandem with this second phase of commemoration, the Delhi Ridge, Lucknow Residency, and the Cawnpore Well grew in importance as sites of memory, and over the course of the late nineteenth century, they each featured among the most instantly recognisable and perpetually reproduced images of India. Appearing on postcards, within the pages of guidebooks, and even in early colonial films, these mnemonic signifiers reached an enormous audience beyond the populations of their immediate surroundings.[34] Indeed, when James Ricalton came to compile *India through the Stereoscope: A Journey through Hindustan*, some fifty years after the mutiny, the author no doubt thought it only natural that he should include these mutiny monuments among the 100 most important sites of India.[35] If these visual and textual sources provided remote access to these mutiny monuments, then, for the more wealthy or adventurous, what Bernard Cohn has perceptively termed the 'mutiny pilgrimage' offered an opportunity to personally bear witness to these sites.[36]

Travelling to South Asia in order to fulfil work commitments or visiting the subcontinent purely for leisure, thousands of individuals included visits to the principal sites of the conflict among the most important components of their travel itinerary in India. Though the great majority of visitors left no account of their trip, a minority of primarily middle-class visitors of both sexes wrote travelogues, detailing their experiences whilst visiting these locations. Sometimes reported as part of a trip to the subcontinent, and otherwise an element within a 'Grand Tour' taking in extensive parts of the globe, the 'mutiny pilgrimage' is usually contained within a small section of the travel diary set within a standardised journey starting in Calcutta or Bombay and passing through a relatively regimented series of towns and cities that typically included Agra, Jaipur, and Mysore among others. Primarily written by civil servants, missionaries, and tourists – and motivated for the most part by a mixture of financial and social gain – these accounts of the mutiny pilgrimage further help us to understand what it meant to remember the mutiny over this period.

In evaluating these tour diaries, this section of the chapter will be divided into three subsections. The first subsection will consider how numerous individuals responded to the official inducements to celebrate the mutiny as a triumphant imperial victory. The next two subsections will look at how the anxieties that could produce such acts of celebration also animated intense fear.

---

[34] See 'Historic Mutiny Sites', a 1914 short film concentrating on the mutiny sites of Delhi. Held by the British Film Institute, ID: 199944. Accessible on the Colonial Film Catalogue, www.colonialfilm.org.uk/node/109 (accessed 1 August 2015).

[35] Ricalton, *India through the Stereoscope*.   [36] Cohn, 'Representing Authority', p. 179.

Celebration and Self-Assurance on the Mutiny Tour

As was argued earlier, the commemoration of the mutiny attempted to trans-form the uprising into a heroic victory, which eschewed alternative events that might have undermined this collective memory. Presenting the uprising as an exemplary colonial small war that demonstrated the essential quali-ties of the lionised soldier hero of the late nineteenth century, this official memory of the mutiny was indeed reflected in many of the travel diaries writ-ten by those who visited these sites. To take the Lucknow Residency as an example, the words of one journalist seem typical. Describing the 'battered ruins of Lucknow' as 'testifying to a heroism so splendid as to rob even death of its sting', this writer claims that the Residency brings 'an inspiration that is almost joyous. Every crumbling gateway and every gloomy cellar has its tale of heroic endurance and magnificent defense, and the final relief of the beleaguered garrison wrote such a finish to the story as erased much of its earlier bitterness'.[37] As this description of the Residency suggests, for many of those who stood within the shot-pitted walls of the building and remembered the siege, it is clear that they understood that they were supposed to reflect on the bravery and fortitude of the beleaguered garrison, over and above the daily horrors of a bloody and traumatic siege. Remembered in such a way, journalist and cycling enthusiast, John Foster Frasier was probably not alone among British visitors to the site in exclaiming just 'how proud we felt … that we were British!'.[38]

Similarly, for those who stood on the Delhi Ridge and surveyed the site of some of the most intense fighting of the mutiny, there was little doubt about what they were being induced to remember. Thus, John Jackson, who was travelling in India as part of his advocacy for leprosy relief and missionary support, noted that when

driving slowly along the ridge and in by the Kashmir Gate, one could realize the events of the siege, and feel a thrill of admiration for that crowning act of courage – the storm-ing of the gate. It brought the mutiny near, to see the marks made by the British guns which are still visible on the masonry of the walls.[39]

As was the case in Lucknow, the Delhi Ridge, crowned by the Mutiny Memorial, was seen by its visitors as a location of heroic endeavour and ulti-mate triumph. To remember the mutiny whilst standing on the Delhi Ridge was not to remember the frightful and bloody loss of the city on 11 May 1857

---

[37] F. G. A., *The Outlook*, 3 April 1915, quoted in Rai, *Young India*, pp. 106–07.
[38] Fraser, *Round the World on a Wheel*, p. 217.
[39] Jackson, *In Leper-Land: Being a Record of My Tour of 7,000 Miles among Indian Lepers Including Some Notes on Missions and an Account of Eleven Days with Miss Mary Reed and Her Lepers*, p. 226.

but rather, guided by the official sites of memory located within the city, a visitor was implored to recall the siege that ultimately led to the city being stormed and decisively retaken four months later.

If remembering the mutiny within these memorial landscapes in Delhi and Lucknow helped establish a shared memory of sacrifice, endurance, and victory, then the presence of mutiny veterans at these sites proved decisive in shaping the experiences of many visitors. Although one guidebook told its readers that the Delhi Ridge was best explored with just a 'guide book, but no guide, a packet of sandwiches' and 'a solar topee', many visitors chose to employ a mutiny veteran to accompany them around the commemorative landscapes of the two cities.[40] Whilst the most influential visitors could occasionally secure the services of such exalted veterans as Lord Napier or Lord Roberts, many veterans from the 1880s onwards found gainful employment acting as tour guides in these cities.

Indeed, it is often when accompanied by a guide that these spaces of memory seemed to possess the most power to draw their visitor into the past. Therefore, according to renowned surgeon Sir Frederick Treves, who remains well known today through his work with Joseph Merrick, if one visits the Residency 'just after sundown, when the light is failing' the 'tortured little place of refuge becomes peopled again'.[41] Going on to evocatively describe the strange scene that seems to unfold directly in front of his eyes, Treves tells his readers that he could see that:

pallid women have crawled out of the cellars into the still air, holding their ragged clothing about their necks. They ask of the first passer-by the old monotonous question: 'Any news? Any signs of their coming?' ... There is a wine-coloured stain on the road, with rounded edges. It is plain enough to the women in spite of the dust which has been scrapped over it. It was where a man, shot through the chest, died in the morning.... In what may be called the street men are already forming up for a night attack. Within the darkened rooms of the Residency there is a kind of gipsy camp, with all its miscellaneous untidiness of dishes and clothes, beds, and cooking pots, mixed up with the sofas and chairs and delicate decorations of a drawing room.[42]

In this way, the Residency seems to possess the power to imaginatively interpolate its visitor into the bloody conflict of 1857. Spatially locating them within the very walls that offered shelter to the beleaguered party decades earlier, the temporal line seems to be momentarily interrupted. As a result, the mutiny pilgrim is thrust into the scene as either a member of the courageous defence force or, alternatively, as one of Havelock's band of brave

---

[40] Anon, *The P&O Pocket Book*, p. 62.
[41] Sir Treves, *The Other Side of the Lantern*, p. 187.   [42] Ibid.

soldiers who succeeded in fighting their way to Lucknow and reinforcing the position. In this respect, the mutiny tour was more than just a celebration of the British soldier hero; it also helped visitors directly identify with this subject position and, for the time they spent at the Residency or on the Ridge at least, embody the values of this idealised British subject.

Terror and Anxiety on the Mutiny Tour

If tourists who embarked on the Mutiny Pilgrimage remembered the uprising as a glorious victory, however, then British memories of the mutiny could also be connected with contemporary concerns over the security of British India resulting in an altogether different experience of the Mutiny Tour. As has been noted previously, the late nineteenth century was replete with events that raised the prospect of a widespread revolt against British power and which resulted in a habitual anxiety that helped frame the everyday experiences of the British community in India. If British memory of the mutiny could be shaped by the confidence and values of popular imperialism, then it could also be formed by these perpetual fears and pronounced sense of vulnerability. In this respect, the mutiny of 1857 was seen by many as a lens through which to evaluate the security of contemporary India and consider the prospect of a 'second mutiny'. In so doing, the potential uprising is made known, and even familiar, although its encoding as a second event is not intended or effective in quelling the fear associated with the prospect of such a revolt by articulating it with a moment of imperial confidence – on the contrary, it elevates the sense of fear and dread by providing a framework in which an otherwise imagined revolt seems to become real.

In this way, Lady Layard, reflecting on the government's decision to preserve buildings such as the Kashmiri Gate and the Lucknow Residency after the mutiny, noted in her diary that she could not 'understand the idea of the necessity of nursing such ruins. It is said to be a warning to natives—it seems to me a warning to us English'.[43] Writing at the end of 1905 and in the wake of the enormous anti-partition protests and riots that had gripped British attention throughout the year, it is easy to understand how Layard was not filled with pride or confidence when coming into contact with such mnemonic sites, rather she seems to have been filled with acute trepidation as she inspected these battered buildings.

Surprisingly perhaps, Layard's assessment of these monuments seems to find some resonance in the writings of Lord Roberts who, as we have seen, played a significant role in commemorating the mutiny during this second

---

[43] Lady Layard, 28 December 1905, 'Vol. XVI, 5 August 1903–14 April 1906', Journals of Mary Enid Evelyn Layard, fol. 224, British Library, Add. MS 46168.

phase of memorialisation. After considering whether 'the monument on the Ridge at Delhi should be levelled, and the picturesque Residency at Lucknow allowed to fall into decay', Roberts argues that these mutiny monuments served an invaluable purpose in the present.[44] Noting that such memorials commemorated a heroic struggle in which British and Native soldiers fought side by side, Roberts goes on to argue that they are even more 'valuable as reminders that we must never again allow ourselves to be lulled into fanciful security'.[45] Published in the same year as anti-colonial sentiments reached their peak as a result of the measures introduced by the British administration to tackle the plague that spread from Bombay to Pune in the late 1896–97, it is again easy to appreciate why Roberts felt that the British administration could not afford to feel secure. With the governmental response to the plague seen as excessively draconian and authoritarian, many Indians rose up in protest. Ultimately, these agitations saw a small number of political radicals assassinate the chairman of the Special Plague Committee, Commissioner W. C. Rand, followed by a British crack down on sedition that not only led to the execution of those responsible for the murder but also the subsequent imprisonment of popular radical nationalists such as Bal Gangadhar Tilak, who were charged with sedition and incitement to violence.[46]

If the mutiny could be remembered by many as an anxiety provoking warning against complacency and feelings of inviolability, then this was accentuated when tourists found themselves recalling the mutiny whilst no longer within the vicinity of these official signifiers of meaning and memory. If the various mutiny monuments could provoke anxieties concerning the security of British India, then travelogues betray their author's apprehensions and fears most readily when recounting their experiences of the broader mnemonic landscapes of these cities. One tourist, whose travel diary evinces such memories and associated anxieties, is Isabel Savory who remains famous today as one of the most prominent female adventurers of her time.[47] Staying in a hotel just outside the city, Savory notes that 'all the morning I had been looking at the great stone walls and the gates, picturing Delhi on that memorable day in May only forty-four years ago'.[48] If the thought of the unexpected assault in 1857 appears to have fascinated Savory whilst she was outside the city walls, the author seems to have been filled with a sense of dread and pronounced

---

[44] Roberts, *Forty-One Years in India: From Subaltern to Commander-In-Chief*, p. viii.

[45] Ibid, pp. viii–ix.

[46] For a brief treatment of this event that sets it within a broader trend of revolutionary terrorism, see Heehs, *The Bomb in Bengal. The Rise of Revolutionary Terrorism in India, 1900–1910*, pp. 8–12.

[47] See McKenzie, *The Right Sort of Woman*, Chapter 5, 'Isabel Savory in India', pp. 85–106.

[48] Savory, *A Sportswoman in India*, p. 300.

vulnerability once she stepped within the city and found herself on 'those very streets which were once crowded with an infuriated, fanatical Eastern mob, and stained with our own countrymen's blood'.[49] Remembering the brutal massacres of British civilians, Savory found herself staring into the eyes of 'many an old, wizened native' and thinking '"that very man probably saw it all"; that in those Mutiny days he may have stood by at the butchery of our ancestors and our friends'.[50]

Another English woman who likewise found herself remembering the massacres of 11 May and surveying the crowds of Delhi in search of mutineers was Harriet Murray-Aynsley. Like Savory, Murray-Aynsely discovered that when walking through the city, she 'could not help picturing the whole of these events so vividly to myself as to render it quite painful to me to look at any native of the place who might have been at that time of an age to have taken an active part in them'.[51] In so doing, Savory and Murray-Aynsley seem to be unable to walk through the streets of Delhi without seeing themselves as potential victims of the mutiny, despite the many decades that separated them from the violence of 1857. However, if this paranoia and anxiety resulted in a somewhat fraught visit to Delhi, then this was exponentially heightened by Savory when she noted that the 'dark faces of the Sepoys belonging to the native infantry regiment' presently stationed in the city 'were typical of the vast lines of rebel soldiery, variously estimated at from fifty thousand to seventy thousand disciplined men, who must have surged up and down these very thoroughfares, after they had shot down all their own English officers and had thrown all restraint to the winds'.[52] In so imagining the past in the present, Savory decidedly brings the mutiny onto the streets of Delhi once again. Connecting the present crop of Indian troops with those who mutinied, and refusing to see any difference between the two bodies of men, Savory can only conclude that a second mutiny would most likely occur with as little warning as the first owing to what she felt was 'a great gulf' fixed by 'racial laws' between 'the white man and the black man'.[53]

If Savory and Murray-Aynsley each saw Delhi as a hostile and potentially threatening space when remembering the mutiny, then this depiction of the city is well summed up by noted artist Alexander Henry Hallam Murray who, after visiting the city, found himself agreeing with those who thought that 'living in Delhi was like living on a volcano'.[54] Following his own tour of the Ridge, and inspection of the city, Alexander Murray concluded that he felt the

---

[49] Ibid.   [50] Ibid.
[51] Murray-Aynsley, *Our Visit to Hindostan, Kashmir and Ladakh*, p. 45.
[52] Savory, *A Sportswoman in India*, p. 301.   [53] Ibid.
[54] Murray, *The High-Road of Empire*, p. 227.

same spirit that animated the uprising in 1857 still existed in Delhi. Confiding in his readers that 'I fear there is still amongst the Mohammedan natives, a smoldering feeling of political animosity towards us: many of the men are not yet dead whose hands were dyed in our blood', Alexander Murray concluded that a 'section of the vernacular fanatics are doubtless busy, in many quarters, stirring the embers'.[55]

Fear and Loathing in Cawnpore

As we have seen previously, the mutiny tour in Delhi and Lucknow was not a straightforward celebration of British martial prowess. For many of those tourists who travelled to these sites, their experiences of remembering the mutiny were riven by anxieties and fears over the contemporary security of British India. Seen in this way, the mutiny was not only a signifier capable of provoking feelings of pride, confidence, and power, it also reminded many that India remained a turbulent colonial possession and that a 'second mutiny' would likely arrive as suddenly as the first and result in equal devastation. However, if this was undoubtedly true of Lucknow and Delhi, then it was even more pronounced in Cawnpore. Faced with an event that seemed to eschew being sewn into a narrative of heroic endurance and ultimate victory, those tourists who travelled to the city in order to remember the mutiny did so in a rather different way.

For some visitors to the Memorial Church and the Angel of the Resurrection, these official spaces of memory proved capable of producing the very effect desired by Lord and Lady Canning. As we explored in the previous chapter of this book, the commemoration of the mutiny in Cawnpore was undertaken in such a way as to help promote reconciliation and forgiveness on the part of the British community in India. Whilst the conservation of the ruins of the Residency and the Kashmiri Gate helped suspend memory within the moment of heroic endeavour, Canning was careful to efface all signs of the mutiny in Cawnpore and replace them with carefully cultivated gardens and classical European architecture.

With all references and outward appearance of the conflict carefully removed, the official monuments constructed in Cawnpore seem to have had their desired effect on many of those who visited them and thus, to quote the prolific author Amy Charlotte Menzies,

it is difficult to prevent bitter and revengeful feelings taking possession of us as we remember all that happened in that historic place, but after looking at that calm, peaceful and dignified figure, a certain feeling of 'Father, forgive them, for they know not what they do', takes the place of revenge. It is seldom that a monument appeals to us in

[55] Ibid.

that way; many are grand, great works of art and manipulation, but that white angel at Cawnpore is something more.[56]

However, whilst some visitors to Cawnpore seem to have adhered to the official inducements to 'forget Cawnpore!' many others found such a proposition quite impossible. Indeed, for some visitors to the city, it was not even necessary to disembark the train to feel filled with anxieties and fears stemming from their memory of the mutiny within the city. In this respect, the experiences of biologist and botanical artist, Marianne North, encapsulate the debilitating paranoia and apprehensions that many felt when arriving in the city. Having already admitted to her readers, whilst describing her time in Lucknow, that the 'graves and the stories of the mutiny ... sickened me', Marianne North can be read as building a short allusion to the ill-fated siege of Cawnpore in her description of her arrival in the city at midnight.[57] Informing her readers that she was first awoken by a pleasing cup of tea that was passed to her through her carriage window, North goes on to tell her readers that she was soon besieged by street hawkers who shoved all manner of goods into her carriage through the open windows including a variety of comestibles, toys and, most alarmingly, unsheathed knives. Besieged within her carriage and surrounded by a crowd, it is apparent that North is building a narrative of her own siege in such a way as to remind her readers of the events of 1857. Seen in this way, the conclusion of the event is telling. Just as the siege of Cawnpore concluded in Bibighar, so too does North's narrative end with an allusion to the massacre. Surveying the array of commodities on offer, North noticed there were 'pith models of the memorial reminding one of that awful mutiny-time'.[58] Reflecting on what the sight of the commemorative object meant to her, North admitted that it 'made me wonder if it would not someday come again. No one can tell; we really know nothing of what natives think, and few make real friends among them'.[59]

If the train station in Cawnpore was a setting in which such fears and apprehensions could be staged, then there was one spot, more than any other, which seemed to be imbued with such emotions and memories. Satichaura Ghat or, as it was more commonly known by its visitors, The Massacre Ghat, retained an unnerving aura for almost all who travelled to the spot. Unlike the greatly sanitised and sumptuously planted gardens which surrounded the Angel of the Resurrection, or the imposing neo-gothic Memorial Church which marked the site of Wheeler's entrenchments, the place where the surrendering garrison was ambushed and slaughtered remained uncared for and officially un-commemorated. Indeed, according to an editorial published in

[56] Menzies, *Lord William Beresford, V.C.*, p. 77.
[57] North, *Recollections of a Happy Life*, p. 23. For arrival in Cawnpore, see p. 40.
[58] Ibid, p. 40.   [59] Ibid.

The Times of India in 1874, this obscure site was seldom visited and even 'English people who have been living in Cawnpore for years cannot tell where it is to be found'.[60]

In sharp contradistinction to Cawnpore's official monuments, a tourist wishing to visit the Massacre Ghat was therefore required to not only first locate the site, which was well concealed about a mile from the Memorial Church, but also to negotiate a sheer ravine where it was necessary for visitors to abandon their carriage and continue on foot down the 'rough scrambling path' until they emerged at the river's edge where it was necessary for them to trace the bank until the river opened out, marking the site of the Massacre Ghat.[61] Though not marked by any official monument or served by a convenient road, mutiny veterans acting as tour guides helped make this unofficial site of memory an equally important mnemonic site in the late nineteenth century, and as the mutiny tour grew in popularity and the numbers of mutiny pilgrims gradually increased, the Massacre Ghat proved as essential a destination as the officially licensed sites of memory. Placed within the heart of the memorial landscape of Cawnpore, this unofficial memorial elicited a dramatically different reaction to the authorised sites of memory installed within the city. Whilst standing in the neo-gothic memorial church or among the carefully cultivated flowers, shrubs, and trees which surrounded the mournful Angel of the Resurrection, one was induced to forget the massacres which once took place in these locations, but the Massacre Ghat, as its informal name implies, retained the ability to deliver a powerful mnemonic experience to its visitors.

As described by one individual who visited the spot, the river appeared 'very wide here, with islands of sand in midstream' whilst in 'the late afternoon sunlight, a low caste native was washing his scant clothing in the muddy water, while beyond him floated a decaying body upon the sluggish current, with kites hovering over it and vultures sitting motionless on the sandbank toward which it was veering'.[62] The apparent authenticity of the site, when compared with the official monuments, seems to have been captured by Sir George Trevelyan as early as the mid-1860s when, writing the history of the mutiny in Cawnpore whilst employed by the Indian Civil Service, he compared the three spaces of memory available to a visitor.[63] Whilst noting that 'it is interesting to observe the neat garden that strives to beguile away the associations which haunt the well of evil fame' and acknowledging that 'it may gratify some minds, beneath the roof of a memorial church that is now building, to listen as Christian worship is performed above a spot which once resounded with ineffectual prayers and vain ejaculations addressed to

[60] Anon, 'Editorial', *The Times of India*, 6 November 1874, p. 2.   [61] Ibid.
[62] Forbes, *Twice around the World*, p. 138.   [63] Trevelyan, *Cawnpore*, pp. 228–29.

quite other ears', Trevelyan asserts that he found Satichaura Ghat a more appropriate location to remember the mutiny.[64] Noting that the site has not been 'transformed by votive stone and marble', Trevelyan tells his readers that it was here that an 'Englishman' should make a prayer for assistance in the 'conciliation of races estranged by a terrible memory'.[65] However, if Trevelyan felt that the apparently more authentic site induced him to pray for rapprochement, the great majority of visitors seem to have been moved to rather different emotions. As opposed to the conciliatory though mournful aura of Cawnpore's official monuments, the Massacre Ghat projected a dramatically different meaning and memory. Summing up the attitude many experienced on the spot, Treves tells his readers that in his own opinion, 'this is probably the very bitterest spot on the earth, this murderer's stair, this devil's trap, this traitor's gate! The very stones are tainted and festered with mean hate, and, until it rots, the mud-covered colonnade will be foul with the sneaking shadows of the cowardice'.[66]

Further, though it appears to have been impossible for visitors to actively imagine the gruesome events, they were asked to forget within the confines of the neo-gothic Memorial Church or whilst standing in the Memorial Garden surrounded by flowers and shrubs in full bloom, the same was not true at the Massacre Ghat. In the same way as we have seen earlier for visitors to the Residency and the Ridge, those who ventured to the Massacre Ghat almost immediately found themselves imaginatively interpolated into the events that they were there to remember. However, unlike the Residency and the Ridge, the effect of this process was dramatically different. Rather than joining in the storming of Delhi or imagining themselves as the courageous defenders of Lucknow, the individual was forced into the subject position of victim; duped by the treacherous mutineers. Indeed, for many, this process seems to have begun even before they reached the waterfront. As reported in *The Times of India,* when walking between the Memorial Church and the Massacre Ghat, it was possible, 'step by step', to 'in imagination accompany the broken remnants of the brave little band, as they marched forth from their intrenchment, on that June morning'.[67]

Indeed, just as Treves had experienced the uncanny ability of the Residency to transport him back to 1857, so too did he find the same effect as he wound his way down towards the waterfront. Retracing the exact path taken by the beleaguered garrison as they left Wheeler's entrenchment and made their way towards the boats, Treves begins to imagine the scene enacted over fifty years earlier. At first describing what he imagined the scene would have been like, the temporal line of Treves's narrative suddenly becomes distorted and he is

[64] Ibid.   [65] Ibid.   [66] Treves, *The Other Side*, p. 177.
[67] Anon, 'Editorial', *The Times of India*, 6 November 1874, p. 2.

once again surrounded in the present by 'worn-out soldiers, ragged and lean; pallid women; terror-stricken, wondering children … together with much untidy luggage and hastily packed bundles'.[68]

A dazed woman walks by the litter that carries her wounded husband. He turns his throbbing head to look at the green slope of the gully, and she talks of a combe in Devonshire they both know well. She tells how the journey on the river will make him strong, and how there is no need any more to measure his water in a wine glass. A soldier, with a bullet in his foot, limps along with his hand on a comrade's shoulder. They are wild, unshaven men, burnt by the sun to the colour of a lava stream. They go over the tale of the trenches and of the sepoys they have shot, and when something about the path to the river reminds them of home they lapse in to rhapsodies upon beer. A small, toddling child pulls at his mother's hand to show her two squirrels who are playing in a tree, but she hears nothing, and her gaze is far away. Her husband and two children are lying in the well outside the entrenchment, and she and the small boy are now on their way to the river alone.[69]

Surrounded by the remnants of Wheeler's entrenchment as they made their death march to the ghat and into the waiting ambush, the mutiny pilgrims who visited the Massacre Ghat experienced the site of memory as an anxiety provoking and deeply disturbing site. The untreated and apparently authentic memorial environment offered by the Massacre Ghat quickly led its visitors to a heightened sense of fear verging on paranoia as they, unlike those who had trusted in the fidelity of Indians decades earlier only to be slaughtered as they boarded the boats, turned away from the water both literally and metaphorically and walked away. A good example of this effect is given in the travelogue of Scottish singer, David Kennedy, and his daughter, Marjory Kennedy-Fraser, who were booked to perform in the town as part of an extensive tour of India.[70] Making their way to the Massacre Ghat under the care of Joe Lee, a particularly eccentric mutiny veteran and well known tour guide, the group reported that after witnessing the spot and listening to Lee's narration of the massacre, the party left the site and continued over a bridge en route to the Angel of the Resurrection when they noticed that beside the bridge sat an Indian deep in prayer.[71] Considering what the man might be praying for, Kennedy concluded that he was no doubt praying for the same thing he prayed for every day, that 'some white man might fall through' the bridge into the water beneath.[72] Even starker was the experience of Alexander Murray who, having been led to the spot by the ever-present Joe Lee, noticed 'A wild-looking fanatical Yogi …

---

[68] Treves, *The Other Side*, pp. 175–76.   [69] Ibid.   [70] Kennedy, 'Singing Round the World'.
[71] Ibid, p. 355. Accounts of tours led by Joe Lee are unmistakable, even when Lee isn't mentioned by name. For more on the delightfully eccentric Joe Lee, see Yalland, *Boxwallahs*, pp. 366–70; Fraser, *Round the World*, p. 213. For Joe Lee's own narrative of 1857 and tour guide of Cawnpore, see Lee, *The Indian Mutiny*.
[72] Ibid.

haranguing an attentive crowd of natives near the Temple of Shiva, on the bank of the river at the Massacre Ghat'.[73] Apparently asking Lee what the yogi was telling his audience, the party were duly informed that 'he was recounting the story of the wretched defenders, decoyed on that fatal June 27 into open boats, under a safe conduct, and then shot down defenseless from the banks'.[74] This strange reversal of perspective proved telling for Murray. Faced with what Lee told him was a parallel commemorative tour being taken in a rather different spirit and propagating a radically different story of the massacre and mutiny, Murray concludes that his party 'could not feel then that Marochetti's beautiful angel over the well represented the presiding genius of Cawnpore, but rather that the fiendish spirit which had animated Nana Sahib was only smoldering, and that fifty years of Western secular education, as assimilated by the Hindu, would not protect us from another outbreak of treacherous fanaticism'.[75]

Interestingly, as noted by journalist Edgar Allen Forbes, British visitors seemed to elicit a greater emotional connection to the commemorative landscape of Cawnpore than did tourists of other nationalities. Telling his readers that whilst, to an American visitor, The Angel of the Resurrection 'stands there as a monument of forgiveness, and its silent influence is as powerful as the fragrance that comes from crushed jasmine and mignonette', 'to the Englishman, with all the bitter memories brought back to him by the sight of the memorials, Cawnpore has a different meaning. He does not merely *see* Cawnpore; he *feels* it'.[76] This is a fascinating perspective which perhaps could only be given by a visitor who did not carry with him Britain's anxious collective memory of 1857. As Forbes seems to correctly argue, the mnemonic force of Cawnpore resides in a space abstracted from official commemoration for British visitors, for whom the experience of remembering the mutiny never conformed to the official inducements that surrounded them. If this is true for those British visitors who did not witness the events of 1857, then perhaps predictably, the effect was magnified for those who did. In this respect, American doctor, Arley Isabel Munson, relays a not entirely different insight based on her own visit to Cawnpore.[77] Having visited the principal sites of memory within the city and acknowledged, like many others, the ability of the Memorial Garden and statue over the well 'to banish all hatred against the perpetrators of the deed which she commemorates', Munson was forced to reassess her views after dining with a mutiny veteran who seemed to harbour a great deal of hatred towards the Indian population, an attitude which Munson felt was demonstrated whenever the veteran had to deal with the Indian waiting staff. This low-level animosity soon rose to the surface, however, when Munson engaged the old soldier about his own memories of the mutiny in

---

[73] Murray, *The High-Road*, p. 154.   [74] Ibid.   [75] Ibid.
[76] Forbes, *Twice around the World*, p. 138.   [77] Munson, *Jungle Days*, p. 151.

Cawnpore. As he recounted the mutiny to his audience, Munson noted that his 'eyes flashed hatred and he seemed as bitter about the Mutiny as if it had occurred last week', concluding by exclaiming 'The dogs! The devils! The lying, thieving rats! I hate every one of them! I'll never forgive them! Don't you trust them! They'll do you every time'.[78] Assessing the wild outburst of her dining companion, Munson concluded that it was apparent to her that the 'shadow of the Peace Angel's wings had not fallen across his wounded spirit'.[79]

[78] Ibid.   [79] Ibid.

4   The Mutiny of 1907
Anxiety and the Mutiny's Golden Jubilee

The previous chapters of this book have focused on practices of commemoration employed to memorialise the mutiny over the course of a fifty-year period. As we have seen, commemoration over this period was a sometimes conscious but always active response to perceived imperial vulnerability and the apparent likelihood of further armed insurrection in the mould of the mutiny. With intense colonial anxieties gripping the Anglo-Indian community, the British administration attempted to shape the uprising into a more usable form capable of reassuring the alarmed population by presenting the uprising as an instance of native fidelity and an example of British military might. As has further been shown, however, this official memory of the mutiny was never entirely accepted. Whilst some individuals adhered to these powerful mnemonic inducements, the process of commemoration was always stained by an overwhelming sense of fear and loathing. Shifting our attention now to how the mutiny was remembered and commemorated in Britain, this chapter will consider the mutiny's Golden Jubilee in 1907. As will be shown, the mnemonic acts employed to mark the fiftieth anniversary of the mutiny are best understood as an extension of what we have identified in Chapter 3 as the second phase of commemoration, and therefore, they must be read alongside the intense fear of insurrection that developed over the previous decades and which dominated how India was imagined as the mutiny's anniversary approached, and the spectre of mutiny once again appeared to loom.

The colonial panic predicated on the apparent inevitability of the 'mutiny of 1907' has attracted considerable attention from scholars who have assessed the growth of disaffection in Punjab that resulted in considerable unrest spreading throughout the territory in early 1907.[1] As has been shown, persistent anxieties stemming from Britain's memory of the mutiny played a significant role in structuring how this disorder was understood and imagined, leading to a colonial panic over the apparent immediacy of a 'second mutiny'.[2] Further, the role of rumour and misinformation together with the speed and breadth of

---

[1] Barrier, 'The Punjab Disturbances of 1907', pp. 353–83.
[2] Wagner, *The Great Fear of* 1857, pp. xv–xxiv.

transmission by the electric telegraph has been shown to have helped exasperate this panic, leading to a breakdown of intelligence predicated on the volume of available information and the state's inability to manage and evaluate it.[3] However, despite this considerable interest, rather less attention has been paid to how this panic was reflected in Britain, and even less concern has been shown towards understanding how political elites responded to this panic through practices of commemoration aimed, ostensibly at least, at 1857.

Our purpose of revisiting the 'mutiny of 1907' is therefore twofold. First, we will chart the development of fear of insurrection in Britain through the popular press and pay close attention to how memories of the mutiny came into contact with reports of contemporary disturbance and disorder. In so doing, we will argue that not only did Britain's memory of the mutiny help structure how contemporary events in Punjab were imagined, but further that contemporary anxieties themselves helped mould how the mutiny itself was remembered. Second, by focusing on acts of memorialisation held at the end of the year, this chapter will examine how commemoration was utilised to establish the contemporary significance of remembering the mutiny in Britain. By investigating these two areas, this chapter will argue that both fear and celebration were responses to anxieties connected to growing unrest in India, and the rise of liberalism and radicalism within the metropole. As was considered in Chapter 3, the 1890s were replete with many of the most serious threats to British hegemony in the subcontinent since the mutiny itself, leading many to suffer considerable apprehensions concerning the security of British India. As will further be explored here, this growth of disaffection and agitation came to maturity in the first years of the twentieth century following the explosion of protest which greeted the controversial Partition of Bengal in 1905 and which spread quickly to other theatres of disturbance across India. If India was therefore seen to be more unstable than at any time since 1857, political developments in Britain were seen by many to further imperil the Indian empire in its moment of greatest need. In the face of domestic political changes that had resulted in the dramatic defeat of the Conservative-Liberal Unionist coalition at the ballot box in 1906, conservative and imperialist elements within Britain grew increasingly anxious that the Liberal government would fail the empire. Men such as John Morley, the new secretary of State for India, were considered by those described by M. N. Das as 'orthodox imperialists', to be quite unequal to the growing challenges confronting British rule in India, whilst radicals like James Keir Hardie were considered antithetical to the imperial project and a growing threat to empire.[4]

This growth of liberalism and radicalism within Britain coupled with the growing crisis within India were seen by orthodox imperialists to present a

---

[3] Choudhury, 'Sinews of Panic and the Nerves of Empire', pp. 965–1002.
[4] Das, *India under Morley and Minto*, see Chapter 3, 'Politics in England', pp. 62–87.

perfect storm in which a 'second mutiny' was almost inevitable. Whilst the mid-Victorian generation could muster great soldier heroes capable of quelling such an uprising, orthodox imperialists harboured doubts that the present generation would be equal to the challenges presented by a popular rebellion against colonial rule. Whilst the mutiny had underpinned British claims to be a naturally martial race which was capable of winning great victories against overwhelming odds, Britain's rather more recent experience of the Boer War had convinced many that the current generation was not imbued with the same physical advantages and fighting spirit epitomised by men such as Brigadier-General John Nicholson and Field Marshal Lord Clyde. Whilst the Boer War had been greeted with an unprecedented surge of popular support, the conflict had developed into a protracted and brutal conflict in which Britain's inability to swiftly and decisively defeat the smaller army consisting of Boer farmers had led to considerable introspection concerning the apparent weakness of Britain's military machine.[5] These colonial anxieties were further compounded by reports that around half of all those who volunteered to join the army in the wake of the upsurge in popular support of the war had been deemed physically unsuitable for military service.[6]

With India in a state of unrest, a Liberal government regarded as unsuited to the task of quelling the rise of sedition and agitation, and an army viewed as lacking the qualities required to suppress a large-scale armed rebellion in India, 1907 was a year of considerable colonial anxiety concerning the security of British India. As this chapter will show, these pervasive anxieties played a considerable role in shaping how the mutiny was remembered in 1907, as well as how it was commemorated at the end of the year. As will be shown, commemoration was once again an anxious response to the perceived vulnerability of British India which was deployed by hard-line imperialists in an attempt to reaffirm the values that had helped underpin colonial rule in the late Victorian era and were now thought necessary to combat growing unrest in India, but imperilled by political and social developments in Britain. In developing this argument, this chapter will be divided into three principal sections. The first will begin by discussing the spread of unrest over the first years of the twentieth century, which resulted in a debilitating fear of insurrection developing in India over the first month of 1907. The second will start by reviewing the political climate in Britain at the start of the year, before considering how the panic in India was reported in the conservative press in Britain, and specifically how these

---

[5] For a concise and inciteful discussion on how and why the Boer War became imbued with such significance within the British imagination, see the introduction to Judd, Surridge and Surridge, *The Boer War.*

[6] Searle, *Eugenics and Politics in Britain 1900–1914*, Chapter 3 'The Issue of Racial Degeneration', pp. 20–33.

reports developed within a mutually constitutive process with how the mutiny of 1857 was remembered. Finally, this chapter will consider the practices of commemoration employed by staunch imperialists to celebrate victory over the mutiny. As will be argued here, the celebration of the mutiny responded to colonial anxieties over the security of British India through an inducement to the present generation to emulate the imperial spirit that had saved the empire fifty years previously and which was now thought both lacking and yet necessary to save India in the present.

Partition, Punjab, and Political Unrest

As the fiftieth anniversary of the mutiny approached, the British administration in India was confronting its greatest challenge since 1857 due, in large measure, to the Partition of Bengal in 1905. Whilst it is possible to trace the growth of Indian nationalism over the course of the late nineteenth century, partition proved to be a catalysing event, which resulted in the emergence of a rather more radical and militant voice within the nationalist movement. Whilst Curzon initially saw the question of partition as a relatively straightforward proposal that offered innumerable administrative advantages to his government, others responsible for the decision also recognised it as a powerful political tool that would fracture the unity of the province and weaken an area known to be increasingly hostile to British rule.[7] Regardless of the motivations that lay behind these proposals, the moment they became publicly known in late 1903, the Indian National Congress was instrumental in organising a series of protests and petitions against the plan. Recognising that partition carried designs beyond administrative efficiency, the Congress was successful in organising some of the largest political gatherings that had been seen in British India.[8]

Despite the apparent widespread support for the anti-partition movement, the British administration continued their deliberations on the subject. Indeed, the protests only helped consolidate British thinking by providing, what many saw as, yet further proof of the dangers of a unified Bengal. Not only were the protests seen to support the proposed measures, they also helped expedite their enactment. Believing that the anti-partition protests would only intensify and gather momentum the longer discussion was allowed to continue, Curzon pressed for a decisive and immutable resolution to be reached and enforced at the very earliest juncture.[9] As a result, the Partition of Bengal was officially announced in mid-1905 and effected just months later. Ultimately, the controversial policy would not only be Curzon's most enduring legacy of his time in India, but it would also be his last of any real import. An unrelated and

[7] Sarkar, *Swadeshi Movement in Bengal.*   [8] Ibid.   [9] Ibid.

protracted disagreement between the Viceroy and the commander-in-chief of India came to a head over the course of the summer causing Curzon to decide that his position had become untenable.[10] With Curzon's resignation accepted in London, Lord Minto arrived in India in November to assume his responsibilities as Viceroy.

Though Curzon had hoped that a swift and decisive decision on partition would curtail further agitations, he was ultimately proved wrong. Minto's appearance in India, occurring just weeks before the Liberal Party came into power in Britain, had an immediate impact on the anti-partition movement with many harbouring hopes that the new government might revisit the question of partition and rescind the earlier decision.[11] However, when these hopes were shown to be ill-placed, protest once again began to destabilise the region. Further, the agitations led to the popularisation of a rather more militant and openly belligerent voice from within the Congress. Formed in 1885, the Congress had provided a platform from which generally western educated, and overwhelmingly moderately minded, Indians could question the British administration and make calls for political reform. However, it is also possible to trace the emergence of a rather more radical line of thought over the late 1890s, which began to gain traction at the end of the decade for a number of reasons but especially as a result of anti-British feeling arising in response to the measures taken to combat the spread of plague in Pune during the final years of the nineteenth century.[12] Not content with constitutional protest and administrative reform, men such as Bal Gangadhar Tilak began to promote a far more radical and combative approach to political agitation that announced, as its ultimate goal, the total overthrow of the British administration. Following partition, this militant strain of nationalism that often combined reactionary Hinduism with European influences gained a significant number of adherents, resulting in the formation of underground groups committed to a course of revolutionary terrorism.[13]

If the political unrest in Bengal was the cause of great apprehension, then reports of disturbances in Punjab were the source of even more immediate concern.[14] As is well recognised, military recruitment practices in India underwent a significant transformation in the years that followed the mutiny. Whilst pre-mutiny recruitment had drawn heavily on high-caste Brahmins and Rajputs from Awadh and Bihar, from 1858 onwards recruitment began

---

[10] Cohen, 'Issue, Role, and Personality', pp. 337–55. See also Gilmour, *Curzon*.
[11] Das, *India under Morley and Minto*, pp. 35–36.
[12] For a good discussion of Bal Gangadhar Tilak's involvement, see Wolpert, *Tilak and Gokhale*, pp. 88–97.
[13] Heehs, *The Bomb in Bengal*; Heehs, *Nationalism, Terrorism, Communalism*, See Chapter 4, 'Foreign Influences on Bengali Revolutionary Terrorism 1902–1908', pp. 68–95.
[14] Barrier, 'The Punjab Disturbances of 1907'.

to focus on new territories and demographics.[15] Guided in large measure by the official memory of the mutiny developed in the immediate wake of the conflict, this resulted in a shift towards Punjabi recruits who, due to their exemplary service during the uprising, were now seen as overwhelmingly loyal. This post-mutiny shift in recruitment patterns was further accentuated from the 1880s onwards due to the perceived threat posed by Russia.[16] With the second Anglo-Afghan War concluding in 1880, and caused largely by fears of Russian designs on Central and South Asia, the Northwest of India took on a tremendously important strategic significance and was, accordingly, at the heart of Britain's military and security policies. This shift in British thinking was enshrined in the categorisation of 'martial races' that, it was widely believed, possessed a biologically or culturally predetermined aptitude for the rigors of active service and made Punjab home to a high percentage of the most naturally martial communities of India. As a result of these factors, Punjab supplied an incredibly high percentage of the Indian Army by 1907.[17]

With Punjab so central to Anglo-Indian security, the British administration had worked hard to ensure that the province was predisposed to British rule through a number of social and economic policies. However, from 1900 onwards, various issues began to arise. This was especially true in the Chenab Canal Colony where a combination of corruption among lower officials, problems over irrigation, and crop failure had been steadily building over the previous few years and, by the time Minto arrived in India, had led to considerable financial hardship for many.[18] Indeed, the new viceroy arrived just in time to preside over what should have been the annual cotton harvest, however, due to blight, this was a time of increased frustrations and financial ruin in the region. If these festering issues were the cause of disaffection in the area, then two British policies, enacted in the latter half of 1906, had the effect of considerably exasperating them. The first of these was the Punjab Colonisation of Land Bill, which extended administrative control of the region and formalised the much-hated system of fines. On top of this, a dramatic increase in the Bari Doab Canal Rates further infuriated many cultivators. Water rates had previously been artificially reduced as a further inducement of loyalty but this policy was now thought to be cutting profits and was accordingly abandoned. These two measures induced an almost immediate reaction from many in Punjab leading to large-scale protests and agitations in the region that grew throughout late 1906 and the first month of 1907.[19] Though disaffection would be treated

---

[15] Omissi, *The Sepoy and the Raj. The Indian Army, 1860–1940.*   [16] Ibid.
[17] Ibid. See also Streets, *Martial Races.*
[18] Barrier, 'The Punjab Disturbances of 1907'.   [19] Ibid.

seriously no matter where it occurred, activism in Punjab clearly carried additional threats. Due to its geographical position in relation to Afghanistan along with the strong connection between the province and the army, the possibility that anti-British feeling could destabilise the region and potentially reach Punjabi sepoys serving in the army was the cause of considerable consternation.

The intersection of these issues in early 1907 was the cause of considerable alarm within the colonial administration, as well as within the Anglo-Indian community more generally, and their proximity to the fiftieth anniversary of the mutiny appeared to portend a widespread rebellion. Read alongside the anxious experiences resulting from remembering the mutiny discussed in Chapter 3, this should come as little surprise. Indeed, it is no coincidence that the unrest assumed its most desperate form within the British imagination around the fiftieth anniversary of the start of the mutiny. With 1857 featuring prominently within the British imagination, contemporary unrest was quickly accentuated and structured around the mutiny itself. Accordingly, a broad range of British administrators searched for the slightest shred of intelligence which could be seized upon and imbued with overwhelming significance. To take one example of how rumour of an impending mutiny was taken seriously at this time within the government, J. M. Holms, the Financial Secretary to the Government in the United Provinces of Agra and Oudh, reported a series of anecdotes collected from a range of sources which purported to show that several regiments in Meerut, Allahabad, and Delhi were preparing for, or were on the edge of, an uprising.[20] Generally in the form of half-heard conversations aboard trains or in waiting rooms, Holms seems to have become convinced of the veracity of these stories, and they caused him to reach out for assistance in quelling the uprising. Though such unsubstantiated intelligence could have been passed off as unimportant, the paranoia that surrounded the anniversary helped them appear to be an invaluable warning of a violent explosion within the army.[21]

If the British administration was showing signs of paranoia as the jubilee approached, then the same was amply true for the Anglo-Indian community. With 1857 dominating their thoughts around its anniversary, British communities grew increasingly wary of their surroundings and even the most insignificant scrap of information could cause mass panic at the prospect of a 'second mutiny'. To take Delhi as an example, the Anglo-Indian community appears

[20] J. M. Holms to Sir Herbert, 23 May 1907, 'Printed copies of letter and telegrams to and from persons in India, Jan–Jun 1907', The Indian Papers of the 4th Earl of Minto, Ms.12766, Centre for South Asian Studies Archive, University of Cambridge, Reel 48.
[21] For the breadth and depth of reports, see Choudhury, 'Sinews of Panic and the Nerves of Empire', See in particular pp. 978–85.

to have become convinced that 10 May 1907 would undoubtedly see the start of a violent revolution within the city. British soldiers began preparing for such an eventuality, and the civilian community started to plan escape routes out of Delhi or to points of refuge within it. The Zenana Mission in Delhi even sent two priests to the local fort to appeal for help in the event of an uprising. With large numbers of school children under their care, the mission felt certain that they would find it impossible to reach the fort without a military escort. As the tenth approached, priests kept a watch for signs of disturbances at night and looked out anxiously towards the fort for a red light accompanied by three gun shots signifying an uprising, whilst the 'girls all slept at night with their Bibles and hymn books by them, and boys … with sticks'.[22] This intense terror and acute sense of vulnerability was certainly not isolated to missionaries, however. The entire British community of Delhi was showing signs of debilitating anxiety, and the slightest report of violence, no matter how poorly corroborated, was sufficient to cause panic. To take one such incident, an erroneous rumour that two British people had been 'massacred' in the city 'spread quickly in the Civil lines, and Europeans were requested to make for the club, which in a short time was crowded with them and their families, the men being armed with all sorts of weapons'.[23] With growing nationalism, political unrest, and reports of conspiracies all intersecting with the mutiny's anniversary, panic spread throughout the colonial administration and the Anglo-Indian community, which became convinced that a violent uprising was almost an inevitability.

The Mutiny of 1907 in Britain

As has been briefly outlined previously, the fiftieth anniversary of the mutiny was greeted by the colonial administration and the Anglo-Indian community with a widespread panic over the possibility of a 'second mutiny'. Driven by anxieties over the security of the Indian empire, and focusing on the unfolding unrest within Punjab, this intense fear of insurrection was productive of a panic that both prevented the colonial administration from responding to the potential threats in a measured manner, and seemingly paralysed the Anglo-Indian community as they waited patiently for the anticipated uprising. If British memory of the mutiny was therefore implicated in these feverish panics in India, then it was having a similar effect in Britain. The full gamut of newspapers carried alarming reports of extreme unrest and were all quick to connect it with the mutiny of 1857 to produce a heightened sense of

---

[22] Anon, 'The Unrest in India: Missionaries' Letters', *The Manchester Guardian*, 6 July 1907, p. 6.
[23] Anon, 'An Episode at Delhi', p. 7. For an amusing description of this panic, see Hardie, *India*, p. 60.

fear within the metropole. *The Times*, for example, began carrying alarming articles on the condition of Punjab which appeared all the more unsettling to its readers given the newspaper's representation of the province a little over a year earlier. Discussing the condition of Punjab whilst describing the Royal Tour of India by the Prince of Wales, the newspaper had described Lahore as a 'capitol of a thoroughly settled British province, where it is as safe for a visitor to wander through the back streets at midnight as it is to walk down Piccadilly, and a good deal safer than in many parts of London'.[24] However, with *The Times* now detailing the unrest which gripped the city, the change in representation must have appeared dramatic. Describing several mass mobilisations within the city, *The Times* presented Lahore as a dangerous space, seething with animosity towards any Englishmen unfortunate enough to find themselves caught up in the events. Recounting, for example, the transportation of two Indian journalists who had been charged on counts of sedition and incitement relating to an earlier agitation within the city, the newspaper described how

the prison van was stopped and assailed by a riotous mob, the police in charge were pelted with mud, and the two convicts were greeted as popular heroes and crowned in Oriental fashion with garlands. Nor was this all. The mob, we are told, afterwards proceeded in a procession through one of the chief thoroughfares of Lahore and assaulted every European they met with until the police firmly dispersed them. Such an explosion of anti-British feeling in a great Indian centre has hardly occurred since the days of the Mutiny.[25]

In fully understanding how the panic unfolded within Britain, it is first necessary to consider the domestic political climate of 1907. With the Conservative government losing a great deal of its legitimacy over the previous three years, primarily as a result of debates over tariff reform and the use of Chinese labour in South Africa, Arthur Balfour resigned as Prime Minister, leading to the formation of a minority Liberal government at the end of 1905.[26] Following the hastily convened General Election held in January 1906, which saw a dramatic victory for the Liberals alongside the first electoral successes for candidates representing the Labour Party, the Liberals were able to form a majority government and thus brought a lengthy period of Conservative rule to a conclusive close. With the make-up of the House of Commons reflecting a number of important sociopolitical changes that would continue to shape Britain's political climate for many years to come, the Liberals found themselves occupying the middle ground in terms of imperial policy between the opposing poles of the Conservatives and the more radically minded members of the House.[27]

---

[24] Anon, 'Indian Affairs', p. 4.   [25] Anon, *The Times*, 20 April 1907, p. 11.
[26] For the politics of tariff reform that resulted in the 'crisis of Conservatism', see Green, *The Crisis of Conservatism*.
[27] Das, *India under Morley and Minto*, pp. 62–87.

Though in no way in favour of dissolving the empire, or even in presiding over an erosion of British territorial possessions abroad, the Liberal Party was nonetheless unwilling to involve itself in imperial expansion and was certainly opposed to the militarism that had reached its apogee in the years leading up to the Boer War.[28] Perhaps even more significantly John Morley, the Secretary of State for India, had proved himself to be staunchly opposed to anything that could be accused of resembling tsarist repression whilst acting as the Chief Secretary for Ireland in the last decade of the nineteenth century.[29] As a result, many conservative commentators felt uneasy when contemplating whether the current administration would have the necessary resolve to contain Indian unrest and utilise repressive measures against sedition and agitation when deemed necessary. Indeed, as the troubles in Punjab began to assume colossal proportions within the British imagination around the fiftieth anniversary of the uprising, the conservative minded *Manchester Courier and Lancashire Advertiser* told its readers that it 'is unfortunate that the accession of a Liberal government to office in this country should coincide with a recrudescence of unrest in the Punjab'.[30]

Such fears as were betrayed by the conservative press had been confirmed for many during the previous year, when the actions of Sir Bampfylde Fuller, the Lieutenant Governor of the newly created province of East Bengal, met with wide-scale opposition from Liberals and radicals in the House of Commons. In particular, concerns were raised in relation to his use of force to break up a conference held in Barisal in April 1906, which resulted in the assault and arrest of several notable congressmen including Surendranath Bannerjee.[31] Ultimately, Fuller's time in office was curtailed when he felt compelled to tender his resignation in response to the refusal of the central government to support the draconian measures he wished to apply in connection with the involvement of students from schools in Sirajganj in the Swadeshi movement. Though the Anglo-Indian press made its disappointment abundantly clear, as did a range of conservative newspapers in Britain, Morley and Minto appear to have been largely united in their decision and relieved to see Fuller leave without the ignominy of being actively removed from his post.[32]

The 'Fuller Episode', as it became known, convinced much of the Anglo-Indian community that the Liberal government was not equal to the task in front of it, as well as persuading many old India Hands and diehard imperialists in Britain that the current administration would fail to address the mounting

[28] Porter, *The Lion's Share*, pp. 200–4. See also Porter, *Critics of Empire*.
[29] Jackson, *Morley of Blackburn*, see especially Chapters 8–10.
[30] Anon, 'The Morning's News', p. 6.
[31] For Banerjea's own account of what happened at Barisal, see Banerjea, *A Nation in Making*, pp. 220–27.
[32] Das, *India under Morley and Minto*, pp. 36–41.

threat to British supremacy in India with due urgency and vigour. In particular, these quarters harboured concerns that the central government would fail to recognise the seriousness of the current situation in Punjab and would accordingly fail to support whatever course of action was deemed necessary by the Lieutenant-Governor, Denzil Ibbetson, himself a vocal supporter of Fuller's draconian policies in East Bengal. For many of these orthodox imperialists, the folly of such a course of action was only compounded by the British military's apparent weaknesses, which had been so candidly revealed by the Boer War. Whilst the Boer War had at first generated enormous popular support, its conclusion had proved the cause of considerable consternation rather than celebration. British failure to swiftly and decisively defeat a numerically inferior enemy had convinced many commentators that Britain was not the military superpower which colonial conflicts such as the Battle of Omdurman had seemed to suggest. Further, the Boer War had undermined British claims to be a naturally imperial and martial race. Whilst the mutiny of 1857 was met by a generation imbued with all the essential attributes of the late nineteenth-century soldier hero, the public had been distressed to learn that around half of all volunteers for the war in South Africa had been deemed physically unsuitable for the rigours of armed combat.[33]

Indeed, many orthodox imperialists including men such as Lord Roberts became so concerned with what this might mean for the future of the British empire that they turned their attention to what practical solutions might be found to halt, or even reverse this martial decline.[34] However, with pronounced anxieties concerning the ability of the present generation to supply soldiers of the calibre required to defeat a widespread rebellion in India, coupled with doubts that the Liberal government was equal to the task of responding with due urgency to the first signs of disturbance and thus succeed in preventing such an uprising, many looked to India with profound apprehension as reports of disturbances and political agitation were received. It is with this political background that one must attempt to understand the mutually constitutive relationship that developed in early 1907 between what it meant to remember the mutiny of 1857 and how the existing unrest in India was imagined and understood.

In paying close attention to how the panic in India came into conversation with the mutiny of 1857, it becomes clear that in 1907 British memory of the mutiny was structuring present fears of unrest at the same time as contemporary fears were colouring how the mutiny itself was remembered. As we saw in Chapter 1, immediate responses to news of the uprising in India were critical of the colonial administration and the military hierarchy who were

---

[33] See Searle, *Eugenics and Politics in Britain 1900–1914*, pp. 20–33.
[34] See Semmel, *Imperialism and Social Reform*, see especially Chapter 12, 'Lord Roberts and Robert Blatchford', pp. 208–25.

held jointly responsible for the first signs of mutiny. Further, the military in general and certain army officers in particular, who were accused of failing to respond with sufficient urgency and vigour to the first signs of unrest, were singled out for considerable opprobrium. As was also explored in Chapter 1, however, this initially critical response first gave way to an intensely anxious imagination of the conflict which focused on the Cawnpore Massacres and then to an excessively triumphant depiction of the conflict following news of the Relief of Lucknow and the fall of Delhi in late 1857. Pushed to the margins of memory over the following fifty years from where it could only fleetingly resurface and only then primarily in historical appraisals of the conflict, this critical discourse on the mutiny which focused on the multiple failings of the British administration and army now returned to the surface and characterised countless popular accounts of the conflict which entered circulation around its anniversary.

In interrogating this process, it is useful to begin by considering a commemorative article written by Perceval Landon and published in *The Telegraph* of 10 May, exactly fifty years after the mutiny in Meerut signalled the start of the uprising.[35] Though the article drew attention to several notable and praiseworthy mutiny veterans who had lived long enough to see the anniversary, the central message of the article was contained in its leading columns. Dedicated to a discussion on the causes of the mutiny and whether it should have been anticipated and mitigated against or at least immediately suppressed when the first signs of violence occurred, this article constructed a very particular memory of the mutiny that must be considered a reflection of contemporary anxieties. In this account of the mutiny, the Indian population do not seem to shoulder any blame, rather they are portrayed as credulous and superstitious as opposed to treacherous and conniving. Instead of assigning blame to the mutineers, the author reserves his vitriol for the British administration and senior officers who failed to recognise the brewing storm and, crucially, failed to act with due courage, strength, and determination when the moment demanded it. In this respect, blame seems to lie with men such as Governor-General Charles Canning; 'a man with that academic subtlety which has in every century lost or risked a nation' and whilst surrounded by portents of insurrection 'was busy reconciling with preconceived ideas the stern and illogical facts of a brewing storm'.[36] If Canning had failed to recognise the impending uprising, then the article also apportions blame on the inaction of men such as General Hewitt, of whom there 'is not a drearier picture of cowardice and ineptitude in all the Indian Mutiny', a man 'who sat with palsied brain while the murder of his fellow-countrymen was going on under his eyes'.[37]

[35] Perceval Landon, '"1857" Outbreak of the Mutiny, May 10 at Meerut', p. 5.
[36] Ibid.   [37] Ibid.

This account of historical events and criticism of men who had long since died cannot simply be seen as of antiquarian interest, rather this memory of the mutiny was being shaped in large measure by present events and contemporary concerns. Indeed, within this commemorative account of the mutiny, and specifically the description of Canning and Hewitt, it is hard not to see Morley and Minto being described by Landon. Morley, a man whose literary accomplishments included several volumes dedicated to liberal political philosophy and economics, and Minto, whose failure to support Fuller's decisive measures in East Bengal had come in for such intense criticism, are seen to be imperilling contemporary India and may yet be responsible for a 'second mutiny', and the attendant horrors and bloodshed that had characterised the first.

Such a memory of the mutiny and its apparent relevance to the present was certainly not limited to *The Telegraph,* rather it was shared by numerous conservative publications who felt compelled to remember 1857 over this period. To take another clear example, one may turn to *The Manchester Courier and Lancashire Advertiser.* Writing in the days immediately preceding the anniversary of the outbreak of the mutiny in Meerut, the newspaper told its readers that 'Mrs. Flora Annie Steel, in her wonderful story of the Indian Mutiny "On the Face of the Waters" has shown how mysteriously yet irresistibly, disaffection widens its area, and how great is the danger which results from feeble treatment of the early outbreaks' before, in the same article, going on to bemoan the apparent leniency of the legal system in India which was only encouraging further sedition and unrest and tying the hands of the police in Lahore who were apparently emasculated as a result.[38] A few days later the newspaper returned to the same subject writing that the 'police of Lahore have complained that they are powerless as long as the magistrates refused to support them. It can never be forgotten that divided authority and the want of a few strong men at Meerut were the main causes of the outbreak of the Indian Mutiny. In the present case, the area of disturbance is largely the same as it was in the fateful May of half-a-century ago'.[39]

If, for many, the recollection of 1857 demanded urgent and decisive action in the present, then the conservative press was again under no illusions of exactly what this meant. As the *Nottingham Evening Post* told its readers, the 'lesson of the Mutiny is never again to hold danger cheap ... peace must ever be preserved in India by the firm hand, and sedition only raises its head when it fancies the government to be weak'.[40] Or, as put by one correspondent in *The Times*

---

[38] Anon, 'The Morning's News', 4 May 1907, p. 6.   [39] Ibid, 9 May 1907, p. 6.
[40] Anon, 'Disturbed India', p. 4.

we must realize that the spirit of the Mutiny is not dead and that a very large proportion of the educated classes hate us.... New India has been tried and found wanting, and again we must hold the country with the power of the sword, and in the interests of ourselves, of our women and children, and of the Empire, we must see that the edge of the sword is not dulled ... the British Government will fall when men find that it is no longer strong.[41]

Seen in this light, British memory of the mutiny in its jubilee year appears to be structured, in large part, by anxieties stemming from the contemporary condition of India, and fears relating to the willingness and capability of the Liberal government to respond with due urgency and strength. Further, it should be noted that this discourse was not limited to conservative publications, rather it quickly permeated the great majority of liberal and even radical newspapers and magazines published over this period.[42]

Ultimately, the unrest in Punjab was exposed as largely baseless with peace returning to the region in June following the utilisation of both oppressive and conciliatory measures. Though Morley and Minto had opposed Fuller's policies in East Bengal, they supported Ibbetson in Punjab, resulting in Lala Lajpat Rai and Ajit Singh being deported without due legal procedure.[43] The fact that these authoritarian measures were readily accepted as both desirable and necessary by not only Morley and Minto, but the great bulk of the conservative and liberal press is certainly significant and can only be fully explained when considered in relation to the impact of the mutually supportive construction of 1857 and 1907.[44]

Formal Commemoration and the Celebration of the Mutiny Jubilee

With unrest in Punjab quickly dissipating, the intense fear that had characterised Britain's response to the fiftieth anniversary also faded over the summer months of 1907. However, from September onwards, national attention once again turned to the mutiny as several important anniversaries encouraged a desire to recollect the conflict. Indeed, September alone witnessed the anniversaries of the reoccupation of Delhi and the First Relief of Lucknow. As a result, in a number of towns, small commemorative events

---

[41] Anon, 'Riots and Unrest in the Punjab', p. 7.

[42] To take one example, in the form of *Reynolds Newspaper*, initial equivocation seems to give way to support of, or at least acquiescence to, oppressive measures. Anon, 'The Government of India', p. 6.

[43] Barrier, 'The Punjab Disturbances of 1907'.

[44] Whether they were necessary is another matter. Certainly, Barrier suggests that they were not and that peace was a result of the conciliatory measures that saw a repeal of the controversial bill. Ibid. Nonetheless, their support is evidence of the fact that the mutually constitutive relationship between 1857 and 1907 helped bolster orthodox imperial ideology.

were held arranged by, or for the benefit of, local mutiny veterans by a range of well-wishers motivated for the most part by a mixture of philanthropy and self-publicity.[45] In addition, a number of small-scale acts of commemoration were conducted across the country, primarily arranged by the various regional veteran associations that had grown up in the late nineteenth and early twentieth centuries, and thus, for example, wreaths were laid and decorations hung at a number of mutiny memorials in Britain including at Havelock's Trafalgar Square statue where, on 25 September, The Committee of Survivors of Havelock's Relief of Lucknow decorated the monument to mark the fiftieth anniversary of the First Relief.[46] According to the London correspondent of one newspaper, the 'statue was viewed during the day by crowds of people, including many Indian Mutiny veterans, who willingly recounted real and fictitious reminiscences for the benefit of the bystanders'.[47] Similarly, The Corporation of Sunderland arranged for flowers to be laid two months later at monuments dedicated to Havelock in Sunderland and London to commemorate the General's death during the Second Relief of Lucknow.[48]

In addition to these modest localised events, many regional and national newspapers began including articles celebrating the suppression of the mutiny. Most notably, *The Times* serialised a historical account of the mutiny written by Field Marshal Sir Henry Evelyn Wood, himself a mutiny veteran, over sixteen parts and eighteen days.[49] Just as was the case earlier in the year, this coverage made it abundantly clear what it meant to remember the mutiny in 1907. Just as the newspaper, alongside the great majority of the conservative press, had explicitly connected their recollection of the mutiny with the contemporary state of India, so too did it tell its readers ahead of the first part of Wood's account, that 'In relation to the present unrest in India, and also to the future trend of affairs in that great Dependency, Sir Evelyn Wood's opening chapter has an immediate and not merely an historical interest and importance'.[50] However, upon an assessment of all sixteen parts, it is clear that the same is true of the entire series of articles. Thus, whilst the first part continues largely from where *The Times* had left off when the unrest in Punjab began to subside in June and thus continues to bemoan 'The inability of our officers

[45] See, for example, Anon, 'Indian Mutiny Veterans', p. 4.
[46] The Secretary HM Office of Works to General Sir George D. Parker, 7 September 1907, 'Trafalgar Square: Statue of General Sir Henry Havelock', TNA, WORK 20/34.
[47] London Correspondent, 'Gossip from the Capital', *Lancashire Evening Post*, 26 September 1907, p. 2.
[48] Town Clerk, Sunderland, to Secretary, Office of Works, 19 November 1907, 'Trafalgar Square: Statue of General Sir Henry Havelock', TNA, WORK 20/34.
[49] For the first instalment, see Field Marshal Sir Wood, 'Revolt in Hindustan, 1857–9', p. 11.
[50] Anon, 'Advert', p. 7.

to read the signs' of revolt in 1857 and the 'regrettable supineness amongst senior officers' and especially those in Meerut, the remainder of the series is entirely more celebratory in nature.[51] Wood's historical treatment of the mutiny returns to the triumphant memory inculcated over the second phase of commemoration explored in Chapter 3, and therefore, focuses on the courage, sacrifice, and ultimate victory of British soldiers who suppressed the uprising and saved the empire in its moment of need. In this respect, the explicit justification for the series given by *The Times* is instructive when they wrote that 'of such matters it is good to read, not because fighting and bloodshed are in themselves admirable but because if you have to fight for your country and to preserve your comrades and even your wives and children from massacre, it is well to do it in the whole-hearted spirit of these heroes'.[52] In this respect, the series seems to be best read as an inducement to the reader to follow in the footsteps of these heroes and be ready to 'fight for your country'. In this regard, Wood's concluding paragraph of his final instalment is telling. Informing his readers that the greatest benefit of British rule in India was the 'maintenance of internal peace', Wood reminds his readers that this 'can only be assured while Princes and peoples realize that the paramount Power "beareth not the sword in vain"'.[53]

This meaning and memory of 1857 was readily developed in a host of other publications from September onwards. To take just one more example, this time published in *The Leamington Spa Courier*, another conservative newspaper, the writer begins by angrily telling his readers that 'many of us have wholly forgotten the story of the Indian Mutiny'.[54] The article then goes on to openly praise the account of the mutiny given by Wood and serialised in *The Times* and goes as far as to recommend that it be 'adopted as a text book by the Board of Education, for then might our youth have some conception of what it cost to make and keep the British Empire'. Going on to recollect the various mutiny heroes such as Nicholson, Outram, and Havelock, the newspaper told its readers that the response given by Clyde when he was asked to come out of retirement and leave Britain for India summed up the attitude evinced by the mutiny heroes and provided the most important lesson for the present generation. Unquestioningly accepting his country's call, *The Leamington Spa Courier* recalls that Clyde told the government that he would be ready to leave for India in 'Half-an-hour'.[55]

---

[51] Wood, 'Revolt in Hindustan, 1857–9', p. 11.   [52] Anon, 'The Indian Mutiny', p. 9.
[53] Wood, 'Revolt in Hindustan, 1857–9', p. 14.   [54] Anon, 'Lest we Forget', p. 4.
[55] Ibid. It should be noted that this is of course an inaccurate account of Clyde's acceptance of the position. He asked for 24 hours. The shortening of time might be seen to represent hyperbole on the part of the author. However, it is better explained by considering the perceived distance of India from Britain. With the advent of the telegraph and modern transportation India seemed closer. Therefore, the threat seemed closer and the time of response also needed to be quicker.

This inducement to hold India by the sword and learn the lessons of duty to country and empire from immortal mutiny heroes like Clyde is fully appreciated when once again embedded within the contemporary political situation in Britain. With a growing number of radicals in Britain taking up an anti-imperialist stance and, for the first time, a significant number of these speaking from positions within the House of Commons following the General Election of 1906, the empire was facing a serious ideological threat. Indeed, at precisely the same moment that the mutiny once again enters imperial discourse in September and October, James Keir Hardie arrived in India as part of his global voyage.[56] Hardie had become one of the most famous and successful voices for socialism within mainstream British politics over the previous two decades, but the breakthrough General Election of 1906 came, in many respects, a little too late for Hardie who was beginning to suffer from a range of health problems even as he became the first leader of the newly formed Labour Party.[57] Indeed, it was precisely because of his failing health that Hardie had embarked on his grand-tour which had seen him visit Canada, Japan, and Singapore before arriving in Calcutta on 18 September, exactly fifty years after Bahadur Shah II had fled the Red Fort in search of sanctuary a few days ahead of the fall of Delhi. If Hardie's journey up to that point had been pursued for the purpose of relaxation and convalescence, then his arrival in India, apparently coinciding with the return of his health, saw the aging socialist spokesman pursue an altogether different agenda. Travelling with nationalist leaders and leading Swadeshi proponents such as Tilak and Jagesh Chowdhuri, Hardie spent his time in India meeting Congressmen and addressing large crowds on the subject of British policy and Indian nationalism as he travelled through East Bengal, the United Provinces, and Punjab before heading south to Bombay and Pune before finally travelling to Madras where he left India for Australia and South Africa after stopping in Ceylon.[58]

Reports of Hardie's speeches in India were the cause of considerable outrage in Britain with the conservative press accusing Hardie of inciting another mutiny. Of particular concern was the content of Hardie's speeches in Barisal where he reportedly compared British suppression of legitimate protest to

---

[56] For an account of Hardie's journey that situates his time in India within a broader consideration of his time in Australia and South Africa and that specifically focuses on the apparent political connection between metropole and periphery, see Hyslop, 'The world voyage of James Keir Hardie', pp. 343–62.

[57] Though neglecting issues of imperialism, for a study of the Independent Labour Party in the two decades that preceded the breakthrough elections of 1906, see Howell, *British Workers and the Independent Labour Party*. For a useful discussion of Keir Hardie's opposition to the Boer War and attitudes towards British imperialism in the years proceeding his trip to India, see Porter, *Critics of Empire*, pp. 95–137, see especially pp. 124–31. See also Prior, 'Empire before Labour', pp. 23–40.

[58] Hyslop, 'The world voyage of James Keir Hardie'.

Czarist oppression in Russia and even accused British officials of committing atrocities comparable to those of the Armenian genocide. Indeed, at precisely the same time that British newspapers carried stories of Hardie's speeches and accused him of inciting rebellion, the same newspapers celebrated loyalty and duty to empire in relation to the mutiny with this juxtaposition often present in the same article. Just as the enormous fear that arose earlier in the year is best understood as an important element within the ideological struggle for empire and ultimately supported oppressive measures to combat the growth of unrest in the country, so too is the emergence of a celebratory discourse from September onwards best understood in precisely the same way. In opposition to radicals and liberals, the celebration of mutiny heroes was intimately tied to conservative calls for the maintenance of empire as an indispensable component of what it meant to be British and thus to hold India with a strong arm.

Formal Commemoration and a Commitment to Empire

This chapter has thus far focused on how the panic of 1907 reported in the conservative press was both a product of fears emanating from India, as well as anxieties rooted in Britain over growing liberalism and radicalism, together with the perceived threat this posed to empire. In this respect, memories of the mutiny both reflected these anxieties and were used by imperialist elements within Britain in the face of challenges at home as much as from abroad. It is precisely in this context that we should evaluate the principal ostensive attempt to memorialise the mutiny when, on 23 December, *The Telegraph*, in conjunction with orthodox imperialists, helped arrange a grand event to mark the Jubilee year.

Discussion on what form the Jubilee celebrations should take began in 1906 with discussion on a wide variety of possible events. Perhaps, the most controversial suggestion came from Frank Hugh O'Donnell, a prominent Irish politician and critic of the British empire who, as early as the 1870s, had linked Irish demands for home rule with early Indian nationalist aspirations when, in corroboration with several other Irish MPs, Gyanendramohan Tagore, and J.C Meenakshya, he had helped form the Constitutional Society of India.[59] Suggesting a very different memory of the mutiny than was promoted by the government or had been adopted by the great majority of the population, O'Donnell suggested that British commemoration should take the form of reparation services at three sites in India readily connected with

---

[59] Mehrotra, *The Emergence of the Indian National Congress,* pp. 324–31. For more, see O'Donnell, *A History of The Irish Parliamentary Party.* For more on the connection between how Indian nationalism and Irish nationalism came into contact and conversation, see Silvestri, 'The Sinn Fein of India', pp. 454–86.

injustices in 1857. The first of these services would commemorate the manu-
facture of cartridges greased with pork and cow fat in Dum Dum to 'dishon-
our and degrade hundreds of thousands of brave and gallant soldiers'. The
second would acknowledge the cruel punishments inflicted on sepoys who
refused the cartridges in Meerut and which resulted in the soldiers being
'forced into insurrection'. Finally, the third should mark British cruelty and
vengeance on the spot where Major William Hodson executed Bahadur Shah
Zafar's two sons and grandson. A ceremony at which O'Donnell hoped the
government would willingly join 'Hindus and Mahomedans, who should
meet in hundreds of thousands, to commemorate the cruel massacre of the
princely prisoners'.[60]

O'Donnell's suggestion is interesting for many reasons, but not least because
it highlights the sheer breadth of possibility in how Britain could remember the
mutiny. However, as is perhaps inevitable when considered alongside the dominant memory of the mutiny, O'Donnell's provocative suggestion did not meet
with assent from many quarters.[61] A potentially more likely suggestion was
championed by Field Marshal Lord Roberts who saw the upcoming anniversary as an appropriate occasion to celebrate the contributions of mutiny veterans in securing India. As we have already seen in Chapter 3, Roberts had been
at the forefront of British commemorative activities during the second phase
of commemoration and had taken a prominent position within the memorial
committees established to help arrange for the construction of monuments
dedicated to Brigadier-General John Nicholson and General Alexander Taylor
in Delhi. Himself a mutiny veteran and, at least since the Boer War, one of the
foremost military heroes of his era, it would be easy to account for Robert's
interest in remembering the mutiny on its fiftieth anniversary as a nostalgic
activity. However, when read alongside Robert's robust stance on the need for
widespread military reform, it is apparent that remembering 1857 in 1907 was
of contemporary significance for the Field-Marshal.

With the Boer War highlighting numerous failings within Britain's military
machinery, Roberts became one of the most vocal proponents for a system of
conscription to be adopted by Britain. A military model employed on the con-
tinent and, most significantly, by the German army, conscription had always

---

[60] This article was originally published in the Shyamji Krishnavarma's *Indian Sociologist*
though was pejoratively reprinted in *The Times*. See Imperialist to the Editor of the Times,
The Times, 6 June 1907, p. 15; O'Donnell, 'A Triple Reparation', p. 15.

[61] Frank Hugh O'Donnell's brother, colonial administrator, and fellow critic of aspects of British
rule, Charles James O'Donnell, wrote to *The Times* pointing out that his brother had written
the letter over a year earlier and noting that 'I regret he expressed himself so strongly'. C. J.
O'Donnell to the editor, *The Times*, 10 June 1907, p. 4. For more on the O'Donnell brothers in
particular, and the relationship between Ireland and empire in general, see Bender, 'Ireland
and Empire', pp. 343–60.

been rejected as antithetical to Britain's national character but in the light of what now seemed to be systemic failings in the wake of the Boer War, groups such as Roberts's National Service League began to attract more favourable attention with their proposals for a moderate system of 'national service' to be introduced. For Roberts, British security and global supremacy could only be maintained by a greatly reinvigorated military system capable of not only tackling threats, which might develop within Britain's imperial possessions but, more pressingly, within continental Europe. Particularly wary of the German military and industrial strength, Roberts anxiously warned the public about the precarious geopolitical position occupied by Britain at the start of the twentieth century.[62] Though conscription was not introduced until demanded by the Great War, the Territorial Army gained Crown consent in August 1907 and grew rapidly over the following twelve months until it numbered some 188,000 recruits by the end of 1908. Similarly, Lord Robert Baden-Powell, another Boer War Hero with extensive service in India, held the first meeting of his nascent scouting movement in August 1907. Designed to prepare young men physically and mentally for the rigorous of imperial duty, Baden-Powell's exertions in establishing The Boy Scout organisation was roundly praised by orthodox imperialists for promoting an important message to the next generation who would in time be charged with defending the empire.[63] Though not convinced that these developments were sufficient, Roberts was extremely supportive of both the territorial army and the Scouting movement and further helped organise a great number of rifle clubs across Britain with the intention of helping prepare the nation for armed combat in any way possible. Given Roberts' preoccupations, it would be misguided to dismiss his desire to commemorate the mutiny as driven by pure nostalgia. On the contrary, it is clear that his desire to celebrate the great martial heroes of a previous generation was significantly motivated by his own anxious ambition to encourage young men to accept the duty of empire at a time when it was reaching a crisis point.

However, if orthodox imperialists such as Roberts saw the proposed commemoration ceremony as an opportunity to help promote the martial values which were needed to save the empire, then the suggestion also met with fierce criticism. In light of the continued anti-partition movement, Morley was adamantly opposed to any attempt to formally remember the mutiny in the present. Hearing about the plans for jubilee celebrations, Morley wrote to Minto to secure the Viceroy's support in opposing the idea of any 'commemoration whatsoever, great or small', adding that as 'soon as the King comes back from Marienbad I mean to bring the matter before him and I trust that

---

[62] Semmel, *Imperialism and Social Reform*, see especially Chapter 12, 'Lord Roberts and Robert Blatchford', pp. 208–25.

[63] MacDonald, *Sons of the Empire*.

he will encourage us to veto any commemoration'.[64] In response, Minto was rather more vociferous, writing that:

Anything of the sort is, in my opinion, utterly out of the question. I cannot imagine anyone, who has ever thought twice about it making such a proposal ... I cannot say how wrong I feel it would be to revive the memory of those times throughout India.... The Indian troops, who stood by us, may well be proud of that terrible time, but neither they nor we should ever care to commemorate its anniversary.[65]

The vociferous nature of Minto's rebuttal of a commemoration ceremony is made all the more surprising given his involvement in the inauguration ceremony of a monument dedicated to the memory of Major-General John Nicholson erected near Kashmiri Gate just months earlier. As was discussed in Chapter 3, the monument had been initially approved by Lord Curzon whilst acting as Viceroy and was arranged by a memorial committee headed by Lord Roberts and Sir Henry Norman who entrusted its production to Thomas Brock.[66] As detailed earlier, Minto utilised the unveiling ceremony as an occasion primarily concerned with celebrating Indian loyalty during the mutiny and as a further inducement to the Indian army to continue supporting the British administration. However, other parties had been unsure if, given the political situation within India, remembering the mutiny was prudent. Indeed, the Lieutenant-Governor of Punjab suggested that the viceroy's presence at the unveiling of Nicholson's monument might not be advisable in the present climate.[67] This opinion was further elaborated by *The Tribune* which, after informing its readers that it did not begrudge Nicholson any honour which it was possible to award such a courageous and important hero, went on to argue that 'anything which is likely to revive the memories of the Mutiny is to be strongly depreciated in the best interests of the country' as remembering it in the present is 'hardly likely to promote friendly relations between Europeans and Indians in this country'.[68] Ultimately, the newspaper felt that it

---

[64] Morley to Minto, 15 August 1906, 'Letter from Morley to Minto', Papers of John Morley as Secretary of State for India, fol. 167, OIOC, MSS EUR D573/1.

[65] Earl Minto to Right Hon. Morley, 3 September 1906, 'Printed copies of telegrams to and from the Secretary of State for India', The Indian Papers of the 4th Earl of Minto, Ms.12741, No. 15, Centre for South Asian Studies Archive, University of Cambridge, Reel 41.

[66] Earl Minto, 'Unveiling of the Nicholson Statue at Delhi', Speeches made by Lord Minto 1905-10, The Indian Papers of the 4th Earl of Minto, Ms.12686, Centre for South Asian Studies Archive, University of Cambridge, Reel 35.

[67] See J. R. Dunlop Smith to E. D. Maclagan, 11 March 1906, 'Printed copies of letters and telegrams to and from persons in India, Nov 1905–June 1906', The Indian Papers of the 4th Earl of Minto, Ms.12764, No. 101, Centre for South Asian Studies Archive, University of Cambridge, Reel 47.

[68] Anon, *Tribune*, 11 April 1906, in 'Press Cuttings, Aug 1905–Mar 1907', The Indian Papers of the 4th Earl of Minto, Ms.12720, p. 127, Centre for South Asian Studies Archive, University of Cambridge, Reel 36.

would have been better if Minto had declined to have anything to do with one of the 'Imperialistic freaks of his erratic predecessor'.[69]

Clearly, the events in Barisal combined with the spread of the Swadeshi movement beyond Bengal and the first signs of unrest in Punjab over the course of the following few months helped Minto share the opinion of *The Tribune*. The fiftieth anniversary is therefore remarkable as for the first time within official discourse the centrality of the memory of the mutiny is brought into question. Whilst successive viceroys and administrators had helped cement the significance of the mutiny within official memory, Morley and Minto questioned the desirability of remembering the mutiny at all. Thus, whilst conflict had always characterised the trajectory of official memory as regards the mutiny, what is at stake in 1907 is not *how* the mutiny is remembered, but whether the mutiny *should* be remembered.

Though the commemoration ceremony proposed in mid-1906 garnered support from a number of traditionally minded imperialists including Roberts, Kitchener, and King Edward VII, resistance from the Viceroy and the Secretary of State, along with the continued unrest in India, appears to have resulted in these plans being set aside until they were revived by a number of popular calls in September and October 1907 for a suitable commemoration event. Of the various parties who proved amenable to such proposals, it was *The Telegraph* through its owner, Lord Burnham, that resolved to arrange and fund such a ceremony. Though writers of letters addressed to the editor of *The Telegraph* had wished to see celebrations held on either the anniversary of the capture of Delhi or that of the second relief of Lucknow, the amount of work involved in preparing such a ceremony was considered excessive for the time available.[70] Accordingly, the newspaper resolved to hold a grand celebration at the Royal Albert Hall in late December, with invitations extended to all surviving mutiny veterans who saw service in 1857.[71] Accordingly, a memorial

---

[69] Ibid.
[70] For the first public announcement, see Anon (Perceval Landon), "'1857' Indian Mutiny Golden Commemoration, Daily Telegraph Christmas Dinner at the Albert Hall, to the Veterans who Survive, In the Roberts', *The Daily Telegraph*, p. 11.
[71] In fact, the sheer abundance of dates seen worthy of celebration from September onwards complicated the decision. Many small local celebrations were held on various dates to commemorate specific events. For example, wreaths were laid and decorations hung at a number of memorials including the statue of Havelock in Trafalgar Square where, on 25 September, The Committee of Survivors of Havelock's Relief of Lucknow decorated the monument to mark the fiftieth anniversary of the First Relief of Lucknow. The Secretary HM Office of Works to General Sir George D. Parker, 7 September 1907, 'Trafalgar Square: Statue of General Sir Henry Havelock', TNA, WORK 20/34. The Corporation of Sunderland likewise arranged for flowers to be laid two months later to mark the Second Relief of Lucknow and the General's death. Town Clerk, Sunderland, to Secretary, Office of Works, 19 November 1907, 'Trafalgar Square: Statue of General Sir Henry Havelock', TNA, WORK 20/34.

committee was quickly formed with Roberts taking the chair and Perceval Landon of *The Telegraph*, appointed the honorary Secretary. Over the following weeks, the memorial committee grew quickly to include a venerable selection of mutiny veterans and staunch imperialists such as Lord Curzon, Lord Walter Kerr, and Rudyard Kipling. With the newspaper making its plans public in mid-November, *The Telegraph* proceeded to keep the anniversary of the mutiny alive within its readers' memory through daily updates on the progress made by the memorial committee and the numbers of applications received and checked by the War Office. In addition to this, the newspaper solicited original first-hand accounts of mutiny anecdotes, which were published alongside a number of poems and letters written by an assortment of veterans and well-wishers.

After many weeks of preparations and mounting excitement, the event began with a parade of mutiny veterans led by Colonel Sir Neville Chamberlain. Chamberlain, who had served under Roberts in Afghanistan, India, and South Africa, was not involved in the mutiny but, in addition to his own long service, was thought a suitable candidate for the task as he was the nephew of Field Marshal Sir Neville Chamberlain, who had served as adjunct-general during the mutiny before being seriously injured during the siege of Delhi.[72] Starting promptly at 13:00 outside the Royal Albert Hall, Edward Wrench, who had served in both the Crimean War and the mutiny as a military surgeon, was one of the first to arrive for what he evocatively titled in his diary, 'my last parade'.[73] He was not alone for long, however, and was soon joined by a host of aged mutiny veterans before Lord Roberts made his appearance for the inspection. Describing the event, Wrench noted that 'there was no formal falling in – but as old soldiers we arranged ourselves in three lines as naturally as a flight of wild fowl form in a V' (Figure 4.1).[74]

Following the inspection, the veterans retired inside the Royal Albert Hall for the banquet. Sitting on the high table, Chamberlain records that 'I sat next to my intimate friend, Rudyard Kipling, and we had a merry time, recalling happy days, in India'.[75] The evening witnessed speeches from a number of dignitaries including Lord Curzon and Field Marshal Lord Roberts who, fifty

---

[72] Perceval Landon to Sir Neville Chamberlain, 5 December 1907, Letter attached to inside back cover of a copy of Landon, '*1857: In Commemoration of the 50th Anniversary of the Indian Mutiny*', annotated by Chamberlain. Sir Neville Francis Fitzgerald Chamberlain papers, OIOC, Mss EUR A180.

[73] Edward M. Wrench, 'My Last Parade', diary entry for Monday 23 December 1907, 'Diaries of Edward M. Wrench', Papers of Edward M. Wrench, Nottingham University, Manuscripts and Special Collections, Wr D52.

[74] Ibid.

[75] Chamberlain, note made on the inside copy of his annotated copy of Landon, *In Commemoration*, Sir Neville Francis Fitzgerald Chamberlain papers, OIOC, Mss EUR A180.

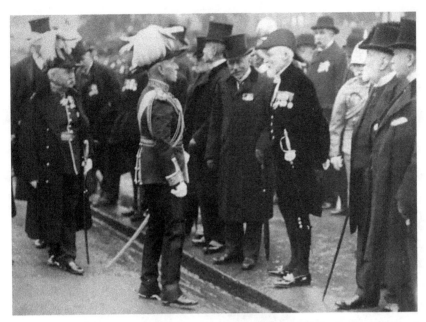

Figure 4.1 Photograph of Lord Roberts, Colonel J. P. Robertson, and Edward M. Wrench at the Inspection of Mutiny Veterans at the Royal Albert Hall, London. Papers of Edward M. Wrench, 21–23 December, pp. 184–85, Nottingham University, Manuscripts and Special Collections, Wr D52. Picture also published in *Daily Mirror*, 24 December 1907.

years earlier, had been a lieutenant in India during the mutiny.[76] In addition to this, the evening saw the first public reading of a commemorative poem written for the occasion by Rudyard Kipling. *The Veterans*, like the speeches that came before it, made the true purpose of the commemoration ceremony abundantly clear. After introducing the purpose of the poem, to commemorate and celebrate the veterans of a desperate struggle who ultimately 'cleansed our East with steel', the final stanza is revealing

> One service more we dare to ask –
>   Pray for us, heroes, pray,
> That when Fate lays on us our task
>   We do not shame the day.[77]

---

[76] For an account of Roberts' Mutiny experiences, see Roberts, *Forty-One Years in India*. For further details on the commemoration ceremony, see Anon (Perceval Landon), 'Indian Mutiny Golden Commemoration, "The Daily Telegraph" Christmas Dinner to the Veterans Who Survive'", pp. 9–12; Landon, *In Commemoration*.

[77] Kipling, 'The Veterans', p. 315.

The final lesson of Kipling's poem can be taken as the central theme contained within the practices of commemoration and memorialisation utilised to mark the jubilee year of the mutiny. Whether remembering the ineptitude and inactivity of British officers who failed to anticipate the uprising or respond to the first signs of unrest with due vigour, or recalling a generation of mutiny heroes who fought so desperately and valiantly to suppress the uprising, commemoration is best understood as an inducement to the present generation to take up the sword and defend British supremacy in India. With India in a state of unrest, a Liberal government who many still doubted had the resolve to hold India, and men like Keir Hardie finding a new platform from which to criticise British colonial policy and undermine imperial ideology, the practices of commemoration which were employed to mark the Golden Jubilee of the Mutiny are once again best understood as an anxious response to perceived imperial vulnerabilities, connected to both the rise of Indian nationalism in the late nineteenth century along with the growth of liberalism and radicalism within the metropole.

5   The War of Indian Independence
A Struggle for Meaning, Memory, and the Right to Narrate

Thus far, this study has concentrated on identifying and understanding the first two phases of British commemoration deployed in India and Britain over the course of the fifty years that followed the mutiny. As we have seen, both phases were responses to specific anxieties that developed over the course of this period. Whilst the first stage of commemoration was used by the colonial administration as an attempt to produce a less divisive and debilitating memory of the mutiny in the immediate wake of the conflict, the second was a reaction to growing anxieties during the late nineteenth and early twentieth centuries and attempted to mould British memory into a celebration of British mutiny heroes. Both an attempt to reassure the British public in a period of growing fears over the rise of Indian nationalism and an inducement to emulate the imperial spirit of those who had held India in a moment of crisis, commemoration played an important ideological role during this time of colonial anxiety.

This chapter will now turn to Indian attempts to remember the mutiny and specifically look at how this was partially achieved through the subversion and appropriation of British mnemonic symbols. As we will see here, whilst it is difficult to uncover the content of Indian counter-memories in the immediate aftermath of the mutiny and through much of the nineteenth century, it is possible to locate their presence – always challenging and troubling British constructions of the past from the margins of mnemonic space. However, as we will argue, the mutiny's jubilee year not only saw acts of British commemoration, it also witnessed the emergence of a rather more robust Indian counter-memory that not only challenged the hegemonic nature of British memory but more significantly British hegemonic control of India. Articulated as an inducement to further resistance and even as a guide for future insurrection, this counter-memory encouraged further acts of insubordination and resistance to British rule.

In highlighting the struggle for meaning, memory, and the right to narrate which characterised Indian attempts to construct alternative memories of the past within the sociopolitical realities of the twentieth century, this chapter will also highlight a number of significant debates between Indian nationalists as to what should be remembered when recalling the mutiny, and how it should inform contemporary debates concerning the trajectory of Indian national-ism and the practices of resistance most suitable for prevailing concerns. In this respect, this chapter sets out to both highlight the political implications of Indian constructions of the past in contradistinction to imperial memory, whilst at the same time paying close attention to the significant differences within nationalist constructions of 1857 which gradually consolidated over the course of the early twentieth century into a Congress endorsed memory of the First War of Independence.

In so doing, this chapter will be divided into three principal sections. The first of these will consider how a focus on British symbols of commemoration helps us begin to uncover alternative Indian conceptions of the past. Just as we paid close attention to the British Mutiny Pilgrimage in Chapter 3 of this study, so too can we consider the quite different commemorative tours taken by Indians over the same period to the same locations. The second section of this chapter will consider the emergence of counter-memories in the years that followed the mutiny's jubilee year. Through a continued focus on resistance to British built mnemonic signifiers, this chapter will investigate how nationalist thinkers utilised these spaces of memory to explore the nature of British rule and the multiple forms that resistance could take. The third section will focus on the emergence of what appears to be the first large-scale acts of organ-ised commemoration for the nationalist memory of 1857 within India during the late 1930s. Occurring at the very moment when the British administration began to actively censor its own memory of the mutiny, this significant shift in commemorative power is indicative of broader changes within the power relations of the subcontinent.

Subversion, Sedition, and Vandalism

Although it is possible to uncover a host of nineteenth-century works imbued with British attempts to remember the mutiny, it is rather more difficult to do the same when considering Indian memories. In many ways, the work of writ-ers including Carol E. Henderson and Stephen Legg helps us to both appreci-ate the existence of counter-commemorative landscapes, whilst recognising the inherent difficulty that researchers encounter in recovering them today.[1] Whilst it would be naïve to imagine that Indian counter-memories did not exist, or failed to attach themselves to physical spaces, these memories were very often constructed from rather more furtive and entirely less enduring materials than their colonial equivalents and, as a result, often faded without

---

[1] Henderson, 'Spatial Memorialising of War in 1857', pp. 217–36; Legg, 'Sites of Counter-memory', pp. 180–201.

ever leaving a trace within the imperial archive. Indeed, this was often a conscious strategy employed by those Indians who might otherwise have wished to propagate alternative memories but who made a shrewd assessment of the balance of power and took the rational decision to conceal their potentially insurrectionary memories of 1857. An interesting anecdote that has been rehearsed by several writers goes some way to further illustrate this point. It is said that a missionary at the start of the twentieth century asked his Indian students to write an essay on the mutiny. Rather than reflecting the British licenced memory of the mutiny for the benefit of the teacher, each student submitted a single piece of blank paper. This action, which seems to lie on the seam between a space of false compliance and that of overt resistance, highlights the existence of a 'hidden transcript' on the mutiny which was nonetheless unspeakable for the great majority within imperial interactions.[2]

Largely unrecorded and leaving few traces of its existence, this counter-memory is hard to recapture today although one potentially fertile source of subaltern memory is the understudied folksong. Just as Projit Bihari Mukharji has argued that broadsides printed and circulated in Britain contain an often marginalised vernacular memory of the mutiny associated with Britain's working classes, traditional Indian folksongs perpetuate an alternative conception of the mutiny within India's subordinated classes.[3] Through the compilations of such songs collected by Puran Chandra Joshi and earlier by William Crooke, it is possible to begin to see alternative conceptions of the conflict emerging in which the bravery of rebel leaders is eulogised in contradistinction to British brutality.[4] These songs demonstrate the existence of alternative ways of remembering and commemorating the conflict that challenge the authoritative narrative of the State.[5]

A no less useful lens through which to view those vernacular memories which stood opposed to the dominance of British memory is through a focus on British built monuments. Though these spaces of memory were constructed and imbued with British remembrance, they also provided a space around which alternative memories could be produced. This is apparent when one considers the assessment made by prolific author and nationalist leader Lala Lajpat Rai

---

[2] For an example of this anecdote, see Mehta, *1857*, p. 7. For James C. Scott's notion of the 'hidden transcript', see Scott, *Domination and the Arts of Resistance*. See also Scott, *Weapons of the Weak*.

[3] Mukharji, 'Ambiguous Imperialisms', pp. 110–34; Mukharji, 'Jessie's Dream at Lucknow', pp. 77–113.

[4] Joshi, *1857 in Folk Songs*; Crooke, 'Songs about the king of Oudh', pp. 61–67, pp. 91–92; Crooke, 'Songs of the Mutiny', pp. 123–24, pp. 165–69. See also Nayar (ed.), *The Penguin 1857 Reader*, 'Indian Responses', pp. 294–326.

[5] For an interesting, though brief discussion of these folk songs focusing on their gendered nature, see Amin, 'A Hanging Twice Over'.

who, in considering the way in which Britain remembered the mutiny and specifically how British visitors to the sites of memory established in Lucknow and Cawnpore responded to these commemorative spaces, informs his readers that there existed a dramatically different interpretation of the event among many Indians.[6] Arguing that British visitors to the Residency and to the Angel shared a conflicted memory of the mutiny which revolved around a celebration of the courage and bravery required to defend the Residency tempered by a deep-seated sense of anguish and attended desire for revenge as they stood around the Memorial Well, Rai tells his readers that the 'English are mistaken if they think that a reading of the history of the mutiny and the excesses and cruelties indulged in by the British does not excite similar feeling in the minds of the Indians'.[7] However, whilst Rai thus attests to the presence of these radically alternative sets of meaning and memory still harboured by the Indian population, he further tells his readers that the main difference between British memory and Indian memory is that whilst the 'British can express their feelings freely. The Indians cannot; their feelings must be repressed'.[8]

A remarkably similar example of how British monuments provided a space in which radically different counter-memories could be constructed is likewise recorded by noted anti-imperialist, Wilfrid Scawen Blunt. According to the diary of his 1883–84 tour of India, he had the opportunity of visiting the Residency in company with his host in Lucknow, Rajah Amir Hassan.[9] A man of considerable wealth and influence in the region, the Rajah personally guided Blunt around the battered remains of the compound where

he told us the history of the mutiny from his own point of view. His father had sided with the mutineers and been the chief leader of the Shiah faction among them, till the massacres occurred, when he left them in disgust and went to his own fort, at Mahmudabad, where he took ill and died. Twelve of Amir Hassan's brothers and cousins were shot, blown up, or hanged by the English, and he alone was left, a boy of ten, to be educated by them. All the family property in Lucknow was confiscated and destroyed, for the English destroyed one third of the city, and so he comes in for an inheritance of woe. Looking, however, at the ruins, which are very beautiful, he said: 'We have agreed to forget our history, and the days of our glory. But the English refuse to forget it. They leave their ruins standing to perpetuate the memory of bloodshed. If I could do it, I would persuade the Lieutenant-Governor to have them razed or rebuilt.[10]

Here again, just as Rai suggested previously, it is possible to see how British mutiny monuments provided a mnemonic space in which counter-memories of the mutiny could be propagated. However, if these monuments could be used in such a way, then it is also possible to trace even more direct attempts to resist and occasionally subvert official memory, as represented by these structures,

[6] Rai, *Young India*, p. 107.   [7] Ibid.   [8] Ibid.   [9] Blunt, *India under Ripon*.
[10] Ibid, pp. 151–52.

from the moment they were built. If subaltern memory therefore leaves little positive trace of its existence, then it may only be seen opaquely, through its reflection in the edifices which it opposed. In this respect, the incidents at the monument erected in Lucknow to the memory of members of the 93rd Highland Regiment were typical. Erected, as we have already noted, more than forty years after the mutiny, the monument was repeatedly damaged and vandalised following its unveiling. Its brass plaques, recording the monument's dedication, were stolen on at least two separate occasions in the early twentieth century.[11] In Delhi too at the Kashmiri Gate which, like the Residency, had been maintained in its ruined state following the mutiny, frequent episodes of vandalism defaced the large and centrally located structure resulting in the posting of an undercover, plain-clothed policeman in the vicinity at night.[12]

Such acts were largely depoliticised by the British administration and blamed on either thoughtless destruction or, in the case of the theft of the brass plaques, on the potential value of scrap metal. However, in these official evaluations, anxiety over a potentially more political background to the acts is revealed through the occasional slippage between the word 'vandalism' and the word 'sabotage' to describe the damage done. Despite the general tendency to depoliticise such actions, however, the motives which lay behind them are largely unrecoverable owing to their very nature. Regardless of intention, the result was the same. In their frequently marred condition, the monuments, which were designed to speak of an uncontested and authoritative representation of the mutiny, became imbued with a rather more ambivalent meaning for their onlookers. Standing in their damaged state until they could once again be repaired, the monuments became a testimony to the struggle for meaning, memory, and the right to narrate which they were designed to obscure.

In addition to these smaller, everyday acts of resistance, the monuments also became the occasional target of rather larger acts of protest. One of the most significant of these came in 1901 when a series of demonstrations were organised against the admission policies of the Memorial Well in Cawnpore that prohibited natives from entering the confines of Yule's gothic screen unless they had applied in advance for an entry permit from the monument's managing committee.[13] As we saw in Chapter 2, the admission policies that were in force at the monument were as central to its meaning as its form or location and thus these protests challenged the monument directly.

[11] Bullock to C. B. Duke, Deputy High Commissioner for the UK, 5 June 1948, 'File 12a Military Memorials of the Argyll and Sutherland Highlanders in India and Pakistan', fol. 95, OIOC. IOR/R/4/87.
[12] Hilary Waddington to The Senior Superintendent of Police, 22 July 1938, 'Kashmiri Gate', NAI, ASI/Delhi Circle/Monuments/29/1938/Monuments.
[13] W.H.L. Impey to J. P. Hewett, 15 January 1902, 'Admission of Natives to the Cawnpore Memorial Gardens', Judicial and Public Annual Files 73–160, File 142, OIOC. IOR/L/PJ/6/591.

Intriguingly, the acts of protest that were levelled at the monument were triggered by a visit from an English magistrate, John Smedley, whose actions provided the spark to overt dissent. Travelling across North India on a lecture programme sponsored by the Anglo-Indian Temperance Association, Smedley first heard of the rules governing admission to the monument whilst in the city. Appalled by the prohibition of Indians within the monument, Smedley decided to contest the rule by attempting to enter the monument whilst accompanied by an Indian companion. When confronted by Ram Charan, the garden's gatekeeper, and subsequently by Private Whelan, who was on duty at the monument, Smedley is reported by Rex Mayer, the Superintendent of the monument, to have attempted to physically force his companion into the enclosure before being decisively turned away.[14] Smedley gave the event a great deal of exposure during the remainder of his speaking engagements by rehearsing the story and his condemnation of the rule, repeatedly. During one well-attended meeting, arranged by the Congress Party in Lucknow, Smedley pointed out that there was no sign posted in the Memorial Gardens explicitly stating the admittance regulations except, as reported by Special Branch in a classified report on his activities, a 'board put on the outside of the Memorial Well at Cawnpore which says that no dogs are admitted on the grounds'. Smedley suggested to his audience that in the absence of any other sign, 'This most insulting remark refers to the natives of India ... Why should any Government professing to be guided by the spirit of Him who came into the world to seek and to save, allow such an insulting statement to hang outside such a place'.[15]

Smedley's remarks sparked outrage among many Indians, some of whom wrote letters to a number of newspaper editors to protest. Others took more direct action and sought to gain admittance to the monument regardless of regulations, resulting in the British administration being forced to investigate photographs circulating among the population featuring groups of Indians at the monument.[16] One such photograph was traced back to Kanhaiya Lall, a local resident who had obtained a pass from the district judge and entered the monument with 'a great gang'.[17] According to Sir James La Touche, the Lieutenant

---

[14] Rex H. T. Mayer, 1 January 1902, 'statement of what took place at the Memorial Gardens between Mr. Medley [Smedley], the Gate Keeper, the Private at the Well, and lastly with the Superintendent', Copy of note by L. B. Goad, 11 January 1902, Admission of Natives to the Cawnpore Memorial Gardens, Judicial and Public Annual Files 73–160, File 142, OIOC. IOR/L/PJ/6/591.

[15] Extract from *The Advocate*, 8 December 1901, in 'Note' by L. B. Goad, 11 January 1902, 'Admission of Natives to the Cawnpore Memorial Gardens', Judicial and Public Annual Files 73–160, File 142, OIOC. IOR/L/PJ/6/591.

[16] J. P. Hewett to W. H. L. Impey. 15 February 1902, 'Admission of Natives to the Cawnpore Memorial Gardens', Judicial and Public Annual Files 73–160, File 142, OIOC. IOR/L/PJ/6/591.

[17] Sir J. D. LaTouche to Lord Curzon, 1 March 1902, 'Correspondence with People in India, Jan 1902–Jun 1902', Papers of Marquess Curzon of Kedleston, No. 79, p. 104, OIOC, Mss EUR F111/205.

Governor of the North Western Provinces and Chief Commissioner of Oudh, the administration succeeded in confiscating the photographic plate from Lall, which was summarily destroyed to prevent further copies being made.[18]

The apparent incongruity of the protests being started by an English magistrate was captured by William Impey in his report on the disturbances when he wrote, 'It has been reserved for a European Justice of the Peace to create a disturbance in the gardens'.[19] However, whilst it was indeed Smedley's stand against what he perceived to be a gross injustice that had the effect of raising wider overt dissent, it is unlikely that such feelings were not already in circulation. Rather, Smedley provided a legitimised space of protest enabling simmering discontentment to pass from the community's hidden transcript into plain view.

Discussion and debate on the matter was not limited to India but reached further, sparking debate in England where it eventually reached the House of Commons.[20] Ultimately, the protests and agitation did little to change the rules, however. Lord George Hamilton, speaking as the Secretary of State for India, felt that it was unwise to interfere with the Government of India who in turn informed the local government that it was hoped they 'will maintain the existing rule'.[21] The reasons for this were explained by the Viceroy, Lord Curzon, in a letter to La Touche in which he adamantly exclaimed that 'I see no necessity why you should give way about admission to the Cawnpore Memorial site. The spot is sacred to the British, not to the Hindus. It is, further, consecrated ground; and, just as the Hindus keep us out of the sacred places of their faith, an exclusion which we never dispute, so we have an equal right to keep them out of ours, particularly in a place with such memories as Cawnpore'.[22] Going on to further consider the potential ramifications of allowing Indians into the enclosure, Curzon added that 'You can never be certain, if Hindus were admitted, that they might not insult English visitors, or in some way defile the spot'.[23] The protests did, however, result in the management committee being asked to erect a sign outside the monument expressing the terms of admission for Indians, alongside that which prohibited dogs.[24]

---

[18] Ibid.

[19] J. P. Hewett to W. H. L. Impey, 15 January 1902, 'Admission of Natives to the Cawnpore Memorial Gardens', Judicial and Public Annual Files 73–160, File 142, OIOC. IOR/L/PJ/6/591.

[20] Question Mr. Caine to Lord G. Hamilton, *HC Deb, 27 January 1902, Vol 101, Cols. 959–60.*

[21] J. P. Hewett to W. H. L. Impey, 15 February 1902, 'Admission of Natives to the Cawnpore Memorial Gardens', Judicial and Public Annual Files 73–160, File 142, OIOC. IOR/L/PJ/6/591.

[22] Lord Curzon to Sir J. D. LaTouche, 22 February 1902, 'Correspondence with People in India, Jan 1902–Jun 1902', 'Letters and Telegrams to persons in India', Papers of Marquess Curzon of Kedleston, No. 46, p. 42, OIOC, Mss EUR F111/205.

[23] Ibid.

[24] Impey to Hooper, 15 January 1902, 'Admission of Natives to the Cawnpore Memorial Gardens', Judicial and Public Annual Files 73–160, File 142, OIOC. IOR/L/PJ/6/591.

James Young, in his outstanding study on *The Texture of Memory: Holocaust Memorials and Meaning* and in a number of articles, has written extensively on what he has termed 'counter-monuments: brazen, painfully self-conscious memorial spaces conceived to challenge the very premises of their being'.[25] Looking specifically at the German case, Young has argued that among many individuals charged with attempting to commemorate the holocaust, there exists a profound distrust in the traditional monumental form with its claims of mnemonic and discursive closure around an uncontested representation of the past. In such a form, a monument may appear as a suturing signifier which assures all those who come into contact with it that the work of memory has been done for them, replacing contestation with consensus. A counter-monument, on the other hand, operates in a radically different way by eschewing closure in favour of communicating a responsibility to engage with the past. One such counter-monument discussed by Young takes the form of a hollow aluminium pillar located in a suburb of Harburg, which may at first glance appear rather unremarkable, though two things distinguish this monument from others. First of all, passers-by are invited to write upon the monument and second, it is designed to sink into the ground – a little each year. As Young explains, this monument acts as a social mirror in which the attitudes, memories, and beliefs of the community are captured and included in the memorial form. Whilst monuments generally claim a monopoly on meaning and memory, the Harburg monument has become a testimony to the range and diversity of meanings which, at any one time, are associated with the holocaust by its visitors.[26]

Though clearly not by British design, the result of the perpetual struggle between official memory and vernacular memories was also inscribed upon many mutiny monuments. Through vandalism, graffiti, theft, and protest, the struggle for meaning, memory, and the right to narrate was written onto many mutiny monuments resulting in a rather more ambivalent meaning being communicated to all those who came into contact with them. In this respect, the inscription of dissent upon British monuments undermined their claim on the past, revealing the struggle for meaning which they were designed to obscure.

A Struggle for Memory and the Mutiny's Jubilee Year

As we have seen previously, resistance to mutiny monuments was a crucial part of their ontology, which contested their authorised meaning from the very moment of their inception onwards. Revealing the presence of radically different ways of remembering the mutiny, British monuments not only gave a space in which alternative memories of 1857 could be articulated, but they

---

[25] Young, 'The Counter-monument', pp. 267–96, p. 269. See also Young, *The Texture of Memory*.
[26] Ibid.

also provided a canvas on which these counter-memories could, however fleetingly, be recorded. It was not until Indian nationalism began to garner popular support, however, that it became possible for a diverse selection of individuals to publicly propagate a different memory of the mutiny to that licensed by the British administration. These alternative memories were not purely a matter of reclaiming the past, or even seizing the right to narrate in the present, rather they were also deeply entwined with conceptions of the contemporary realities of British rule, and the multiple means of resistance available to the subordinated Indian population.

It is perhaps unsurprising that these attempts to (re)remember the mutiny began to emerge in the years that followed the Partition of Bengal and the start of mass political mobilisation in centres across India.[27] As we have noted in Chapter 4, the Indian National Congress was instrumental in organising a series of protests and petitions against the proposals to partition Bengal.[28] Since its inception in 1885, the Congress had been dominated by moderate leaders, such as Gopal Krishna Gokhale, who placed their faith in western institutions of administration and education and simply wished to secure a wider role for Indians within the government. However, anger stemming from the unilateral decision to partition Bengal married to a growing sense of frustration at the lack of tangible results that could be boasted from twenty years of Congress-led constitutional protest, encouraged the emergence of a rather more radical voice. Headed by men such as Bal Gandahir Tilak, this brand of Indian nationalism was driven by the desire to win total independence for India and advocated direct action in support of this goal.[29]

The fundamental divide which existed between these two schools of Indian nationalism famously led to the split of the Congress in late 1907. Whilst the Congress moderates continued to work with the British administration in an attempt to secure greater Indian representation within the highest levels of government, the extremists promoted a range of strikes, agitations, and boycotts in an attempt to disrupt British control and win total independence.[30] With neither faction proving successful in its stated aims, and both losing credibility as a result, many young nationalists, particularly those located in Bengal, Maharashtra, and Punjab, began turning increasingly to more overtly violent forms of resistance. Driven underground by British repression, and animated by a blend of anger and frustration, a wave of revolutionary terrorism hit India and Britain from 1907 onwards.[31] Combining Reactionary Hinduism

---

[27] See Sarkar, *Swadeshi Movement in Bengal*.
[28] Ibid. [29] Wolpert, *Tilak and Gokhale*.
[30] For a useful treatment of the split that focuses specifically on Tilak and Gokhale, see Wolpert, *Tilak and Gokhale*, see specifically Chapters 5–6. See also Das, *India under Morley and Minto*, pp. 88–104.
[31] Heehs, *The Bomb in Bengal*.

with European influences from countries such as Russia, these small groups of revolutionary terrorists quickly increased in number and spread to different parts of India with the avowed intention of disrupting smooth governance and, in some cases, preparing an armed vanguard which would be capable of leading a future uprising against the British raj.[32] This tripartite division between moderate, extremist, and revolutionary was in reality never absolute or total, rather these three idealised approaches to resistance against the administration were porous and allowed for significant leakage between them.[33] Nevertheless, it is useful in beginning to conceptualise the divergent aims and courses of action pursued by those aligning themselves in opposition to British rule in the years that followed the Partition of Bengal.

In some respects, the trends and divisions that were set up over this period were reflected in the continued rise of Indian nationalism in the years that followed the First World War. Many nationalist leaders had harboured hopes that India would be granted greater autonomy and potentially self-governance following the Great War. When these concessions were not forthcoming the Congress, led by Mohandas Gandhi, proved successful in extending beyond their traditional middle-class base to reach a broader cross-section of the population during the non-cooperation movement of 1921–22.[34] With popular nationalism beginning to take a hold, debates over how independence should be achieved took on added urgency. In this respect, the debates between Gandhi and Vinayak Damodar Savarkar in the mid-1920s came to reflect significantly different philosophies of resistance. Famously, the two great nationalist leaders met in Britain whilst Savarkar was studying in London and living in India House. Established in 1905 by Shyamji Krishnavarma as student accommodation for Indian students studying abroad, India House quickly developed into a centre for Indian nationalism and political philosophy.[35] Well-funded and organised India House quickly became the heart of radical Indian nationalism in Britain, hosting or housing many influential thinkers and revolutionaries over its short history.[36]

The initial mutual suspicion which is said to have developed between Gandhi and Savarkar at India House would later become a concerted struggle when, in later years, Gandhi would return to India and rise to the leadership of the Congress. Already an ardent advocate of non-violent resistance to British rule from his time in South Africa, Gandhi consistently encouraged complete non-cooperation with the British in India.[37] Stressing the vital significance of

---

[32] Heehs, *Nationalism, Terrorism, Communalism*, see Chapter 4, 'Foreign Influences on Bengali Revolutionary Terrorism 1902–1908', pp. 68–95.

[33] Ibid, p. 2.   [34] Brown, *Gandhi's Rise to Power*.

[35] Tickell, 'Scholarship terrorists', pp. 3–18, p. 9.   [36] Ibid.

[37] For a foregrounding of Gandhi's formative experiences in South Africa and Britain with relevance for his later emergence in Indian politics, see Guha, *Gandhi before India*.

Indian economic independence, he advocated the complete boycott of British goods and encouraged domestically produced alternatives. Though imprisoned for two years in 1922 and prohibited from engaging in political activities upon his release, Gandhi remained the most prominent voice of Indian nationalism in the 1920s and 1930s. In stark contrast, Savarkar had been implicated in the assassination of Sir William Curzon Wyllie in 1909 and was formally convicted of sedition in 1911 and imprisoned on Andaman Island. Upon his conditional release in 1924, Savarkar became a leading proponent of Hindu nationalism which he married with an often overtly militant attitude towards cultural and political struggle against British imperialism.[38]

It is within these debates and tensions that we must understand how memories of the mutiny came into contact with these disparate approaches to resistance against British rule. From at least 1907, the mutiny became a weapon in the hands of extremist and revolutionary elements within the Congress as well as the wider population. Just as this period saw intense British memorialisation of the mutiny, so too did it offer a new focus for Indian nationalist thinkers across the world. However, it was at India House, located a little over seven miles away from the imperial celebrations hosted at the Royal Albert Hall discussed in Chapter 4, that a nationalist memory of the mutiny was most conspicuously and influentially emerging. Largely in reaction to the programme of memorialisation being pursued across London and discussed in Chapter 4, Krishnavarma organised a series of counter-hegemonic commemoration ceremonies in which the mutiny was reconceived as a national freedom struggle.[39] In so doing, Krishnavarma organised celebratory feasts, meetings, and speeches to mark what he perceived to be an important moment within India's fight for freedom, at which he distributed a range of mementos that celebrated the Indian heroes of the conflict.[40] However, for Krishnavarma and the other authors of this alternative conception of the mutiny in which men like Nana Sahib and Tantia Tope were recast as freedom fighters and heroes, the aim was not simply to redress an academic imbalance in the historiography of the mutiny. Their goal was specifically political, and 1857 seems to have provided an important conceptual space in which contemporary debates concerning India's self-rule could be refashioned and reimagined.[41]

If Krishnavarma was able to challenge Britain's official memory of the mutiny by co-opting one of the principal instruments utilised to mark it, the

---

[38] For a useful biography of Savarkar, see Keer, *Veer Savarkar*; For a wider assessment of Hindu nationalism that situates Savarkar within the broader movement, see Jaffrelot, *The Hindu Nationalist Movement in India*.

[39] Kerr, *Political Trouble in India 1907–1917*, pp. 172–73, pp. 176–78, 'Official printed material on India: miscellaneous internal affairs', Papers of Marquess Curzon of Kedleston, OIOC. Mss EUR F111/441.

[40] Ibid.   [41] Ibid.

commemoration ceremony, then it was Savarkar who put forward one of the most complete attempts to dismantle it. Savarkar who, at the age of twenty-three, had come to London on a scholarship offered by Krishnavarma's Indian Home Rule Society had been involved in underground organisations campaigning against British rule long before his arrival in London. However, it was through his relationship with India House that his radicalism began to cement. Krishnavarma's resistance to Britain's official memory of the mutiny and determination to rearticulate the struggle as a fight for freedom greatly influenced and meshed with Savarkar's own thinking on the subject, and in 1908, the young political dissident completed an ambitious and polemical work entitled *The Indian War of Independence, 1857.* Putting forward an alternative and highly emotive conception of the conflict presented as a unified and legitimate revolution against foreign rule, Savarkar's work found a large readership among Indian nationalists in Europe, America, and India despite being banned by the British Government.

Like Krishnavarma's own co-option of 1857, Savarkar's provocative work should not be read as an inert piece of academic scholarship. On the contrary, it was a call to action in which the War of Independence is utilised as a symbol of, and model for, resistance within the present. As Chakravarty has argued, 'as a remembered figure' within the writings of Savarkar, 'the rebellion gives lineage to the violent underbelly of Indian nationalism' and thus 'recovering a story of heroism and martyrdom is to give legitimacy to contemporary armed resistance'.[42] Accordingly, Savarkar's work proved to be an important conceptual rallying point for Indian nationalists propagating an extremist or revolutionary course of action, who used it as an appeal for armed resistance against British rule. This was reflected in many calls to action authored in its wake. *Ghadar*, to take one important anti-British journal which was published outside of India in the early twentieth century, always carried an item on the front page containing a fourteen-point list of grievances with British Rule in India which ended with the emotive lines: 'fifty six years have passed since the Ghadar of 1857, now there is urgent need of the second one'.[43] Thus, as 1857 was rearticulated by these nationalist thinkers in the wake of Savarkar's work, many concerned with India's struggle for freedom began to draw a lineage of the contemporary freedom struggle which saw it rooted within 1857. As William Faulkner famously wrote, 'the past is never dead, it is not even past', so it is for the mutiny as it was brought into public conversation and debate as a mechanism to understand and think through contemporary issues.[44]

However, despite its growing significance among nationalist thinkers, not everyone saw the mutiny as a potential model on which contemporary resistance

---

[42] Chakravarty, *The Indian Mutiny and the British Imagination*, p. 53.
[43] See Puri, *Ghadar Movement.*   [44] Faulkner, *Requiem for a Nun*, p. 81.

should be built. For more moderately minded nationalists like Gokhale, who fully supported western institutions and values, the mutiny was a bloody uprising fomented by the dying feudal order and not the basis for engagement with the British government in the present. Although guided by a rather different light, Gandhi broadly shared this memory of the mutiny.[45] Committed to a programme of non-violent civil disobedience, Gandhi appears to have remembered the mutiny as a poignant warning against the horrors of armed insurrection. However, at the same time as he saw it as yet further evidence against the effectiveness of violent revolt, Gandhi actively acknowledged that it also demonstrated the brutality of British rule in India. Thus, whilst the mutiny represented an important moment within the history of British rule which underscored British oppression and violence against the Indian population, it did not offer a practical model for contemporary resistance – on the contrary, it was a clear reminder of the futility of violent insurrection.

Seen in this way, the struggle for meaning, memory, and the right to narrate that centred on the mutiny in the early twentieth century was clearly more than a historiographical disagreement. Just as we have shown in Chapter 4, British memory of the mutiny in 1907 was an inducement to defend India by the sword and respond to all forms of Indian unrest with due urgency and virility. On the other hand, Indian memories of the mutiny undermined the supposed justice of British rule, whilst at the same time offered a prescribed course of resistance in the present. However, if Indian memories of the mutiny agreed in their condemnation of British violence, then they were divided on the moral value of Indian violence. Thus, a close study of the struggle for meaning and memory over this period must necessarily highlight the contest within an as yet unconsolidated nationalist memory of the mutiny as much as between an official imperial memory and those vernacular memories that opposed it.

The Struggle for Memory and Mutiny Monuments

Just as we argued was the case within the late Victorian era, this chapter will now show how a focus on British-built mutiny monuments enables us to better analyse how this struggle for meaning and memory developed and played out during the crucial interwar years. Just as we have shown how British mutiny monuments provided a site in which alternative memories could be constructed and recorded, so too was this the case during this period. With such an intense focus on the events of 1857 among Indians fighting for independence, British mutiny monuments came under redoubled attack.

---

[45] As Faisal Devji has argued, who otherwise traces the trajectory of Mahatma's resistance projects back to the mutiny, 'Gandhi's own references to the Mutiny were invariably negative, and he saw it much like the British did'. Devji, *The Impossible Indian*, p. 11.

In addition to new instances of anonymous and transitory forms of resistance, such as the smashing of one of the marble tablets erected at the Mutiny Memorial in Delhi which prompted the ASI to plead with the Delhi police to investigate and 'bring the offender to book', there were also a number of examples of overt protest and resistance.[46] One notable case occurred in connection with a monument erected in 1860 to the memory of Brigadier-General James Neill who, as we have seen, played a crucial role in the reoccupation of Cawnpore and the relief of Lucknow.[47] Whilst the monument had almost certainly been subject to the same evasive forms of protest that had been inflicted on other mutiny monuments, unequivocal overt protest and demonstration against the memorial and in favour of its removal from the public space of Madras began spontaneously in 1927 when two men attempted to destroy the monument using a hammer and an axe. In justifying and explaining their act, one of the two men stated in court that according to 'his study of history he knew that Neill had done much harm to the country, and thought that his statue should not be there'.[48]

The protest was soon joined by an independent group calling itself the Tamil Nadu Volunteer Corps and received added publicity through the support of Mahatma Gandhi who, during a speech made at Royapuram, told his audience that 'The cause appeals to me most forcibly. I have not a shadow of doubt that that statue must be removed from that site' as it was 'a standing insult to the nation'.[49] Expanding on these views in a later article, Gandhi wrote that the inscription on the monument, which informed its reader that Neill was a 'brave, resolute, self-reliant soldier ... [who] fell gloriously at the relief of Lucknow', was 'false history'. Going on to expound upon the multiple atrocities committed by Neill, Gandhi opines that he could 'never forgive Neill for his very bloody work' before concluding that this was 'the true character of the "hero" in whose honour the statue was erected by "public subscription"'.[50]

Gandhi was so concerned with the removal that he met with around twenty of the protestors over the course of two days. During these meetings, and in subsequent writings on the subject, Gandhi once again expressed his support for the cause though continued to reiterate his commitment to non-violence

---

[46] Superintendent ASI to the senior superintendent of Police in Delhi, 9 December 1936, NAI, ASI/Delhi Circle/Monuments/476/1936/Monuments/Mutiny monument.

[47] Mahatma Gandhi, 'Discussion with Neil Statue Volunteers 6 and 7 September 1927', pp. 34–44.

[48] *The Hindu*, quoted in Mahatma Gandhi, 'Insolent Reminders', *Young India*, 25 August 1927 in The *Collected Works of Mahatma Gandhi*, Vol. XXXIX, (Electronic Book), (New Delhi: Publications Division Government of India, 1999) No. 448, pp. 453–55.

[49] Mahatma Gandhi, 'Speech at Royapuram, Madras', 7 September 1927 in *The Collected Works of Mahatma Gandhi*, Vol. XXXX, (Electronic Book), (New Delhi: Publications Division Government of India, 1999) No. 24, pp. 51–53.

[50] Gandhi, 'The Neill Statue and Non-Violence', pp. 178–80.

as the method of effecting change.[51] Gandhi was not the only high-profile political dissident to offer support to the campaign, however. Savarkar, who had only recently been released from imprisonment on a charge of sedition, also lent his support to the removal. Harbouring little sympathy for any of the British generals he discussed in *The War of Indian Independence*, Savarkar reserved special venom for his assessment of Neill as a soldier and as a man. Recounting the many atrocities performed under the General's orders, Savarkar writes that:

> It is difficult to find a parallel, even in the history of savages, to the cruel brutality which Neill showed in the provinces of Benares and Allahabad! ...Neill burnt old men; Neill burnt middle-aged men; Neill burnt young men; Neill burnt children; Neill burnt infants; Neill burnt babies in cradles; and Neill has burnt babies suckling at the breasts of their mothers![52]

With such antipathy towards Neill, it is of little surprise to learn that Savarkar was greatly supportive of the campaign against the monument. However, he was also scathing of Gandhi's public insistence that only non-violent action should be used to achieve it. Savarkar ridiculed Gandhi's stance on the matter and, in two separate satirical pieces of prose, can be read as subtly equating the protesters' attempts to remove the monument with the broader objective of expelling the British from India.[53] In so doing, Savarkar questioned Gandhi's entire philosophy of resistance and highlighted his own attitudes towards the freedom struggle, arguing that it was only through the progressive potential of violence, in this case, violence against the monument, that the protestors' goals could reasonably be achieved.

In making his arguments, Savarkar asked the protestors to learn from the demonstrations that had taken place earlier in the decade against a monument to John Lawrence, another British figure associated with the mutiny.[54] John Lawrence, brother of Henry Lawrence who, as we have seen, died during the siege of the Residency, had served in Punjab during the mutiny earning the moniker, 'the hero of the Punjab' before being made Viceroy of India in 1864. The monument had originally been intended for London but was ill-favoured by Lawrence's family, resulting in its eventual transportation to Lahore. As

---

[51] Gandhi, 'Discussion with Neil Statue Volunteers 6 and 7 September 1927', pp. 34–44.

[52] Savarkar, *The War of Indian Independence*, p. 166.

[53] Vinayak Damodar Savarkar, 'Non-violent pseudo-code', *Shraddhananda*, 10 January 1928 and Vinayak Damodar Savarkar 'Speech and Action', *Shraddhananda*, 8 December 1927, in Vinayak Damodar Savarkar, *Gandhian Confusion [Gandhi Gondhal]*, translated by Swatantryaveer Savarkar Rashtriya Smarak Trust and available as e-book, accessed 3 March 2011, www.savarkarsmarak.com/bookdetails.php?bid=81 No. 12 and No. 13.

[54] For more details on the change of inscription of the Lord Lawrence Statue, see 'The Lord Lawrence Statue, Lahore: change of inscription and questions of its removal', Judicial and Public Department Files, Files 7001–7178, File 7098, OIOC. IOR/L/PJ/6/1776.

remembered by Maude Lawrence, John's youngest surviving child, the principal reason for rejecting the monument was the inscription which read 'Will you be governed by the pen or the sword?' which was disliked by the family because it 'was quite fictitious, as we can never trace that he ever said anything of the kind'.[55]

If the inscription proved unpopular among Lawrence's family, then it was rather more controversial in India where it became the subject of a sustained campaign in the 1920s.[56] Large-scale mobilisation pressed for an alteration to the wording of the inscription or else the monument's removal from public space. The British administration remained resolute, however, and posted a police officer to guard the monument to prevent further damage.[57] Eventually, in the face of continued vandalism and protest, it was finally agreed by the government that the inscription would be altered to the more acceptable, 'I served you with pen and sword'.

By suggesting that it was only through violence against Lawrence's monument that the activists succeeded in achieving their aims, Savarkar urged the protestors associated with the campaign against Neill's monument to likewise pick up weapons or else be condemned to follow Gandhi's teachings and impotently 'keep on making faces to the statue from a distance' as this 'will be more befitting a pure satyagrahi'.[58] For Savarkar then, the political agitations concerning the monument to Neill were used as an allegory through which he could explore broader questions on the multiple forms resistance to British rule could take. By equating the removal of the monument with the removal of the British, Savarkar could use the episode to argue that it was only through violence that change could be facilitated. Just as non-violent protest would never result in the removal of the monument, so too would it never convince the British to leave India.

---

[55] Maude Lawrence to Sir Lionel Earle, 23 December 1926, 'Statue of Lord Lawrence: Waterloo Place', TNA, WORK 20/160. Indeed, according to Maude Lawrence, the inscription was no more popular among the British public leading to *Punch* ridiculing the memorial with a pictorial caricature accompanied by the satirical caption, 'who the Devil has been cutting pens with my sword?'. The monument was replaced in London with an alternative depiction and accompanied by a simple inscription noting that John Lawrence was the 'ruler of the Punjaub [sic] during the Sepoy Mutiny of 1857 and Viceroy of India from 1864 to 1869'. For more information on this statue, see 'Statue of Lord Lawrence', TNA, WORK 20/94.
[56] See 'The Lord Lawrence Statue, Lahore: change of inscription and questions of its removal', Judicial and Public Department Files, Files 7001–7178, File 7098, OIOC. IOR/L/PJ/6/1776.
[57] One of the most important causes of their apprehension to acquiesce stemmed from their fear that 'the mischief-makers may cast their eyes around and find some other statue or monument to which they could take objection', J. E. Ferrand, 'Minute', 22 June 1923, 'The Lord Lawrence Statue, Lahore: change of inscription and questions of its removal', Judicial and Public Department Files, Files 7001–7178, File 7098, OIOC. IOR/L/PJ/6/1776.
[58] Vinayak Damodar Savarkar, 'Non-violent pseudo-code', *Shraddhananda*, 10 January 1928, in Vinayak Damodar Savarkar, *Gandhian Confusion [Gandhi Gondhal]* translated by Swatantryaveer Savarkar Rashtriya Smarak Trust and available as e-book, accessed 3 March 2011, www.savarkarsmarak.com/bookdetails.php?bid=81 No. 12.

If the construction of a monument is indicative of the production of memory, then campaigns to destroy, alter, or remove monuments should themselves be seen as practices of memorialisation. Seen in this way, the practices of memorialisation which attached themselves to the monument of Neill reveal as much about opposition to Britain's official imperial memory of the mutiny as they do the differences between disparate vernacular memories which were uneasily brought together within a loosely united campaign. In this way, not only the objective but also the method employed to achieve it became a point of contention and formed a debate in which broader disagreements over how British rule should be opposed were aired and understood. Ultimately, the movement floundered for around a decade before the monument was finally moved due to the strength of public support and a vote from the Madras Corporation in favour of relocating the monument to a local museum.[59] With its new surroundings excluding the memorial from the field of living memory, the campaign was ultimately successful in figuratively consigning Neill to the annals of history. However, even as British mutiny monuments were being contested, resisted, subverted, and occasionally relocated or altered, new mutiny monuments continued to appear. Indeed, even as the decision to relocate Neill's monument was being made, the discovery of a skeleton in Badli-ki-serai put in process the construction of Britain's last mutiny monument; a full eighty years after the conflict began.

Located around six miles from Delhi, Badli-ki-serai had witnessed a pivotal engagement between the Delhi Field Force and the rebels, which resulted in heavy losses on each side though a decisive victory for the British. Following British success at Hindan Bridge on 30–31 May 1857, the Delhi Field Force had proceeded slowly and hesitantly towards Delhi, inadvertently allowing the rebels time to begin fortifying and preparing a strong defensive position at an old caravanserai which stood between the advancing field force and Delhi. According to Dalrymple, Badli-ki-serai presented 'an ideal place for a stand. With marshland on either side, a line of artillery had been entrenched between the serai and a small hillock to the west, straddling both sides of the road and providing a small but bristling Mughal Maginot Line: any force coming from the direction of Alipore would have no option but to charge down a narrow causeway straight into the face of the massed Mughal guns'.[60]

Advancing on the rebel position during the early morning of 8 June, the 75th Highlanders were ordered to take the lead and charge the enemy battery. According to Richard Barter, who found himself in the front lines of the assault party, no sooner was the order given than the men began to storm the battery:

---

[59] Agitation over the monument abated a short while later, but the monument was eventually removed in 1937 under order of the newly appointed Madras Legislative Assembly following the Government of India Act, 1935, a matter of months after their election. This, predictably, raised debate in Britain. See HC Deb, 29 November 1937, Vol. 329, Cols. 1661–2 ; HC Deb, 06 December 1937, Vol. 330, Cols. 1–2.

[60] Dalrymple, *The Last Mughal*, p. 250.

Soon our fellows were dropping fast ... their shot striking the line at every discharge. I remember one in particular taking a man's head off, or rather smashing it to pieces and covering my old Colour Sergeant Walsh with blood and brains so that it was some time before he could see again.... I saw a shrapnel shell burst exactly in the faces of one of the Companies of the right wing. It tore a wide gap and the men near it involuntarily turned away. I called out, 'Don't turn men, don't turn', and was at once answered 'Never fear Mister Barter sir, we ain't agoing to turn'. And on they went quietly closing up the gap made by their fallen comrades. The time had come to end all this and ... the order was given '75th prepare to charge' and down went the long line of bayonets ... a wild shout, or rather yell of vengeance went up from the line as it rushed to the charge. The enemy followed our movements, their bayonets were also lowered and their advance was steady as they came to meet us, but when the exultant shout arose, they could not stand it, their line wavered and undulated, many began firing with their firelocks at their hips, and at last, as we were closing on them, the whole turned and ran for dear life followed by a shout of derisive laughter from our fellows. In three minutes the 75th stood breathless but victors in the Enemy's battery.[61]

With fifty men wounded and twenty-three dead including Lieutenant Alfred Harrison who received a fatal headshot as he led his men towards the enemy's battery, the victory came at a high price for the British but with Delhi now in sight, there was precious little time to attend to the dead. Gathering the bodies together for a hasty burial within a mound before moving on towards Delhi, the location of their last resting place was lost within the mists of war and remained a mystery over the following decades until a partial collapse of the mound caused by heavy rains and the activities of local villages collecting mud for their homes revealed the skeletal remains of one soldier.[62] Largely through the enterprise and imagination of one Mrs. A.H. Lloyd, the mound was identified as the mass burial site for the twenty-three soldiers and the exposed human remains were quite remarkably and improbably identified as those of Lieutenant Alfred Harrison. With the burial site finally identified, Mrs Lloyd, supported by the Gordon Highlanders, which had been formed in 1881 out of the 75th and 92nd Regiments of Foot, swiftly began planning how the site might be commemorated leading to the erection of a large monument dedicated to the dead and a separate grave in which Harrison's remains were interred.[63]

With construction work completed in late 1938, a grand ceremony was coordinated for 1 December. Draped in a Union Jack which had flown over the ruins of the Lucknow Residency, both day and night, before being specially donated for the occasion, the memorial was formally unveiled by the commander-in-chief, Sir Robert Cassels, who then gave way to the Chaplain of

[61] Ibid, pp. 251–52.
[62] Anon, 'Form and Order of the Unveiling and Dedication of the Memorial to the Gordon Highlanders at Badli-ki-serai near Delhi on Thursday, December 1st, 1938', 'Correspondence as Colonel of the Gordon Highlanders 1912–49', Papers of Gen. Sir. Ian Standish Monteith Hamilton, Liddell Hart Military Archives, Kings College London, HAMILTON-10-31.
[63] Ibid.

Figure 5.1 Sir Robert Cassels unveils the monument at Badli-ki-serai. 'Correspondence as Colonel of the Gordon Highlanders 1912–49', Papers of Gen. Sir Ian Standish Monteith Hamilton, Liddell Hart Military Archives, Kings College London, HAMILTON-10-31.

Delhi, Rev. C. J. G. Robinson.[64] As the chaplain concluded the dedication ceremony to 'the glory of God and in memory of His servants, Alfred Harrison, and twenty-two others of this Regiment whose names are known only to God', buglers of The Royal Norfolk Regiment sounded 'Last Post', as all present reflected on the occasion. Describing the ceremony in a letter to General Sir Ian Hamilton, Mrs Lloyd told the colonel of the Gordon Highlanders that she felt that '[e]verything went off splendidly and I have never been to a simpler or more impressive and beautiful service. I think you would be very pleased with the monument, and the work on the grave and gate is really most beautifully done.... I cannot express to you my feelings when the "Last Post" sounded over these men, hastily buried in the terrible heat of a June day so long ago without a prayer or a word said over them. I wish you could see it all'.[65]

---

[64] Mrs. A. H. Lloyd, 'List of Photographs of unveiling ceremony at Badli-ki-serai, 'Correspondence as Colonel of the Gordon Highlanders 1912–49', Papers of Gen. Sir Ian Standish Monteith Hamilton, Liddell Hart Military Archives, Kings College London, HAMILTON-10-31.

[65] Mrs. A. H. Lloyd to Sir Ian Hamilton, 15 December 1938, 'Correspondence as Colonel of the Gordon Highlanders 1912–49', Papers of Gen. Sir Ian Standish Monteith Hamilton, Liddell Hart Military Archives, Kings College London, HAMILTON-10-31.

However, if the monument was considered a success by those who conceived and constructed it, it was seen as an insult and aggravation by many Indian nationalists culminating in a motion of adjournment being tabled in the Central Legislative Assembly by Sri Prakasa and Radhabai Subbarayan to 'censure and condemn' the Government of India for their involvement in its construction.[66] As Prakasa explained, whilst 'I have no objections to private friends and relatives raising memorials to the dead' as even 'murderers have their friends and those friends may hold their memory dear ... when the Commander-in-Chief of the army in India goes down and associates himself with this ceremony, he puts the *imprimatur* of official approval on this transaction. It is that to which I strongly object'.[67]

Described by Lord Zetland, the Secretary of State for India and Burma, as 'a small storm in a teacup' the ensuing debate on the monument would ultimately represent an important watershed moment in Britain's official memory of the mutiny by ushering in a period of greater concern over how Indian audiences might react to official recognition of the mutiny.[68]

Of particular concern to Prakasa and those who supported the motion were the terms used to describe those who fought and died against the British at Badli-ki-serai. Not only during the ceremony but also recorded on the monument itself, the rebels were referred to as mutineers and thus the monument's inscription recorded its dedication to 'those men of H.M 75th Regiment ... who fell while charging the mutineers' guns on this mound at the battle of Badli-ki-Serai'. Though Defence Secretary C.M.G. Ogilvie argued that the term mutineer was not 'opprobrious and insulting to India' and was further the only appropriate term 'for troops who have risen in arms against their Government', Prakasa argued that the only intrinsic difference between the American War of Independence and India's own struggle for independence in 1857 was that India was unsuccessful and that this explained the dramatically different nomenclature applied to each event; 'The Americans fought and won, and so they became the warriors of freedom; we fought and lost, and we are dubbed as mutineers'.[69] Addressing what he felt was therefore an insulting

---

[66] Extracts from Central Legislative Assembly Debates, 2 December 1938, Vol. III, 1938, published in Basudev Chatterji and Sarvepalli Gopal (eds.), *Towards Freedom: Documents on the Movement for Independence in India, 1938, Part 1* (New Delhi: Oxford University Press, 1999), pp. 995–1001, p. 998.

[67] Ibid, p. 997.

[68] 'Extract from Lord Zetland to Lord Lithgow, 6 December 1938', p. 14, Films Offensive to Indian Public Opinion Pts. XIII-XIX, OIOC, IOR/L/PJ/8/128 Coll. 105/A. See also Lord Lithgow to Lord Zetland, 13 December 1938, p. 570, 'Letters from Lord Lithgow to Lord Zetland dated Jan-Jun 1938 and Oct-Dec 1938', Papers of 2nd Marquees of Zetland, OIOC, Mss. Eur. D609/15.

[69] Extracts from Central Legislative Assembly Debates, 2 December 1938, Vol. III, 1938, published in Basudev Chatterji and Sarvepalli Gopal (eds.), *Towards Freedom: Documents on the Movement for Independence in India, 1938, Part 1* (New Delhi: Oxford University Press, 1999), pp. 995–1001, p. 996.

inscription, Prakasa suggested an alternative dedication which he argued would be acceptable: 'Sacred to the memory of the brave men who fought and died here on either side for the case each holds dear, in the Badli-ki-serai battle on the 8th June, 1857'.[70]

Similarly, Madhav Aney, who also spoke in favour of the motion, argued that the term 'mutineer' was certain to cause offence to many Indians and whilst it was once 'the fashion to describe them as mutineers and give them all sorts of bad names', the Government of India should now realise that 'the story of 1857 is looked upon as the first brave attempt made by the Indian people to regain the liberty of which they were robbed'. Indeed, so prevalent was this counter-memory of 1857 that, according to Aney, 'stories and traditions are heard in every village where there was a mutiny ... and those people who fought for independence in those days are today remembered much more than all the other names whom you try to crowd the pages of history with'.[71] In addressing what was thus seen by many to be a seriously distorted memory of 1857, Syed Ghulam Bhik Nairang likened the British representation of the conflict in monuments and literature to the popular fable about a painting of a man emerging victorious from a bloody encounter with a lion. Though soliciting pride from all humans who saw the painting, lions simply retorted that the picture was obviously painted by a man and had it been painted by a lion, an observer 'would have found the lion on top of the man'.[72]

As is apparent in this debate centring on the Badli-ki-serai memorial and the others discussed previously, mutiny monuments not only served as physical sites around which British memories of the mutiny could be organised but also presented a space in which radically different memories of the conflict could be conceived and rehearsed. However, this debate also seems to reveal the existence of a dramatically different mnemonic topography altogether which, though not formally marked by any official monument or structure, nevertheless persisted informally within local tradition. Arguing that 'Our people remember the cruel deeds that were committed against us; but we have not been able to express them because we had been stifled', Prakasa asked Ogilvie if it would be considered acceptable to raise a monument at the 'Gate of Blood' in Delhi, 'where, tradition says, hundreds of my people were blown at the cannon's mouth from day to day' in 1857, or if he would be allowed to construct a monument to Ijarat Jehan, a leader celebrated by both Muslims and Hindus 'whose memory is still fresh in the countryside and who was hanged by the British for his patriotic activities on an open mound which is still pointed out' by those who lived around the site.[73] With all those who

---

[70] Ibid, p. 997.   [71] Ibid, pp. 999–1000.   [72] Ibid, p. 1001.   [73] Ibid, p. 996.

spoke, with the exception of Ogilvie, supporting the debate, the motion was carried and the Assembly was accordingly adjourned as a calculated censure on the Government.

As we have seen earlier, the interwar struggle for meaning memory and the right to narrate was more than a contest over the past, it was a desperate fight for the present. Over this period, imperial memory came into contact with a range of counter-memories that sought to propagate a quite different conception of 1857 that used the event to undermine British rule by demonstrating the extreme brutality of British counter-insurgency. However, if these Indian memories uniformly used the mutiny as a moment around which it was possible to question British rule, then they also utilised it as a lesson for future resistance. Whilst extremists and revolutionary terrorists saw the mutiny as a model on which future resistance could be based, more moderate and non-violent advocates used the mutiny to demonstrate the futility and cost of armed resistance.

Counter Commemoration and the Growth of Nationalist Memory

With such a level of resistance to Britain's official memory of the mutiny and with the Indian nationalist movement continuing to grow in strength as Britain was drawn into the Second World War, the monument at Badli-ki-serai proved to be Britain's last mutiny monument. Not only did the debate which surrounded the Badli-ki-serai memorial make any future monument dedicated to the mutiny unthinkable, it also ushered in a new era in Britain's official memory of the mutiny. This study has shown how successive administrations saw 1857 as an essential component of Britain's story in India; however, the final years of Britain's South Asian empire witnessed the first steps towards suppressing this memory. Indeed, in no small part due to the adverse reception of the Badli-ki-serai memorial, the production of a film based on *The Relief of Lucknow* was banned by the Government of India in the wake of the controversy, due to the belief that the film would have likely led to yet further unrest within the charged political climate of the late 1930s.[74] As argued by Lord Lothian, 'to us the Mutiny was a glorious episode in our history in which British soldiers and civilians showed extraordinary heroism in resisting a singularly brutal collection of rebels. To the Indians – it was a heroic if unsuccessful attempt to strike for freedom'. Thus, the release of a British film on the mutiny would almost certainly

---

[74] For a detailed analysis of the reasons behind this decision and its part in a broader process of censorship, see Chowdhry, *Colonial India and the Making of Empire Cinema*.

have been greeted by films covering the same topic, in a radically different way, made by Indian companies. The administration therefore, fearing the propagation of anti-hegemonic memories, censored further expressions of British memory.

In marked contrast, the second half of the 1930s and the 1940s saw Indian nationalists begin to find it possible to open up a space for overt memorialisation for the first time. If, as we have noted previously, earlier in the century, Lajpat Rai was able to compare the freedom with which the British administration was able to commemorate 1857 with the manifest impossibility for Indians to likewise memorialise the event, then the final years of British India ushered in a remarkable reversal of fortunes. As Britain began to censor its own memory of the mutiny for fear that its expression would consolidate anti-imperial sentiment and occasion new spaces of protest, an overtly nationalist memory of the War of Independence began to emerge from the shadows and dominate the imagination of many individuals engaged in the freedom movement.

Indeed, the 1930s began to see the first overt attempts by nationalist elements to actively commemorate Indian heroes of 1857. Though India House had been able to hold such events for a few years around the time of the mutiny's jubilee, it was not until the mid-1930s that such events could find something approaching free expression in India. Among the many events and heroes seen worthy of commemoration, it was the memory of one individual in particular which came to dominate these early attempts to openly commemorate the War of Independence; Rani Lakshmibai.

Lakshmibai, who had been viewed with ambivalence by British commentators following the conflict, was seen by many in India to embody the spirit of resistance.[75] Credited along with Tantia Tope for organising and leading the uprising following the reconquest of Lucknow in 1858, Lakshmibai was famed for her remarkable bravery, determination and leadership qualities displayed in countless popular stories drawn from her life story as much as from the war itself. Commonly depicted dressed as a man, and with her young child strapped to her back as she led the rebels from the front, Lakshmibai was celebrated for her tactical awareness as much as for her physical courage, which resulted in her forces enjoying a series of victories before their inevitable defeat. Killed in action around Gwalior on 17 June 1858, Rani Lakshmibai died a martyr and thus secured her legacy within the Indian imagination of resistance.[76]

---

[75] For a useful study of British attitudes towards Lakshmibai as reflected in fiction, see Sen, 'Inscribing the Rani of Jhansi in Colonial "Mutiny" Fiction', pp. 1754–61.
[76] For an excellent study of the construction of Lakshmibai within popular Indian texts, see Deshpande, 'The making of an Indian Nationalist Archive', pp. 855–79.

With stories of Lakshmibai's exploits enjoying wide circulation through-out India, a number of groups and organisations began to arrange annual events to commemorate significant moments in her life. Among these, the annual Anniversary Ceremony held in Gwalior to mark the day of her death proved to be among the best attended, and this was particularly so on the eightieth anniversary which was celebrated just months before the monument at Badli-ki-serai was unveiled. Building on the popularity of the event in 1938, seasoned Congress campaigners Maulvi Nuruddin Bihari and Musamat Satyavati Devi helped organise a similar event the following year during which they sought to not only celebrate the life of Lakshmibai but further demonstrate the contemporary significance of the great military leader in the present day.[77]

Telling the assembled crowd that it 'is no secret as to why you have all gathered at this meeting. We're celebrating the 81st anniversary of Maharani Laxmibai who lost her life fighting with the English', recently elected president of the Delhi District Congress Committee, Maulvi Nuruddin Bihari, shaped the Rani into a nationalist hero who 'did not fight for her throne, her children and comfort; but she fought only to save her poor subjects from the slavery of English people'.[78] Going on to examine the ways in which British industry exploited both Indian labour and natural resources, Bihari concluded that 'the conditions of Indians is continuously going from bad to worse' and that in the present 'hundreds of Indian labourers and farmers are starving, but there is nobody to take care of them'.[79] Further, Bihari argued that Britain had relied on India's support during the First World War, and yet all that Indians had received as a 'reward for their taking part in the Great War' were the well-known draconian measures enforced by the Rowlatt Act of 1919.[80]

With Rani Lakshmibai established as a national hero and with the present urgency for action underlined, the conclusion of Bihari's speech was self-evident, although the orator stressed that 'we cannot be benefitted by acting exactly as Maharani Laxmi Bai did. By using the weapon of non-violence and with unity such as it was among us before we can achieve' political and economic independence which would lead to a more affluent and just nation.[81]

---

[77] See 'Objectionable speeches made by Maulvi Nur-ud Din Behari and Musammat Satyavati Devi on the occasion of the anniversary celebrations of the Rani of Jhansi at Gwalior', OIOC, IOR/R/1/1/3228.

[78] 'Translation of the Speech delivered by Maulvi Nuruddin Bihari of Delhi, in Daulatganj Park, Lashkar, Gwalior State, on the occasion of the anniversary celebrations of the Rani of Jhansi, on 17th of June 1939', Objectionable speeches made by Maulvi Nur-ud Din Behari and Musammat Satyavati Devi on the occasion of the anniversary celebrations of the Rani of Jhansi at Gwalior, OIOC, IOR/R/1/1/3228.

[79] Ibid.   [80] Ibid.   [81] Ibid.

In this way, the anniversary ceremony marking Rani Lakshmibai's death may be seen to mark the successful appropriation of 1857 into the ideological discourse of the Congress Party. Here, the War of Independence is deployed as an incitement to non-violent resistance to British rule. What the conflict may be said to successfully teach the present is the need for unity and an alternative 'weapon' to that utilised by the rebels of 1857. If, as we have shown previously, the conflict was seen as an incitement to violent resistance by men such as Savarkar, then this co-option of the narrative, and its deployment as part of a Congress sanctioned nationalist narrative which prizes non-violence as the central weapon of resistance, refashioned how 1857 should be remembered and used in the present.

6   Remembering the Mutiny at the End of Empire: 1947–1972

As India's tryst with destiny approached, the Anglo-Indian community found itself concerned with a great variety of issues that demanded immediate and urgent attention. From post-independence security implications to the logistics of partition, a vast and varied range of considerations prompted great anxiety in the weeks that surrounded 15 August 1947. Among the often-fevered deliberations that accompanied these concerns, one topic seemed to generate a disproportionately high level of discussion within official and popular circles alike: what would be the post-colonial fate of British-built monuments and especially those marking the Cawnpore Well, the Lucknow Residency, and the Delhi Ridge?

The sight of monuments being destroyed at moments of political and social rupture is a common phenomenon. Whether in the Ukraine, Iraq, Libya, or any number of other locations, political transformation is frequently marked by the destruction of monuments erected by discredited regimes. Of no less import are those cases where monuments to past rulers are allowed to remain unmolested, or even remain as important ideological markers which connect the past with the present after moments of sociopolitical rupture. Accordingly, the study of the divergent policies pursued by new governments in relation to such monuments has been seen as a way of better understanding how nations in transition relate to, and try to remake, their collective pasts. In this respect, the markedly different fates of Soviet monuments in various east-European nations have been seen to underscore very different attitudes towards remembering the Soviet Union, as well as reflecting different contemporary aspirations, political systems, and questions of identity.[1]

Though the 'after-life' of colonial era monuments remains an understudied issue within broader discussions on decolonisation, the events of the past few years promise to change this. With sociopolitical movements, such as

---

[1] See for example Forest and Johnson, 'Monumental Politics', pp. 269–88; Frances W. Harrison, 'Reviving Heritage in Post-Soviet Eastern Europe: A Visual Approach to National Identity', *Totem: The University of Western Ontario Journal of Anthropology*, 20 (2012). See also Nadkarni, 'The Death of Socialism and the Afterlife of Its Monuments', pp. 193–207; Lankauskas, 'Sensuous (Re)collections', pp. 27–52.

the Rhodes Must Fall Campaign, using colonial monuments as symbols of how colonial era ideas persist in the present and are implicated in contemporary structures of inequality and racism both in former European colonies and metropoles, greater attention is now being paid to what these mnemonic signifiers can teach us about the past and the present. Addressing this question with specific reference to India, the work of Mary Ann Steggles on the fate of British monuments is most important. Focusing on cataloguing and tracing the history of colonial statuary in India, Steggles has shown that the popular belief that British monuments were immediately damaged, destroyed, or discarded in the aftermath of formal independence is inaccurate; as she shows it was a slow and contingent process over many decades and in fact some British monuments can still be found well cared for in their original locations or otherwise preserved in museums or spaces purposely dedicated to them.[2]

If the years that followed formal Indian independence did not witness significant enmity towards colonial monuments, those dedicated to the mutiny of 1857 seem to present an exception. Indeed, as will be explored in more detail below, the frequent low-level violence directed towards British mutiny monuments studied in Chapter 5 escalated at independence and continued over the course of the following years accompanied by increasingly vociferous calls for the central government to remove, destroy, or otherwise appropriate such monuments which in their current state were seen as standing affronts to independent India. Equally notable were the popular demands that emanated from several quarters for the construction of new monuments dedicated to 1857 and its principal Indian heroes including such revered characters as Tantia Tope, Mangal Pandey, and Rani Lakshmibai. Whilst it might be assumed that such proposals were greeted with enthusiasm, the actual response was entirely more reticent, with the central government proving reluctant to place too much commemorative emphasis on 1857, and preferring instead to propagate a narrative of Congress-led non-violent resistance to colonial rule and its ultimate success in achieving Indian freedom. Whilst this official reluctance to celebrate 1857 might in part be attributed to international diplomacy given the economic importance of India's continued relationship with Britain, it also served significant ideological interests by affirming the Congress Party's domestic political legitimacy which, over the course of the twenty years that followed formal independence, remained indisputable. By placing the Congress Party at the heart of a rigidly disciplined story of the independence movement, the party emerged as the natural rulers of post-colonial India with their unrivalled political dominance justified by virtue of their role in securing national freedom from colonial rule.[3]

---

[2] Steggles and Barnes, *British Sculpture in India*. See also Steggles, *Statues of the Raj*.
[3] For an informative assessment of how this official Congress-sponsored discourse disciplined the 'Indian Independence Movement', see Amin, *Event, Metaphor Memory*.

If the Indian Government was hesitant to commemorate 1857 in the first twenty-five years of independence, then the British Government proved strenuously resistant to any suggestion that it be remembered at all. Accordingly, not only was their reaction to popular enthusiasm in India to celebrate the First War of Independence predictably disagreeable, but they also refused to sanction any celebration of the event and its principal imperial heroes in Britain. Once again, this decision was undoubtedly influenced by diplomatic considerations given the mutual significance of Britain's economic relationship with India, but it was also of broader significance given Britain's post-war imperial aspirations. Whilst the process of decolonisation has often been considered a prolonged calculated withdrawal resulting from Britain's perception of its post-war economic weakness and geopolitical position, more recent scholarship has questioned such a narrative. Far from portraying decolonisation as a conscious part of Britain's reassessment of its global position and priorities, it is now clear that Britain remained intent on re-establishing itself as a genuine global power alongside the US and the USSR.[4] Further, it is also now clear that at least until the Suez Crisis, but most likely through until at least the very end of the 1950s, Britain saw the empire and the commonwealth as essential components of this endeavour for a disparate range of geopolitical, strategic, and economic reasons.[5]

Whilst this desire to reinvigorate the empire undoubtedly required economic and military commitment, it also necessitated a carefully established ideology which could not only justify the venture at 'home' but also to the leaders of nationalist movements which developed in many African colonies in the 1950s, and to the US which remained, ostensibly at least, strenuously anti-imperialist and committed to a philosophy of self-determination.[6] This ideology was founded around an official memory of Britain's Indian empire as the fulfilment of Thomas Macaulay's famous prophecy that Indian self-rule would be 'the proudest day in British history', and thus something to be emulated in the present, in other parts of the world.[7] Accordingly, a long and careful narrative of the Indian empire was built around consensual rule and amicable instruction resulting in the gradual and meticulously planned withdrawal of British control resulting in the establishment of two new legitimate nation states.[8] Such a memory required a careful

---

[4] See for example Kent, *British Imperial Strategy and the Origins of the Cold War, 1944–49*; Darwin, *Britain and Decolonization*.

[5] For a stimulating collection of essays on this period which, though not presenting a coherent view, offer a number of useful insights, see Lynn (ed.), *The British Empire in the 1950s*.

[6] For American attitudes towards the British empire in the context of cold war strategy and planning, see Louis and Robinson, 'The Imperialism of decolonization', pp. 462–511.

[7] Macaulay, 'A speech delivered in the house of commons on the 10th of July, 1833', pp. 111–42, p. 142.

[8] For more on Britain's post-war memory of empire, see Darwin, 'Memory of empire in Britain', pp. 18–37; Darwin, 'British decolonization since 1945', pp. 187–209, see in particular pp. 188–90.

negotiation of the past and present and particularly relied on a sanitised memory of Indian independence shorn of the many horrors that resulted from partition.[9] Likewise, those violent episodes which punctuated colonial rule in India had to be elided and the mutiny, as the bloodiest of all, completely silenced. As an event which not only highlights the many horrors of empire but also reveals the non-consensual nature of imperial rule, 1857 was anathema to Britain's official memory of British India and an impediment to the reinvigoration of empire.

As this chapter will show, the fate of British built mutiny monuments in general, and those which marked the Cawnpore Well, Lucknow Residency, and Delhi Ridge specifically, was largely a product of this struggle for meaning, memory, and the right to narrate between popular memories of empire, which emphasised the events of 1857, and the official ideologies of the British and Indian governments which did not. In tracing the post-colonial history of these three sites, this chapter will be divided into two principal sections. The first of these will investigate the acts of popular protest against these sites which erupted over the first ten years following independence, alongside an analysis of how the British state responded, not as might have been expected by endeavouring to protect these sacred sites of empire, but by actively facilitating their removal from the cultural field. The second section will consider the British and Indian governments' responses to the centenary of the uprising in 1957. Placed within the long history of exuberant commemoration and celebration studied in the previous chapters of this book, the absence of any official large-scale attempt to remember 1857 may at first be surprising. As this section will show, however, this was not an innocuous omission nor was it a simple oversight, rather it was a conscious decision to actively forget the uprising in the context of present interests. Nevertheless, this section will finally show how a range of popular and unofficial actors refused to accept these inducements to forget the mutiny, resulting in the appropriation and conversion into national iconography of the Cawnpore Well, Lucknow Residency, and Delhi Ridge, to help mark the twenty-fifth anniversary of Independence in 1972.

Mutiny Monuments: The Politics
of Contestation and Relocation

Although British monuments were not generally the target of violence or damage at Independence, mutiny monuments appear to be a clear exception. Whilst the hundreds of monuments dedicated to various colonial administrators and British royalty, including the ubiquitous statues of Queen Victoria, generally

---

[9] For how partition has been remembered in different communities and by different individuals see, among other studies, Pandey, *Remembering Partition*; Bhalla, *Stories about the Partition of India*, Volumes I–III; Roy and Bhatia, *Partitioned Lives*; Kamra, *Bearing Witness*; Saint, *Witnessing Partition*.

survived the turbulent period unscathed, those associated with the mutiny immediately became the target of popular outbursts. Indeed, the likelihood of mutiny monuments becoming the focus of violence following Independence was foreseen by many members of the British communities based in both Lucknow and Cawnpore, where the future of these monuments had been discussed for about a year before Independence. In Lucknow, a strong sentiment expressed its desire to see the Residency destroyed and levelled before handover to prevent the site becoming a target for vandalism or desecration; however, such proposals were resisted by the governor of the United Provinces, Sir Francis Wylie, and the Viceroy, The Earl Mountbatten, who were of the opinion that the building represented an important link to the past which should not be severed at Independence and which might, at any rate, be preserved in an Independent India.[10] A similar debate had been held in Cawnpore concerning the future of the monument above the well, and whilst Wylie had favoured handing over the site to the Allahabad Diocese Trust as this, in his opinion, would 'give site religious cover and thereby possibly protect it from interference', the local society immediately responsible for its maintenance was not keen on relinquishing ownership and preferred to retain it under its own management.[11]

However, the belief of the responsible society in its ability to secure the well from harm was severely challenged by the events of 15 August. Required to abandon the controversial admittance policy and enable the place to be freely available to everyone during the Independence Day celebrations, the British community in Cawnpore could only watch in horror as a large group gathered around the extensive site, damaging trees and uprooting plants before turning their attention to the 'Angel of the Well'. According to the British High Commission, 'a mob of tens of thousands overwhelmed the Well and garden and committed much wanton damage and desecration. The face of the angel was blackened, the palms of its hands were broken' and further damage done to the walls of the enclosure and its paving.[12]

---

[10] Sir Francis Wylie to The Earl Mountbatten, 4 August 1947, 'File 11, Historical Monuments in India', fol. 172, OIOC. IOR/R/4/82. At any rate, both men were optimistic that the monument could be reasonably preserved owing to measures taken some ten years previously to safeguard the site. For details, see Tuker, *While Memory Serves*, Appendix X 'The Residency at Lucknow', pp. 647–48.

[11] Wylie to Mountbatten, 4 August 1947, 'File 11, Historical Monuments in India', fol. 172, OIOC. IOR/R/4/82. See also Brigadier H. Bullock, 'Short History of the British Monuments and Graves Section Office of the High Commissioner for the United Kingdom New Delhi', 'File 11/1b Historical Monuments in India: Mutiny Memorial Well at Cawnpore', OIOC. IOR/R/4/84.

[12] Upon representation from the British High Commission, the United Provinces Government provided an official apology and offered to have the memorial fully repaired. However, with the new open access policy in place, the Society reportedly found it impossible to maintain the gardens, Brigadier H. Bullock, 'Short History of the British Monuments and Graves Section Office of the High Commissioner for the United Kingdom New Delhi', 'File 11/1b Historical Monuments in India: Mutiny Memorial Well at Cawnpore', OIOC. IOR/R/4/84.

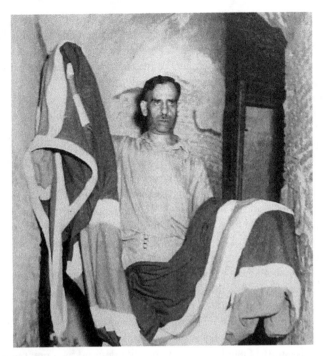

Figure 6.1 Mr Ireland, Residency Caretaker, with the last Residency Flag; '2 photograph albums and 2 envelopes of loose photographs', Sir Francis Tuker Papers, IWM, 71/21/13.

In Lucknow too, crowds gathered on 15 August and congregated at the Residency, one of the most recognisable symbols of British rule in the country, with the intention of marking the change of power through the subversion of the mnemonic site. As we have noted, the Residency was famous for being surmounted by the only Union Jack which flew both day and night as a constant reminder of the siege and of British victory in 1858. The crowd was reportedly intent upon removing this flag and replacing it with India's tricolour; however, they found themselves forestalled upon arrival. At the suggestion of Mountbatten, the flag had been 'quietly hauled down' on 13 August by Warrant Officer Ireland in front of a small collection of British officers.[13] To ensure that no flag could ever be flown from the same spot again, the flag post had been removed and the foundations cemented by a

[13] R. G. Chisholm to Lieutenant commander P. N. Howes, 22 August 1947, '10893 Disposal of Union Jack Flown at Residency', fol. 62, OIOC. IOR/L/PJ/7/12506. For a rather more detailed description of this event, see Tuker, *While Memory Serves*, pp. 342–43.

team of engineers the following evening.[14] Unable to complete their purpose, the crowd grew restless, prompting the police to call for Govind Ballabh Pant, the Chief Minister of the United Provinces who, according to General Sir Francis Tuker, successfully turned back the crowd after imploring them to not damage a British monument dedicated to the dead.[15]

Following the large-scale outpouring of emotion witnessed on 15 August, frequent low-level acts were continually aimed at mutiny monuments in the weeks and months that followed Independence. These varied in type and degree but the example of the monument erected in Lucknow by the 93rd Highland Regiment was typical. Upon finding the monument 'somewhat knocked about and many bricks displaced' as a result of being pelted with rocks, some protection had been added in the form of a tall barbed wire fence around the perimeter of the monument.[16] This attempt to protect the memorial was not at all successful, however, as within a few months it was reported on a subsequent inspection that a 'lot of the barbed wire has already been stolen, and the enclosure is being used as a latrine'.[17]

In Delhi too, monuments that once celebrated British suppression of the mutiny were quickly subverted. During British rule, the Kashmiri Gate had been maintained in much the same way as had the Residency, with strict instructions stating that, even when repairs were thought absolutely necessary for public safety, 'None of the holes made by shot should be refilled'.[18] By 1948, however, the Kashmiri Gate had become heavily defaced by a great amount of graffiti and had further become the temporary residence of numerous refugees

[14] Tuker, *While Memory Serves*, p. 417. The event was equally quietly communicated to Mountbatten by a simple telegram reading 'The Union Jack on Lucknow Residency was lowered at 20 hours on 13th August'. 'Telegram from Governor of the United Provinces to Viceroy, 14.45 hours 14 August, 1947', 10893 Disposal of Union Jack Flown at Residency, fol. 79, OIOC. IOR-L-PJ-7-12506.

[15] Tuker, *While Memory Serves*, p. 417. The fate of the final flag to fly from the Residency became a keenly debated point of contention in the weeks after Independence with many coming forward to claim it. Ultimately, the flag was transferred to Windsor Castle. See 10893 Disposal of Union Jack Flown at Residency, fol. 27, OIOC. IOR-L-PJ-7-12506. However, there are those who believe that Field Marshal Sir Claude Auchinleck, contrary to expectation, decided to send the flag to his alma mater, Wellington College. I would like to thank Jill Shepherd of Wellington College for sharing their considerable correspondence on the subject which sadly fails to resolve the question, though asks many more!

[16] C. B. Duke to H. Bullock, 1 June 1948, 'File 12a Military Memorials of the Argyll and Sutherland Highlanders in India and Pakistan', fol. 100, OIOC. IOR/R/4/87.

[17] Hashman to Swingler, 15 February 1949, 'File 12a Military Memorials of the Argyll and Sutherland Highlanders in India and Pakistan', fol. 74, OIOC. IOR/R/4/87.

[18] Gordon Sanderson to W. M. Haily, 17 February 1913, NAI, ASI/Delhi Circle/Monuments/97D/1913/Monuments/Preservation of Kashmiri Gate and proposal to drive a road through it. See also M. Hailey to the Superintendent, Muhammadan and British Monuments, Northern Circle, Agra. 6 June 1918, NAI, ASI/Delhi Circle/ Monuments/ 533/ 1918/ Monuments/ Kabuli Bagh, Delhi.

fleeing communal violence.[19] Such was the national crisis that the refugees were allowed to remain on the site until longer-term accommodation could be found, leaving the ASI to impotently complain that:

Not only have the refugees converted these monuments into vast latrines but everywhere here and there heaps of refuse and peelings mixed with overripe eatables stink badly in the corners; also smoke coming out of their improvised ovens has defaced the facades spotted here and there with spitting of batch ... some of the headstrongs amongst the refugees have fitted door leavers and chowkats and raised unsightly wooden stalls dwindling and cramping upon the aesthetics about these monuments.[20]

Taken together, the fate of British mutiny monuments in the months which followed Independence had a dramatic impact upon their meaning. If, as we have already argued, attempts to sabotage, subvert, or appropriate monuments should be seen as so many commemoration ceremonies, then these persistent acts highlight the extent to which the mutiny remained an important point of contention, especially when compared to the lack of popular protest aimed at other British monuments.[21] Clearly then, these monuments were not simply targeted as symbols of British power, in which respect they were indivisible from other British monuments, but rather they were specifically resented for the way in which they commemorated the mutiny. By targeting these monuments, in particular, individuals were attempting to rewrite the history of 1857 and the path to self-rule, by incorporating the mutiny into a history of colonial oppression and Indian resistance which ultimately culminated in independence. Of perhaps even more significance for us, however, was how a range of British voices responded to these attempts to destroy or, more exactly, remake the mutiny.

With growing concerns in both India and England over the condition and future of British monuments and cemeteries, Sir Terence Shone, the British High Commissioner to India, decided to establish the British Monuments and Graves Section of the High Commissioner's Office (BMGS) at the end of 1947. Appointing Brigadier Humphrey Bullock, the responsible officer, this department was tasked with planning and implementing a strategy in which British monuments and graves could be preserved from damage or at least

---

[19] Graffiti had appeared before independence but had always been taken very seriously and a plain clothed policeman was stationed on the spot to catch culprits when thought necessary. Hilary Waddington to the senior Superintendent of Police Delhi, 22 July 1938, NAI, ASI/ Delhi Circle/Monuments/ 29/1938/Monuments/Kashmiri gate.

[20] Assistant Superintendent, Archaeological Department, Delhi Circle, Curzon Road Barracks to the chief commissioner, 18 March 1948, NAI, ASI/Delhi Circle/Monuments/ D.78/1949/ Monuments/Kashmiri gate.

[21] For a number of useful discussions on the politics of destruction and reconstruction of monuments, see the essays collected together in Nelson and Olin (eds.), *Monuments and Memory, Made and Unmade*.

disposed of with as much dignity as possible. To this end, Bullock resolved to do all he could to maintain these structures out of what he described as 'a blend of sentiment and historical significance, and additionally ... patriotism'.[22]

Bullock, an enthusiastic amateur historian and author of several works on the history of British India, was fiercely in favour of attempting to preserve as many monuments as possible and adamantly opposed any proposal which would see monuments or gravestones destroyed by the British themselves in an attempt to curtail controversy and prevent further acts of desecration.[23] Therefore, Bullock saw the principal challenge faced by the BGMS as the allocation of the scarce funds available for the upkeep of monuments and cemeteries made on the basis of 'their historical importance' and 'their interest as part of the British story in India' whilst holding, 'on behalf of HMG a watching brief, to see how monuments of British rule were being treated and to think out ways and means of persuading the Government of India and Pakistan that such monuments when important ought to be maintained by them'.[24] However, Bullock seems to have seen mutiny monuments as a particularly difficult category, as they 'have evoked adverse comment from Indians in the past and may do so again' and thus comprised one of the largest and most controversial classes of monument under his care.[25] Further, Bullock's own attitude towards these mutiny monuments appears to be rather ambivalent. For example, in assessing the mutiny monument raised on the Delhi Ridge to commemorate the siege of Delhi, Bullock describes the structure as an 'architectural monstrosity which British opinion would nevertheless probably consider to deserve preservation'.[26] Similarly, in correspondence with Brigadier Clark who, writing from the depot of the Argyll and Sutherland Highlanders, had raised concerns about the mutiny monument raised in honour of the 93rd Highlanders, Bullock records his view that 'monuments of the Indian Mutiny, which are particularly profuse at Cawnpore and Lucknow, are a source of some potential

---

[22] Humphrey Bullock, 'Minute: Preliminary note on the preservation of monuments of British Rule in India and Pakistan', 15 December 1947, File 11 Historical monuments in India, p. 160, OIOC. IOR/R/4/82.

[23] In this vein, it had been widely suggested that unpopular monuments, or those which could no longer be reasonably maintained, should be buried in situ; however, Bullock felt that 'any proposal to bury or destroy such monuments' was 'savouring of wanton iconoclasm. Nothing is more reprehensible to the historian than the deliberate destruction of documentary evidence'. Humphrey Bullock, 'Minute: Disposal of unwanted churches and of memorials in them', File 11 Historical monuments in India, p. 155, OIOC. IOR/R/4/82. Bullock had already written a number of books on military history including Bullock, *Indian Infantry Colours*, and Bullock, *Indian Cavalry Colours*.

[24] Humphrey Bullock, 'Minute: Preliminary note on the preservation of monuments of British Rule in India and Pakistan', 15 December 1947, File 11 Historical monuments in India, p. 160, OIOC. IOR/R/4/82.

[25] Ibid.   [26] Ibid.

embarrassment in present conditions' before adding that nonetheless, 'We are doing our best to keep an eye on them'.[27]

Ultimately, in consultation with the various interested parties, Bullock pursued a policy of relocating such monuments to places where they would effectively be hidden from view. Whilst this may be considered a pragmatic course of action given the circumstances, it appears to have in fact been part of a broader desire to essentially help forget the mutiny. Thus, in the case of the aforementioned monument to the 93rd Highlanders, Bullock in consultation with Brigadier Clark resolved not to further consider proposals to safeguard the memorial but instead to relocate it to an alternative site where, it was hoped, the monument would quietly avoid attention.[28] Selecting the Cantonment Cemetery in Lucknow as the most suitable location, the monument was quietly moved without ceremony and successfully re-erected by the end of 1949.[29] A short distance away in Cawnpore, a similar debate was ensuing concerning the memorial over the well. Following the violence meted out to the monument over the course of the Independence Day celebrations in 1947, the United Provinces Government had repaired the monument to its former condition. Once repaired, however, fears for its long-term safety encouraged the Memorial Well Garden Society to consider its options. The UP Government had proposed that the Memorial Well and a small portion of the gardens might be bounded by a six-foot wall for protection and maintained by the Society, but upon consideration by a number of affected bodies, it was widely agreed that the best course of action would be to move the entire monument into nearby All Souls' Church which, as we saw earlier, was itself a monument to the mutiny. As the Standing Memorandum held by the Commonwealth Relations Office would relate, this course of action was the only option available as 'the funds at the Governor's disposal were insufficient and had had over a year or two to be supplemented from private pockets' and further the maintenance of a small plot within the gardens would likely be an 'aggravation to Indian susceptibilities'.[30]

With dwindling funds, and nothing further coming from Bullock's Graves and Monuments Section to supplement the upkeep of the monument, Christopher Ackroyd, Secretary of the Lucknow Diocesan Trust Association (LDTA), wrote

---

[27] Humphrey Bullock to Brigadier Clark, 2 April 1948, 'File12a Military Memorials of the Argyll and Sutherland Highlanders in India and Pakistan', fol. 137, OIOC. IOR/R/4/87.

[28] For alternative proposals to safeguard the monument in situ, see Hashman & Son to Mr Swingler, 3 March 1949, 'File12a Military Memorials of the Argyll and Sutherland Highlanders in India and Pakistan', fol. 68, OIOC. IOR/R/4/87.

[29] Humphrey Bullock to J. R. Mendis, 14 November 1949, 'File12a Military Memorials of the Argyll and Sutherland Highlanders in India and Pakistan', fol. 101, OIOC. IOR/R/4/87.

[30] Sir Robert Menzies, 'Cawnpore Memorial Well, 8 March 1949, 'File 11/1b Historical Monuments in India: Mutiny Memorial Well at Cawnpore', fol. 73, OIOC. IOR/R/4/84.

that he favoured 'removal entirely whilst we have the money and once out of sight in the Memorial Church Compound there would I think be no further trouble',[31] a sentiment echoed in the LDTA's committee meeting which 'heartily agreed with the idea of wiping out all traces on the site of the tragedy'.[32]

When Sir Robert Menzies, Acting President of the Memorial Well Garden Society, was approached on the proposed course of action, he immediately responded directly to Brigadier Bullock informing him that 'I entirely agree with Ackroyd's idea of wiping out all traces on the site of the tragedy',[33] and following a meeting with Christopher Robinson, Bishop of Lucknow, it was reported that:

He is not very keen on the Angel ... He feels ... after a certain time a grave has no special value ... one should not be unduly sentimental on the subject ... What has happened had happened, but there is no point in rubbing it in ... in a few years time there should be no certainty as to the site of the Well, one person saying it is here, another over there.[34]

This decision was finalised at a meeting of the Society's Governors towards the end of 1948, when it was resolved that the removal of the monument represented the best solution to the problem. It was further added that it was hoped 'there will be no trace left of the tragedy. "Grass grows over a battlefield but never a scaffold"',[35] a decision fully supported by Bullock following his fact-finding trip to Cawnpore a few weeks later.[36] By early 1950, Ackroyd could send a postcard to Bullock letting him know that 'the work is practically done ... The whole effect extremely good now.... I have also made a separate enclosure for some grave monuments from other places with spare railings'.[37]

This process of removing mutiny monuments to locations described as 'out of sight' clearly went beyond simply erasing controversial symbols from the physical landscape of the United Provinces. The removals were aimed far more specifically at the community's collective memory. The monuments and, it was hoped, their memories were being actively removed from the cultural field and quietly hidden away. As recorded by the monument's own governing

[31] Christopher Ackroyd, quoted in letter from C. J. Toyne to Bullock, 13 August 1948, File 11/1b Historical Monuments in India: Mutiny Memorial Well at Cawnpore, fol. 35, OIOC. IOR/R/4/84.

[32] Christopher Ackroyd to Sir Robert Menzies, 14 November 1948, File 11/1b Historical Monuments in India: Mutiny Memorial Well at Cawnpore, fol. 40, OIOC. IOR/R/4/84.

[33] Sir Robert Menzies to Bullock, 17 November 1948, File 11/1b Historical Monuments in India: Mutiny Memorial Well at Cawnpore, fol. 40, OIOC. IOR/R/4/84.

[34] Christopher Ackroyd to Sir Robert Menzies, 14 November 1948, File 11/1b Historical Monuments in India: Mutiny Memorial Well at Cawnpore, fol. 40, OIOC. IOR/R/4/84.

[35] Christopher Ackroyd to C. J. Toyne, 14 November 1948, File 11/1b Historical Monuments in India: Mutiny Memorial Well at Cawnpore, fol. 42, OIOC. IOR/R/4/84.

[36] Bullock, 'Memorandum: Cawnpore Memorial Well', File 11/1b Historical Monuments in India: Mutiny Memorial Well at Cawnpore, fol. 53, OIOC. IOR/R/4/84.

[37] Ackroyd to Bullock, 20 February 1950, 'Extract from postcard', File 11/1b Historical Monuments in India: Mutiny Memorial Well at Cawnpore, fol. 84, OIOC. IOR/R/4/84.

Figure 6.2 The Angel of the Resurrection at All Souls' Church. Photograph by the author, 4 August 2012.

body, 'Grass grows over a battlefield but never a scaffold'.[38] As this resolution points out, for the governing body this process of forgetting went beyond stone and metal, but was designed to reach the memories of all those living in Cawnpore. The 'Cawnpore Massacre', which, for over ninety years, had been at the heart of Britain's memory of empire, was being quietly forgotten and its memorial edifice appropriately relocated to a cemetery.

The Lucknow Residency may be seen to have suffered a similar fate. In a letter to Sir Francis Tuker, who had been the commander of the Lucknow District shortly before independence, R. Fyres-Clinton noted his concern about the future of the Residency. Writing from his home in England, Fyres-Clinton stated that from his time in India forty years before, 'one of the most vivid recollections I have is of my visit to the Residency at Lucknow' before noting that he feared it 'may have been razed to the ground by now ... at any rate I fear that will be its fate sooner or later'.[39] Whilst, as this letter shows, some individuals located in Britain were still concerned about the condition of the structure, the site was not in fact under a direct threat from the Indian Government. Rather it had been safely preserved by a predominantly British committee, but after its transfer to the ASI in the 1950s had little care or attention spent on it. Largely neglected, the area gradually reverted to nature over the following years until one concerned resident could eventually write that it had largely 'degenerated into a jungle'.[40]

If the uncoordinated acts of vandalism and desecration which accompanied independence challenged and subverted these symbols of British imperialism, then it is also apparent that the BMGS, along with local sentiment, also

[38] Christopher Ackroyd to C. J. Toyne, 14 November 1948, File 11/1b Historical Monuments in India: Mutiny Memorial Well at Cawnpore, fol. 42, OIOC. IOR/R/4/84.

[39] R. Fyres-Clinton to Sir Francis Tuker, 21 June 1953, Sir Francis Tuker Papers, IWM, 71-21-5-6.

[40] B. N. Chaubey to the Director General ASI, 17 August 1972, 'Improvements of Lucknow residency Premises suggestion by B. N. Chaubey', NAI, ASI/HQ/Monuments/26/97/72-M. See also B. N. Chaubey to the Director General ASI, NAI, ASI/HQ/Monuments/ 22/20/70-M/1970. For administrative arrangements at independence until transfer to the ASI, see Tuker, *Whilst Memory Serves*, Appendix X, pp. 647–48.

favoured their removal. Monuments which had been constructed over the preceding ninety years as a celebration of British victory over the mutiny were carefully and discreetly hidden from popular attention or otherwise actively forgotten. In better understanding the local interests that contributed to this process, it is useful to consider for a moment the aspirations and intentions of the local British community that remained in India following independence, as well as other British émigrés who came to India for employment in the various British businesses that continued to thrive in the first decade that followed independence. Whilst the vast majority of the British population returned 'home' in 1947, nearly 28,000 British expatriates remained in India in 1951.[41] Consisting primarily, but certainly not entirely, in members of the non-official British community of India, which had grown gradually since the Charter Act of 1833, many of the individuals who elected to stay did so out of a combination of interests. Whilst some were already of retirement age and saw no future beyond India, for others the decision was based on a careful consideration that weighed the socio-economic advantages of remaining in India against those of returning to Britain and concluded that their future was better served by staying in India. Following the aspirations of British traders and industrialists who had travelled to India for over 100 years, many hoped to make their fortune before very probably returning to Britain. For the majority of these, running tea plantations in northeast India or employed in industry or commerce in various Indian centres, the following years proved discouraging. Whilst many found the 1950s conducive to their interests, few remained by the end of the following decade.[42] Particularly hard hit by the devaluation of the rupee in the 1960s and taxes which increased during the same decade, most of the last stayers-on returned to Britain over the course of the 1960s.[43]

However, at least whilst they remained in the subcontinent, the history and legacy of British India was clearly a pressing concern for the local communities continued social and economic well-being. This is especially true for those located in areas where the spectre of the mutiny yet still lingered, and for whom the reverberations of 1857 in the first decade that followed independence did not seem conducive to their interests. To take one such individual, Sir Robert Menzies, the President of the Memorial Well Garden Society and the Managing Director of the British Indian Corporation (BIC), it is clear to see the economic interests that helped motivate his desire to forget the mutiny. Known locally as the 'uncrowned King of Cawnpore', Menzies had helped the BIC enjoy a period of considerable prosperity during the war.[44] Just as the Boer War, fifty years earlier, had stimulated the fledgling industries in Cawnpore,

[41] Purcell, *After the Raj*, p. 15.   [42] Ibid.
[43] Ibid, p. 129; For a broader discussion, see Lipton and Firn, *The Erosion of a Relationship*.
[44] Yalland, *Boxwallahs*, p. 434; Christie, *Morning Drum*, p. 129.

which were contracted to provide large quantities of equipment for the British army, so too did the Second World War prove lucrative for many of the mills producing textiles for the war effort, as well as the thriving leather industry in the city.[45] As a major industrial conglomerate comprising primarily of several wool mills, tanneries, and military equipment manufacturers specialising in boots, the BIC had been kept extremely busy during the war and intended to continue growing in the years which followed. Though British control of the BIC would end acrimoniously in 1956 following Menzies decision to return to Britain and sell his shares to Haridas Mundhra, the prosperity of the company during the intervening years relied significantly on its workforce.[46] Therefore if, as was clearly the case, the mutiny continued to be a live issue disrupting the continued harmony between the British owners and the thousands of Indians employed in the city, then acrimony could only have a negative impact on the business interests of the BIC in general and Menzies in particular, and thus business considerations most likely helped stimulate his sudden decision to support the proposals to remove the Angel of the Resurrection, and 'hide' it away out of sight.

However, if a range of British interests converged on helping forget the mutiny, as indicated by the debates over the fate of British mutiny monuments, then these practices of forgetting were applied with equal vigour in response to fears of any counter-memory materialising. This is most apparent in the case of a number of controversial regimental colours which had been laid up in Allahabad Cathedral at the end of the nineteenth century. Concerned about the adverse impact on his congregation and the wider community, Christopher Robinson, Bishop of Lucknow, wrote to the High Commission around a year after independence to request that the regimental colours be removed. He pointed out that not only did many members of his congregation 'not wish to have the colours in the cathedral', but more importantly when

…non-Christians come to our services, and we want to encourage them to come, they invariably ask 'what is the Union Jack doing here?' Actually it is of course not the Union Jack but the colours of the Cheshire Regiment. It is one more thing that we have to try and explain to non-Christians and as they are draped around the Chancel Arch it is not possible to avoid seeing them. I will, therefore, say that they incite adverse comments and for political reasons they are much better not there.[47]

Whilst against the removal of colours from churches in principle, the BMGS was sympathetic towards such considerations and immediately began arranging

---

[45] Yalland, *Boxwallahs*, p. 402, p. 434; Purcell, *After the Raj*, pp. 245–46.

[46] For an overview of the 'Mundhra scandal', 'independent India's first major financial scandal', see Dadabhoy, *Barons of Banking*, pp. 144–49.

[47] Christopher Lucknow to Lt. Col. H. C. Druett, 3 September 1948, 'File 12/1 Monuments: Regimental Colours in Churches in India and Pakistan', fol. 15, OIOC. IOR/R/4/86.

for the colours to be sent to Sandhurst, as the most suitable location for such colonial military memorabilia. Bullock, however, who eighteen years earlier had visited Allahabad on a research trip for his two-volume history of Indian military colours, suspected that Robinson was incorrect in his identification of the regiments concerned.[48] Indeed, among the several colours within the church, there existed a number which had belonged to regiments that had been disbanded in 1857 after they mutinied. Among these, those of the 37th and 38th Bengal Native Infantry were perhaps the most prominent. Interestingly, in both cases, the fate of the regimental colours has been recorded. In the case of the 37th who mutinied in Benares, Brigadier-General Neill recorded that following the 'expulsion of the 37th regiment ... I sent out parties and brought in the arms, accoutrements, and colours of the 37th that had been left in their lines'.[49] Similarly in the case of the 38th, Lieut Peile records that, following the outbreak of mutiny in Delhi on 11 May, he endeavoured to recover the colours. 'After a great deal of persuasion, I was allowed to take the regimental colours, but on arriving outside, to my horror I found that my syce had decamped with my horse. I was, therefore, compelled to place the standard again in the quarter-guard'.[50]

Following the suppression of the mutiny, these regiments were disbanded and their colours returned to the Allahabad Arsenal. They were subsequently transferred to the Allahabad Cathedral in 1899 where, displayed securely in British possession within the tranquillity of the cathedral, they were stripped of their menace and likely hung as a reassuring reminder of British authority. Given the history of the colours and the need for approval from the Government of India to transfer them to the United Kingdom, Bullock thought it advisable to seek the counsel of the Commonwealth Relations Office in London (CRO). Writing that 'There seem to me to be reasons why we should not invite attention to the existence of these Colours', Bullock reminds CRO that

...there is, as you know, a school of thought in this country, which now extols the Mutineers as the first fighters for Indian freedom. This school of thought would no doubt like to get hold of such colours as material for hero worship.... The whole question is rather a difficult one, and perhaps it would be better to leave the Colours of the Mutinous Regiments, at least, in the decent obscurity which surrounds them at present.[51]

Upon consultation with the defence department, CRO agreed with Bullock's assessment and advised that the colours be left where they were 'in order to

---

[48] Bullock, *Indian Infantry Colours* and Bullock, *Indian Cavalry Colours*.
[49] Lieutenant-Colonel J. G. Neill, of the Madras Army, to the Adjunct-General of the Bengal Army, in Chick, *Annals of the Indian Rebellion*, p. 372.
[50] Narrative of Lieut. Peile of the 38th N. I., printed in Chick, *Annals of the Indian Rebellion*, pp. 181–84, p. 182.
[51] H. Bullock to R. G. Chisholm, 10 May 1949, 'File 12/1 Monuments: Regimental Colours in Churches in India and Pakistan', fol. 6, OIOC. IOR/R/4/86.

avoid any danger of creating unnecessary ill-feeling'. Adding that 'It is perhaps conceivable that the Colours may be unearthed ... but this risk does not seem to outweigh the other consideration'.[52]

With both British and Indian monuments safely concealed by the BGMS, the department appears not so much interested in repressing an emerging official Indian memory of the mutiny in favour of preserving British official memory, rather the department seems equally eager that both be forgotten. So seen, it may reasonably be said that contrary to his official designation, Bullock was not interested in how the mutiny may be remembered, rather he was actively interested in how the mutiny may be forgotten.

The Mutiny's Centenary: A Struggle for Meaning, Memory, and the Right to Narrate

The BGMS and the local British community seem to have been largely successful in removing the last physical traces of the 'Cawnpore Massacre' and, over the following years, the Angel of the Resurrection, along with the monument dedicated to the 93rd originally erected at Sikander Bagh, rapidly lost all significance. Situated within graveyards in Uttar Pradesh, the monuments were rapidly forgotten and fell into obscurity. The Residency too, deteriorating to the state of a 'jungle', went largely disregarded; a relic lost in the realms of time. However, if this process of active forgetting is apparent from the first months and years of independence, then it reaches its apogee ten years later during the mutiny's centenary year. Though a number of unofficial groups in both India and England attempted to propagate the mutiny's memory, official actors did all they could to block such attempts or at least subdue and temper them.

In considering the likelihood of extensive celebrations, Stephen Whitwell wrote from the United Kingdom High Commission in India (UKHCI) to CRO to express his concern that 'the occasion may lead to demonstrations directed particularly against UK persons or monuments'.[53] Fearing such a backlash, High Commissioner Malcolm Macdonald, son of the first Labour Party Prime Minister, Ramsay MacDonald, arranged a meeting with Dr Sarvepalli Radhakrishnan, Vice-president of India and president of a central government committee tasked with organising the centenary celebrations. In his note on the meeting, Macdonald reports that he raised the concerns of Christopher Robinson, Bishop of Lucknow, 'that some plaques and memorials in churches which had been erected after the Mutiny were couched in

---

[52] R. G. Chisholm to Bullock, 16 June 1949, 'File 12/1 Monuments: Regimental Colours in Churches in India and Pakistan', fol. 5, OIOC. IOR/R/4/86.
[53] S. J. Whitwell (UKHCI) to V. C. Martin (CRO), 20 October 1956, 'Celebrations of Indian Mutiny Centenary in 1957', fol. 2, TNA, DO 35/9144.

language which may have seemed appropriate one hundred years ago, but which might now be offensive to Indian nationalist sentiment ... ardent celebrators of the Mutiny might feel moved to enter churches and cemeteries and smash such plaques'.[54]

For his part, Radhakrishnan thought such eventualities unlikely, but agreed to keep the matter in mind as preparations for the anniversary were finalised. Surprisingly, perhaps, Macdonald concluded that the Indian Government seemed as unwilling to remember 1857 as its British counterpart. Radhakrishnan and Dr Kailash Nath Katju, Defence Minister and President of the All-India Congress Sub-Committee likewise charged with preparing the centenary celebrations, had both informed UKHCI that there would be no official celebrations of the Mutiny as such, rather the anniversary would be celebrated in August as part of the annual Independence Day celebrations. Recording his conversation with Radhakrishnan, Macdonald noted that:

> He told me that so far as the Central Government is concerned, there would be no celebrations on the anniversary of the Mutiny in May. His Committee had decided to celebrate in August, and to put the emphasis on the fact that this is the tenth year of independence.... The central committee had been deliberately packed with old I.C.S officers like [Mullath Kadingi] Vellodi with a view to any anti-British sentiments being reduced as far as possible, if not wholly eliminated. The celebration would be an occasion for mutual friendliness between the Indians and the British, not the reverse.[55]

In keeping with this spirit, Radhakrishnan likewise informed Macdonald that his central committee was opposed to the construction of monuments or other memorials dedicated to 1857, a sentiment shared by other veteran members of the Congress including Morarji Dessai, Chief Minister of Bombay, who in conversation with Henry Twist, Deputy High Commissioner in Bombay, is reported to have 'expressed strong disapproval of the idea of commemorating the Mutiny at all', a sentiment also shared by the governor of Bombay, Sri Prakasa, who was nevertheless also acting as the president of a regional committee tasked with the mutiny's commemoration.[56]

Taking their lead from the expressed intentions of these committees concerned with official acts of commemoration on behalf of the Indian Government, CRO and UKHCI likewise went about ensuring that in Britain the anniversary would be passed over with as little attention as was possible. In Pakistan, where similar celebrations were anxiously expected, the

---

[54] Malcolm Macdonald, 'Note from High Commissioner', 'Celebrations of Indian Mutiny Centenary in 1957', fol. 25, TNA, DO 35/9144.
[55] Ibid.
[56] S. J. Whitwell (UKHCI) to V. C. Martin (CRO), 20 October 1956, 'Celebrations of Indian Mutiny Centenary in 1957', fol. 2, TNA, DO 35/9144; Malcolm Macdonald, High Commissioner, to The Rt. Hon. Harold Macmillan, MP, Commonwealth Relations Office, 1 October 1957, 'Celebrations of Indian Mutiny Centenary in 1957', fol. 52, TNA, DO 35/9144.

High Commission had earlier outlined what they saw as possible responses. Writing on the subject, first secretary Charles Thompson had suggested that Britain could engage in a policy of counter commemoration designed to challenge Pakistan's official memory of the mutiny. Thompson outlined several ways in which this might be achieved, most provocatively exhibitions and commemorations of the mutiny to be held in London, official visits and deputations to Pakistan and the exchange of messages between military regiments in Pakistan and Britain who fought together in suppression of the mutiny.[57]

In response to these proposals, the UKHCI made its own views abundantly clear, arguing that 'any kind of large-scale, counter-offensive ... in India [would] be a major error.... Our main object during the whole affair will be, by whatever means, to damp down the fires of controversy rather than to stoke them up'.[58] Accordingly, the UKHCI was especially concerned about UP, where it was widely felt the greatest risk of counter celebrations was likely. Accordingly, John Rob, counsellor at the UKHCI, travelled with Whitwell to both Cawnpore and Lucknow where, it was reported by John Christie of the Citizens Association, they

...did some excellent work ... over our own rather special local problems – in Lucknow, for instance, we could happily celebrate a glorious feat of British arms, and elsewhere the 200th anniversary of the battle of Plassey! In Cawnpore we are all so backward, and most of what happened was so bloody that it would not be difficult for anyone to put a foot wrong and commit unintentional bêtises, if care and forethought is not taken.[59]

As noted previously, the concern of UKHCI extended beyond Indian borders and encompassed any proposal to commemorate the mutiny in England where, it was felt, it was equally important that no official commemoration ceremony should be considered. Despite this, however, a number of interested parties planned to hold their own private events. Principal among these were a number of regiments that wished to hold parades or events in Britain, including Sandhurst, the Royal Military Academy, which planned to host a mutiny exhibition to mark the occasion. Discussing these arrangements, Godfrey Boyd Shannon, former Deputy High Commissioner in India, opined that 'it is distressing that some British regiments certainly will hold commemorative parades', adding that 'From the point of view of United Kingdom-Indian

---

[57] C. A. Thompson to V. C. Martin, 3 October 1956, 'Celebrations of Indian Mutiny Centenary in 1957', fol. 31, TNA, DO 35/9144.

[58] S. J. Whitwell (UKHCI) to V. C. Martin (CRO), 20 October 1956, 'Celebrations of Indian Mutiny Centenary in 1957', fol. 2, TNA, DO 35/9144.

[59] Extract from a letter dated 19 December 1956 from W. H. J. Christie, CSI OBE, President Designate U.K. Citizens Association, India, to Sir Gilbert Laithwaite, 'Celebrations of Indian Mutiny Centenary in 1957', fol. 15, TNA, DO 35/9144.

relations' such events are 'rather horrifying, since commemorative parades could only provoke bitter comment and counter celebrations in India'.[60]

Shannon's opinions were widely shared, and as relayed by Sir Claude Auchinleck to Sir J. Gilbert Lathwaite, whilst 'he yielded to no one in his admiration for what our people had done in 1857 to 1859 and his abhorrence of the excesses committed by the Mutineers ... there is no gainsaying the fact that our people too, in the heat of anger, committed many atrocities in putting down the Mutiny and it was in no one's interest that either set of atrocities should be given publicity now'.[61]

Of particular concern were the plans of the 60th Rifles and the 2nd Gurkhas to celebrate the centenary. These regiments had forged a bond in 1857 during their defence of Hindu Rao's House and had remained close from this time. A central feature of the shared experience of these two regiments was a large wooden table located in Hindu Rao's House that, in addition to dining, was used as an operating table during the more frenetic periods of the conflict.[62] Following the successful recapture of Delhi, the two regiments were anxious to cement their relationship and initially achieved this by each taking a portion of the table as a memorial to their shared suffering; a powerful symbol of their enduring connection which remains a prized possession of each regiment to this day (Figure 6.3).

Eager to continue this relationship and together mark the anniversary, the 60th Rifles planned to hold a parade to which current and past members of the 2nd Gurkhas based in England were invited. In addition, the 2nd Gurkhas were to hold their own celebration of 'Delhi Day' in Singapore where the regiment was then stationed. As communicated by Shannon to CRO, 'The proposal for celebration by Gurkha regiments raises particular difficulties, in that the Government of India are already jealous of our continued recruitment of Gurkhas for the British Army and would particularly resent Gurkha regiments celebrating the defeat of Indians'.[63]

Adopting a 'policy ... to ensure that any celebrations and publicity here are played down and kept to a minimum', CRO wrote to the War Office expressing its concern over regimental plans to hold a commemoration ceremony,

---

[60] Godfrey Boyd Shannon to Mr Snelling, 10 January 1957, 'Celebrations of Indian Mutiny Centenary in 1957', fol. 13, TNA, DO 35/9144.

[61] Sir J. Gilbert Laithwaite, 'Note for record on meeting with Sir Claude Auchinleck', 10 December 1956, 'Celebrations of Indian Mutiny Centenary in 1957', fol. 14, TNA, DO 35/9144.

[62] A picture of the 'Delhi Table' was included in the commemorative booklet released as part of this event. 'Delhi Day Programme', Sir Francis Tuker Papers. IWM, 71/21/14/2. The Gurkha Museum commissioned Jason Askew to paint a seven-foot depiction of the 60th Rifles and the 2nd Gurkhas dining together at the 'Delhi Table' as part of the 2007, 150th Anniversary of the event.

[63] Godfrey Boyd Shannon to Arthur W. Snelling (CRO), 9 January 1957, 'Celebrations of Indian Mutiny Centenary in 1957', TNA, DO 35/9144.

Figure 6.3 The 'Delhi Table', photograph taken from the regimental commemorative booklet produced as part of the 100th Anniversary, 'Mutiny – Gurka', Sir Francis Tuker Papers, IWM, 71-21-5-6.

a view which was fully supported by Sir F. Stanley Tomlinson, Head of the South East Asia Department at the Foreign Office, who also wrote to the War Office to register his anxieties on the subject.[64] In response, the Army Council wrote to all regiments to stress that 'the greatest care should be taken in planning the centenary celebrations to ensure that no offence is given and that the occasion is used to express the mutual friendliness between the British and Indian peoples'.[65] Adding that it was particularly important that 'as little attention as possible is directed to atrocities and aspects likely to engender hatred of former enemies'.[66] In keeping with this policy, the colonel of the regiment, Major-General Lewis Pugh, wrote to the War Office to inform it that '... we intend to commemorate the bravery of our officers and men with the 60th at Winchester. There is no intention of commemorating the Indian Mutiny as such, although the Indians will by this date have completed their celebrations of the first attempt to throw off the foreign yoke!'.[67]

---

[64] F. S. Tomlinson to Major-General Hamilton, Director of Military operations, War Office, 14 December 1956, 'Celebrations of Indian Mutiny Centenary in 1957', fol. 11, TNA, DO 35/9144.
[65] 'Draft confidential' from Army Council to All Commands, 1 May 1957, 'Celebrations of Indian Mutiny Centenary in 1957', TNA, DO 35/9144.
[66] Ibid.
[67] Major-General L. H. C. Pugh to Major-General Hamilton, Director of Military operations, War Office, 1 December 1956, 'Celebrations of Indian Mutiny Centenary in 1957', TNA, DO 35/9144.

In keeping with these demands and this emphasis, the celebration on 14 September was confined to the Green Jacket's Depot and eschewed a focus on the mutiny in favour of a broader celebration of the regiment's involvement in many conflicts over the course of a long and glorious history.[68] The centenary was likewise marked in Singapore on the same day with a similar emphasis on proceedings. As part of these celebrations, the regiments traded gifts to mark the occasion and, in Winchester, a Deodar tree was planted. As explained by the Chaplain-General, Canon Victor Pike, the native Nepalese tree was a fitting tribute to the day's activities as in its native land it had 'to withstand powerful winds, and often when two branches were rubbed together by the force of the gale they gave forth a sap which united the branches, so that they grew together as one in strength and unity'.[69] With the wind acting as a metaphor for the mutiny and the branches for the two regiments, the tree was thought to be 'a wonderful symbol of what was being done to-day'.[70] Although of great significance to those participating in these ceremonies, the events followed the direction that had been given by the Army Council and accordingly avoided media attention and wider publicity. Therefore, they passed with little public attention in either Britain or India.

If the British Government was therefore largely successful in suppressing acts of commemoration in Britain, then, as promised by those in charge of the Congress committee tasked with organising events to mark the centenary of the mutiny in India, the Indian Government seems to have tried its best to likewise eschew directly commemorating the event. Indeed, this is immediately apparent if one considers how Nehru attempted to negotiate memories of the mutiny over the course of the year. Indeed, 1957 was seen by many in India as an auspicious year for multiple and often conflicting reasons. Not only did the year represent the 100th anniversary of 1857, it also marked the 200th anniversary of the Battle of Plassey as well as the tenth anniversary of Independence. Of no less immediate political significance, the start of the year would also witness India's second national elections since independence. Accordingly, given the nature of the highly emotive and disparate events brought readily to mind, Nehru expressed his belief that 'Nineteen hundred and fifty seven is a strange year'.[71] Speaking at an election rally in Nagpur at the start of the year, Nehru told his audience that:

---

[68] See the commemorative booklets printed for each event. Neither focuses on the mutiny but rather sets it within a broader history of the regiment. 'Mutiny – Gurka', Sir Francis Tuker Papers, IWM, 71-21-5-6.

[69] Anon, 'The Delhi Centenary', pp. 126–33, pp. 129–30. The Royal Green Jackets (Rifles) Museum.

[70] Ibid.

[71] Nehru, 'What the Congress stands for, speech given at an election meeting, Nagpur, 21 February 1957', pp. 143–59, p. 154.

Two hundred years ago the British won the battle of Plassey in Bengal which is supposed to mark the beginning of the British empire in India.... Then a hundred years ago, in 1857, a great war of independence broke out with the armed forces in open rebellion against the British. The rebellion was crushed. It took another twenty-eight years before Congress was established which ultimately led India to freedom. We will be celebrating the tenth anniversary of Indian independence in August. So 1957 is a very special year.[72]

Although these three disparate events may at first seem to be quite distinct and largely disassociated, Nehru's speech brings them into conversation with each other and further co-opts them into a linear narrative which appears to present an ultimately triumphal account of 200 years of Indian history culminating in Congress led resistance to British imperialism. The position occupied by 1857 within this memory is, however, ultimately ambivalent. As powerfully argued by Shahid Amin, India's authorised discourse on the Indian Independence Movement has been built around a narrative of Congress-led non-violent resistance to British imperialism with all events deemed to be out of keeping with this narrative excluded.[73] Therefore, as Amin tells his readers, this disciplined discourse 'induces a selective national amnesia in relation to specified events which would fit awkwardly, even seriously inconvenience, the neatly woven pattern'.[74] To say that such events are excluded from the independence movement is not to imply an entirely negative process, however. Such incidents are not simply forgotten but used to help define those events that are legitimised by the nationalist narrative, and in this way, inside and outside are bound into a deeply intimate relationship and like 'buyer and seller or teacher and pupil are interdependent – together they authorise each other'.[75]

With the memory of the mutiny so much alive within so many Indian communities, an outright disqualification of the event, as Amin demonstrates is the case with the 'Chauri Chaura riots of 1922' and is manifestly the case with other struggles deemed essentially violent by the central government such as the 'RIN Mutiny of 1946', was not possible. It was, however, incorporated into Indian official memory only to be again officially forgotten. Indeed, just months after Nehru had deployed the memory of 1857 in his election speech considered previously, he again invoked the memory of the mutiny. Speaking following the overwhelming electoral success of the Congress Party, in which its dominant position in post-colonial India was further underlined by an increase in its seat count and vote share, Nehru addressed a considerable crowd in Delhi on 10 May 1957.[76] Beginning his speech by stressing that

[72] Ibid.
[73] Amin, *Event, Metaphor, Memory,* see specifically 'Prologue'.
[74] Ibid, p. 3.
[75] Jenny Edkins, *Trauma and the Memory of Politics* (Cambridge: Cambridge University Press, 2003), p. 187.
[76] Roach, 'India's 1957 Election', pp. 65–78.

he was required to confirm that the newly constituted Lok Sabha had been sworn in on that day, Nehru emphasised that it was purely 'a coincidence' that this event fell 'exactly a hundred years from the day on which the first war of independence, or the mutiny as some people call it, began in the city of Meerut'.[77] However in so doing, the newly re-elected Prime Minister of India took the opportunity of discussing the event. Whilst emphasising to his audience that he was in no doubt that the war was indeed a national uprising against the many injustices of British rule, he also found much to praise about the British.[78]

The main purpose of Nehru's speech, however, was not to remember the mutiny but to forget it. In fact, Nehru specifically introduced the subject so that it could be forgotten. Bringing the mutiny into conversation with Congress-led freedom struggles and debates on how India should behave in a geopolitical landscape in which political and strategic contours had been dramatically refashioned by the introduction of nuclear weapons, Nehru told his audience that it was

...by a strange coincidence, exactly a hundred years ago today on the 10th of May, our war of independence began in Meerut.... Three days hence falls Buddha Purnima, which is yet another landmark. They are reminders of two different ways of life and we will have to choose one in this age of nuclear weapons. An arms race is not the solution. Until the world opinion chooses the other path, the danger of nuclear weapons will continue to hang over our heads like the sword of Damocles.... I appeal to you to think of all those brave warriors who had lit the torch of India's independence. That torch continued to burn for a century until India became free. Let us pay homage to those brave heroes and the others who came after them and carried the torch. Let us think of Gandhiji and remind ourselves that unless we see reason and defeat violence, it will bring ruin to mankind.[79]

In so positioning 1857, Nehru remembers the mutiny only so he can compel his audience to forget it. The event was significant as the first freedom struggle, but ultimately its value in the present is that it, along with all forms of violence, is left in the past. In fact, for Nehru, the only lesson which the event may fruitfully be said to teach is the value of unity between Muslim and Hindu. For this, as a model, the mutiny was exemplary.[80]

Whilst British and Indian official memories forged around the Mutiny's centenary were thus designed to complement one another and steer their respective publics away from remembering the event at all, not all those concerned with how the mutiny should be remembered were equally accommodating.

---

[77] Nehru, 'The First War of Independence', pp. 3–15, p. 3.
[78] Ibid, p. 7.   [79] Ibid, pp. 14–15.
[80] This point was made very forcefully by the Minister for Education, Maulana Abul Kalam. See his forward in Sen, Eighteen-Fifty-Seven.

In particular, those political parties that had competed in the elections earlier in the year took the opportunity presented by the 100th anniversary of 1857 to organise large-scale commemoration ceremonies to mark the anniversary. Among the most ardent of these was a loose coalition of otherwise factious left-wing parties including the Communist Party of India, the Praja Socialist Party, and Dr Ram Manohar Lohia's Socialist Party, which came together in a rare moment of unity to organise widespread celebrations of the anniversary in Uttar Pradesh. Holding up 1857 as a symbol of revolution which was as urgent in the mid-twentieth century as it was in the mid-nineteenth century, these left-wing organisations mobilised in protest around British mutiny monuments demanding that the government removes them immediately.[81] These agitations were heavily policed but nevertheless extensive damage resulted. In Benares, a monument to Queen Victoria was pulled down by protestors and at Etawah demonstrations outside the Victoria Memorial Hall resulted in the building being forcibly 'renamed' in honour of the Indian mutiny hero, Rani of Jhansi, by protestors using red paint.

Similarly at Gorakhpur, the Hindu nationalist party, Jan Sangh, used the opportunity of the mutiny's anniversary to demand political change. Though the anniversary had earlier been muted as a potential date for another 'mutiny' by the Party, this time against the policies of the secular Congress Party, and designed to establish a state founded on the principles of Hindutva, the resulting agitations proved rather less ambitious if nonetheless provocative. Taking aim at British monuments by draping a large black piece of material over a monument to Queen Victoria and placing a life-size portrait of the Rani of Jhansi in front, the Jan Sangh orchestrated a striking allegory for the contemporary political situation as a strong police presence descended on the protestors who resolutely kept a vigil over the subverted monument.[82] With the police appearing to be protecting a statue dedicated to British rule of India from those celebrating one of the greatest heroes of 1857, the Jan Sangh successfully equated the Indian State with the British empire and the protestors with the nationalist heroes who fought for the nation 100 years earlier. So severe were these agitations, which resulted in the arrest of around 400 protestors, that the Government of Uttar Pradesh felt that it was left with little alternative but to remove all monuments in the State that were 'reminiscent of foreign domination' resulting in a clean

---

[81] See Malcolm Macdonald to Rt. Hon. The Earl of Home, Secretary of State CRO, 22 June 1957, 'Celebrations of Indian Mutiny Centenary in 1957', TNA, DO 35/9144; Anon, '400 Indians Arrested after Anti-British Protests', *The Times*, 12 May 1957, p. 10. For more on the factious relationship between these parties, see Angela Sutherland Burger, *Opposition in a Dominant-Party System: A Study of the Jan Sangh, the Praja Socialist Party, and the Socialist Party in Utter Pradesh, India*, (Berkeley: University of California Press, 1969).

[82] Anon, 'Socialists Launch Satyagraha: Over 103 arrests in U.P.', *The Times of India*, 11 May 1957, p. 1.

sweep of monuments which, ten years earlier, had been feared by Bullock.[83] As Macdonald reported to Harold Macmillan, the UKHCI had been notified around a year earlier by the Indian Government that it was its policy to gradually remove British monuments to purpose built museums, but that it was 'not surprising that this process should have been somewhat speeded during the Mutiny Centenary Year or that this should have happened principally in the province which was most heavily affected by 1857'.[84]

On the Delhi Ridge too, British monuments became the target of protest over this period. The protests were most significantly aimed at the Kashmiri Gate and the statues of Brigadier-General John Nicholson and General Sir Alexander Taylor who each played central roles in the recapture of Delhi in 1857. As we saw in Chapter 3, both monuments were erected in the early twentieth century with most attention paid to Sir Thomas Brock's monument in honour of Nicholson. Following a series of protests primarily led by the same socialist and communist parties, Nehru sanctioned the removal of both monuments to curtail further agitation. Commenting on the removal of Taylor's memorial, Lohia is quoted as conceding that, unlike a statue, it is impossible to 'whisk away history. But history, particularly evil history, should not be there all the time to look at. Evil history belongs to the archives and museums'.[85] Interestingly, it seems certain that Nehru would have agreed, though might have added that 'evil history' was simply better forgotten.

Though every attempt was made to ensure that the removal of these monuments was achieved with as little public knowledge as possible and was therefore conducted under the cover of darkness, Brigadier Perry of the Commonwealth Graves Commission, who had been invited to be present as a representative of British interests, noted in his diary that the removal of Nicholson's statue attracted a small crowd of policemen and workmen. Inquisitive of their interest in the proceedings, Perry asked the superintendent of police why the crowd had assembled and was told 'rather sheepishly that "Jan Nikalsayn" had been a very "zubberdast" man, and that they could not be sure that his spirit would not return to haunt those who disturbed him'.[86] Given Nicholson's apparent ability to continue instilling fear and apprehension despite being dead for 100 years, the sight of his impotent statue lying supine on the ground waiting to be sealed inside a crate with an as yet uncertain future must have detracted from his aura. Even today, the image can't help but appear as a most pathetic depiction

[83] Malcolm Macdonald, High Commissioner, to The Rt. Hon. Harold Macmillan, MP, Commonwealth Relations Office, 1 October 1957, 'Celebrations of Indian Mutiny Centenary in 1957', fol. 52, TNA, DO 35/9144.

[84] Ibid.

[85] Dr Ram Manohar Lohia speaking at a press conference, quoted in Anon, 'Removal of Statues: Dr. Lohia's Call', The Times of India, 8 June 1957, p. 5.

[86] Brigadier Perry's Diary quoted in Steggles, Statues of the Raj, p. 147.

Figure 6.4 The Nicholson monument in a shipping crate. The photo appears to be credited to Ian Cowes. Dungannon School Archives. A no less poignant image is Taylor's plinth standing devoid of its statue. See Anon, 'Statue Removed', *The Times of India*, 12 June 1957, p. 8.

of the end of empire, and perhaps a rather more fitting one than the pomp and ceremony which attended the official handover of power and which frequently is used to represent the end of British India (Figure 6.4).

Though the fate of both Nicholson's and Taylor's statues remained unresolved as their storage crates were sealed, both would ultimately find their way back to Britain in the years which followed their removal from Delhi. In fact, even before orders had been submitted for their ejection, interested parties had begun to discuss what should be done in the event of their removal. In the case of Nicholson, one missionary stationed in Bombay had encouraged her cousin living in Northern Ireland to consider the question in a Christmas card sent in 1956 in which she reminded her cousin that 'this being "57" memories are roused & are bitter & there is danger it might be destroyed'.[87] Considering possibilities for its transportation back to Britain, the missionary noted that she felt that Brock's depiction of Nicholson had 'a good North of Ireland look!' and accordingly suggested that her cousin enquire with either Lisburn, as the probable birthplace of the mutiny hero, or else with Nicholson's Alma Mater, The Royal School Dungannon, to see if either place had any interest in acquiring the statue.[88] Though Dungannon's Board of Governors did indeed make tentative enquires on the subject, they were at first rebuked and told that given the Government of India's intentions concerning the centenary, it was felt 'unwise to arouse any undue interest in

---

[87] Identity of Missionary censored, quoted in Author Censored to A. de. G. Gaudin, Headmaster of The Royal School Dungannon, 28 December 1956, The Royal School Dungannon Archives.
[88] Ibid.

Figure 6.5 Mountbatten unveils the Nicholson monument at the Royal School. The Royal School Dungannon Archives.

the statue at present', however, following the monument's removal and uncertain future, the question gained a greater urgency.[89] Following a protracted discussion between several governmental departments and the school it was finally agreed that as Dungannon's expressed interest in acquiring the statue was purely 'sentimental and in no way political', arrangements were indeed made for the transferal of the statue to the school, with the costs being met in part by the Ministry of Education and in part by the school itself.[90] Arriving at the school in late 1958, the monument was finally unveiled by Mountbatten in its new location close to the Headmaster's house within the school grounds on 13 April 1960 (Figure 6.5).

Likewise, Taylor's statue quickly became of interest to parties in England who felt an enduring connection with the mutiny hero. Among these, the Cooper's Hill Society proved to be one of the most proactive. As noted earlier, following the mutiny, Taylor had gone on to have a successful career in the Royal Engineers and had ultimately been appointed the principal of the Royal Indian Engineering College at Cooper's Hill. Following the

[89] R. S. Brownell, Ministry of Education to A. de. G. Gaudin, Headmaster of The Royal School Dungannon, 27 June 1957, The Royal School Dungannon Archives.
[90] Gaudin to Brownell,14 December 1957, The Royal School Dungannon Archives.

closure of the college in 1906, the Cooper's Hill Society took on the task of maintaining an active network of former students and as soon as news of Taylor's statue being removed reached Britain, the society in communication with Alex Taylor's granddaughter, Dorothy Taylor, began to make arrangements for the statue's transportation to England with a view to erecting the memorial on the former site of the college which was now being used by the Shoreditch Training College.[91] With help coming especially from Lord Hailey who, when acting as Chief Commissioner of Delhi, had helped with the original erection of the statue, the monument was successfully transported back to England and unveiled at a ceremony attended by Lord Hailey, Sir Alexander Rouse, and an extensive number of Taylor's descendants among others.[92] The ease with which these monuments found new homes in Britain should alert us to the fact that, at least for certain sections of the population, the mutiny and its British heroes remained a relevant component of collective memory and identity. Just as the protests in India demonstrate the extent to which the mutiny remained a live issue, so too must their ready welcome 'home' demonstrate that the mutiny continued to help define the meaning of empire for many.

However, these monuments dedicated to Nicholson and Taylor were not the only statues to be removed from public spaces over this period. West Bengal, for example, which had noted the violent protests in neighbouring states, responded pre-emptively by removing John Henry Foley's equestrian monument to Sir James Outram which had been erected in 1874. Indeed, such was the number of monuments removed over this period that *The Times* could bitterly complain of a 'holocaust of British statues' in India, adding that 'it now rests with Mr Nehru to prevent August 15 marking a new milestone in Indo-British estrangement'.[93] The Indian press was rather more torn on the subject. Though some elements of the media supported the campaigns to rid India of British mutiny monuments, others were rather more reflective on the subject perhaps seeing the politics behind the rush to rename streets and tear down statues to reflect R. K. Narayan's satirical short story, *Lawley Road*, which had been published presciently in 1956.[94] One publication that became particularly concerned with the issue was *Shankar's Weekly*, a satirical journal in the mould of *Punch*. Through a number of engagements with the protests, the publication mocked the campaign in general and Lohia in particular

---

[91] Anon, 'Minutes of the Committee Meeting held at Over-Seas House on 18th April 1958', 'Committee Meetings', Cooper's Hill Society Papers, OIOC, Mss EUR F239/3.

[92] Anon, 'Annual Report', *The Coopers Hill Magazine*, Vol. XVI. No. 4, 1961, 'Cooper's Hill Society: Cooper's Hill Magazine', Cooper's Hill Society Papers, OIOC, Mss EUR F239/20.

[93] Our Own Correspondent, 'Everything waits for Mr Nehru: Indian Prime minister returns to pressing problems', *The Times*, 15 July 1957, p. 8.

[94] Narayan, *Lawley Road and Other Stories*.

for taking such an uncompromising stance on a subject which it seems to have thought frivolous.[95]

In tandem with these popular demands to remember the mutiny in India by subverting or removing British mutiny monuments, the first proposals to formally commemorate the mutiny through monumentalisation also arose in various quarters. Once again, the central Indian Government in general and Nehru in particular were not in favour of the proposals and attempted to block their realisation. However, in the end, several proposals did indeed come to fruition including the erection of a 25-foot equestrian statue dedicated to Rani Lakshmibai, constructed close to the National Institute of Physical Education in Gwalior which was also named after the rebel leader.[96] Of rather more concern to Nehru were proposals made by the Government of West Bengal to likewise commemorate Mangal Pandey by building a monument in Barrackpore. Whilst historians remain divided on the significance of Mangal Pandey's actions in terms of the broader uprising, he was none-the-less seen by many to have fired the shot which catalysed the rebellion.[97] At least following the publication of Savarkar's work on 1857 in which Mangal Pandey's contributions were eulogised, the rebel had begun to evolve into an important national hero and was accorded the double honour of not only firing the first shot of the rebellion but also, following his execution, of being the first martyr of the independence movement.[98] The Government of West Bengal seems to have seen it as appropriate to take the opportunity of the centenary of the uprising to commemorate the hero in Barrackpore and accordingly applied to the Defence Ministry for a plot of land on which to construct a suitable commemorative structure.

The proposal was greeted with much concern and some alarm by both the Defence Ministry and other senior members of the government. Nehru, in response to the proposal, made his own feelings clear on the subject, writing to Bidan Chandra Roy, the Chief Minister of West Bengal, to inform him that:

I rather doubt if it will be proper or advisable to use a piece of land belonging to our Defence establishments for this purpose. Whatever we may think of Mangal Pandey's act, it is not a good example to set to the men in our Army, and to have this memorial in land appertaining to the Army would be to draw very particular attention to this. Personally, I do not think an ornate memorial is necessary for this purpose. Perhaps, a plaque

---

[95] See, for example, the cartoon by K. A. Sarkar published in *Shankar's Weekly*, K. Shankar Pillai, *Shankar's Weekly Volume 10, May–November 1957* (New Delhi: Indraprastha Press, 1957).

[96] For more details on the construction of a monument at Poona dedicated to Rani Lakshmibai, see Anon, 'Memorial in Poona: Rani of Jhansi Statue', *The Times of India*, 24 July 1857, p. 3; Anon, 'President Unveils Statue of Rani Laxmibai', *The Times of India*, 19 June 1958, p. 1.

[97] Cf. Mukherjee, *Mangal Pandey*; Misra, *Mangal Pandey*; Wagner, *The Great Fear of 1857*.

[98] Savarkar, *Indian War of Independence, 1857*.

somewhere will be enough. But, if you want some kind of a memorial, I would suggest that it should be put up somewhere else, and not on land belonging to our military.[99]

Ultimately, the monument championed by the Government of West Bengal and intended for Barrackpore was realised, much against Nehru's wishes, with construction beginning in the centenary year. However, if the monument dedicated to Mangal Pandey raised concerns within the central government, it was those acts of commemoration proposed by the Government of Uttar Pradesh that proved to be the most contentious among the remaining British community within the state. Announcing on the ninety-ninth anniversary of the conflict that a large sum of money was to be made available for the erection of monuments in a number of locations associated with 1857 to be unveiled at the conflict's centenary, the local government stressed both a desire and a willingness to find meaning in the memory of 1857. One of the grandest of these monuments was erected in Lucknow near to the Residency and comprised a tall tower on the banks of the River Gomti dedicated to all those who fought for freedom in 1857.

However, the most provocative monument to a rebel leader was reserved for Cawnpore. As High Commissioner Malcolm Macdonald correctly assessed, 'Memories of events there during 1857 were particularly bitter and controversial, and it seemed by no means unlikely that there would be celebrations of a kind wounding to British sentiment'.[100] The monument planned for Cawnpore took the form of a bust depicting Tantia Tope to be sited on the former location of Marochetti's Angel of the Resurrection and for the gardens as a whole to be renamed after Nana Sahib. Predictably enough, news of this decision was not greeted with any enthusiasm among the British community in Uttar Pradesh and, as John Christie of the Citizens Association, and a director of the BIC, pointed out to Sir Gilbert Laithwaite, 'without being particularly stuffy about such things, no one can feel happy about a statue to the Nana Sahib's Chief Military Advisor on that particular spot'.[101]

The situation found an uneasy compromise after several members of the British community in Cawnpore appealed to the District Collector and pointed out that under the terms of the transfer of the gardens to the municipality, it was strictly required that no building was to be constructed on the former site

[99] Jawaharlal Nehru to Bidan Chandra Roy, 3 August 1957, reproduced in *Selected Works of Jawaharlal Nehru Second Series,* Vol. 39, 1 August–31 October 1957, H. Y. Sharada Prasad, A. K. Damodaran and Mushirul Hasan (eds.) (New Delhi: Oxford University Press, 2007), pp. 165–66, pp. 165–66.

[100] Malcolm Macdonald to Rt. Hon. The Earl of Home, Secretary of State CRO, 22 June 1957, 'Celebrations of Indian Mutiny Centenary in 1957', TNA, DO 35/9144.

[101] W. H. J. Christie, President designate UK, Citizens Association, India, to Sir Gilbert Laithwaite, 19 December 1956, 'Celebrations of Indian Mutiny Centenary in 1957', TNA, DO 35/9144.

Figure 6.6 Bust of Tantia Tope in Nana Rao Park. Photograph by the author, 2012.

of the well.[102] Accordingly, the monument's plinth, which had already been put in situ, was removed to an alternative location within the gardens from where Tantia Tope to this day looks out over the former site of the well which, though no longer present, is still marked by an indentation in the landscape conspicuous to anyone who knows the history of the park.

The appearance of Tantia Tope in what was no longer the Memorial Gardens, but Nana Rao Park, underlines the failure of the British community to facilitate forgetting. Just as we noted earlier in the chapter how Menzies in cooperation with the BGMS attempted to remove 1857 from the cultural field of Cawnpore when they removed the Angel of the Resurrection, it is clear that grass did not grow over the battlefield with the removal of the scaffold, to the contrary, the scaffold was replaced and memory lived on.

With the Cawnpore Well rededicated in honour of the principal Indian heroes associated with the uprising in the city, the attention of many now swung to the Lucknow Residency and the Delhi Ridge. Among the most august of the voices calling for the sacred sites to be claimed in the name of Indian nationalism belonged to Major-General Enaith Habibullah, founder commandant of the National Defence Academy who had been born in Lucknow in 1917. Writing to the ASI in 1963, Habibullah requested that the monuments in Lucknow, given their association with 'the "1857 Upserge" [sic] could be kept

---

[102] Malcolm Macdonald to Rt. Hon. The Earl of Home, Secretary of State CRO, 22 June 1957, 'Celebrations of Indian Mutiny Centenary in 1957', TNA, DO 35/9144.

to a more fitting standard'.[103] Similarly, B. N. Chaubey in 1970 wrote to the ASI as he felt it necessary to point out the 'woeful state of the "Residency Garden", Lucknow, in every respect, whether it is the maintenance of the garden-lawns, flowerbeds or the roads in these premises'.[104] As these letters suggest, for many local residents of Lucknow, the Residency was no longer seen as a monument of British endurance, sacrifice, and ultimate victory against which an alternative counter-memory could be fashioned, rather it was being seen as itself a direct space of memory connected to the First War of Indian Independence.

This redefinition and appropriation of the site was completed in 1972 to celebrate the Silver Jubilee of Independence when a grand pageant was organised on 30 June, the sixty-fifth anniversary of the Battle of Chinhut and the start of the siege. Beginning with a large assembly around Sikander Bagh which, in 1857, had witnessed fierce fighting from rebels who courageously held the position to the last man, the crowd, led by Nana Sahib's grandson, began their progress towards the Residency after observing a two-minute silence to commemorate all those who died laying siege to the British, followed by a rendition of the national anthem played by a military band.[105] It may well be said that this 'storming of the Residency' not only helped mark the anniversary but further enacted the appropriation of the site as a memorial space dedicated to the freedom struggle. Indeed, as B. N. Chaubey reported to the ASI, the occasion was a grand one with all those who addressed the audience on the occasion 'emphasising the sanctity of these premises, which was declared to be saturated with the blood of the Indian Martyrs, who had thus laid the First Foundation of the Freedom Fight, discounting the erstwhile belief that it was reminiscent of British Glory'.[106]

Similarly in Delhi, the remaining British-built monuments became the subject of great debate as the silver anniversary of independence approached. As regards the Mutiny Memorial located on the Ridge, the Chief Executive of the Delhi Municipal Council had proposed that the monument should either be demolished or at least rededicated by removing the plaques recording the original citation and replacing these with new plaques celebrating the independence struggle in 1857. Similarly, regarding the Kashmiri Gate, Banarsi Dass Garg of the Delhi Municipal Corporation wrote to the ASI to bitterly complain against the existence of the plaque erected under Napier's orders in

[103] Major-General Enaith Habibullah to Director ASI, 1968, NAI, 3/2/UP/10/1968/M.
[104] B. N. Chaubey to the Director General ASI, NAI, ASI/HQ/Monuments/ 22/20/70-M/1970.
[105] Anon, 'Residency Stormed', *Pioneer Lucknow*, 1 July 1972; Anon, 'Lucknow Pageant', Hindu Times, 21 July 1972. Newspaper clippings enclosed with B. N. Chaubey to the Director General ASI, 17 August 1972, 'Improvements of Lucknow residency premises suggestion by B. N. Chaubey', NAI, ASI/HQ/Monuments/26/97/72-M.
[106] Ibid.

1876 giving the details of how the gate was stormed in 1857. Claiming that 'existence of such monuments in the Silver Jubilee year of Freedom seems improper', Garg suggested that the memorial 'be removed to some museum and replaced (if necessary) by one citing the tales of those freedom fighters who bravely encountered the English'.[107]

The ASI, for their part, opposed on principle any alteration to nationally protected monuments and was fully supported by Prime Minister Indira Gandhi who, two years after the death of her father in 1964, had taken control of the Congress Party and had recently been returned to power in the 1971 general elections. Though the ASI and the central government therefore opposed any alteration to the mutiny monument, both accepted that supplementary inscriptions 'giving the nationalist point of view' could be installed. Accordingly, new plaques and tablets were erected at each site in 1972 giving an alternative history of the event. In the case of the Mutiny Memorial, the site was officially renamed Ajitgarh on Independence Day and, at a ceremony hosted some weeks later and presided over by the Lt.-Governor of Delhi, Baleshwar Prasad, a new tablet was unveiled giving its readers a brief history of the monument before informing them that the monument was now considered 'a memorial for those martyrs who rose and fought against the British during 1857 A.D.' and not the British forces who ultimately succeeded in retaking the city.[108]

With the Cawnpore Well, Lucknow Residency, and Delhi Ridge converted from emblems of empire into nationalist iconography, it is clear that by India's Silver Jubilee in 1972 the events of 1857 had been fully incorporated into the nation's story. Widely celebrated as India's First War of Independence, the conflict and its principal heroes were firmly rooted in the public's consciousness, even if only reluctantly assimilated into the central government's official memory of the freedom struggle. However, at the exact same time that the appropriation of these sacred sites of empire reflected the symbolic incorporation of 1857 into official nationalist discourse in India, the British Government was continuing to reject the event as a defining moment in their own history of empire. With Britain locked in what now appeared a precipitous period of decline as it faced a series of financial, political, and military setbacks in the late 1950s and 1960s

---

[107] Banarsi Dass Garg to Shrimati D. Mitre, Director (Monuments) ASI, 6 September 1972, 'removal of Memorial stone slab affixed on Kashmiri Gate Delhi', NAI, ASI/HQ/Monuments/26/112/1972/M.

[108] Written on sign erected at Ajitghar. See also Anon, 'Monument Renamed', *The Times of India*, 29 August 1972, p. 4. For a further analysis of the transformation of the Kashmiri Gate, see Mrinalini Rajagopalan, 'From Colonial Memorial to National Monument: The Case of the Kashmiri Gate, Delhi' in Mrinalini Rajagopalan and Madhuri Desai (eds.), *Colonial Frames, Nationalist Histories: Imperial Legacies, Architecture and Modernity*, (Farnham: Ashgate, 2012), pp. 73–101.

which saw its post-war colonial aspirations rapidly unravel, the government was forced to seriously reappraise Britain's place in the new world order and shift attention towards its position in Europe; a goal which was significantly achieved by the European Communities Act of 1972, which saw Britain join the EEC at the start of the following year. With Britain losing the last real vestiges of its empire by the end of the 1960s, and forced to come to terms with its radically diminished place on the world stage, many looked upon the nation's colonial legacy with renewed pride and as a potentially powerful way of raising Britain's prestige and contemporary relevance during a period of decline.

Accordingly, when the BBC aired a series of documentaries designed to introduce the history of empire to a new generation during the twenty-fifth anniversary of Indian independence, a great many interested parties tuned in enthusiastically. The subjects covered in the documentary varied greatly, but few generated as much discussion as an episode entitled 'Remember Cawnpore!'. Indeed, following the broadcast of this episode, a flood of letters was received by a number of newspapers, variously complaining that the programme needlessly focused upon the massacre and the British retaliation, when what *should* be remembered is not the bloodshed, but the great modernisation of India through Empire and the many other benefits of colonialism. Such was the public reaction to the television programme that it sparked a debate in the House of Lords introduced by Lord Ferrier:

Having served and worked for many years in India, as did my father before me … I felt that I owed it to my forebears … to monitor these Indian programmes … The first, entitled 'Remember Cawnpore', caused me to address a letter to the editor of The Times … in protest at such macabre scenes.… I cannot recall any emphasis on the fact that long before the mutiny Britain had declared her intention to enable the Indians to govern themselves. There was no mention of great names such as Macauley, John Lawrence, John Nicholson, Dalhousie, Cornwallis…[109]

This sentiment was reflected throughout the debate by almost all who spoke, thus Lord Milverton reminded the House 'one must not forget that the British Empire is at an end, and the question arises: would one, from this series, get any conception of what the Empire meant, and still means, in the world – in other words, the good which it has done and which still remains?'[110] and Lord Barnby claimed that '[i]n the series there was much talk of bloodshed and disorder, but very little relating to praise about what Britain had done.… Let us hope that some future producer will produce another series that will show what Britain did in the development of her Empire for the benefit of humanity'.[111] Essentially, this calls for a sanitisation of Empire; the mutiny is not worth

---

[109] HL Deb, 6 July 1972, vol. 332, cc.1521.   [110] HL Deb, 6 July 1972, vol. 332, cc.1538.
[111] HL Deb, 6 July 1972, vol. 332, cc.1533.

remembering because what should be remembered is the good that the Empire achieved, not what Barnby calls the 'bloodshed and disorder' which may at times have accompanied these benefits. What seems to have motivated Lord Ferrier is not the fact that the episode 'Remember Cawnpore!' was inaccurate, or produced a false or one-sided account of the events, but rather that the event itself was not worthy of memory.

This official attitude towards remembering empire continues to predominate up to the current day and was in evidence again, for example, in 2007 when the 150th anniversary of the conflict passed with little popular attention and no official acts of commemoration.[112] Indeed, the great mutiny heroes whose names were once catchwords for the indomitable spirit of empire have long been forgotten, and those who pass by the grave of Sir James Outram located in the nave of Westminster Abbey, the memorial to Lord Clyde in Waterloo Place, or the statue of Sir Henry Havelock staring out towards Admiralty Arch from its south-facing plinth in Trafalgar Square fail to remember the men whose memory were once thought important enough to etch into the heart of empire. Indeed, then mayor of London, Ken Livingston, was no doubt correct in the year 2000 when he highlighted the dismal obscurity into which such men have sunk when, speaking specifically about the statue of Henry Havelock, he claimed that it represented a man about whom 'not one person in 10,000 going through Trafalgar Square knows any details'.[113] In India, on the other hand, the significance of remembering 1857 has only grown since 1972 and today the conflict is a defining feature of empire and the subject of enormous commemorative attention. As will be explored in Chapter 7, however, this should not be taken as evidence that the struggle for meaning, memory and the right to narrate, which has characterised commemoration over the past 160 years has finally come to an end.

---

[112] This may be seen as a component of the broader process discussed in Gilroy, *Postcolonial Melancholia*.

[113] Ken Livingston quoted in Paul Kelso, 'Mayor Attacks Generals in Battle of Trafalgar Square', *The Guardian*, 20 October 2000, p. 3.

7 Celebrating the First War of Independence Today
Caste, Gender, and Religion

When traveling through much of north India today, it is hard not to be astonished by the sheer number of statues dedicated to the principal Indian heroes of 1857. Proudly occupying conspicuous locations, and almost permanently festooned with fresh garlands, these memorials range from modest and often crudely produced busts standing in rural villages to grandiose statues located in major cities. If the memories of 1857 are therefore spatially mapped onto the landscape of contemporary India, then they also occupy a significant temporal place on the national calendar. Though 10 May remains a focal point for various national, regional, and local organisations which choose the anniversary of the uprising in Meerut as a suitable date for arranging remembrance ceremonies, other events associated with the conflict such as the Battle of Chinhut, the birth of Rani Lakshmibai, and the execution of Mangal Pandey are also formally remembered with acts of commemoration.

Whilst this uninhibited national outpouring underscores the significance of remembering 1857 in twenty-first-century India, this chapter will show that this does not indicate that the struggle for meaning, memory, and the right to narrate that characterised commemoration over the preceding century and a half in India has finally drawn to a close and been replaced by a national consensus. Based on participant observation at memorial ceremonies held by a range of organisations to mark the 160th anniversary of 1857 in 2017–18, along with semi-structured interviews with participants and organisers at these events, this chapter will show that what it means to remember the conflict remains as contingent and contested today as it has been at any point in the past.[1] Thus, whilst all those involved in the commemoration of the First War of Independence agree that they are coming together to mark a pivotal moment in the history of Indian Independence which is deserving of enthusiastic celebration in the present, this chapter

---

[1] Interviews, when possible and preferable, conducted in English by author or else in Hindi with the aid of my interpreter, Pankaj Singh. Field recordings of interviews and speeches, as well as leaflets and other documents collected during such events, were subsequently translated by Harpreet Singh.

will show that their reasons for doing so vary widely and are, in fact, often diametrically opposed. Reflecting the contemporary aspirations of groups organised around very different identity positions, the respective practices of commemoration organised by each group to celebrate the First War of Independence are intimately bound up with specific conceptions of caste, class, gender, and religion.

In this regard, contemporary commemoration of 1857 once again tells us more about the present than it does about the past and may be used as a prism through which to understand the rise of identity politics in India which from the onset of the post-Congress polity has come to characterise the political landscape of India. As was noted in Chapter 6, the first two decades that followed formal independence was a period of unrivalled dominance for the Congress Party owing, in large measure, to its strong identification with the independence movement.[2] From the 1970s onwards, however, the party entered a period of decline that would ultimately lead to the end of the one-party dominant system which characterised Indian politics until the 1990s.[3] From this point onwards, a new political system which is characterised by the formation of often unstable coalitions between a range of parties began to arise and is particularly marked by the formation of national and regional parties which increasingly mobilise the electorate based on a plethora of often intersecting identity positions including class, caste, religion, ethnicity, gender, and even language.[4] Though the interactions between these overlapping social identities have made themselves known in myriad ways over the past three decades, the political reverberations caused by 'Mandal and Mandir' have made caste and religion the two categories to most fundamentally reorient the sociopolitical landscape over this period.

'Mandal' as a term is today frequently used to refer to the rise of the Other Backward Classes (OBC) self-assertion movement and stems from the popular name of the Second Backward Classes Commission which was chaired by B. P. Mandal. Reporting in 1980, the 'Mandal Commission' had made the politically contentious recommendation that OBCs be granted 27 per cent reservations in both public sector employment and higher education. Although the proposal was greeted with alarm by members of higher caste groups who were immediately opposed to the scheme on the grounds that it adversely affected their own aspirations, and with at least initial ambivalence from many Dalit

---

[2] The so-called 'Congress System'. See Kothari, 'The Congress "System" in India', pp. 1161–73.
[3] Candland, 'Congress Decline and Party Pluralism in India', pp. 19–35.
[4] For an interesting study concerning the period of intense political instability that resulted in three general elections being held in as many years at the end of the twentieth century, see Singh and Saxena, *India at the Polls*.

groups who feared that there might be negative consequences for their own already existing quotas, the proposals were duly implemented in 1990 by V. P. Singh's coalition government resulting in the greater politicisation of caste and an attendant transformation of national and regional politics along this cleavage.[5]

It is with this background that 'Mandir' should be understood. Translating literally as 'Temple', 'Mandir' refers most directly to the ongoing campaign to build a Hindu temple dedicated to Lord Ram on the site of a Muslim mosque called the Babri Masjid in Ayodhya, Uttar Pradesh. Infamously, this campaign took on national, and even international significance when, in 1992, up to 150,000 Hindu activists launched an attack on the mosque. Wielding a variety of implements including hammers and pickaxes, the mob succeeded in demolishing the Babri Masjid, and instigating a wave of communal riots across the country which would ultimately result in more than 2,000 deaths.[6] Thus, whilst Mandal resulted in intra-Hindu conflict drawn up on caste lines, Mandir unified Hinduism by driving inter-religious conflict. However, whether emphasising caste or religious difference, 'Mandal and Mandir' has helped instigate a period of identity politics since the early 1990s, with consequences which are still unfolding in the present.

With the decline of the Congress Party accompanied by the politicisation of identity came in new ways of remembering the past. As was explored in Chapter 6, the two decades of Congress dominance which followed formal independence in 1947 was supported in large measure by an official memory of the independence movement which emphasised Congress-led non-violent resistance to colonial rule and therefore presented the party as the natural successor to the British.[7] As the legitimacy of Congress rule began to wane, however, alternative memories began to bubble to the surface and a plethora of previously marginalised events and individuals were added to the official pantheon by a diverse range of grassroots activists who were eagerly supported in their endeavours by various political actors. Accordingly, the 1980s and 1990s witnessed the re-emergence of various events 'forgotten' by the Congress Party's licensed history of the freedom struggle, such as the RIN Mutiny of 1946 and the Chauri Chaura Riots of 1922, with each becoming the subject of various national and regional commemoration events over this period resulting, most enduringly and conspicuously, in the erection of monuments and

---

[5] For an excellent study that situates the impact of 'Mandal' within a longer story of the lower caste movement in North Indian politics, see Jaffrelot, *India's Silent Revolution*.
[6] For an illuminating collection of documents charting the Babri Masjid issue, see Noorani, *The Babri Masjid Question 1528–2003*.
[7] Amin, *Event, Metaphor, Memory*.

memorials dedicated to these events and their principal actors.[8] Whilst such previously maligned events have today been incorporated into the national story, however, it is the First War of Independence, which has become the subject of the most intense acts of commemoration in keeping with its status as a cultural lodestone in contemporary India. As suggested earlier, however, this clamour for commemoration should not be read as an indication of a consolidated and unified history. On the contrary, when these disparate voices are disentangled, it becomes clear that contemporary commemoration of 1857 reflects the divergent identities, values, beliefs, and conceptions of self and society, which lie behind the contested nature of the contemporary Indian polity. When carefully investigated, therefore, these commemoration ceremonies reveal the fractured nature of contemporary Indian society, at the same time as uncovering the fractured nature of contemporary Indian memory.

2017 and the Politics of Commemoration: Identity, Aspiration, and Assertion

The 160th anniversary of the First War of Independence was greeted by a tremendous outpouring of commemorative activities arranged by a diverse selection of organisations and individuals and hosted in various locations across India. These commemorative activities took various forms including, but not limited to, the construction of new monuments such as that dedicated to Jhalkaribai sited in Bhopal, and unveiled by the President of India, Ram Nath Kovind; the production of a major film entitled *Manikarnika: The Queen of Jhansi* written by K. V. Vijayendra Prasad, and starring Bollywood legend, Kangana Ranaut; and dozens of smaller events and activities hosted by various groups in locations as disparate as Mumbai, Bikaner, and Bihar.[9]

In investigating the anniversary, however, this chapter will concentrate on commemorative activities that took place in the north Indian state of Uttar Pradesh (UP). The reasons for doing so are twofold. First, as the state which witnessed the greatest proportion of the fighting in 1857, it is unsurprising that

---

[8] In the case of the 'RIN Mutiny', the event was honoured at a ceremony in August 1997 to mark the fiftieth anniversary of independence during which the mutiny was celebrated for its role in securing freedom and officially renamed 'The Naval Uprising of 1946'. Ships were named after prominent leaders of the uprising and a monument located in south Mumbai opposite the Taj Wellington Mews was unveiled on Navy Day 2001, and dedicated to all those who participated in the uprising. Today, the event is regularly the subject of various acts of commemoration.

[9] In Mumbai, a play dedicated to the memory of Jhalkaribai written by theatre practitioner and author, Neha Singh, was performed. In Bikaner, the Sakdrupi Brahmin Bondu Charitable Trust hosted a commemoration ceremony in honour of Mangal Pandey. In Bihar, there was a three-day festival named Veer Kunwar Singh Vijayotsav.

UP is also the state which witnessed the greatest number of commemoration ceremonies held to mark the anniversary in 2017–18. Accordingly, a focus on commemoration within the state gives us access to a large and diverse array of events to consider and analyse.

Second, UP is often referred to as 'a microcosm of the Indian nation' with many of the most prevalent sociopolitical issues which dominate the national scene also characterising the state.[10] Indeed, this is especially true of Hindu nationalism, and the politicisation of caste, which have each gained momentum in UP since the 1980s and have helped radically transform the political landscape since the Congress Party lost power at both the national and state levels following the general elections of 1989. From this point onwards, the state has witnessed the rise of the Bahujan Samaj Party (BSP) as a tool for Dalit emancipation, and the Samajwadi Party (SP) as a vehicle of OBC assertion, with each party enjoying significant electoral success over the past three decades. Equally, at least since the demolition of the Babri Masjid, itself located in Faizabad District of UP, the state has come to be seen as a centre of Hindu nationalism. Indeed, the right-wing Bharatiya Janata Party (BJP) has also experienced significant success in the state including the 2014 General Elections, and the 2017 Legislative Assembly Elections, as well as during the subsequent 2019 General Elections. With this in mind, therefore, focusing on UP will enable us to give a nuanced treatment of the local and specific issues which provide the immediate background to those practices of commemoration held within the state, whilst at the same time allowing us to draw broader conclusions with relevance to the nation as a whole.

In beginning to consider what commemoration can tell us about India today, this chapter will start by focusing on acts of memorialisation dedicated to the Indian hero Uda Devi (Pasi). Investigating the disparate commemorative activities conducted by various grassroots and political organisations in UP to honour the memory of the revered freedom fighter, this section will use the commemoration of Uda Devi as a device to better understand the intersecting politics of caste, religion, and gender in contemporary India.

Dalit Assertion and Electoral Strategy:
The Emergence of Uda Devi (Pasi)

Speaking at a ceremony to honour the 160th anniversary of Uda Devi's death, Mahesh Prasad, principal organiser of the event and president of a local organisation dedicated to uplifting the Pasi caste, began by outlining

---

[10] Jeffery and Lerche, *Social and Political Change in Uttar Pradesh*, p. 17; see also Govinda, 'On Whose Behalf? Women's Activism and Identity Politics in Uttar Pradesh', pp. 165–87, p. 165.

the great freedom fighter's glorious deeds which had won her eternal fame in 1857.[11] Addressing about eighty people who had assembled for the occasion around a permanent memorial dedicated to Uda Devi in Hargaon, a small town located in the Sitapur district of UP, Mahesh Prasad recounted what little is known about the heroine by first commenting that she had been the wife of Makka Pasi, a renowned commander of Begum Hazrat Mahal's army which had taken control of the region following the uprising of 1857. Commensurate with her husband's rank in the military, Uda Devi was herself responsible for commanding the 'women's brigade', which not only took an active role in armed combat but was also charged with caring for the wounded during and after engagements with the enemy. It was whilst performing the latter of these duties, in the aftermath of the Battle of Chinhut, that Uda Devi uncovered the lifeless body of her husband who had fallen in the hour of victory. Going on to describe the scene, Mahesh Prasand explained how Uda Devi broke down in 'mournful tears' whilst cradling her husband's dead body, prompting:

Begum Hazrat Mahal to console Uda Devi Pasi by telling her not to be disheartened because one lion has fallen. Instead understand that the enemy has killed one person, and in return you should kill thousands. This would be Uda Devi's revenge. Hearing this, Uda Devi Pasi plotted her revenge until the opportunity presented itself during the battle of Sikander Bagh. Uda Devi Pasi dressed as a man, and climbed a peepal tree under which some earthen water pots were kept. When the British soldiers were exhausted, they went there to quench their thirst. So, this way, one by one, she shot 36 soldiers. Later Captain Wallace and Captain Dawson approached the tree and saw the dead bodies of the 36 soldiers. They looked up and caught the glimpse of a shadow. They drew back and ordered fire at the tree. On doing so, a corpse fell down and they discovered that it was not a man but a woman. Captain Dawson removed his hat and saluted saying that had he known that it was a woman he would not have fired even at the expense of his own life.[12]

This remarkable story of Uda Devi's courage, cunning, and ultimate sacrifice was rehearsed in numerous commemorative ceremonies organised by members of the Pasi caste during the 160th anniversary of 1857, with the largest held in the Lucknow Division of UP where the Pasi community is

---

[11] Mahesh Prasand is the president of a local organisation dedicated to elevating the Pasi Caste. The organisation is called the *Maharaja Chita Pasi Sevaa Sansathan* (Maharaja Chita Pasi Service Organisation).

[12] Mahesh Prasand (President of the Maharaja Chita Pasi Sevaa Sansathan), speaking at a commemoration ceremony in honour of Uda Devi in Hargaon, Sitapur district, UP, 18 January 2018. The most common narrative deviations, as the story was told to me by different people in different locals, include the number of British soldiers killed, which sometimes goes into the hundreds or even thousands, and the device used by Uda Devi which is sometimes said to be a bow and arrow, at other times explosives, and occasionally poison which she is said to have added to the drinking water before hiding in the tree to witness the result.

demographically dominant, even if they remain structurally oppressed owing to their position at the bottom of the Hindu caste hierarchy. A Dalit caste, whose members have traditionally been employed as pig herders, toddy tappers, and *chowkidars*, the Pasi community count Uda Devi among the greatest of their caste icons, with many members travelling large distances from across north India to pay their respects to the great heroine each year. Whilst Uda Devi's memory is emphatically celebrated today, however, this was not the case until as recently as the 1970s, when a number of popular folktales were first recorded among the Pasi community eulogising their caste's contribution to the rebellion of 1857.[13] Arising concurrently with the renovation and rededication of the Lucknow Residency, these folktales emerged at a time and place in which the events of 1857 were enjoying a renaissance within popular memory. No less significantly, they developed alongside other popular calls for the commemoration of hitherto neglected heroes of 1857, including an otherwise anonymous female sniper whose impressive marksmanship at Sikander Bagh was recorded by several contemporary British writers, and which marked her out for special attention.[14] It was, nonetheless, left to Dauji Gupta, the then Mayor of Lucknow, and president of the 1857 Freedom Struggle Festival, which organised the 1972 pageant discussed in Chapter 6, to connect the story of a great female Pasi warrior with that of the anonymous woman sniper, and even achieve the yet more remarkable feat of genealogy in tracing her lineage to a Pasi family which fortuitously continued to live in the Lucknow region of UP.[15]

   If the (re)emergence of Uda Devi Pasi was therefore highly contingent on the various chance factors outlined previously, then it should also be understood in relation to a growing wave of Dalit assertion which was marked, most conspicuously, by the founding of the Dalit Panthers in the western Indian state of Maharashtra.[16] Frustrated by the apparent failure of the Congress Party to sufficiently represent the interests of Dalits, coupled with popular discontentment in the then recently formed Ambedkarite Republican Party of India which, following moderate success in the mid-1960s had been beset by factionalism, the Dalit Panthers were the most influential among a plethora of grassroots

---

[13] Narayan, *Women Heroes and Dalit Assertion in North India*, p. 142.

[14] For example, Major-General Enaith Habibillah, who had only recently been elected to the Uttar Pradesh Legislative Assembly, had expressed this view in 1970. See Major-General Enaith Habibullah to Dr. V. K. R. V. Rao, 20 June 1970, NAI, ASI/18/3/2/70-M.

[15] Indeed, her own great-great-great-granddaughter, Rajeshwari Devi, who now takes on the responsibility of organising an annual commemoration ceremony on the very site where her ancestor is said to have died, freely admits that she, like her parents and grandparents before her, was largely ignorant of her ancestor's glorious story until Dauji Gupta, then mayor of Lucknow and president of the 1857 Freedom Struggle Festival, informed them about it in 1972. Rajeshwari Devi, interviewed in Lucknow, 26 February 2018.

[16] For the earlier history of the Dalit movement in colonial India, see Omvedt, *Dalits and the Democratic Revolution*.

organisations and associations which began to emerge in this period, and which concentrated their efforts on highlighting caste oppression, raising Dalit consciousness, and instilling a sense of pride, worth, and self-confidence among the lowest caste groups in India.[17] With this emphasis on encouraging caste pride came new ways of remembering the past, during which Dalit castes imagined, uncovered, and created their own histories and with them, new and emerging sociopolitical identities for use in the present. Whilst these histories reached back into the distant past with, for example, particular emphasis placed on stories rooted in antiquity as well as the glorious exploits of various medieval Dalit kings, 1857 also became a popular historical moment in which it was possible to discover and recover a range of Dalit heroes.[18]

Accordingly, the 1960s and 1970s appear to be a wellspring for Dalit freedom fighters during which, in 1964 for example, the earliest known reference to Jhalkaribai Kori of Jhansi can be found.[19] A member of the Kori caste, and a trusted advisor to Rani Lakshmibai, Jhalkaribai Kori is said to have volunteered to dress as the Rani and impersonate her in battle in order to create a diversion, which would allow the real Rani to escape the Jhansi Fort and reorganise her army.[20] The emergence of Uda Devi as an important signifier denoting nodal motifs of a newly emboldened Pasi identity which emphasised the caste's natural courage, martial prowess, and self-dignity, therefore appears to be a product of this period of Dalit assertion.

Whilst the story of Uda Devi was initially confined to the Pasi community concentrated in the Lucknow region of UP, the story took on state-wide significance following the formation of the BSP in 1984. Established by the veteran Dalit activist, Kanshi Ram, as a party to unite and champion the causes of all those occupying the lowest levels in the traditional Hindu social system, the BSP reached out to many historically oppressed groups including the members of Dalit castes, many of whom proved especially attracted to the party's message.[21] As part of their effort to mobilise the support of the various Dalit castes who, together, make up over 20 per cent of the population of UP, the BSP adopted a tactic of appropriating the numerous low caste heroes who had risen to prominence during the wave of Dalit assertion which characterised the 1960s and 1970s. With specific relevance to the demographically significant

---

[17] Omvedt, *Reinventing Revolution*, see Chapter 3, 'The Anticaste Movement', pp. 47–75.

[18] Narayan, *The Making of the Dalit Public in North India, Uttar Pradesh 1950-Present*; Narayan, *Women Heroes and Dalit Assertion*.

[19] Narayan, *Making of the Dalit Public*, p. 63.

[20] As with Uda Devi, and other Dalit heroes of 1857, the exact story of Jhalkaribai varies considerably from region to region and from person to person with some narratives going so far as to claim that Rani Lakshmibai was too scared to fight the British from the start and so Jhalkaribai took her place and led the army throughout the conflict, albeit in the Rani's name.

[21] For more on Kanshi Ram, see Narayan, *Kanshiram*.

Pasi caste, which is the second largest Scheduled Caste state-wide, Uda Devi
Pasi proved to be of special significance. Along with other popular Pasi heroes
such as the supposed medieval Pasi king, Maharaja Bijli Pasi, Uda Devi Pasi
became the subject of numerous statues and attendant commemoration ceremonies organised by the BSP from the late 1980s onwards, resulting in the
female warrior becoming a popular and well-known historical figure beyond
the Pasi caste.[22]

Though the BSP initially utilised caste heroes such as Uda Devi Pasi to
mobilise the members of the respective castes from which they were drawn,
from the 1990s onwards, the party has consolidated them into a broader, unified Dalit identity. This amalgamation of individual castes into a unified Dalit
identity is most clearly demonstrated in the subtle shifts in the identification of individual caste idols. Thus, whilst the names of Uda Devi Pasi, and
Jhalkaribai Kori, for example, emphasised the separate caste identities from
which these heroes originally hailed, the BSP has elected to celebrate 'Uda
Devi', and 'Jhalkaribai' who, with their names stripped of caste identity and
hence markers of difference, can all the more readily be incorporated into the
unified Dalit identity which underpins the BSP's central ideology and electoral strategy.[23] Further, with the rise of Mayawati as a central spokeswoman
within the BSP during the 1990s, eventually resulting in her serving four separate terms as Chief Minister of UP, as well as assuming formal leadership of
the party in 2003, female Dalit heroes have taken on yet more significance
and have become ever more closely associated with the BSP in general, and
Mayawati in particular, who is symbolically positioned so as to appear to rank
among their number, and thus share in the same reverence which is directed
towards members of this sacred Dalit pantheon.

If these caste idols have been appropriated by the BSP in an attempt to
mobilise support for the party, however, then they have also been co-opted into
the electoral strategy of other political parties in UP; most notably the BJP.
Though the BJP has tended to focus its efforts on different idols to those celebrated by the BSP such as the eleventh-century Pasi king, Maharaja Suheldev,
who is presented by the party as a Hindu martyr who died nobly whilst fighting Muslim invaders, the BJP has also used the commemoration of Uda Devi
to help mobilise the Pasi community within the state, resulting in the female
warrior gaining yet more institutional support and greater mainstream acceptance.[24] Indeed, it was the BJP's Chief Minister, Yogi Adityanath who, during
the celebrations of the 160th anniversary, announced that hitherto neglected
Pasi icons including Uda Devi would be officially inducted into the school

---

[22] Ibid.
[23] Narayan, *Women Heroes and Dalit Assertion*, pp. 86–87.
[24] Narayan, *Fascinating Hindutva*, pp. 85–89.

curriculum and accorded a central place within future editions of school text-books.[25] Whilst the BSP identifies Uda Devi as first and foremost a Dalit hero in the practices of commemoration which they organise, in keeping with its own ideology and electoral strategy, the BJP identifies Uda Devi as a national hero who fought in defence of her religion and culture against British colonialism and who stands in a long line of courageous Pasi icons who have distinguished themselves by resisting foreign invaders of all stripes.

With both the BJP and the BSP vying for the sizeable Pasi vote in the run up to the 2019 General Elections, Uda Devi was therefore deployed by both parties in an attempt to mobilise the Pasi community in their favour. Although the BSP repeatedly used Uda Devi as an important symbol within their campaign strategy, it was the BJP who ultimately went the furthest in using Uda Devi's memory in an effort to secure the Pasi vote when, days after Narendra Modi released a postage stamp honouring Suheldev, the BJP championed a proposal to construct a 100-foot statue of Uda Devi in UP.[26]

Grassroots Pasi Activism and What It Means to Commemorate Uda Devi

As has been explored previously, following the emergence of Uda Devi as an icon in the early 1970s, her commemoration has not infrequently been the result of crass electoral strategy employed by different political elements vying for the support of a significant demographic in central UP; a fact readily seen, for example, in the build-up to the 2019 General Election. If we turn away from these largely cynical attempts to attract votes and secure political office, however, and instead focus on how Uda Devi is commemorated at the grassroots, it becomes possible to better understand just why she has become such a totemic character for the Pasi community, and more fully understand what significance her commemoration plays today.

In so doing, one is presented with no shortage of commemorative ceremonies to consider. The 160th anniversary of 1857 witnessed a wide range of events from small and intimate affairs to large and well-publicised gatherings. Among these, however, that organised by Rajeshwari Devi, supposedly the Great-Great-Great Granddaughter of Uda Devi, in cooperation with the Uttar Pradesh Pasi Awakoti Mandal proved among the most significant. Held at Sikander Bagh and based around a simple bust that claims to mark the very spot where Uda Devi died, the event was held on 16 November 2017 to mark the anniversary of her death. Addressing the crowd of people who had turned out to pay their respects to her ancestor, Rajeshwari Devi began by outlining

---

[25] Anon, 'UP Government to Introduce Pasi Community Icons in School Syllabus'.
[26] Anon, 'BJP bats for freedom fighter Uda Devi Pasi's 100-foot statue in Uttar Pradesh'.

the martyr's story, before going on to explain the great truths from which the Pasi community should learn. High among these was that, contrary to accepted history, Pasis are a 'heroic and bold' people who have played a leading role in the history of the country.

In fact, the Pasis are the only people in the world who ruled an area non-stop for one thousand years. The Muslims only ruled for seven-hundred-and-fifty years. In the 10th Century, 11th Century, and 13th century, the Muslims came and fought with us. The Pasis fought very bravely and many were killed, however we never surrendered, even in defeat, because we were a warrior community. This same bravery and courage was displayed by Uda Devi in her fight against the British and so our whole community must be courageous now.[27]

In this speech, Uda Devi is sewn into a glorious Pasi history and serves as an emblematic figure who embodies the courage, valour, and martial spirit which have become recurring motifs for the Pasi community since at least the 1970s. In this respect, to commemorate Uda Devi today is to raise Pasi's dignity and self-respect, and project an exemplary image of Pasi identity for members of the caste to emulate and for others to admire. What it means to use Uda Devi as a model for behaviour and action in the present is further explained by Sandeep, a thirty-eight-year-old participant at a Pasi rally held in nearby Baribanki. Carrying a large, framed poster depicting a typical representation of the caste icon, Sandeep explained why he considers it so important to remember Uda Devi today, and what the Pasi community must learn from her great deeds:

we celebrate Uda Devi because we want to teach our people self-respect – we want to make our people powerful again. That is why we celebrate Uda Devi.... Uda Devi stood up against oppression from the British by using the only thing she had available to her; a gun. We tell our sons and daughters that they can stand up to oppression from the upper castes but they don't have to resort to using a gun. They have to use the book. They can read and become clever, and then become doctors, lawyers, or politicians and then they can lead their community forward.... They must concentrate on education and working hard at school and then they too can become like Uda Devi.[28]

Here, British oppression of India is equated with high caste oppression of the Pasi community, and Uda Devi is used as a symbol of resistance against both forms of tyranny. For this speaker, the importance of remembering Uda Devi today is to encourage the next generation of Pasis to fight back against the ongoing subjugation that their community faces from upper caste India by studying hard at school and attaining positions of power and

---

[27] Rajeshwari Devi, speech made at commemoration ceremony in honour of Uda Devi in Lucknow, 16 November 2017.
[28] Sandeep (name changed by request), interviewed in Barabanki, 28 February 2018.

Figure 7.1 Woman dressed as a soldier stands in front of a bust of Uda Devi during a ceremony organised by the Maharaja Chita Pasi Sevaa Sansathan in Hargaon, Sitapur district, UP, 18 January 2018. Photograph by Pravin Rajwanshi.

responsibility in society from where they can affect change for the community as a whole.

If Uda Devi is seen as a symbol of resistance to oppression, however, then she is also seen as a victim of oppression. Although it was the British who were responsible for her death, it is the 'ruling castes' who are blamed for the suppression of her legacy. In this way, Kamla Rawat, a community leader and social activist in central UP, spoke at length during her address at a commemoration ceremony dedicated to Uda Devi in Sitapur, claiming that Uda Devi had been deliberately forgotten at the national level.[29] Reflecting on why Uda Devi does not enjoy a more prominent place within the national

---

[29] Kamla Rawat spoke at the event in October 2017. She was interviewed on 27 February 2018 in Lucknow, when she was kind enough to provide a printed copy of the speech she made in Sitapur, from which the following quotes are drawn. Kamla Rawat, interviewed in Lucknow, 27 February 2018.

consciousness, Kamla Rawat argued that 'The Pasi caste made a brave contribution to the revolution of 1857, but upper caste Indian historians keep in mind their hatred for the Pasi caste. They ignored the brave history of the Pasi caste and they did not mention them in Indian history ... The story of the *Virangana* [brave woman] Uda Devi Pasi should have been written down in golden letters ... it is a matter of great grievance that she has not got to-date the respect she deserves'.[30]

With this in mind, the commemoration of Uda Devi appears to be essentially conflicted. On the one hand, Uda Devi is remembered as a victim of upper caste oppression, and on the other hand, she is celebrated as a symbol of resistance to all forms of oppression. These two opposed aspects of Uda Devi as a remembered figure are resolved, however, in the very act of her commemoration. This is well summed up by Rajiv Kumar, a thirty-two-year-old teacher at a local school in Sitapur, and a member of the Maharaja Chita Pasi Sevaa Sansathan that organises the annual commemoration ceremony in Hargaon, mentioned previously. Discussing why he plays such an active role in helping organise the annual commemoration ceremony, which is now entering its fifth year, Rajiv Kumar explained that:

In the writing of history there has been a great deal of bias because of caste discrimination ... [People like Uda Devi, Jhalkaribai, and Marta Dingi] fought with such bravery when fighting for freedom but when it came to writing history, these figures were forgotten. People like Rani Lakshmibai have become a mythised figure about whom so much literature has been written but these other marginal figures are forgotten. Now we have knowledge about these figures we are fighting against caste oppression by trying to give them the place they deserve among the other great heroes of India. First, we must educate our own people about Uda Devi, because many still haven't heard about her, then we need to educate the whole country and make sure nobody can ignore her anymore.[31]

For Rajiv Kumar, then, commemorating Uda Devi is itself a method for Pasi activists and community leaders to resist caste oppression. As a method of propagating a caste icon whose memory has been suppressed by members of the upper castes, commemoration is itself a direct challenge to the structures of power responsible for subjugating the Pasi caste and confining it to the lowest levels of the traditional social system. It is in this respect that commemoration resolves the tension between remembering Uda Devi as a victim of oppression and as a symbol of resistance. For members of the Pasi caste, to commemorate Uda Devi is to fight against the evils of the caste system directly by propagating what they see as illicit memory concerning the true history and character of their caste and thus help elevate their community's position within contemporary India.

[30] Ibid.
[31] Rajiv Kumar, interview in Haragoan, Sitapur District UP, 27 February 2018.

Indeed, this becomes ever more apparent when talking to the people who come together to commemorate Uda Devi each year. Whilst conversations with attendees at commemoration ceremonies invariably begin with discussions about Uda Devi's bravery and patriotism, they almost invariably continue with an impassioned discussion about the history of her commemoration, and in particular, the caste oppression which resulted in the first monument to be unveiled in her honour on 30 June 1973 at Sikander Bagh, being officially dedicated to an 'Unknown Heroine'. From that day on, 30 June became an important date of commemoration and protest for the Pasi community of Lucknow, who came together to honour Uda Devi Pasi, whilst at the same time protesting the omission of her name from the official plinth. This annual event quickly became sufficiently prominent to attract members of the Pasi community from across central UP, who gathered together to honour Uda Devi's memory by, for example, hanging pictures glorifying the Pasi martyr from a tree, which many believed to be the very one from which she was shot. Further, speakers would both celebrate Uda Devi's bravery, courage, and sacrifice during the battle of Sikander Bagh, whilst denouncing the caste oppression which they held responsible for her official anonymity.[32] The ceremony was often concluded by painting over the prefix of 'Unknown Heroine', to leave what they saw as the more accurate inscription of 'known Heroine'.[33] This concerted campaign ultimately proved successful when the bust was unveiled for a second time in 1997, this time with an inscription which identified the sniper as Uda Devi followed, a year later, by the unveiling of a statue dedicated to her and located just a few meters away.

It can be seen that for the Pasi community, Uda Devi is a potent signifier, with connotations extending far beyond the struggle for national independence in 1857. As a somewhat conflicted symbol which represents caste oppression at the same time as it symbolises resistance to all forms of tyranny, what it means to remember Uda Devi is synthesised by the very act of commemoration which is itself seen as a form of direct action against caste oppression. By refusing to accept what is seen as a distorted history of India concocted by high caste actors intent on marginalising the members of Dalit castes, the Pasi community believes that they are directly challenging the long-standing systems of power which continue to oppress them in the present. By coming together in opposition to what they believe amounts to a high caste conspiracy to forget Uda Devi, the Pasi community of central UP honour a historical personage who embodies what they see as essential components of Pasi identity which have long been the subject of systematic suppression.

---

[32] Rajeshwari Devi and M. P. Singh, interviewed in Lucknow, 26 February 2018. Ram Lal Rahi (former member of the Lok Sabha for Mishrikh, UP), interviewed in Sitapur, 27 February 2018.
[33] Ibid.

Uda Devi and the Fight for Female Empowerment

If many members of the Pasi community see the commemoration of Uda Devi as a way of resisting caste oppression, others see it as a way of resisting female subjugation which, they argue, is exceptionally prevalent within the Pasi caste. Daya, a thirty-eight-year-old editor of a small online newsletter serving the Pasi community, is an especially vocal proponent of this point of view.[34] Explaining that she was not born into a Pasi family and had never heard of Uda Devi before moving to central UP when she married a Pasi man, Daya expressed how shocked she was to discover the lowly position many women occupy within the broader Pasi community. And thus whilst:

Many women are performing in Bollywood, and many women are politicians, in ortho-dox Pasi families women aren't given the same opportunities. In orthodox Pasi families I know women with Batchelors degrees, even Master's degrees, who are just hidden away by their families – and I know many more women who could have studied at uni-versity but were never even given the opportunity because they are women.[35]

It was at least partially in response to this that she started editing the online newsletter, with a view to helping change entrenched attitudes shared by many Pasi men and women alike regarding the role women should play in the house-hold, and in society more generally. It is in service of this cause that Daya believes the memory of Uda Devi can help. 'If women can use the gun and fight in wars, and even kill 36 British soldiers, why should they not then be trained as teachers, and lawyers? Become Community leaders?... We must remember *Viranganas* [brave women] like Uda Devi because they have much to teach men who think women are second-class citizens, and those women who let themselves be treated in this way'.[36]

For Daya, therefore, participation in the commemoration of Uda Devi is a component of an intra-caste struggle against female subjugation, rather than the inter-caste struggle against caste oppression espoused by many above. Whilst this gendered attitude towards the commemoration of Uda Devi can certainly be found among the Pasi community of central UP, and especially when talking to young, wealthy Pasi women who have enjoyed the benefits of a university education, it is more prevalent outside central UP. When one leaves the Lucknow Division to consider what it means to remember Uda Devi elsewhere in UP, where a lower concentration of Pasis prevails, one discov-ers that caste frequently stops being a factor at all in her remembrance, or else is deliberately elided to emphasise an alternative identity position. This is certainly the case for a small group of activists known as the Lakshmibai Brigade, an NGO led by Manjeet Kaur, a female lawyer working in Jaunpur, a

---

[34] Daya (name changed by request), interviewed in Barabanki, 11 February 2018.
[35] Ibid.   [36] Ibid.

city in eastern UP. This group, which is overwhelmingly made up of women, but also contains a small number of male members who play a supporting role in the organisation, has existed for over eighteen years during which they have campaigned for all downtrodden peoples, but especially women to whom the NGO has been officially dedicated for nearly a decade.[37]

As part of this campaign for female empowerment, the Lakshmibai Brigade has been responsible for several different initiatives in the local area which, most recently, has involved training women in martial arts to equip them with a defence against domestic battery and sexual abuse.[38] Whilst the hope is that this skill will help reduce incidence of assault and rape, the group is most active in seeking justice for women who have been the victims of such crimes. To this end, Manjeet Kaur and Rakesh Yadav, both trained lawyers, are prepared to provide legal counsel and representation on a pro bono basis to female victims who would normally be unable to afford such services, or else to take a reduced fee based on whatever the victim is able to pay.[39]

Among the many cases they dealt with during the 160th anniversary year of 1857, the rape of an impoverished Dalit Muslim teenager by the son of a wealthy high caste shopkeeper most clearly highlights the intersection of class, caste, and gender in such cases. Molested whilst urinating in a field close to her home, the young lady appealed to Manjeet Kaur and the Lakshmibai Brigade, for help in attaining justice. However, whilst Manjeet Kaur was still helping her prepare a written report to file with the police and thus begin official proceedings against the perpetrator, the victim decided to withdraw her allegations on the advice of her family and friends who feared that she would face stigma from the wider community, as well as potential intimidation and recriminations from the assailant's well-placed family, should she further pursue the matter. The case came to what Manjeet Kaur considered an ultimately unsatisfactory conclusion when she was at least able to convince the victim to seek some private recompense from her attacker's family, resulting in a small out-of-court cash settlement. Commenting on the case, Manjeet Kaur explained that such an outcome was frustratingly common, but at least it offered some small justice to those who would otherwise get none.[40]

It is as part of their broader advocacy work that the Lakshmibai Brigade arrange annual commemoration ceremonies which are primarily in honour of great Indian women, including many associated with 1857. Indeed, during the 160th anniversary, for example, the group arranged separate events in honour of Rani Lakshmibai, Jhalkaribai, Begum Hazrat Mahal, and Uda Devi. Surprisingly, perhaps, the last of these, which was held in November 2017 to mark the anniversary of Uda Devi's death, made no mention of the Pasi icon's caste, and indeed, when later discussing her motivation for organising

---

[37] Manjeet Kaur and Rakesh Yadav, interviewed in Jaunpur, 22 March 2018.
[38] Ibid.   [39] Ibid.   [40] Ibid.

the event, Manjeet Kaur explained that it was a mistake to think that Uda Devi was a Pasi, rather she was simply a woman, and not from any one caste in particular.[41] Much as the BSP had begun to elide Uda Devi's caste to portray her as first and foremost a Dalit hero, Manjeet Kaur takes this one stage further by completely erasing her caste identity, enabling her to instead symbolise every Indian woman. It is this which enables Uda Devi to fulfil the role intended for her in the commemoration ceremonies organised by the Lakshmibai Brigade.

Therefore, whilst the ceremony placed a great deal of emphasis on the heroic actions which won Uda Devi fame in much the same way as is typical in the acts of commemoration hosted in central UP by Pasi activists, the central message was not concerned with the on-going struggle against caste oppression, but rather with the fight against female oppression. Further elaborating on this point, Manjeet Kaur explained that she helps organise these events to celebrate the life of Uda Devi because she is a powerful role model for young women; 'Uda Devi was willing to fight and sacrifice her life in the fight for freedom from the British Government. Today, it is the same. We want to teach our members and all women that they must stand up to the government and fight for their fundamental rights. This too is a dangerous fight but unless we have the courage to take part we will never win'.[42] For Manjeet Kaur, and the Lakshmibai Brigade therefore, Uda Devi plays a parallel symbolic function to that played in the Pasi community's fight against caste oppression. Symbolising women's ability to courageously fight against all forms of government to secure their fundamental human rights, Uda Devi acts as a powerful signifier within the discourse of female empowerment.

If the Lakshmibai Brigade celebrate Uda Devi as a symbol of the fight for female empowerment, then the same is undoubtedly true for the acts of commemoration that they host in honour of other great women including the Rani of Jhansi, after whom the group is named. Celebrated as a glorious warrior queen who embodies leadership, strength, and power, Rani Lakshmibai is likewise celebrated by the Lakshmibai Brigade as a role model to which all women can aspire. Remembered as a glorious warrior queen who, with her son strapped to her back, rode into battle and led her troops from the front, Rani Lakshmibai symbolises women's ability to be both a mother and a leader or, as Manjeet Kaur puts it, 'Mahrani Lakshmibai was a working mother! If she could both fight for what was right and raise a son, then so can we.... She reminds us of woman's power and encourages me to fight for women's empowerment today'.[43] If the many great female warriors associated with the events of 1857 such as the Rani of Jhansi are therefore important signifiers within the discourse on female

---

[41] Ibid.   [42] Ibid.   [43] Ibid.

empowerment employed by the Lakshmibai Brigade, then, when travelling about forty miles further east to the sacred city of Varanasi, it becomes apparent that what it means to remember Rani Lakshmibai is no less contested than in the case of Uda Devi (Pasi).

Contested Nationalisms: Maharani Lakshmibai Nyas and Hindu Rashtra

Located on the western bank of the River Ganges in the south-east of UP, Varanasi is one of India's most sacred cities.[44] Famously described by Mark Twain as being 'older than history, older than tradition, older even than legend and looks twice as old as all of them put together', the city is one of the most important sites of pilgrimage for Hindus who travel there due to its association with the legends of Lord Shiva and to bathe in the purifying waters of the Ganges.[45] Descending one of the city's many *ghats* at sunrise whilst chanting from Hindu scriptures, millions of pilgrims bathe in the river each year, believing that the holy water will wash away their earthly sins.

Just a short walk away from the Assi Ghat, which is among the most popular places for pilgrims to engage in this ritual act of purification, is another site considered sacred by many. Marked by an imposing golden equestrian statue standing in an ornate garden and surrounded by a series of relief sculptures, the site marks the birthplace of the great warrior queen, Rani Lakshmibai. Plans for a monument on the site had first been mooted in 1969 by a recently formed memorial committee concerned with the commemoration of the Rani. The memorial committee's proposals found significant support and were ratified by the Varanasi Municipal Corporation who pledged a generous sum of money to construct a suitable monument; however, the project became mired in legal disputes when concerns about the project were raised by the landowners. Though members of the memorial committee continued to periodically raise the subject with the Municipal Corporation and its officers over the following years, it was not until the issue was taken up by the *Maharani Lakshmibai Nyas* (Maharani Lakshmibai Trust, shortened hereafter to MLN) in the late 1990s that the project once again gained momentum.[46] Formed in 1998 by prominent local lawyer, Rajendra Pratap Pandey, the MLN energetically campaigned for the erection of the statue and finally succeeded in breaking the legal deadlock which had thus far thwarted the project, resulting in the memorial gardens being laid out and opened to the public in the years that followed.[47]

[44] Eck, *Banaras*.
[45] Twain, *More Tramps Abroad*, p. 332.
[46] Rajendra Pratap Pandey, Vivek Shanker Tiwari, Meena Chaubey, and Durga Pandey interviewed in Varanasi, 21 March 2018.
[47] Ibid.

Figure 7.2 Maharani Lakshmibai Nyas procession through Varanasi in 2018. Photograph used with permission of Rajendra Pratap Pandey.

Since the official inauguration of the commemorative gardens, the MLN has overseen annual events on the site in honour of the great freedom fighter. With their prominence steadily growing over the intervening years, the MLN now succeeds in drawing very considerable crowds and enjoys significant exposure in the local media. This was the case in 2018 when the group organised a procession through the city led by a young lady on horseback who, with raised sword and shield, represented the warrior queen (Figure 7.2). The procession terminated at the commemorative gardens, where a small deputation had been praying since sunrise. With the arrival of the procession the main ceremony could begin, which consisted in a series of speeches made by senior members of the MLN interspersed by several short plays and dances depicting scenes from the life of Rani Lakshmibai.

Though the MLN formally operates as an independent organisation, it has strong links with many of the right-wing Hindu nationalist organisations that make up the Sangh Parivar, and especially the Rashtriya Swayamsevak Sangh (RSS) and its women's wing, the Rashtra Sevika Samiti. Both organisations have long histories dating back to the first half of the twentieth century and developed in a tradition of Hindu nationalism that can be traced back to the nineteenth century.[48] Dedicated to the establishment of a Hindu Rashtra,

---

[48] For the early history of Hindu nationalism, see Zavos, *The Emergence of Hindu Nationalism in India.*

understood to be an independent India in which Hindu cultural and religious concerns are deeply enshrined within the national fabric, these organisations have enjoyed a period of considerable growth over the past thirty years which has helped mainstream many of their values and beliefs.[49]

The growth of the RSS as a cultural organisation has occurred alongside the formation of their political wing, the BJP, and its emergence as a powerful political force at both the state and national levels. Founded in 1980, the BJP grew in stature during the period of Congress malaise presided over by Rajiv Gandhi, before experiencing rapid growth in the years which followed the demolition of the Babri Masjid in Ayodhya leading to their eventual electoral success in the late 1990s.[50] Though the Congress-led United Progressive Alliance surprised the BJP in the 2004 General Election, and secured re-election in 2009, it would be wrong to see these defeats as signalling the decline of Hindu nationalism in these years, indeed explicit displays of Hindu religiosity became ever more normalised over this period leading to an equally everyday brand of Hindu nationalism extending its reach across the country.[51] This normalisation of Hindu nationalism contributed to the electoral success of the BJP in the 2014 and 2019 General Elections, as well as in many of the intervening Legislative Assembly elections including that held in UP, which resulted in the BJP's Yogi Adityanath being appointed the Chief Minister on 8 March 2017. It was, however, the selection of Narendra Modi to lead the party in 2014, which had the most decisive impact on the BJP's electoral success.[52]

A member of the RSS since childhood and whose reputation as Chief Minister of Gujarat during the 2002 communal violence won him support from many on the Hindu right, Modi perhaps need not have selected the sacred city of Varanasi as his parliamentary constituency in 2014 as a way of sending out a clear message to the Hindu heartland which was already looking to him as an ardent champion of Hindu Rashtra. At the same time, Modi could rely on his strong economic record in Gujarat as evidence that a BJP government under his leadership could steer the nation towards greater development and prosperity, and ultimately ensure that India emerged as a major player on the world stage. Accordingly, many saw Modi as representing the convergence of powerful cultural and economic aspirations and turned towards the BJP in 2014 as a vehicle which could help realise their ambitions.[53]

---

[49] For an excellent study that places the growth of the BJP since the 1980s within a longer narrative of the Hindu nationalist movement since the 1920s, see Jaffrelot, *The Hindu Nationalist Movement in India*. See also Hansen, *The Saffron Wave*.

[50] Ibid.

[51] Harriss, Jeffrey, and Corbridge, 'Is India becoming the "Hindu Rashtra" sought by Hindu Nationalists?', pp. 12–13. See also Nanda, *The God Market*.

[52] For an informative discussion on the populist appeal of Narendra Modi, see Jaffrelot and Tillin, 'Populism in India', pp. 179–94, pp. 184–88.

[53] Ibid.

The MLN's ties to the Sangh go back to its establishment, with lifelong member of the RSS, Rajendra Pratap Pandey, founding the organisation. Whilst not uncritical of the BJP's record during their earlier term in office where the party had to appease its coalition partners by tempering many of their more controversial policies, Pandey became an ardent supporter of Modi as far back as 1999.[54] Accordingly, Pandey ensured that he used his senior position within the RSS to support Modi and the BJP during the 2014 election campaign in Varanasi and started campaigning ahead of the 2019 General Election as early as 2017.[55] Pandey is not the only member of the MLN with ties to the Hindu right, indeed its current president, Sharad Renu, is the *Boudhik Pramukh* (Intellectual Head) of the Rashtra Sevika Samiti, and other senior members include Vivek Shankar Tiwari, Meena Chaubey, and Durga Pandey who each enjoy positions of varying responsibility within the RSS, Rashtra Sevika Samiti, and BJP, respectively. Indeed, the connection between the MLN and the Sangh is made explicit in many of the pamphlets and leaflets distributed at events organised by them, with one noting the Trust's 'gratitude to the Rashtriya Swayamsevak Sangh for its support' before going on to unequivocally state that 'the Mahrani Laxmibai Nyas is a part of the Rashtra Sevika Samiti'.[56]

Unsurprisingly, given their close ties, many of the aspirations and concerns which motivate the Hindu right are deeply embedded in the practices of commemoration organised by the MLN and have the effect of colouring what it means for them to remember Rani Lakshmibai at such events. This is immediately apparent if one considers the commemoration event held in 2018, and the speech given by Sharad Renu, the organisation's president, and the Intellectual Head of the Rashtra Sevika Samiti.[57] Beginning her address by explaining that the Rani was a symbol of woman's indomitable power and spirit in overcoming the many challenges that life presents, Renu's depiction of Lakshmibai seems to have much in common with how the warrior queen is celebrated by the female empowerment activists who make up the Lakshmibai Brigade considered earlier. However, the narrative begins to deviate significantly as Renu goes on to explain that there are many lessons which her audience should learn from the Rani, and not least that 'we should have everything that reflects or depicts India in our heart, be it its food, costumes, garments, traditions, or

[54] Rajendra Pratap Pandey, interviewed in Varanasi, 21 March 2018.
[55] For more on Rajendra Pratap Pandey's role during the 2014 election, see Praveen Donthi, 'How Amit Shah and the RSS Managed the BJP's Varanasi Campaign', *The Caravan*, 11 May 2014, https://caravanmagazine.in/vantage/shah-rss-varanasi. Rajendra Pratap Pandey is a *Sanghchalak* within the RSS.
[56] Rajendra Pratap Pandey, 'Foreword', *181st Birth Anniversary of Rani Lakshmibai*. A pamphlet circulated at commemoration ceremony.
[57] Sharad Renu, speaking at commemoration ceremony in honour of Rani Lakshmibai, 6 November 2018, Varanasi.

culture. Everything that is a part of India should be a part of your life.... This is how Maharani Lakshmibai formed her own character, based on the character of India'.[58] Going on to explain more about the Rani's past, Renu clarified that she had been inspired from a very young age to follow the teachings and example of Shivaji Bhonsle.[59] Celebrated by the Sangh as a devout Hindu who led the fight against Muslim Mughal rule ultimately resulting in him succeeding in founding the Maratha Empire in the late seventeenth century, Shivaji is frequently employed by the Sangh as an idealised symbol of the values and beliefs that define Hindutva today.[60] By drawing a direct connection between Shivaji's wars against the Mughals and Lakshmibai's motivations in leading the rebellion against the British, Renu is presenting the Rani as an idealised defender of her nation's faith and culture.

With Rani Lakshmibai standing in as a symbol of Hindu nationalism, the president of the MLN continued by telling her audience that the spirit of Rani Lakshmibai was still alive today and exemplified in the stories of three girls who courageously risked their lives for the nation. The first of these was a young girl who was supposedly attending an event at her school in Bihar to celebrate Republic Day on 26 January 2015, when a group of terrorists armed with machine guns hijacked the event and ordered that the national flag be lowered 'or there would be dead bodies all over the place'.[61] Whilst everyone else was too scared to do anything, 'one girl, I am going to call her *Prerana* (inspiration) ... grabbed the pole of the flag and stood there and in a sharp voice she dared them to try and take the flag down but that they must know that the first thing they would have to do is shoot her down. "It is only after my dead body has fallen to the ground that you will succeed in taking the flag down", she told them'. Remarkably, *Prerana* inspired the rest of the school to likewise join her in defence of the national flag and succeeded in repulsing the terrorists who realised that they would be unable to achieve their goals when confronted by so determined a defence.[62]

The other two young girls to be highlighted in Renu's speech as being imbued by the spirit and teaching of Rani Lakshmibai found themselves on the frontlines of armed conflict between India and Pakistan in 1999, during the Kargil War. Accustomed to navigating the mountain paths around their houses thanks to their experience shepherding goats in the area, the two young girls volunteered to help deliver much needed supplies to a number of

[58] Ibid.   [59] Ibid.
[60] For a detailed examination of how Shivaji has been imagined and deployed by different actors over time, see Laine, *Shivaji*. See also O'Hanlon, 'Maratha History as Polemic, pp. 1–33. For an interesting study which compares how the Sangh and Samiti narrate Shivaji's life with specific reference to how the Samiti emphasises the role played by Jijabai, Shivaji's mother, see Menon, *Everyday Nationalism*, pp. 26–53.
[61] Ibid.   [62] Ibid.

under-provisioned soldiers who had been tasked with holding a strategically significant, if remote, position. Travelling the treacherous mountain paths at night to avoid detection, the two girls succeeded in delivering large quantities of rice donated by their village to the grateful Indian troops over the course of several days 'which is a clear demonstration of love of country and bravery. So, the girls in our times are no less brave than those of the past'.[63] Read alongside the tale of *Prerana*, the moral of the story seems clear. To learn from Rani Lakshmibai and to tap into the spirit of the great warrior queen means to become an ardent nationalist, and stand against India's enemies, both domestic and foreign, who continue to threaten the nation in the same way as the Mughal and British empires did in the past. Thus, just as Renu's narrative begins with Shivaji's defeat of the Muslim Mughal Empire, followed by Lakshmibai's valiant, if ill-fated rebellion against the British, the story ends with victories over the enemy within, and the enemy without, represented by the terrorists and Pakistan, respectively. When talking to some of the hundreds of people who participated in the event, it is clear that this point had not been missed by the great majority of those in attendance and was taken a good deal further by others. Tanuj, for example, who was present for the majority of the proceedings, explained that in his opinion, the greatest lesson that 'Mahrani Lakshmibai teaches us today is that we must always fight to protect our culture, just as she did in 1857'.[64] Going on to expand upon what relevance this has for the present, Tanuj explained that the difference is that it is no longer the British who threaten Indian culture, rather it is the 'Muslims and Christians who daily pollute India.... Muslims must be reconverted to Hinduism or else driven from India altogether'.[65] Similarly, another spectator named Anil felt that India was threatened by 'foreign elements' and that just as 'India rose up with nationalist pride' in 1857, 'to protect their land, their culture, and their Dharma', so too must 'we protect the nation from all enemies who mean us harm'.[66]

Contested Nationalisms: 1857 Rashtravaadi Manch and Communal Unity

Remembering 1857 as a revolt led by Hindu nationalists in defence of India's fundamental cultural and religious identity is deeply rejected by the loose coalition of left-wing activists who, in 2017 and 2018, united under the banner of the 1857 Rashtravaadi Manch (1857 Nationalist Forum), to help organise a programme of commemorative events known by the acronym, RAVA, or the

---

[63] Ibid.
[64] Tanuj, interviewed in Varanasi, 6 November 2018.
[65] Ibid.
[66] Anil, interviewed in Varanasi, 6 November 2018.

Rashtriya Apmaan Virodhi Abhiyaan (National Anti-Insurgency Campaign).[67] Though many of the members of this umbrella group belong to a range of regional and national political parties and profess adherence to a spectrum of left-wing political ideologies including socialism, Marxism, and communism, they all share a deep-seated aversion to the direction taken by Indian politics over the past few decades and especially since the 2014 General Election.[68]

Indeed, the group's founding member, Amaresh Misra, had been considering launching such an organisation for some time but felt that 'the election of the BJP in 2014 with their version of fascist nationalism spurred me on. I said "OK", now we must do something to oppose this Hindu pseudo nationalism'.[69] An avowed Marxist, and author of a two-volume history of 1857 published in 2007 to mark the event's 150th anniversary, Misra decided to inaugurate the 1857 Rashtravaadi Manch, with the intention of opposing the conception of Hindu nationalism which animates the Sangh by promoting a form of nationalism based on an ethos of unity, and intercommunal harmony, which he believes characterised the 1857 War of Independence.[70] Misra's conception of what he calls 1857 nationalism has proved appealing to many other left-wing activists who joined the organisation, and who share his distaste for the sociopolitical developments that they believe were inaugurated by Modi's election in 2014 and exasperated by the appointment of Yogi Adityanath as Chief Minister in 2017. To take the case of Peeyush, a member of the 1857 Rashtravaadi Manch and a designated youth leader within the organisation, the young activist claims that he felt compelled to respond to what he identifies as the growing persecution of minority groups in India.[71] Influenced by a number of high-profile cases involving the violent persecution of minorities in India since 2014, Peeyush joined the 1857 Rashtravaadi Manch as he felt that 'we must learn from the past and 1857 has much to teach us today about how the whole country is stronger when Hindus and Muslims are united'.[72] Likewise, Fahim, another teenage member of the organisation, felt that it was the appointment of Adityanath that convinced him to join the 1857 Rashtravaadi Manch.[73] 'I can't understand how we got here. These fascists are taking control of everything and most people don't care or don't know but I wanted to do something … In 1857, Hindus and Muslims fought together

---

[67] The group's main website can be found at www.instamojo.com/1857/1857-nationalist-forum/, last accessed 1 July 2019. See also www.milligazette.com/news/15597-join-mangal-pandey-march-to-build-a-new-anti-fascist-nationalism, last accessed 1 July 2019.

[68] Amaresh Misra, interviewed in Lucknow, 19 January 2018. Deepak Kabir, interviewed in Lucknow, 5 April 2018. Focus Group, hosted in Lucknow, 21 March 2018.

[69] Amaresh Misra, interviewed in Lucknow, 19 January 2018.

[70] Misra, *War of Civilisations*.

[71] Focus Group with members of 1857 Nationalist Forum, 7 March 2018.

[72] Ibid.   [73] Ibid.

against their enemies ... 1857 was our past but it can be our future too if we stand together against the new fascist enemy'.[74]

If the 2014 General Election was won on the promise of Hindutva and development, then many members of the 1857 Rashtravaadi Manch believe that they have experienced more of the former than the latter. Indeed, the appointment of Yogi Adityanath as Chief Minister following the BJP's victory in the Legislative Assembly election in 2017 seems to underscore this. As one of the BJP's most aggressive spokesmen whose international reputation, like that of Modi, has been tarnished by past accusations of complicity in communal riots and pogroms in his own constituency of Gorakhpur, Yogi Adityanath's elevation to a position which may be considered second only to that of Prime Minister in terms of national importance is considered deeply concerning by many.[75] Indeed, it was only in 2014 that Yogi Adityanath was censured by the Election Commission for stoking intercommunal tension when repeatedly warning that the nation was facing a 'Love Jihad', an Islamist conspiracy which encouraged and rewarded Muslim men for seducing young vulnerable Hindu women and enticing them to convert to Islam.[76] Responsible for heightened intercommunal suspicions and recriminations, fears of a 'Love Jihad' continue to result in violent outbursts against individuals and groups of Muslims accused of involvement or complicity in the alleged conspiracy.[77]

Likewise, Yogi Adityanath is a leading proponent of the controversial *ghar wapsi* (homecoming) campaign championed by the Sangh.[78] Aimed at converting or, as the Sangh frame it, reconverting adherents of other religions including Christianity and Islam, incidence of *ghar wapsi* has resulted in considerable intercommunal tension in UP which has seen some of the largest mass (re)conversions, including that of over 300 people in Varanasi in 2015.[79] Though such campaigns have had a profound impact on the daily lives of many minorities in India, it is the vigilante violence associated with cow protection, which has proved the most disturbing. A sacred animal under Hinduism, cow slaughter has

---

[74] Ibid.
[75] Harriss, Jeffrey, and Corbridge, 'Is India becoming the "Hindu Rashtra" sought by Hindu Nationalists?'
[76] Ibid, p. 6.
[77] One of the most notorious cases occurred in Rajasthan when Shambhu Lal Regar streamed himself murdering Muslim labourer Mohd Afrazul on social media in 2017. The case became the subject of much national media attention, as did the decision of a small extreme right wing political group in UP to nominate Regar to stand for their party in the 2019 General Elections. See Anon, 'Shambhulal Lal Regar set to contest from Rampur against Azam Khan', https://timesofindia.indiatimes.com/city/meerut/shambhulal-regar-who-hacked-man-to-death-on-camera-set-to-contest-from-rampur-against-azam-khan-on-up-navnirman-senas-ticket/articleshow/68587066.cms
[78] Harriss, Jeffrey, and Corbridge, 'Is India becoming the "Hindu Rashtra" sought by Hindu Nationalists?', p. 6.
[79] Rajeshwar and Amore, 'Coming Home (Ghar Wapsi) and Going Away', p. 313.

become the subject of special attention for the BJP. Accordingly, among the first actions of Yogi Adityanath as Chief Minister was to act against illegal slaughter-houses.[80] Whilst Adityanath has since claimed that the clamp down has helped stop vigilante violence, the reality is likely the reverse. With the BJP placing such emphasis on policing and outlawing the practice, they have created a space in which right-wing cow protection groups feel legitimised in violently enforc-ing the laws. This vigilante justice has led to countless incidents of people, and overwhelmingly Muslims, accused of cow slaughter, or even just the possession of beef, being lynched by mobs of Hindus.[81] One of the most notorious incidents occurred in 2015 and involved a fifty-two-year-old Muslim named Mohammed Akhlaq who was accused of cow slaughter, leading to a savage mob attack that left him dead in his home village of Bisara in western UP. The case became so notorious that the victim's name, Akhlaq, has entered the lexicon of North India as a verb denoting murder in the name of cow protection.[82]

Motivated by this growth of intercommunal violence which they blame on the brand of Hindu nationalism promoted by the RSS and the BJP, the 1857 Rashtravaadi Manch set about commemorating the 160th anniversary of 1857. Remembered as a moment of intercommunal solidarity in which India united against a common enemy, 1857 provided the organisation with an alternative conception of nationalism to promote in opposition to the Sangh. The first of these events was held on 10 May 2017, to mark the 160th anniversary of the start of the rebellion. Consisting in a somewhat shambolic procession of over 100 motorbikes carrying upwards of three to four banner waving activists each, members of the 1857 Rashtravaadi Manch visited the graves of Major-General Sir Henry Havelock in Alambagh, Brigadier-General Sir Henry Lawrence at the Residency, and Major William Hodson at La Martiniere College to protest the colonial era inscriptions which mark each memorial. This opening event of RAVA was followed by a second around a month later in honour of the rebels' victory in Chinhut. Starting in the early evening, and continuing into the night, the commemoration ceremony featured a torchlight procession which wound its way through the streets of the area and culminated in a minute's silence in honour of all those 'Hindus and Muslims who stood together and stood their ground against the British, and finally won a glorious victory' (Figure 7.3).[83]

A little over two weeks later, and the group was once again active, this time holding a commemoration ceremony on 16 July in honour of the 160th

[80] Anon, 'Yogi Adityanath orders closure of slaughter houses, bans cow smuggling', https://timesofindia.indiatimes.com/india/yogi-adityanath-orders-closure-of-slaughter-houses-bans-cow-smuggling/articleshow/57769068.cms
[81] Bajoria, *Violent Cow Protection in India*, www.hrw.org/report/2019/02/18/violent-cow-protection-india/vigilante-groups-attack-minorities
[82] Rajeshwar and Amore, 'Coming Home (Ghar Wapsi) and Going Away'.
[83] Amaresh Misra, interviewed in Lucknow, 19 January 2018.

Figure 7.3 1857 Rashtravaadi Manch protest the grave of William Hodsen (left) and hold a torchlight procession in Chinhut (right). Photographs used by permission of Deepak Kabir.

anniversary of the Awadh Manifesto, which was written by the rebels and is seen by the group as India's first Bill of Rights embodying the central tenets of equality between castes and religions that defines 1857 Nationalism.[84] With the events generating considerable local interest, and with the numbers of the group swelling, Deepak Kabir, a full-time social political activist and one of the principal organisers of the group, felt that they were succeeding in presenting an alternative vision of India to that promoted by the RSS and the BJP.[85] 'The RSS learned how to organise and even learned their ideology from Hitler and Mussolini, but they are the ones who want to talk about Indian culture!... Our message in these events is a simple one; in 1857 we united and fought the greatest army in the world, if we unite today we are more than a match for these fascists who want to divide us just like the British did after 1857'.[86]

With momentum building over the course of the preceding months, the group announced a further event to be held on 18 March 2018. Consisting in a commemoration event to start at the contested site of the former Babri Masjid in Ayodhya before progressing to nearby Kuber Teela, the event was to be held in honour of all those 'Muslims and Hindus who liberated Awadh in 1857, as well as all those who again stood against the British in 1858' during the reoccupation of the territory and to mark the deaths of two men in particular who were executed side by side on 18 March 1858. One a Hindu Mahant and the other a Muslim Maulvi, Ram Charan Das and Amir Ali are said to have been hanged from the branches of the same tree after together leading armed

---

[84] Amaresh Misra, interviewed in Lucknow, 19 January 2018.
[85] Deepak Kabir, interviewed in Lucknow, 5 April 2018.
[86] Ibid.

resistance to the reconquest of Awadh. The intended purpose of the event was, according to Misra, to bring a 'new perspective to the Ayodhya controversies, which have been the source of so much Hindu-Muslim strife' and promote a new message of 'equality, tolerance, and unity based on the lessons of 1857'.[87] Ultimately, however, this final commemorative event was called off around a month before its scheduled date, after the organisers reported receiving anonymous threats of violence should they go ahead with their plans which had, by then, received considerable media attention.[88]

1857 and the Politics of Commemoration

As should be apparent from the above small sample of commemorative activities held in UP and aimed at marking the 160th anniversary of 1857 in 2017–18, the First War of Indian Independence has become a nodal point within India's memory of British colonialism. The subject of enormous popular interest throughout India, and especially in the north, the conflict and its principal Indian heroes are much feted by a diverse array of individuals and organised groups.

Whilst this commemorative outpouring might well go to prove the relevance of 1857 in India today, it certainly should not be taken to indicate homogeneity. As we have seen, when these different commemorative events are subjected to careful consideration, it becomes apparent that they reflect the hopes and fears, aspirations and ideologies of various groups organised around divergent identity positions. Accordingly, the respective acts of commemoration deployed by each group to celebrate 1857 is inextricably intertwined with specific conceptions of caste, class, gender, and religion. Itself a reflection of the divided nature of contemporary Indian society, the commemoration of 1857 today is no less contingent or contested than it was at any other moment over the past 160 years.

---

[87] Amaresh Misra, personal communication with author, 20 February 2018.
[88] Amaresh Misra, personal communication with author, 10 March 2018.

Conclusion
Memories of the Present and Echoes of the Past

With applause for Viceroy Lord Northbrook's speech still echoing around the Brigade Parade Ground, the commander-in-chief, Field Marshal Lord Napier, rose to address the thousands of people who had gathered to witness the unveiling of the latest monument to be added to those already arrayed outside Calcutta's Fort William. Dedicated to the eternal memory of General Sir James Outram, and coming nearly twenty years after his exploits during the mutiny of 1857 had made the British officer a household name in every corner of the empire, the monument justifiably took its place alongside the scores of other memorials on the Maidan dedicated to great statesmen, soldiers, and colonial administrators. Though the Viceroy would later question the artistic merits of the statue executed by celebrated sculptor, John Henry Foley, when he privately admitted to Sir Richard Temple that he disliked 'equestrian statues in violent movement', wryly adding that one 'longs to ask Outram to get off his fidgety horse and pick up his hat!',[1] Lord Northbrook no doubt agreed with the commander-in-chief's speech, which proudly emphasised that:

India is rich in the memorials of great men; it is a country which has offered a wide field for the glorious deeds of soldiers and a still wider and loftier one for civil administrators who have laid the foundations of justice, order and education, which have raised it to a state of civilisation that has no parallel in its earlier history. If ever we are asked, what has Great Britain done for India? We may point with pride to these monuments, and to hundreds of humbler ones spread over the land, and say, that our country has given to India freely, of her wisest bravest and best![2]

Though Napier felt that the statues dedicated to the memories of great colonial soldiers and civil administrators that surrounded his audience would

---

[1] Northbrook to the Hon. Sir Richard Temple, 23 May 1874, 'Correspondence with persons in India, Part I', Papers of the Earl of Northbrook as Viceroy of India 1872–76, p. 132, OIOC, Mss Eur C144/15.

[2] 'Address by His Excellency Lord Napier of Magdala on the unveiling of the Outram Statue', 23 May 1874, Sir James Outram Papers, NAM, 9210/127-72 (C). For more details on the preparations for the unveiling of this monument, see 'letters written by Lord Napier of Magdala regarding the statue of Outram in Calcutta', Sir James Outram Papers, NAM, 9210/127-108.

Figure C.1 Left: Nagesh Yoglekar's statue of Subhas Chandra Bose, photograph by Biswarup Ganguly which has been slightly edited to remove powerlines obscuring monument. Right: John Henry Foley's statue of James Outram, stock image ID: 10330072a, 12 August 1957, Shutterstock.

ensure that Britain's imperial project would ever be remembered for its benef-icence and justice, their removal in the decades that followed Indian inde-pendence suggests otherwise. Indeed, among the first of these monuments to disappear was that dedicated to General Outram. Removed during the cente-nary year of 1857, the statue's fate was soon shared by its neighbours when they too were replaced over the following decades by a new crop of statues dedi-cated to icons of independent India including Mahatma Gandhi, Jawaharlal Nehru, and Matangini Hazra.

Among the many statues to have been constructed on and around the Maidan since independence, however, it is Nagesh Yoglekar's memorial dedi-cated to Subhas Chandra Bose which is the most revealing. Officially unveiled by the Kolkata Municipal Corporation in 1969, the full significance of the statue can only be appreciated by those familiar with the statue of Outram which had been banished from its prominent location a little over ten years earlier. With both rider and horse adopting near identical poses to those depicted in Foley's portrayal of Outram, the memorial's subtext is per-haps best read as a subtle commentary on the contingent and contested nature of public memory alongside its ultimate mutability. In any case, furnished with memorials dedicated to those who resisted colonial rule, as opposed to those who established, defended, and administered it, the commemorative landscapes of post-colonial cities such as Kolkata have come to tell quite a different story of their colonial pasts than that authored by men like Napier (Figure C.1).

Focusing on monuments which, like Foley's statue of Outram, were dedicated to the memory of individuals or events associated with the Great Mutiny of 1857 and especially those which marked the sacred mnemonic landscapes of the Lucknow Residency, Cawnpore Well, and Delhi Ridge, this book is one of the first serious attempts to understand the role played by commemoration in colonial and post-colonial settings. In so doing, the commemoration of 1857 has been used as a lens through which it has been possible to analyse over 150 years of Indian history. Investigating how commemoration reflected and refracted the colonial state's post-mutiny reconstruction of India, the lived reality of high imperialism, the conflicted nature of Indian nationalism, the politics of decolonisation, and the growth of identity politics in modern India, this study has shown that the commemoration of 1857 has consistently responded to contemporary aspirations, concerns, and exigencies by moulding the past into a useable form for those who come together to collectively remember it within the present.

In so doing, it has become clear that whilst it may be tempting to see this struggle for memory as consisting in two homogenous collective memories of empire locked in a contest for the past, this would be to apply an overly crude model to an infinitely more complex process. Indeed, when taken synchronically, the commemoration of India's colonial past is always a product of dispute and debate waged between innumerable different actors as opposed to an opposition between neatly divided perspectives along nationalist and imperialist lines. As we have shown, this was as true in colonial settings as it remains today in post-colonial India. Thus, just as commemoration in the immediate aftermath of the mutiny pitted evangelical British Christians against the colonial government, so too did the 160th anniversary of 1857 in India witness groups mobilised around a range of identity positions including class, caste, religion, and gender compete against one another in their divergent attempts to mark the anniversary in 2017–18.

Whilst commemoration therefore invariably leads to discord regarding the proper way to remember the past, such debates almost inevitably centre on concerns rooted within the present. To take the divergent attitudes exhibited by Indian nationalists to remembering the events of 1857 during the inter-war years as an example, these debates were not so much concerned with inert questions of historical accuracy so much as they were deeply enmeshed with divergent attitudes towards how best to pursue Indian independence in the present. Accordingly, the respective practices of counter commemoration employed by men like Mahatma Gandhi and Vinayak Damodar Savarkar were explicitly utilised as a way of communicating with those engaged in resistance to British rule and specifically regarding what form that resistance should take.

It is precisely this bond between memory and contemporary concerns that has enabled us to utilise commemoration as a tool to better understand a broad range of historical moments. To take the ostensibly vainglorious and triumphant celebrations which characterised the practices of commemoration deployed by the British during the late nineteenth century as an example, we have shown that these acts were somewhat counterintuitively not an expression of the confidence which is so often attributed to the era of high imperialism, so much as they were responses to a range of deep-seated anxieties which riddled the imperial project. From the growth and consolidation of liberalism and radicalism within the metropole, to growing unrest in the subcontinent, and from fears of the deterioration of British martial capabilities stemming from the army's failures during the Boer War, to growing German militarism, commemoration responded to a broad range of anxiety-provoking concerns which helped define the lived reality of the colonial experience during the high noon of empire. Constructing a victorious memory of 1857 designed to reassure the colonial community of the resilience of the British Raj, whilst at the same time encouraging them to emulate the glorious deeds of an earlier generation of soldier heroes who saved the empire in its hour of need, commemoration served an important role within the imperial project.

If the construction of public memory concerning the British empire has been keenly pursued in both colonial and post-colonial settings, then this must be understood as both a positive and a negative endeavour. Much as an artist chisels away and discards more marble than he keeps when working on a sculpture, so too does commemoration discard all that which is considered extraneous to what should be remembered when deciding who and what is deserving of monumentalisation. For this reason, it is as important to note what has been forgotten when evaluating practices of commemoration as it is to pay attention to what has been remembered. An illustrative example of this is apparent when considering how British memory of the conflict changed over the course of the first year which followed its outbreak, and how this shift was reflected in the amendments made by Sir Joseph Noel Paton to his commemorative painting, *In Memoriam*. Shifting from an anxious portrayal of the conflict which focused on the fate of the imprisoned women in Cawnpore to a victorious celebration of imperial victory exemplified by Lucknow, Paton's painting underwent a significant transformation and reselection of available memory en route to its final form. Paton's painting is also interesting, however, because it not only captures the malleability of public memory, but it also comes to symbolise how what is forgotten can continue to echo in the present. Thus, when read as a palimpsest, Paton's painting reveals both a popular desire to (re)remember the mutiny as a glorious victory, at the same moment as it betrays the lingering doubts, fears, and anxieties that continued to haunt the imperial project in the years that followed the conflict.

The same interplay between remembering and forgetting is apparent when considering how 1857 was commemorated by the colonial administration, in general, and Viceroy Lord Canning, in particular, during the first two decades that followed the conflict. Forming an essential component of the government's avowed policy of post-mutiny reconciliation and consolidation which bridged the transfer of power to the Crown in the immediate wake of the mutiny with the 1877 Proclamation Durbar that announced the elevation of Queen Victoria to Empress of India, commemoration played an important role in helping contain the intercommunal enmity that threatened the smooth administration of India over this period. An overwhelmingly active process that veered away from accentuating divisive memories of brutal insurgency and the no less horrifying acts of counter-insurgency whilst steering towards a sanitised memory of the conflict that emphasised the shared exploits and victories of British and Indian soldiers portrayed as fighting shoulder to shoulder against an amorphous enemy, commemoration was used to broker reconciliation whilst installing a more productive colonial relationship which would provide the foundations for stable British rule in the decades ahead.

Forgetting the multiple horrors of empire was not only an essential component of British rule, however, it remains an apparently avowed national policy. Though 1857 remained one of the most obsessively commemorated events on Britain's national calendar for ninety years, the conflict was quickly erased from official memory following Indian independence in 1947. As an event that highlights the non-consensual nature of colonial rule, alongside the violence and brutality which was always inherent within the imperial project, the mutiny stands in stark contrast to the tale of modernisation and tutelage which characterises Britain's official narrative of empire. Quietly but deliberately removed from the national calendar resulting in the conspicuous commemorative silence with which its centenary and sesquicentenary were met in Britain, official amnesia in relation to 1857 can once again only be explained in relation to the pursuit of national interests over the past seventy years. In stark contrast to official silence in Britain, the First War of Independence is the subject of widespread commemoration in India today. Whilst the bloody revolt was marginalised within the Congress Party's endorsed history of the Indian Independence Movement which dominated until at least the 1970s, the significance of remembering the armed rebellion as a defining feature of British imperialism remains vital for a broad range of actors today. However, whilst there is a national consensus on the need to remember and commemorate the events of 1857, there is only discord when considering how and why. Accordingly, when the various commemoration ceremonies which are performed by various groups across India today are subjected to careful consideration, the divergent identities, values, and beliefs which characterise the tangled condition of India's national memory, as much as the current Indian polity, come to the fore.

When treated diachronically, therefore, the commemoration of empire in colonial and post-colonial settings reveals the extent to which the past is in a perpetual state of becoming, as it is repeatedly (re)remembered within the ever-changing conditions of the present. Less because of what it says about the past and more because of what it tells us about the present, therefore, the history of empire remains a greatly controversial topic. Whilst this book has focused on India and the commemoration of 1857 over the past 160 years, there remains much more work to be done of this type. In particular, comparative research contrasting the practices of commemoration employed in different colonial settings by diverse European nations promises to teach us much about the differences and similarities of the experience of empire of the various imperial powers, as well as how it is remembered and conceived by them today. Equally, comparative research into how nations recovering from the trauma of European imperialism construct and represent their colonial pasts promises to tell us much about their divergent histories since they emerged from colonial domination. With memories of European imperialism proving as contingent and contested as they are malleable and mutable, the struggles for meaning, memory, and the right to narrate which have been waged through practices of commemoration show no sign of abating and, as continued debate over the future of colonial era place names and monuments proves, the past will continue to be (re)written in the future.

Bibliography

Manuscript Sources

British Library, London

Add. MS 37151, 'Account by the Rev. Thomas Moore, chaplain to the forces at Cawnpore, of events at Cawnpore, Lucknow, etc.'.

Add. MS 37152 B, Thomas Moore, 'Plan of the three advances on Lucknow'.

Add. MS 46168, Journals of Mary Enid Evelyn Layard, 'Vol. XVI, 5 August 1903–14 April 1906'.

British Library, London, the Oriental and India Office Collections

India Office Records

IOR/L/MIL/7/10672, 'Regimental Colors & Appointments, Honorary Distinctions & Titles 1871, 16th (Lucknow) Bengal Infantry Grant of Design of "Turreted Gateway" for Colours'.

IOR/P/191/4, Proceedings of the PWD, Jan 1864–Feb 1864.

IOR/P/191/5, India Proceedings, Public Works Department, Military Works, Mar 1864–Dec 1864.

IOR/P/191/7, India Proceedings, Public Works Department, Civil Works Buildings, Aug 1864–Dec 1864.

IOR/P/239/41, Punjab Proceedings, Public Works, Sep 1864–Dec 1864.

IOR/P/239/42, Punjab Proceedings, Public Works, Jan 1865–Mar 1865.

IOR/P/435/9, India Proceedings, Public Works Department, Aug 1869.

IOR/P/977, India Proceedings, Public Works, Military Works, 1876–1877.

IOR/L/PJ/6/1776 File 7098, 'The Lord Lawrence Statue, Lahore: Change of Inscription and Questions of Its Removal'.

IOR/L/PJ/6/591 File 142, 'Admission of Natives to the Cawnpore Memorial Gardens'.

IOR/L/PJ/7/12506, '10893 Disposal of Union Jack Flown at Residency'.

IOR/L/PJ/8/128 Coll. 105/A, Films Offensive to Indian Public Opinion Pts. XIII–XIX.

IOR/L/PS/6/455, Political Letters and Dispatches to India, Vol. 1, Oct 1858–Aug 1861, 31 August 1859, No. 24.

IOR/L/PS/6/459, Collections to India Political Dispatches, Vol. 1, 1858, Col. 4.

IOR/L/PS/6/463, Collections to India Political Dispatches, Vol. 5, 1858, Col. 36/18.

IOR/L/PWD/3/336, Collections to Public Works Dispatches to India: Nos. 1–4, 1861, Col. 83.

IOR/L/PWD/3/344, Collections to Public Works Dispatches to India: Nos. 1–18, 1863, Col. 9.

IOR/R/1/1/3228, 'Objectionable Speeches Made by Maulvi Nur-ud Din Behari and Musammat Satyavati Devi on the Occasion of the Anniversary Celebrations of the Rani of Jhansi at Gwalior'.

IOR/R/4/82, 'File 11 Historical Monuments in India'.

IOR/R/4/84, 'File 11/1b Historical Monuments in India: Mutiny Memorial Well at Cawnpore'.

IOR/R/4/86, 'File 12/1 Monuments: Regimental Colours in Churches in India and Pakistan'.

IOR/R/4/87, 'File 12a Military Memorials of the Argyll and Sutherland Highlanders in India and Pakistan'.

IOR/V/10/14, India Administration Report 1860–61.

IOR/V/10/15, 'Report on the Administration of the North-Western Provinces for the Year 1860–61', Administration Reports of the Government of India.

IOR/V/24/3277, 'Report of Proceedings in the Public Works Department 1861–62'.

IOR/V/25/700/83 No. 53, A. E Orr, 'Note on the Arrangements for Unveiling the Telegraph Mutiny Memorial at Delhi, 19 April 1902'.

India Office Private Papers

Mss. Eur. A180, Sir Neville Francis Fitzgerald Chamberlain Papers.

Mss. Eur. A66, John Ryder Oliver Papers.

Mss. Eur. B298/9, 'The Office for the Consecration of the Memorial Well and Adjacent Graves at Cawnpore', Papers of Robert Bensley Thornhill and Family.

Mss. Eur. C144/15, 'Correspondence with Persons in India, Part I', Papers of the Earl of Northbrook as Viceroy of India 1872–76.

Mss. Eur. C144/17, 'Correspondence with Persons in India 1874–75', Papers of the Earl of Northbrook as Viceroy of India.

Mss. Eur. C144/18, 'Correspondence with Persons in India 1876–77', Papers of the Earl of Northbrook as Viceroy of India.

Mss. Eur. D573/1, 'Letter from Morley to Minto', Papers of John Morley as Secretary of State for India.

Mss. Eur. D609/15, 'Letters from Lord Lithgow to Lord Zetland Dated Jan–Jun 1938 and Oct–Dec 1938', Papers of 2nd Marquees of Zetland.

Mss. Eur. D661, 'Memorial Volume of Photographs, Newscuttings, Letters and Souvenirs, Relating to Charlotte Elizabeth Canning', Charlotte Elizabeth Canning Papers.

Mss. Eur. D905, Frederick Sleigh Roberts' Papers.

Mss. Eur. D983, 'Anonymous Diary, Dated Oct–Nov 1861, by a Member of the Judge Advocate General's Department, Bengal, of a Tour through the North-Western Provinces and to the Foothills of the Himalaya, Describing Ancient Monuments and Scenes of the Indian Mutiny'.

Mss. Eur. F111/205, 'Correspondence with People in India, Jan 1902–Jun 1902', Papers of Marquess Curzon of Kedleston.

Mss. Eur. F111/207, 'Correspondence with People in India, Jan 1903–Jun 1903', Papers of Marquess Curzon of Kedleston.

Mss. Eur. F111/210, 'Correspondence with People in India, Jan 1905–Jun 1905', Papers of the Marquess Curzon of Kedleston.

Mss. Eur. F111/441, 'Official Printed Material on India: Miscellaneous Internal Affairs', Papers of Marquess Curzon of Kedleston.

Mss. Eur. F111/560, *Speeches by Lord Curzon of Kedleston Volume II*', Papers of the Marquess Curzon of Kedleston.

Mss. Eur. F127/479, 'Letters from Lord Lawrence, Viceroy of India, to John Strachey as Chief Commissioner of Oudh 1866–68', Strachey Collection.

Mss. Eur. F239/20, 'Cooper's Hill Society: Cooper's Hill Magazine', Cooper's Hill Society Papers.

Mss. Eur. F239/3, 'Committee Meetings', Cooper's Hill Society Papers.

Mss. Eur. F580/4, 'Letters of Major Ashton Cromwell Warner in India to and from His Family', Journals of Captain Richard Warner and Letters of His Son, Major Ashton Cromwell Warner, to and from Friends and Family.

Mss. Eur. F630/1, 'Letters from Rev Thomas Moore to His Mother', Letters of Rev. Thomas Moore and His Wife Dorothy Moore from India.

Mss. Eur. F630/2, 'Thirteen Letters or Journal-Letters from Rev Thomas Moore and Dora Moore to His Mother, and to His Brother Tony Moore. With Typed Transcriptions', Letters of Rev. Thomas Moore and His Wife Dorothy Moore from India.

Mss. Eur. F630/3, 'Letters from Dora Moore to Mrs. Moore', Letters of Rev. Thomas Moore and His Wife Dorothy Moore from India.

Mss. Eur. F630/8, 'A Wooden Miniature Replica of the Memorial Cross, Commemorating the Women and Children of the 32nd Regiment Massacred at Cawnpore on 16 July 1857', Letters of Rev. Thomas Moore and His Wife Dorothy Moore from India.

Photographs

PHOTO 193/(21), 'View of the Site in Cawnpore Which Was to Become the Memorial Garden', Tytler Collection: Photographs by Robert and Harriet Tytler Depicting Buildings and Sites Associated with the Indian Mutiny.

PHOTO 11/(45), 'The Memorial Well Cawnpore', Album of Photographs Mostly by Samuel Bourne.

PHOTO 11/(67), 'Cashmere Gate', Album of Photographs Mostly by Samuel Bourne.

Centre of South Asian Studies Archive, University of Cambridge

61, Reel 28, Canning, 'Miscellaneous Letters to People in India, 1859', The Indian Papers of the Rt. Hon. Charles John Earl Canning (Wakefield: Microform Academic Publishers, 2007).

62, Reel 28, Canning, 'Miscellaneous Letters from the Governor-General to Persons in India, 1860', The Indian Papers of the Rt. Hon. Charles John Earl Canning (Wakefield: Microform Academic Publishers, 2007).

Box 2, No. 19B, Reid Papers.

ms.12720, Reel 36, 'Press Cuttings, Aug 1905–Mar 1907', The Indian Papers of the 4th Earl of Minto (Wakefield: Microform Academic Publishers, 2007).

ms.12735, Reel 38, 'Printed Copies of Correspondence with the Secretary of State for India, Nov 1905–Jun 1906', The Indian Papers of the 4th Earl of Minto (Wakefield: Microform Academic Publishers, 2007).

ms.12741, Reel 41, 'Printed Copies of Telegrams to and from the Secretary of State for India', The Indian Papers of the 4th Earl of Minto (Wakefield: Microform Academic Publishers, 2007).

ms.12742, Reel 41, 'Printed Copies of Telegrams to and from the Secretary of State for India', The Indian Papers of the 4th Earl of Minto (Wakefield: Microform Academic Publishers, 2007).

ms.12764, Reel 47, 'Printed Copies of Letters and Telegrams to and from Persons in India, Nov 1905–Jun 1906', The Indian Papers of the 4th Earl of Minto (Wakefield: Microform Academic Publishers, 2007).

ms.12766, Reel 48, 'Printed Copies of Letter and Telegrams to and from Persons in India, Jan–Jun 1907', The Indian Papers of the 4th Earl of Minto (Wakefield: Microform Academic Publishers, 2007).

ms.12776, Reel 52, 'Printed Copies of Letters and Telegrams to and from Persons Outside India, 1905–Jun 1908', The Indian Papers of the 4th Earl of Minto (Wakefield: Microform Academic Publishers, 2007).

ms.12686, Reel 35, 'Speeches Made by Lord Minto 1905–10', The Indian Papers of the 4th Earl of Minto (Wakefield: Microform Academic Publishers, 2007).

Imperial War Museum, London

Box 71-21-5-6, 'Mutiny – Gurka', Private Papers of Lieutenant General Sir Francis Tuker.

Box 71/21/13, '2 Photograph Albums and 2 Envelopes of Loose Photographs', Private Papers of Lieutenant General Sir Francis Tuker.

Box 71/21/14/2, 'Delhi Day Programme', Private Papers of Lieutenant General Sir Francis Tuker.

Q 69821, 'Photo by Felice Beato of Residency in March 1858', Royal Artillery Institution Collection.

Lidell Hart Military Archives, Kings College London

HAMILTON-10-31, 'Correspondence as Colonel of the Gordon Highlanders 1912–49', Papers of Gen. Sir Ian Standish Monteith Hamilton.

Manuscripts and Special Collections, Nottingham University

Wr D52, 'Diaries of Edward M. Wrench, 1907', Papers of Edward M. Wrench.

National Archives of India, Delhi

ASI – Archaeological Survey of India

ASI/3/2/UP/10/1968/M, 'Major General Enaith Habibullah to Director ASI'.

ASI/18/1/10/68-M, 'Report of the Subcommittee for the Promotion of Tourism in Lucknow'.

ASI/Delhi Circle/Monuments/533/1918/Monuments, 'Kabuli Bagh, Delhi'.

ASI/Delhi Circle/Monuments/29/1938/Monuments, 'Kashmiri Gate'.

ASI/Delhi Circle/Monuments/476/1936/Monuments, 'Mutiny Monument'.

ASI/Delhi Circle/Monuments/97D/1913/Monuments, 'Preservation of Kashmiri Gate and Proposal to Drive a Road through It'.

ASI/Delhi Circle/Monuments/D.78/1949/Monuments, 'Kashmiri Gate'.

ASI/HQ/Monuments/22/20/70-M/1970, 'B. N. Chaubey to the Director General ASI'.

ASI/HQ/Monuments/26/112/1972/M, 'Removal of Memorial Stone Slab Affixed on Kashmiri Gate Delhi'.

ASI/HQ/Monuments/26/97/72-M, 'Improvements of Lucknow Residency Premises Suggestion by B. N. Chaubey'.

ASI/HQ/Monuments/561/1930/Monuments – Kashmiri Gate, 'Extract from Major General E.R. Kenyon to the Superintendent, Archaeological Survey, Frontier Circle Lahore, 27 March 1930'.

Public Works Department Proceedings, April 1868 No. 13A, 'Report by on the Expense of Constructing the Delhi Memorial Monument'.

National Archives, Kew, London

*DO – Dominions Office and Commonwealth Relations
and Foreign and Commonwealth Offices*

DO 35/9144, 'Celebrations of Indian Mutiny Centenary in 1957'.

HO – Home Office

HO 45/6857, 'A Form of Prayer and Thanksgiving to Almighty God for the Success Granted to Our Arms in Suppressing the Rebellion and Restoring Tranquility in Her Majesty's Indian Dominions'.

WORK – Office of Works and Successors

WORK 20/34, 'Trafalgar Square: Statue of General Sir Henry Havelock'.
WORK 20/94, 'Statue of Lord Lawrence'.
WORK 20/160, 'Statue of Lord Lawrence: Waterloo Place'.

Rhodes House Library, University of Oxford

*USPG – Papers of the United Society for
the Propagation of the Gospel*

USPG/C/CRIMEA/3, 'Crimean War 1854–6', Papers of the United Society for the Propagation of the Gospel.

USPG/CLR/Calcutta/14, 'Copies of Letters Received', Papers of the United Society for the Propagation of the Gospel.

USPG/CLR/Home/219, 'Copies of Letters Received (HOME)', Papers of the United Society for the Propagation of the Gospel.

USPG/Standing Committee Minutes 1857–9/26, 'Minutes of the Standing Committee, 1857–9', Papers of the United Society for the Propagation of the Gospel.

Royal Engineer's Museum and Library Collection, Gillingham

Professional Papers of the Royal Engineers 9 (1860).

Staffordshire Regiment Museum, Whittington

'Major Kenneth Foulkes Memorial Dedication by Rt. Rev. Sydney Bill', 23 April 1939.

Templar Study Centre, National Army Museum, London

1963-09-26, 'Manuscript Extracts from Letters of Lt Gen. F. C. Maisey Relating to Delhi Palace, 1857; Associated with the Indian Mutiny (1857–1859)', Frederick Charles Maisey Papers.
1965-11-113-14, 'Photograph of Wheeler's Entrenchment Taken by Felice Beato'.
9210/127-72 (C), 'Address by His Excellency Lord Napier of Magdala on the Unveiling of the Outram Statue', Sir James Outram Papers.
9210/127-108, 'Letters Written by Lord Napier of Magdala Regarding the Statue of Outram in Calcutta', Sir James Outram Papers.

The Royal Green Jackets (Rifle) Museum, Winchester

Anon, 'The Delhi Centenary', *The King's Royal Rifle Corps Chronicle*, 1957 (Winchester: Warren & Son, 1905), pp. 126–33.

The Royal School Dungannon Archives, Dungannon

Anon [Censored], to A. de. G. Gaudin, Headmaster of the Royal School Dungannon, 28 December 1956.
R. S. Brownell, Ministry of Education to A. de. G. Gaudin, Headmaster of the Royal School Dungannon, 27 June 1957.
A. de. G. Gaudin, Headmaster of the Royal School Dungannon, to R. S. Brownell, Ministry of Education, 14 December 1957.
Photograph of Mountbatten Unveiling Nicholson's Monument at the Royal School Dungannon.

Published Primary Sources

A Volunteer, *My Journal or What I Did and Saw between the 9th June and 25th November, 1857 with an Account of General Havelock's March from Allahabad to Lucknow* (Calcutta, 1858).
Adjunct General's Office Horse Guards, *Instruction of Musketry 1856* (East Sussex, 2009).
Anon, 'The Lucknow Memorial', Extract from the Express, in: E. H. Hilton (ed.), *The Tourists Guide to Lucknow: In Five Parts* (Lucknow, 1894), Appendix B, 'Extract from the Express', pp. vi–xi.
Anon, *The P&O Pocket Book* (London, 1908).

Baden-Powell, Robert, *Indian Memories: Recollections of Soldering, Sport, ETC.* (London, 1915).

Banerjea, Surendranath, *A Nation in Making: Being the Reminiscences of Fifty Years of Public Life* (London, 1927).

Bloomfield, David (ed.), *Lahore to Lucknow: The Indian Mutiny Journal of Arthur Moffatt Lang* (London, 1992).

Blunt, Edward A. H., 'The Tomb of John Mildenhall', *Journal of the Royal Asiatic Society* 42 (1910), pp. 495–98.

Blunt, Edward A. H., *List of Inscriptions on Christian Tombs and Tablets of Historical Interest in the United Provinces of Agra and Oudh* (Allahabad, 1911).

Blunt, Wilfred Scawen, *India under Ripon: A Private Diary by Wilfrid Scawen Blunt* (London, 1909).

Borges, Jorge Luis, 'Funes the Memorious', in: D. A. Yates and J. E. Irby (eds.), *Labyrinths: Selected Stories and Other Writing* (London, 2000), pp. 87–95.

Boucicault, Dion, 'Jessie Brown, or, the Relief of Lucknow: A Drama in Three Acts', in: P. Thomson (ed.), *Plays by Dion Boucicault* (Cambridge, 1984), pp. 101–32.

Butler, William, *Land of the Veda: Being Personal Reminiscences of India Its Religions, Mythology, Principal Monuments, Palaces, and Mausoleums* (New York, 1872).

Chatterji, Basudev and Sarvepalli Gopal (eds.), *Towards Freedom: Documents on the Movement for Independence in India, 1938, Part 1* (New Delhi, 1999).

Christie, W. H. John, *Morning Drum* (London, 1983).

Clark, Francis E., *Our Journey around the World* (Hartford, 1895).

Cotton, Sophia A. (ed.), *Memoir of George Edward Lynch Cotton, D.D., Bishop of Calcutta, and Metropolitan: With Selections from His Journals and Correspondence* (London, 1871).

Crawshay, George, *Proselytism Destructive of Christianity and Incompatible with Political Dominion: Speech of Mr. Crawshay at the India House on the Vote of Annuity to Sir John Lawrence August 25, 1858* (London, 1858).

Darling, Malcolm, *Apprentice to Power: India 1904–1908* (London, 1966).

Dickens, Charles, *Little Dorrit* (London, 1953).

Ewart, John Alexander, *The Story of a Soldiers Life or Peace, War and Mutiny* (London, 1881).

Fanshawe, Herbert Charles, *Delhi: Past and Present* (London, 1902).

Field, Henry Martyn, *From Egypt to Japan* (New York, 1905).

Fitzmaurice, Edmond, *The Life of Granville George Leveson Gower Second Earl Granville 1815–1891* (London, 1905).

Forbes, Edgar Allen, *Twice around the World* (New York, 1912).

Forbes-Mitchell, William, *Reminiscences of the Great Mutiny 1857–59 Including the Relief, Siege, and Capture of Lucknow, and the Campaigns in Rohilcund and Oude* (London, 1910).

Fowle, Fulwar William, *A Thank-Offering for the Quelling of Mutiny and Rebellion in India, and for the Preservation of Dear Children in That Land of Horrors and Heroes* (Salisbury, 1859).

Fraser, John Foster, *Round the World on a Wheel* (London, 1907).

Gandhi, Mahatma, 'Discussion with Neil Statue Volunteers 6 and 7 September 1927', *The Hindu*, 10 September 1927, in: *The Collected Works of Mahatma Gandhi,* Vol. XXXX (Electronic Book), (New Delhi, 1999) No. 22, pp. 34–44.

Gandhi, Mahatma, 'Insolent Reminders', *Young India*, 25 August 1927, in: The Collected Works of Mahatma Gandhi, Vol. XXXIX (Electronic Book), (New Delhi, 1999), pp. 453–55.

Gandhi, Mahatma, 'Speech at Royapuram, Madras', 7 September 1927, in: The Collected Works of Mahatma Gandhi, Vol. XXXX (Electronic Book), (New Delhi, 1999) No. 24, pp. 51–53.

Gandhi, Mahatma, 'The Neill Statue and Non-Violence', *Young India*, 29 September 1927, in: The Collected Works of Mahatma Gandhi, Vol. XXXX (Electronic Book), (New Delhi, 1999) No. 105, pp. 178–80.

Gandhi, Mahatma, *The Hindu*, Quoted in: Mahatma Gandhi, 'Insolent Reminders', *Young India*, 25 August 1927, in: The Collected Works of Mahatma Gandhi, Vol. XXXIX (Electronic Book), (New Delhi, 1999) No. 448, pp. 453–55.

Griffiths, Charles John, *A Narrative of the Siege of Delhi with an Account of the Mutiny at Ferozepore in 1857*, H. J. Yonge (ed.) (London, 1910).

Gubbins, Martin Richard, *An Account of the Mutinies in Oudh and the Siege of the Lucknow Residency* (London, 1858).

Hardie, James Keir, *India: Impressions and Suggestions* (London, 1909).

Herber, Reginald and Amelia Herber, *Narrative of a Journey through the Upper Provinces of India, from Calcutta to Bombay, 1824–25 Volume 1* (London, 1873).

Hilton, Edward H., *The Tourists Guide to Lucknow: In Five Parts* (Lucknow, 1894).

Hodder, Edwin, *Cities of the World: Their Origin, Progress, and Present Aspect* (London, 1882).

Hutchinson, George, *Narrative of the Mutinies in Oude* (London, 1859).

Inglis, Julia, *The Siege of Lucknow: A Diary* (London, 1892).

Jackson, John, *In Leper-Land: Being a Record of My Tour of 7,000 Miles among Indian Lepers Including Some Notes on Missions and an Account of Eleven Days with Miss Mary Reed and Her Lepers* (London, 1901).

Kavanagh, Thomas Henry, *How I Won the Victoria Cross* (London, 1860).

Keene, Henry George, *A Handbook for Visitors to Lucknow: With Preliminary Notes on Allahabad and Cawnpore* (Calcutta, 1875).

Kennedy, David, 'Singing Round the World', in: M. Kennedy (ed.), *The Scottish Singer: Reminiscences of His Life and Work and Singing Round the World* (Paisley, 1887).

Kerr, James Campbell, *Political Trouble in India 1907–1917* (Calcutta, 1917).

Landon, Perceval, *1857: In Commemoration of the 50th Anniversary of the Indian Mutiny* (London, 1907).

Lang, Arthur Moffatt, *Lahore to Lucknow: The Indian Mutiny Journal of Arthur Moffatt Lang*, D. Bloomfield (ed.) (London, 1992).

Lee, Joseph, *The Indian Mutiny: And In Particular, a Narrative of the Events at Cawnpore, June and July, 1857*, 2nd edn. (Cawnpore, 1893).

Low, Sidney, *A Vision of India* (London, 1911).

Macaulay, Thomas Babington, *The Complete Works of Lord Macaulay, Vol. 11, Speeches, Poems and Miscellaneous Writing*, Vol. 1 (London, 1898).

Martin, E. J., 'Delhi Memorial Monument', in: Major A. M. Lang (ed.), *Professional Papers on Indian Engineering 2nd Series*, Vol. IV, No. CLIX (Roorkee, 1875), pp. 199–208.

Menon, Kasturi Gupta, *The Residency: Lucknow* (New Delhi, 2003).

Menzies, Amy Charlotte Bewicke and Lord William Beresford, *V.C.: Some Memories of a Famous Sportsman, Soldier and Wit* (New York, 1917).

Metcalfe, Henry, *The Chronicle of Private Henry Metcalfe*, F. Tuker (ed.) (London, 1953).

Milman, Frances M. (ed.), *Memoir of the Rt. Rev. Robert Milman* (London, 1879).

Moffat, James Clement, *The Story of a Dedicated Life* (New Jersey, 1887).

Moore, Thomas, *Guide to the Model of the Residency, Lucknow, Deposited in the Museum by the Rev. T. Moore* (Lucknow, 1885).

Munson, Arley, *Jungle Days: Being the Experiences of an American Woman Doctor in India* (New York, 1913).

Murray, Hallam A. H., *The High-Road of Empire* (London, 1903).

Murray-Aynsley, Harriet, *Our Visit to Hindostan, Kashmir and Ladakh* (London, 1879).

Narayan, R. K., *Lawley Road and Other Stories* (New Delhi, undated [1956]).

Nehru, Jawaharlal, 'Centenary Celebrations of the 1857 Movement, Note to the Home Ministry, 26 August 1956', in: H. Y. Sharada Prasad, A. K. Damodaran and H. Mushirul (eds.), *Selected Works of Jawaharlal Nehru Vol. 34, 21 June–31 August 1956* (New Delhi, 2005a), pp. 464–65.

Nehru, Jawaharlal, 'The First War of Independence: Speech Made at Delhi's Ramlila Grounds on 10 May, 1957', in: H. Y. Sharada Prasad, A. K. Damodaran and H. Mushirul (eds.), *Selected Works of Jawaharlal Nehru Vol. 38, 1 May 1957–31 July 1957* (New Delhi, 2005b), pp. 3–15.

Nehru, Jawaharlal, 'What the Congress Stands for, Speech Given at an Election Meeting, Nagpur, 21 February 1957', in: H. Y. Sharada Prasad, A. K. Damodaran and H. Mushirul (eds.), *Selected Works of Jawaharlal Nehru Vol. 36, 1 December 1956–21 February 1957* (New Delhi, 2005c), pp. 143–59.

Nehru, Jawaharlal, 'Jawaharlal Nehru to Bidan Chandra Roy, 3 August 1957', in: H. Y. Sharada Prasad, A. K. Damodaran and H. Mushirul (eds.), *Selected Works of Jawaharlal Nehru Second Series, Vol. 39, 1 August–31 October 1957* (New Delhi, 2007), pp. 165–66.

North, Charles Napier, *Journal of an English Officer in India* (London, 1858).

North, Marianne, *Recollections of a Happy Life* (New York, 1894).

O'Donnell, Frank Hugh, *A History of the Irish Parliamentary Party* (London, 1910).

Pillai, K. Shankar, *Shankar's Weekly Volume 10, May–November 1957* (New Delhi, 1957).

Purcell, Hugh, *After the Raj: The Late Stayers-on and the Legacy of British India* (New Delhi, 2010).

Rai, Lajpat, *Young India: An Interpretation and a History of the Nationalist Movement from Within* (New York, 1916).

Reed, Stanley, *The Royal Tour in India: A Record of the Tour of TRH the Prince and Princess of Wales in India and Burma, from November 1905 to March 1906* (Bombay, 1906).

Reid, Charles, *Centenary of the Siege of Delhi, 1857–1957: The Defence of the Main Piquet at Hindoo Rao's House and Other Posts on the Ridge* (London, 1957).

Ricalton, James, *India through the Stereoscope: A Journey through Hindustan* (New York, 1907).

Roberts, Frederick Sleigh, *Forty-One Years in India: From Subaltern to Commander-in-Chief* (London, 1901).

Rossetti, Christina, 'In the Round Tower at Jhansi, June 8, 1857', in: M. Corner (ed.), *The Works of Christina Rossetti* (Ware, Heartfordshire, 1995), p. 160.

Russell, William Howard, *My Diary in India, in the Year 1858–9* Vol. 1 (London, 1860).

Russell, William Howard, *The Prince of Wales' Tour: A Diary in India* (London, 1877).

Savarkar, Vinayak Damodar, 'Non-violent pseudo-code', originally published in *Shraddhananda* 10 January 1928, reproduced in Vinayak Damodar Savarkar, *Gandhian Confusion*, No. 12, translated by Swatantryaveer Savarkar Rashtriya Smarak Trust and available as e-book, accessed 3 March 2011 from www.savarkarsmarak.com/bookdetails.php?bid=81

Savarkar, Vinayak Damodar, 'Speech and Action', originally published in *Shraddhananda* 8 December 1927, reproduced in Vinayak Damodar Savarkar, *Gandhian Confusion*, No. 13, translated by Swatantryaveer Savarkar Rashtriya Smarak Trust and available as e-book, accessed 3 March 2011 from www.savarkarsmarak.com/bookdetails.php?bid=81

Savarkar, Vinayak Damodar, *Indian War of Independence, 1857* (London, 1909).

Savory, Isabel, *A Sportswoman in India: Personal Adventures and Experiences of Travel in Known and Unknown India* (London, 1900).

Sellar, Walter Carruthers and Robert Julian Yeatman, *1066 and All That* (London, 1930).

Shepherd, William Jonah, *A Personal Narrative of the Outbreak and Massacre at Cawnpore during the Sepoy Mutiny of 1857* (Milton Keynes, 2011).

Sherer, John W., *Havelock's March on Cawnpore 1857: A Civilian's Notes* (London, 1910).

Sherer, John W., *Daily Life during the Mutiny* (Allahabad, 1974).

Spooner, David Brainerd, *Annual Report of the Archaeological Survey of India 1921–22* (Shimla, 1924).

Spurgeon, Charles H., *Spurgeon's Fast-Day Sermon: Fast Day Service Held at the Chrystal Palace on Wednesday, October 7th 1857* (New York, 1857).

Storey, Graham and Kathleen Tillotson (eds.), *The Letters of Charles Dickens*, Vol. VIII, pp. 1856–58 (Oxford: Clarendon Press, 1995).

Talmage, T. DeWitt, *The Earth Girdled* (New Haven, 1896).

Taylor, Meadows, *Seeta* (London, 1872).

Tennyson, Alfred, *The Defence of Lucknow: With a Dedicatory Poem to the Princess Alice* (London, 1879).

The Council of Four, *The Royal Academy Review, A Guide to the Exhibition of the Royal Academy of Arts 1858* (London, 1858).

Thomson, Mowbray, *The Story of Cawnpore* (London, 1859).

Treves, Frederick, *The Other Side of the Lantern* (London, 1913).

Tuker, Francis, *While Memory Serves* (London, 1950).

Tull, Barbara M. (ed.), *Affectionately Rachel: Letters from India, 1860–1884* (Ohio, 1992).

Twain, Mark, *More Tramps Abroad* (London, 1897).

Twain, Mark, *Following the Equator Vol. 2* (New York, 1899).

Twing, Mary A. E., *Twice around the World* (New York, 1898).

Wheeler, George, *India in 1875–6: The Visit of the Prince of Wales* (London, 1876).

Wigram, Francis Spencer, *Mutiny at Meerut, 1857–58: Being Extracts from Letters* (Southampton, 1858).

Newspapers and Periodicals

Anon, '400 Indians Arrested after Anti-British Protests', *The Times*, 12 May 1957, p. 10.

Anon, '"1857" Indian Mutiny Golden Commemoration, Daily Telegraph Christmas Dinner at the Albert Hall, to the Veterans Who Survive, In the Chair Lord Roberts', *The Daily Telegraph*, 18 November 1907, p. 11.

Anon, 'Advert', *The Times*, 28 September 1907, p. 7, Col. 5.

Anon, 'An Episode at Delhi', *The Manchester Guardian*, 12 June 1907, p. 7.

Anon, 'BJP to Protest if UK Celebrates "Victory in Sepoy Mutiny"', *The Times of India*, 22 September 2007, retrieved 5 July 2013 from http://timesofindia .indiatimes.com/india/BJP-to-protest-if-UK-celebrates-victory-in-Sepoy-Mutiny/ articleshow/2393099.cms

Anon, 'Crisis of the Sepoy Rebellion', *The London Quarterly Review*, Vol. IX (London, 1858), pp. 530–70, pp. 557–58.

Anon, 'Disturbed India', *Nottingham Evening Post*, 10 May 1907, p. 4.

Anon, 'From Our Own Correspondent', *London Daily News*, 10 December 1857, p. 5.

Anon, 'Editorial', *The Dublin Builder*, 15 November 1861, p. 689.

Anon, 'Editorial', *The Times of India*, 6 November 1874, p. 2.

Anon, 'Everything Waits for Mr Nehru: Indian Prime Minister Returns to Pressing Problems', *The Times*, 15 July 1957, p. 8.

Anon, 'Exhibition of the Royal Academy', *The Times*, 22 May 1858, p. 9.

Anon, 'Extraordinary Murders by a European Soldier', *The Times of India*, 5 June 1876, p. 4.

Anon, 'Inauguration of the Edinburgh Monument to the Highlanders', *Aldershot Military Gazette*, 19 April 1862, p. 2.

Anon, 'Indian Affairs', *The Times*, 10 January 1906, p. 4.

Anon, 'Indian Cities – Lucknow', *Macmillan's Magazine Vol. IV. May–October 1861* (Cambridge, 1861) pp. 155–62.

Anon, 'Indian Mutiny Golden Commemoration, "The Daily Telegraph" Christmas Dinner to the Veterans Who Survive', *The Daily Telegraph*, 24 December 1907, pp. 9–12.

Anon, 'Indian Mutiny Veterans', *Gloucester Citizen*, 23 September 1907, p. 4.

Anon, 'Laying the Foundation of the Lucknow Memorial', *Illustrated London News*, 12 March 1864, Issue 1249, pp. 255–56.

Anon, 'Lest we Forget', *Leamington Spa Courier*, 04 October 1907, p. 4.

Anon, 'Memorial in Poona: Rani of Jhansi Statue', *The Times of India*, 24 July 1857 p. 3.

Anon, 'Monument Erected at Lucknow to the 32nd Foot', *Illustrated London News*, 20 May 1899, Issue 3135, pp. 723–24.

Anon, 'Monument Renamed', *The Times of India*, 29 August 1972, p. 4.

Anon, 'President Unveils Statue of Rani Laxmibai', *The Times of India,* 19 June 1958, p. 1.

Anon, 'Removal of Statues: Dr. Lohia's Call, *The Times of India*, 8 June 1957, p. 5.

Anon, 'Riots and Unrest in the Punjab', *The Times*, 22 May 1907, p. 7.

Anon, 'Socialists Launch Satyagraha: Over 103 Arrests in U.P.', *The Times of India*, 11 May 1957, p. 1.

Anon, 'Statue Removed', *The Times of India*, 12 June 1957, p. 8.

Anon, 'Talk of the Studios', *The Critic*, 26 February 1859, p. 208.

Anon, 'The Cawnpore Massacre Memorials', *The Illustrated London News*, 31 October 1874, Issue 1836, pp. 421–22.

Anon, 'The Day of Humiliation', *Bury and Norwich Post*, 13 October 1857, p. 4.

Anon, 'The Government of India', *Reynolds Newspaper*, 19 May 1907, p. 6.

Anon, 'The Morning's News', *Manchester Courier and Lancashire General Advertiser*, 04 May 1907, p. 6, Col. 3.

Anon, 'The Morning's News', *Manchester Courier and Lancashire General Advertiser*, 09 May 1907, p. 6, Col. 3.

Anon, 'The Problem of the Indian Army', *The Spectator*, 16 December 1905, pp. 5–6.

Anon, 'The Unrest in India: Missionaries' Letters', *The Manchester Guardian*, 6 July 1907, p. 6.

Imperialist to the Editor, *The Times*, 6 June 1907, p. 15.

Kelso, Paul, 'Mayor Attacks Generals in Battle of Trafalgar Square', *The Guardian*, 20 October 2000, p. 3.

Landon, Perceval, '"1857" Outbreak of the Mutiny, May 10 at Meerut', *The Daily Telegraph*, 10 May 1907, p. 5.

London, Correspondant, 'Gossip from the Capital', *Lancashire Evening Post*, 26 September 1907, p. 2.

O'Donnell, Charles James to the editor, *The Times*, 10 June 1907, p. 4.

O'Donnell, Frank Hugh, 'A Triple Reparation', *The Times*, 6 June 1907, p. 15.

Pook, Sally, 'Sikhs Want to Remove Raj Hero's Road Name', *The Telegraph*, 23 May 2002, retrieved 23 July 2011 from www.telegraph.co.uk/news/uknews/1395078/Sikhs-want-to-remove-Raj-heros-road-name.html

Pradhan, Sharat, 'Indian Nationalists Outraged by Colonial Tribute', *Reuters*, 25 September 2007, retrieved 5 July 2013 – from http://in.reuters.com/article/2007/09/24/idINIndia-29695920070924

Wood, Field Marshal Sir Evelyn, 'Revolt in Hindustan, 1857–9', *The Times*, 30 September 1907, p. 11.

Parliamentary Debates

HC Deb – House of Commons Debate

HC Deb, 27 January 1902, vol. 101
HC Deb, 29 November 1937, vol. 329
HC Deb, 06 December 1937, vol. 330

HL Deb – House of Lords Debate

HL Deb, 9 June 1857, vol. 145
HL Deb, 6 July 1972, vol. 332

Lok Sabha Debates

Lok Sabha Debates, English Version, 14th Series, Vol. XXV, 10th Session, Col. 1

Published Secondary Sources

Allen, Brian, 'The Indian Mutiny and British Painting', *Apollo*, 132 (September 1990).

Allen, Charles, *A Glimpse of the Burning Plain: Leaves from the Indian Journals of Charlotte Canning* (London, 1986).

Amin, Shahid, *Event, Metaphor Memory: Chauri-Chaura, 1922–92* (New Delhi, 1995).

Amin, Shahid, 'A Hanging Twice Over', *Outlook India*, 26 March 2007.

Anderson, Benedict, *Imagined Communities: Reflections on the Origin and Spread of Nationalism* (London, 2006).

Anderson, Clare, *Indian Uprising of 1857–8: Prisons, Prisoners, and Rebellion* (London, 2007).

Anderson, Olive, 'The Administrative Reform Association of 1855', *Victorian Studies* 8 (1965), pp. 231–42.

Anon, *The Story of the Cawnpore Mission* (Westminster, 1909).

Assmann, Aleida, 'Canon and Archive', in: A. Erll and N. Ansgar (eds.), *Cultural Memory Studies: An International and Interdisciplinary Handbook* (New York, 2008), pp. 97–109.

Assmann, Aleida, 'From Collective Violence to a Common Future: Four Models for Dealing with a Traumatic Past', in: H. Gonçalves da Silva et al. (eds.), *Conflict, Memory Transfers and the Reshaping of Europe* (Newcastle upon Tyne, 2010), pp. 8–23.

Assmann, Jan, 'Communicative and Cultural Memory', in: A. Erll and A. Nunning (eds.), *Cultural Memory Studies: An International and Interdisciplinary Handbook* (New York, 2008), pp. 109–18.

Baker, Bruce E., *What Reconstruction Meant: Historical Memory in the American South* (Charlottesville, 2007).

Ball, Charles, *The History of the Indian Mutiny* (London, 1959).

Barrier, N. Gerald, 'The Punjab Disturbances of 1907: The Response of the British Government in India to Agrarian Unrest', *Modern Asian Studies* 1 (1967), pp. 353–83.

Bates, Crispin (ed.), *Mutiny at the Margins. New Perspective on the Indian Uprising of 1857. Vol. 5: Muslim, Dalit and Subaltern Narratives* (London, 2014).

Bates, Crispin and Andrea Major (eds.), *Mutiny at the Margins: New Perspectives on the Indian Uprising of 1857, Vol. 2: Britain and the Indian Uprising* (London, 2013).

Bates, Crispin and Marina D. Carter, 'An Uneasy Commemoration: 1957, the British in India and the "Sepoy Mutiny"', in: C. Bates (ed.), *Mutiny at the Margins, Volume 6, Perceptions, Narration and Reinvention: The Pedagogy and Historiography of the Indian Uprising* (London, 2014), pp. 113–35.

Bender, Jill C., *The 1857 Uprising and the British Empire* (Cambridge, 2016).

Bender, Jill C., 'Ireland and Empire', in: R. Bourke and I. McBridge (eds.), *The Princeton History of Modern Ireland* (Princeton, 2016), pp. 343–60.

Bentley, Nicolas (ed.), *Russell's Despatches from the Crimea 1854–1856* (New York, 1966).

Berger, Stefan and Bill Niven (eds.), *Writing the History of Memory* (London, 2014).

Bergson, Henri, and Nancy M. Paul and William Scott Palmer (trans.), *Matter and Memory: Essay on the Relation of Body and Spirit* (New York, 1988).

Bhalla, Alok, *Stories about the Partition of India*, Vols. I–III (New Delhi, 2012).

Blunt, Alison, 'Embodying War: British Women and Domestic Defilement in the Indian Mutiny', *Journal of Historical Geography* 26 (2000), pp. 403–28.

Blunt, Alison, 'Spatial Stories under Siege: British Women Writing from Lucknow', in: R. Lewis and S. Mills (eds.), *Feminist Postcolonial Theory: A Reader* (New York, 2003), pp. 720–39.

Bodnar, John E., *Remaking America: Public Memory, Commemoration, and Patronism in the Twentieth Century* (Princeton, 1994).

Brown, Judith M., *Gandhi's Rise to Power: Indian Politics 1915–1922* (Cambridge, 1972).

Brown, Rebecca M., 'Inscribing Colonial Monumentality: A Case Study of the 1763 Patna Massacre Memorial', *The Journal of Asian Studies* 65 (2006), pp. 91–113.

Brantlinger, Patrick, *Rule of Darkness* (Ithaca, 1988).

Bullock, Humphrey, *Indian Cavalry Colours* (London, 1930).

Bullock, Humphrey, *Indian Infantry Colours* (Bombay, 1931).

Burger, Angela Sutherland, *Opposition in a Dominant-Party System: A Study of the Jan Sangh, the Praja Socialist Party, and the Socialist Party in Uttar Pradesh, India* (Berkeley, 1969).

Burroughs, Peter, 'An Unreformed Army?', in: D. Chandler and I. Beckett (eds.), *The Oxford History of the British Army* (Oxford, 2003), pp. 160–88.

Candland, Christopher, 'Congress Decline and Party Pluralism in India', *Journal of International Affairs* 51 (1997), pp. 19–35.

Cannadine, David, *Ornamentalism: How the British Saw Their Empire* (Harmondsworth, 2002).

Carson, Penelope, *The East India Company and Religion, 1698–1858* (Suffolk, 2013).

Catanach, I. J., 'Poona Politicians and the Plague', *South Asia: Journal of South Asian Studies* 7 (1984), pp. 1–18

CCCS, *Making Histories: Studies in History-Writing and Politics* (London, 1982).

Certeau des, Michael, *The Practice of Everyday Life* (Berkeley, 1988).

Chakrabarty, Dipesh, 'Remembering 1857: An Introductory Note', *Economic and Political Weekly* 42 (2007), pp. 1692–95.

Chakravarty, Gautam, *The Indian Mutiny and the British Imagination* (Cambridge, 2005).

Chakravarty, Gautam, 'Mutiny, War, or Small War? Revisiting an Old Debate', in *Mutiny at the Margins, Vol. IV, Military Aspects of the Indian Uprising* (London, 2014), pp. 135–46.

Chand, Tej Pratap, *The Administration of Avadh, 1858–1877* (Varanasi, 1971).

Charlesworth, Neil, The Myth of the Deccan Riots of 1875, *Modern Asian Studies* 6 (1972), pp. 401–21.

Chatterjee, Partha, *The Black Hole of Empire: History of a Global Practice of Power* (Princeton, 2012).

Chick, Noah Alfred, *Annals of the Indian Rebellion* (Calcutta, 1859).

Choudhury, D. K. Lahiri, 'Sinews of Panic and the Nerves of Empire: The Imagined State's Entanglement with Information Panic, India c. 1880–1912', *Modern Asian Studies* 38 (2004), pp. 965–1002.

Chowdhry, Prem, *Colonial India and the Making of Empire Cinema: Image, Ideology and Identify* (Manchester, 2000).

Cohen, Stephen P., 'Issue, Role, and Personality: The Kitchener-Curzon Dispute', *Comparative Studies in Society and History* 10 (1968), pp. 337–55.

Cohn, Bernard, 'Representing Authority in Victorian India', in: E. Hobsbawm and T. Ranger (eds.), *The Invention of Tradition* (Cambridge, 1983), pp. 165–211.

Condos, Mark, *The Insecurity State: Punjab and the Making of Colonial Power in British India* (Cambridge, 2017).

Confino, Alon, 'Collective Memory and Cultural History: Problems of Method', *American Historical Review* 102 (1997), pp. 1386–403.

Connerney, Richard, 'Uda Devi Zindabad? The Assault on History as Illustrated by the History of an Assault', in: R. Connerney (ed.), *The Upside-down Tree: India's Changing Culture* (New York, 2009), pp. 67–79.

Connerton, Paul, *How Societies Remember* (Cambridge, 1989).

Connerton, Paul, 'Seven Types of Forgetting', *Memory Studies* 1 (2008), pp. 59–71.

Coutu, Joan, *Persuasion and Propaganda: Monuments and the Eighteenth-Century British Empire* (London, 2006).

Crooke, William, 'Songs about the King of Oudh', *Indian Antiquary* 40 (1911a), pp. 61–67, pp. 91–92.

Crooke, William, 'Songs of the Mutiny', *Indian Antiquary* 40 (1911b), pp. 123–24, pp. 165–69.

Crownshaw, Richard, 'History and Memorialization', in: S. Berger and B. Niven (eds.), *Writing the History of Memory* (London, 2014), pp. 219–37.

Curtis, Penelope, *Sculpture 1900–1945: After Rodin* (Oxford, 1999)

Curzon, Lord, 'Mutiny Telegraph Memorial, Delhi', in *Speeches by Lord Curzon of Kedleston Volume II* (Calcutta, 1902), pp. 476–80, p. 479, Papers of the Marquess Curzon of Kedleston, Mss Eur F111/560.

Dadabhoy, Bakhtiar, *Barons of Banking: Glimpses of Indian Banking History* (Noida, 2013).

Dalrymple, William, *The Last Mughal: The Fall of a Dynasty, Delhi, 1857* (London, 2006).

Darwin, John, 'British Decolonisation Since 1945: A Pattern or a Puzzle?', *The Journal of Imperial and Commonwealth History* 12 (1984), pp. 187–209.

Darwin, John, *Britain and Decolonization: The Retreat from Empire in the Post-war World* (Basingstoke, 1988).

Darwin, John, 'Memory of Empire in Britain: A Preliminary View', in: D. Rothermund (ed.), *Memories of Post-imperial Nations: The Aftermath of Decolonization, 1945–2013* (Cambridge, 2015), pp. 18–37.

Das, Manmath Nath, *India under Morley and Minto: Politics behind Revolution, Repression and Reforms* (London, 1964).

David, Saul, *The Indian Mutiny* (London, 2003).

David, Saul, *The Bengal Army and the Outbreak of the Indian Mutiny* (New Delhi, 2009).

Dawson, Graham, *Soldier Heroes: British Adventure, Empire and the Imagining of Masculinity* (London, 1994).

Deshpande, Prachi, 'The Making of an Indian Nationalist Archive: Lakshmibai, Jhansi, and 1857', *The Journal of Asian Studies* 67 (2008), pp. 855–79.

Devji, Faisal, *The Impossible Indian: Gandhi and the Temptation of Violence* (London, 2012).

Dickens, Charles and Wilkie Collins, 'The Perils of Certain English Prisoners', in: C. Dickens and W. Collins (eds.), *The Lazy Tour of Two Idle Apprentices and Other Stories* (London, 1890), pp. 237–327.

Druce, Robert, 'And to Think That Henrietta Guise Was in the Hands of Such Human Demons!: Ideologies of the Anglo-Indian Novel from 1857–1957', in: C. C. Barfoot and Th.D'haen (eds.), *Shades of Empire in Colonial and Postcolonial Literature* (Amsterdam, 1993), pp. 17–35.

Durkheim, Emile, and Joseph Ward Swain (trans.), *The Elementary Forms of the Religious Life* (London, 1915).

Eck, Diana L., *Benaras: City of Light* (London, 1983).

Edkins, Jenny, *Trauma and the Memory of Politics* (Cambridge, 2003).

Engles, Dagmar, 'The Age of Consent Act of 1891: Colonial Ideology in Bengal', *South Asia Research* 3:2 (1983), pp. 107–31.

English, Barbara, 'The Kanpur Massacres in India in the Revolt of 1857', *Past and Present* 142 (1994), pp. 169–78.

Erll, Astrid, 'Re-Writing as Re-visioning: Modes of Representing the "Indian Mutiny" in British Novels, 1857 to 2000', *European Journal of English Studies* 10 (2006), pp. 163–85.

Evershed, Jonathan, *Ghosts of the Somme: Commemoration and Culture War in Northern Ireland* (Indiana, 2018).

Eyerman, Ron, 'Cultural Trauma: Slavery and the Formation of African American Identity', *Canadian Journal of Sociology* (2003), pp. 1–10.

Faktorovich, Anna, *Rebellion as Genre in the Novels of Scott, Dickens and Stevenson* (North Carolina, 2013).

Farooqui, Mahmood, *Besieged: Voices from Delhi 1857* (New Delhi, 2010).

Faulkner, William, *Requiem for a Nun* (Harmondsworth, 1960).

Fentress, James and Chris Wickham, *Social Memory* (London, 1992).

Fentress, James and Chris Wickham, *Social Memory: New Perspective on the Past* (Oxford, 1992).

F.G.A, The Outlook (3 April 1915), quoted in Lajpat Rai, *Young India: An Interpretation and a History of the Nationalist Movement from Within* (New York: B.W. Huebsch, 1916), p. 106–07.

Finlayson, Geoffrey, *The Seventh Earl of Shaftesbury, 1801–1885* (Vancouver, 2004).

Fischer-Tine, Harald (ed.), *Anxieties, Fear and Panic in Colonial Settings: Empire on the Verge of a Nervous Breakdown* (London, 2016).

Fisher, Michael H., *A Clash of Cultures: Awadh, the British, and the Mughals* (Riverdale, 1987).

Fisher, Michael H., 'Multiple Meanings of 1857 for Indians in Britain', *Economic and Political Weekly* 42 (2007), pp. 1703–09.

Forest, Benjamin and Juliet Johnson, 'Monumental Politics: Regime Type and Public Memory in Post-Communist States', *Post-Soviet Affairs* 27 (2011), pp. 269–88.

Forrest, George W. (ed.), *Selections from the Letters, Despatches and Other State Papers Preserved in the Military Department of the Government of India, 1857–58 Vol. 3* (Calcutta, 1902).

Foucault, Michael, *Foucault Live: Interviews 1966–84* (New York, 1989).

Foucault, Michel, *Discipline and Punish. The Birth of the Prison* (London, 1991).

Frith, Nicola, *The French Colonial Imagination: Writing the Indian Uprisings, 1857–1858, from Second Empire to Third Republic* (Lanham, 2014).

Freud, Sigmund, 'A Note upon the Mystic Writing Pad', in: J. Strachey (ed.), *The Standard Edition of the Complete Psychological Works of Sigmund Freud*, Vol. 19 (London, 1961), pp. 227–32.

Fujitani, T., *Splendid Monarchy: Power and Pageantry in Modern Japan* (Berkeley, 1996).

Geppert, Dominik and Frank Lorenz Müller, *Sites of Imperial Memory: Commemorating Colonial Rule in the Nineteenth and Twentieth Centuries* (Manchester, 2015).

Gilmour, David, *Curzon: Imperial Statesman* (New York, 1994).

Gilroy, Paul, *Postcolonial Melancholia* (New York, 2005).

Gooptu, Sharmistha and Boria Majumdar, *Revisiting 1857. Myth, Memory, History* (New Delhi, 2007).

Gopal, Sarvepalli, *British Policy in India 1858–1905* (Cambridge, 1965).

Goswami, Manu, '"Englishness" on the Imperial Circuit: Mutiny Tours in Colonial South Asia', *Journal of Historical Sociology* 9 (1996), pp. 54–84.

Gottlieb, Robert, *Great Expectations: The Sons and Daughters of Charles Dickens* (London, 2012).

Govinda, Radhika, 'On Whose Behalf? Women's Activism and Identity Politics in Uttar Pradesh', in: R. Jeffery, J. Craig, and L. Jens (eds.), *Development Failure and Identity Politics in Uttar Pradesh* (New Delhi, 2014), pp. 165–87.

Graff, Violette (ed.), *Lucknow: Memories of a City* (New Delhi, 1997).

Green, Ewen H. H., *The Crisis of Conservatism: The Politics, Economics and Ideology of the Conservative Party, 1880–1914*, (London, 1995).

Gregg, Hilda, 'The Indian Mutiny in Fiction', *Blackwood's Edinburgh Magazine* 161 (1897), pp. 218–31.

Groseclose, Barbara S., *British Sculpture and the Company Raj: Church Monuments and Public Statuary in Madras, Calcutta, and Bombay to 1858* (London, 1995).

Guha, Ramachandra, *Gandhi Before India* (London, 2013).

Guha, Ranajit, 'The Prose of Counter-Insurgency', in: R. Guha (ed.), *Subaltern Studies II* (New Delhi, 1983), pp. 45–84.

Gupta, Charu, 'Dalit "Viranganas" and Reinvention of 1857', *Economic and Political Weekly* 42 (2007), pp. 1739–45.

Gupta, Charu, 'Condemnation and Commemoration: (En)Gendering Dalit Narratives of 1857', in: C. Bates (ed.), *Mutiny at the Margins: New Perspectives on the Indian Uprising of 1857 Volume 5, Muslim, Dalit and Subaltern Narratives* (London, 2014).

Gupta, Natayani, 'Delhi's History as Reflected in Its Toponymy', in: M. Dayal (ed.), *Celebrating Delhi* (Penguin, 2010), pp. 95–110.

Habib, Reza and Lars Nyberg, 'Neural Correlates of Availability and Accessibility in Memory', *Cerebral Cortex* 18 (2008), pp. 1720–26.

Halbwachs, Maurice and Lewis A. Coser (trans.), *On Collective Memory* (Chicago, 1992).

Hall, Catherine, 'Turning a Blind Eye: Memories of Empire', in: P. Fara and K. Patterson (eds.), *Memory* (Cambridge, 1998), pp. 27–46.

Hannam, Kevin, 'Contested Representations of War and Heritage at the Residency, Lucknow, India', *International Journal of Tourism Research* 8 (2006), pp. 199–212.

Hansen, Thomas Blom, *The Saffron Wave: Democracy and Hindu Nationalism in Modern India* (New Jersey, 1999).

Hare, Augustus, *The Story of Two Noble Lives Being Memorials of Charlotte, Countess Canning, and Louisa, Marchioness of Waterford Vol. 2* (London, 1893).

Harrington, Peter, *British Artists and War: The Face of Battle in Paintings and Prints, 1700–1914* (London, 1993).

Harrison, Frances W., 'Reviving Heritage in Post-Soviet Eastern Europe: A Visual Approach to National Identity', *Totem: The University of Western Ontario Journal of Anthropology* 20:1 (2012).

Harriss, John, Craig Jeffrey and Stuart Corbridge, 'Is India Becoming the "Hindu Rashtra" Sought by Hindu Nationalists?', *Simons Papers in Security and Development* 60 (2017), pp. 1–31.

Heathorn, Stephen, 'Angel of Empire: The Cawnpore Massacre as a British Site of Imperial Remembrance', *Journal of Colonialism and Colonial History* [Online] 8:3 (2007), accessed 1 February 2011 from http://muse.jhu.edu/journals/journal_of_colonialism_and_colonial_history/v008/8.3heathorn.html

Henderson, Carol E., 'Spatial Memorialising of War in 1857: Memories, Traces and Silences in Ethnography', in: B. Crispin (ed.), *Mutiny at the Margins: New Perspectives on the Indian Uprising of 1857, Vol. 1, Anticipations and Experiences in the Locality* (London, 2013), pp. 217–36.

Heehs, Peter, *The Bomb in Bengal. The Rise of Revolutionary Terrorism in India, 1900–1910* (New Delhi, 1993).

Heehs, Peter, 'Foreign Influences on Bengali Revolutionary Terrorism 1902–1908', in: P. Heehs (ed.), *Nationalism, Terrorism, Communalism: Essays in Modern Indian History* (Oxford, 1998), pp. 68–95.

Henty, George Alfred, *In Times of Peril: A Tale of India* (London, 1881).

Herbert, Christopher, *War of No Pity: The Indian Mutiny and Victorian Trauma* (Aldershot, 2004).

Hibbert, Christopher, *The Great Mutiny* (New York, 1978).

Hobsbawm, Eric and Terence Ranger, *The Invention of Tradition* (Cambridge, 2013).

Hoock, Holger, *Empires of the Imagination* (London, 2010).

Hoppen, Theodore, *The Mid-Victorian Generation, 1846–1886* (Oxford, 2000).

Howell, David, *British Workers and the Independent Labour Party* (Manchester, 1984).

Hussain, Syed Mahdi, *Bahadur Shah Zafar and the War of 1857 in Delhi* (New Delhi, 2006).

Hutchins, Francis G., *The Illusion of Permanence: British Imperialism in India* (Princeton, 1967).

Hyslop, Jonathan, 'The World Voyage of James Keir Hardie: Indian Nationalism, Zulu Insurgency and the British Labour Diaspora 1907–1908', *Journal of Global History* 1 (2006), pp. 343–62.

Jackson, Patrick, *Morley of Blackburn: A Literary and Political Biography of John Morley* (Madison, 2012).

Jaffrelot, Christophe, *The Hindu Nationalist Movement in India* (New York, 1998).

Jaffrelot, Christophe, *India's Silent Revolution: The Rise of the Lower Castes in North India* (London, 2003).

Jaffrelot, Christophe and Louise Tillin, 'Populism in India', in C. R. Kaltwasser et al. (eds.), *The Oxford Handbook of Populism* (Oxford, 2017).

Jeffery, Roger, and Jens Lerche, *Social and Political Change in Uttar Pradesh: European Perspectives* (New Delhi, 2003).

Johnson, David A., 'New Delhi's All-India War Memorial (India Gate): Death, Monumentality and the Lasting Legacy of Empire in India', *Journal of Imperial and Commonwealth History* 46 (2018), pp. 345–66.

Joshi, Priti, 'Mutiny Echoes: India, Britons, and Charles Dickens's "A Tale of Two Cities"', *Nineteenth-Century Literature* 62:1 (2007), pp. 48–87.

Joshi, Puran Chandra, *1857 in Folk Songs* (New Delhi, 1994).

Judd, Denis, Keith Terrance Surridge, and Keith Surridge, *The Boer War: A History* (London, 2013).

Kamra, Sukeshi, *Bearing Witness: Partition, Independence, End of the Raj* (Calgary, 2002).

Kansteiner, Wulf, 'Finding Meaning in Memory: A Methodological Critique of Collective Memory Studies', *History and Theory* 41 (2002), pp. 179–97.

Kaye, John W., *A History of the Sepoy War in India, 1857–1858, Vol. 2* (London, 1870).

Keer, Dhananjay, *Veer Savarkar* (Bombay, 1988).

Keller, Ulrich, *The Ultimate Spectacle: A Visual History of the Crimean War* (Oxford, 2013).

Kent, John, *British Imperial Strategy and the Origins of the Cold War, 1944–49* (Leicester, 1993).

King, Anthony D., *Spaces of Global Cultures: Architecture, Urbanism, Identity* (London, 2004).

Kipling, Rudyard, 'The Undertakers', in: D. Karlin (ed.), *The Jungle Books* (Harmondsworth, 1987), pp. 234–55.

Kipling, Rudyard, 'The Veterans', in: R. T. Jones (ed.), *The Collected Poems of Rudyard Kipling* (Hertfordshire, 1994), p. 315.

Klein, Ira, 'Materialism, Mutiny and Modernization in British India', *Modern Asian Studies* 34 (2000), pp. 545–80.

Kothari, Rajni, 'The Congress "System" in India', *Asian Survey* 14 (1964), pp. 1161–73.

Lahiri, Nayanjot, 'Commemorating and Remembering 1857: The Revolt in Delhi and Its Afterlife', *World Archaeology* 35 (2003), pp. 35–60.

Laine, James W., *Shivaji: Hindu King in Islamic India* (New Delhi, 2003).

Lalumia, Matthew, 'Realism and Anti-Aristocratic Sentiment in Victorian Depictions of the Crimean War', *Victorian Studies* 27 (1983), pp. 25–51.

Lankauskas, Gediminas, 'Sensuous (Re)Collections: The Sight and Taste of Socialism at Grutas Statue Park, Lithuania', *Senses and Society* 1 (2006), pp. 27–52.

Legg, Stephen, 'Sites of Counter Memory: The Refusal to Forget and the Nationalist Struggle in Colonial Delhi', *Historical Geography* 33 (2005), pp. 180–201.

Lipton, Michael and John Firn, *The Erosion of a Relationship: India and Britain Since 1960* (London, 1975).

Loftus, Elizabeth F. and Geoffrey R. Loftus, 'On the Permanence of Stored Information in the Human Brain', *American Psychologist* 35 (1980), pp. 409–20.

London, Christopher W., *Architecture in Victorian and Edwardian India* (Bombay, 1994).

Lothspeich, Pamela, 'Unspeakable Outrages and Unbearable Defilements: Rape Narratives in the Literature of Colonial India', *Postcolonial Text* 3 (2007), pp. 1–19.

Louis, Wm. Roger and Ronald Robinson, 'The Imperialism of Decolonization', *The Journal of Imperial and Commonwealth History* 22 (1994), pp. 462–511.

Llewellyn-Jones, Rosie, *Engaging Scoundrels: True Tales of Old Lucknow* (New Delhi, 2000).

Llewellyn-Jones, Rosie (ed.), *Lucknow. City of Illusion* (Munich, 2006).

Llewellyn-Jones, Rosie, 'Africans in the Indian Mutiny', *History Today* 459 (2009), pp. 40–47.

Llewellyn-Jones, Rosie, *The Great Uprising in India 1857–58: Untold Stories Indian and British* (London, 2009).

Luvass, Jay, *The Education of an Army: British Military Thought, 1815–1940* (London, 1964).

Lynn, Martin (ed.), *The British Empire in the 1950s: Retreat or Revival?* (Basingstoke, 2006).

Macdonald, Robert H., *Sons of the Empire: The Frontier and the Boy Scout Movement, 1890–1918* (Toronto, 1993).

Macdonald, Robert H., *The Language of Empire: Myths and Metaphors of Popular Imperialism 1880–1918* (Manchester, 1994).

Mace, Rodney, *Trafalgar Square: Emblem of Empire* (London, 1976).

Mackenzie, John M., *Propaganda and Empire: The Manipulation of British Public Opinion, 1880–1960* (Manchester, 1984).

Mackenzie, John M. (ed.), *Imperialism and Popular Culture* (Manchester, 1986).

Mackenzie, John M. (ed.), *Popular Imperialism and the Military: 1850–1950* (Manchester, 1992).

Maclagan, Michael, *Clemency Canning: Charles John, 1st Earl Canning, Governor-General and Viceroy of India, 1856–1862* (London, 1962).

Major, Andrea, "'Spiritual Battlefields": Evangelical Discourse and Writings of the London Missionary Society', in C. Bates and A. Major (eds.), *Mutiny at the Margins: New Perspectives on the Indian Uprising of 1857*, Vol. 2, Britain and the Indian Uprising (London, 2013), pp. 50–74.

Majumbar, Rochona and Dipesh Chakrabarty, 'Mangal Pandey: Film and History', *Economic and Political Weekly* 42 (2007), pp. 1771–78.

Malik, Salahuddin, *1857. War of Independence or Clash of Civilizations?* (Oxford, 2008).

Markovits, Stefanie, *The Crimean War in the British Imagination* (Cambridge, 2013).

Mazumdar, Shaswati, *Insurgent Sepoy: Europe Views the Revolt of 1857* (New Delhi, 2011).

Mcgarr, Paul M., "'The Viceroys Are Disappearing from the Roundabouts in Delhi": British Symbols of Power in Post-colonial India', *Modern Asian Studies* 49 (2015), pp. 787–831.

Mckenzie, Precious, *The Right Sort of Woman: Victorian Travel Writers and the Fitness of an Empire* (Newcastle, 2012).

Mehrotra, Sri Ram, *The Emergence of the Indian National Congress* (New Delhi, 1971).

Mehta, Asoka, *1857: The Great Rebellion* (Bombay, 1946).

Menon, Kalyani Devaki, *Everyday Nationalism: Women of the Hindu Right in India* (Philadelphia, 2010).

Metcalf, Thomas R., *The Aftermath of Revolt: India, 1857–1870* (New Delhi, 1990).

Metcalf, Thomas R., *The New Cambridge History of India, III.4, Ideologies of the Raj* (Cambridge, 1995).

Mill, John Stuart, *A System of Logic Ratiocinative and Inductive Vol. 1* (London, 1843).

Misra, Amaresh, *Mangal Pandey: The True Story of an Indian Revolutionary* (New Delhi, 2005).

Misra, Amaresh, *War of Civilisations: India AD 1857*, 2 Vols. (New Delhi, 2008).

Misztal, Barbara A., *Theories of Social Remembering* (Philadelphia, 2003).

Mollo, Boris, *The Indian Army* (Poole, 1981).

Moore, Grace, *Dickens and Empire: Discourses of Class, Race and Colonialism in the Words of Charles Dickens* (Aldershot, 2004).

Morris, Henry, *George Hutchinson: A Brief Memorial of a Holy and Useful Life* (London, 1900).

Morris, Jan and Simon Winchester, *Stones of Empire. The Building of the Raj* (Oxford–New York, 1983).

Mukharji, Projit Bihari, 'Jessie's Dream at Lucknow: Popular Memorialisations of Dissent, Ambiguity and Class in the Heart of Empire', *Studies in History* 24 (2008), pp. 77–113.

Mukharji, Projit Bihari, 'Ambiguous Imperialisms: British Subaltern Attitudes towards the "Indian War"', in: C. Bates and A. Major (eds.), *Mutiny at the Margins; New Perspectives on the Indian Uprising of 1857* Vol. II (New Delhi, 2013), pp. 110–34.

Mukherjee, Rudrangshu, '"Satan Let Loose Upon the Earth": The Kanpur Massacres in India in the Revolt of 1857', *Past and Present* 128 (1990), pp. 92–116.

Mukherjee, Rudrangshu, *Spectre of Violence: The 1857 Kanpur Massacres* (New Delhi, 1998).

Mukherjee, Rudrangshu, *Awadh in Revolt, 1857–1858: A Study of Popular Resistance*, 2nd edn. (London, 2002).

Mukherjee, Rudrangshu, *Mangal Pandey: Brave Martyr or Accidental Hero?* (New Delhi, 2005).

Nadkarni, Maya, 'The Death of Socialism and the Afterlife of Its Monuments: Making and Marketing the Past in Budapest's Statue Park Museum', in: K. Hodgkin and S. Radstone (eds.), *Memory, History, Nation: Contested Pasts* (New Jersey, 2005), pp. 193–207.

Nagai, Kaori, 'The Writing on the Wall', *Interventions International Journal of Postcolonial Studies* 7 (2006), pp. 84–96.

Nanda, Meera, *The God Market: How Globalization Is Making India More Hindu* (New Delhi, 2009).

Narayan, Badri, *Women Heroes and Dalit Assertion in North India: Culture, Identity and Politics* (New Delhi, 2006).

Narayan, Badri, 'Reactivating the Past: Dalits and Memories of 1857', *Economic and Political Weekly* 42 (2007), pp. 1734–38.

Narayan, Badri, *The Making of the Dalit Public in North India, Uttar Pradesh 1950– Present* (New Delhi, 2011).

Narayan, Badri, *Kanshiram: Leader of the Dalits* (New Delhi, 2014).

Narayan, Badri, 'Identity and Narratives: Dalits and Memories of 1857', in: C. Bates (ed.), *Mutiny at the Margins: New Perspectives on the Indian Uprising of 1857 Volume 5, Muslim, Dalit and Subaltern Narratives* (London, 2014), pp. 1–16.

Nayar Pramod K. (ed.), *The Penguin 1857 Reader* (New Delhi, 1857).

Nayder, Lilian, *Unequal Partners: Charles Dickens, Wilkie Collins, & Victorian Authorship* (Ithaca, 2002).

Nelson, Robert and Margaret Olin, 'Destruction/Reconstruction', in: R. Nelson and M. Olin (eds.), *Monuments and Memory, Made and Unmade* (Chicago, 2003), pp. 205–09.

Nietzsche, Friedrich, *The Genealogy of Morals* (New York, 1998).

Noorani, Abdul Gafoor Abdul Majeed, *The Babri Masjid Question 1528–2003: 'A Matter of National Honour'*, 2 vols (New Delhi, 2003).

Nora, Pierre, Lawrence D. Krtizman (eds.) and Arthur Goldhammer (trans.), *Realms of Memory: The Construction of the French Past 3 Vols.* (New York, 1996–98).

Nora, Pierre, Mary Trouille and Davic P. Jordan (trans.), *Rethinking France: Les Lieux de memoire 4 Vols.* (Chicago, 2001–2010).

Nyder, Lillian, 'Class Consciousness and the Indian Mutiny in Dickens's "The Perils of Certain English Prisoners"', *Studies in English Literature, 1500–1900* 32:4 (1992), pp. 689–705.

O'Connor, Daniel, *Three Centuries of Mission. The United Society for the Propagation of the Gospel 1701–2000* (London, 2000).

O'Hanlon, Rosalind, 'Maratha History as Polemic: Low Caste Ideology and Political Debate in Late Nineteenth-Century Western India', *Modern Asian Studies* 17 (1983), pp. 1–33.

Oddie, William, 'Dickens and the Indian Mutiny', *The Dickensian* 68 (1972), pp. 3–15.

Oldenburg, Veena Talwar, *The Making of Colonial Lucknow* (New Delhi, 1989).

Olick, Jeffrey, Vered Vinitzky-Seroussi and Daniel Levy, *The Collective Memory Reader* (Oxford, 2011).

Omissi, David, *The Sepoy and the Raj. The Indian Army, 1860–1940* (London, 1994).

Omvedt, Gail, *Reinventing Revolution: New Social Movements and the Socialist Tradition in India* (New York, 1993).

Omvedt, Gail, *Dalits and the Democratic Revolution: Dr Ambedkar and the Dalit Movement in Colonial India* (London, 1994).

Palmer, Julian Arthur Beaufort, *The Mutiny Outbreak at Meerut in 1857* (Cambridge, 1966).

Pandey, Gyanendra, *Remembering Partition: Violence, Nationalism and History in India* (Cambridge, 2001).

Parker, Elizabeth S., Larry Cahill and James L. McGaugh, 'A Case of Unusual Autobiographical Remembering', *Neurocase: The Neural Basis of Cognition* 12 (2006), pp. 35–49.

Pati, Biswamoy, 'Historians and Historiography: Situating 1857', *Economic and Political Weekly* 42 (2007), pp. 1686–91.

Paxman, Nancy, 'Mobilizing Chivalry: Rape in British Indian Novels about the Indian Uprising of 1857', *Victorian Studies* 36 (1992), pp. 5–30.

Peckham, Robert (ed.), *Empire of Panic: Epidemics and Colonial Anxieties* (Hong Kong, 2015).

Pickering, Paul A. and Alex Tyrrell, *Contested Sites: Commemoration, Memorial and Popular Politics in Nineteenth Century Britain* (Aldershot, 2004).

Pionke, Albert, *Plots of Opportunity: Representing Conspiracy in Victorian England* (Ohio, 2004).

Podeh, Elie, *The Politics of National Celebrations in the Arab Middle East* (Cambridge, 2014).

Pollack, Craig Evan, 'Burial at Srebrenica: Linking Place and Trauma', *Social Science and Medicine* 56 (2003), pp. 793–801.

Porter, Bernard, *The Lion's Share: A Short History of British Imperialism 1850–2004*, 4th edn. (Harlow, 2004).

Porter, Bernard, *Critics of Empire: British Radicals and the Imperial Challenge* (London, 2008).

Powell, Avril Ann, *Muslims and Missionaries in Pre-Mutiny India* (London, 2003).

Prasad, Ram Chandra, *Early English Travelers in India: A Study in the Travel Literature of Elizabethan and Jacobean Periods with Particular Reference to India* (New Delhi, 1980).

Putnis, Peter, 'International Press and the Indian Uprising', in: M. Carter and C. Bates (eds.), *Mutiny at the Margins: New Perspectives on the Indian Uprising of 1857*, Vol. III, Global Perspectives (London, 2013), pp. 1–17.

Prior, Christopher, 'Empire Before Labour: The Scramble for Africa' and the Media, 1880–1899', in: B. Frank, C. Horner and D. Stewart (eds.), *The British Labour Movement and Imperialism* (Newcastle Upon Tyne, 2010), pp. 23–40.

Procida, Mary A., *Married to the Empire: Gender, Politics, and Imperialism in India, 1883–1947* (Manchester, 2002).

Puri, Harish K., *Ghadar Movement: Ideology, Organization and Strategy* (Amritsar, 1983).

Rajagopalan, Mrinalini, 'From Colonial Memorial to National Monument: The Case of the Kashmiri Gate, Delhi', in: M. Rajagopalan and M. Desai (eds.), *Colonial Frames, Nationalist Histories: Imperial Legacies, Architecture and Modernity* (Farnham, 2012), pp. 73–101.

Rajeshwar, Yashasvini and Roy C. Amore, 'Coming Home (Ghar Wapsi) and Going Away: Politics and the Mass Conversion Controversy in India', *Religions* [Online] 10 (2019), www.mdpi.com/2077-1444/10/5/313.

Randall, Don, 'Post-mutiny Allegories of Empire in Rudyard Kipling's Jungle Books', *Texas Studies in Literature and Language* 41 (1998), pp. 97–120.

Randall, Don, 'Autumn 1857: The Making of the Indian "Mutiny"', *Victorian Literature and Culture* 31 (2003), pp. 3–17.

Read, Benedict, 'The British Contribution to Statuemania in the 19th Century', in: C. Chevillot and L.de Margerie (eds.), *La Sculpture au XIXe siècle: Melangés pour Anne Pingeot* (Paris, 2008) pp. 370–77.

Reynolds, Edmund George Barton, *The Lee-Enfield Rifle: Its History and Development from First Designs to the Present Day* (London, 1960).

Roach, James R., 'India's 1957 Election', *Far Eastern Survey* 26 (1957), pp. 65–78.

Robb, Peter, 'The Challenge of Gau Mata: British Policy and Religious Change in India, 1880–1916', *Modern Asian Studies* 20 (1986), pp. 285–319.

Robb, Peter, 'On Rebellion of 1857: A Brief History of an Idea', *Economic and Political Weekly* 42 (2007), pp. 1696–702.

Robinson, Jane, *Angels of Albion. Women of the Indian Mutiny* (USA, 1996).

Rothberg, Michael, 'Remembering Back: Cultural Memory, Cultural Legacies, and Postcolonial Studies', in: G. Huggan (ed.), *The Oxford Handbook of Postcolonial Studies* (Oxford, 2012), pp. 359–79.

Rothermund, Dietmar (ed.), *Memories of Post-imperial Nations: The Aftermath of Decolonization, 1945–2013* (Cambridge, 2015).

Roy, Anjali Gera and Nandi Bhatia, *Partitioned Lives: Narratives of Home, Displacement, and Resettlement* (New Delhi, 2008).

Ruskin, John, *Notes on Some of the Principal Pictures Exhibited in the Rooms of the Royal Academy, the Old and New Societies of Painters in Watercolours, the Society of British Artists, and the French Exhibition, No. IV – 1858* (London, 1858).

Said, Edward, *Orientalism* (London, 2003).

Saint, Tarun K., *Witnessing Partition: Memory, History, Fiction* (Oxford, 2010).

Saksena, Vishu S., *India's Freedom Struggle through India Postage Stamps* (New Delhi, 2000).

Sandage, Scott A., 'A Marble House Divided: The Lincoln Memorial, the Civil Rights Movement, and the Politics of Memory, 1939–1963', *The Journal of American History* 80 (1993), pp. 135–67.

Sarkar, Sumit, *The Swadeshi Movement in Bengal 1903–1908* (New Delhi, 1977).

Savage, Kirk, *Standing Soldiers, Kneeling Slaves: Race, War, and Monument in Nineteenth-Century America* (New Jersey, 1997).

Schudson, Michael, *Watergate in American Memory: How We Remember, Forget, and Reconstruct the Past* (New York, 1993).

Schwartz, Barry, 'Social Change and Collective Memory: The Democratization of George Washington', *American Sociological Review* 56 (1991), pp. 221–36.

Schwartz, Barry, *Abraham Lincoln and the Forge of National Memory* (Chicago, 2000).

Schwartz, Barry and Howard Schuman, 'History, Commemoration, and Belief: Abraham Lincoln in American Memory, 1945–2001', *American Sociological Review* 70 (2005), pp. 183–203.

Schwarz, Bill, *Memories of Empire, Volume I, The White Man's World* (Oxford, 2011).

Scott, James C., *Weapons of the Weak: Everyday Forms of Peasant Resistance* (New Haven, 1985).

Scott, James C., *Domination and the Arts of Resistance: Hidden Transcripts* (New Haven, 1990).

Searle, Geoffrey Russell, *The Quest for National Efficiency: A Study in British Politics and Political Thought, 1899–1914* (Berkeley, 1971).

Searle, Geoffrey Russell, *Eugenics and Politics in Britain, 1900–1914* (Leyden, 1976).

Semmel, Bernard, *Imperialism and Social Reform: English Social-Imperial Thought, 1895–1914* (Cambridge, 1960).

Sen, Indrani, 'Inscribing the Rani of Jhansi in Colonial "Mutiny" Fiction', *Economic and Political Weekly* 42 (2007), pp. 1754–61.

Sen, Surendra Nath, *Eighteen-Fifty-Seven* (New Delhi, 1957).

Shackel, Paul, *Myth, Memory, and the Making of the American Landscape* (Gainesville, 2001).

Sharar, Abdul Halim and Abdulhalim Sharar, *Lucknow: The Last Chapter of an Oriental Culture* (Colorado, 1976).

Sharma, Jyotirmaya, 'History as Revenge and Retaliation: Rereading Savarkar's "The War of Independence of 1857"', *Economic and Political Weekly* 42 (2007), pp. 1717–19.

Sharpe, Jenny, 'Allegories of Empire', *Victorian Studies* 36 (1992), pp. 5–30.

Sharpe, Jenny, *Allegories of Empire: The Figure of Woman in the Colonial Text* (Minneapolis, 1993).

Silvestri, Michael, '"The Sinn Fein of India": Irish Nationalism and the Policing of Revolutionary Terrorism in Bengal', *Journal of British Studies* 39:4 (2000), pp. 454–86.

Singh, Ajit Kumar and Syed Shahid Akhtar Jafri, 'Lucknow: From Tradition to Modernity', *History and Sociology of South Asia* 5 (2011), pp. 143–64.

Singh, Mahendra Prasad and Rekha Saxena, *India at the Polls: Parliamentary Elections in the Federal Phase* (New Delhi, 2003).

Singh, Surya Narain, *The Kingdom of Awadh* (New Delhi, 2003).

Smithurst, Peter, *The Pattern 1853 Enfield Rifle* (Oxford, 2011).

Spear, Percival, *Twilight of the Mughals: Studies in Late Mughal Delhi* (Cambridge, 1951).

Spg, *The Story of the Cawnpore Mission* (Westminster, 1909).

Stanley, Brian, 'Christian Responses to the Indian Mutiny of 1857', in: W. J. Shiels (ed.), *The Church and War* (Oxford, 1983), pp. 277–91.

Steggles, Mary Ann, *Statues of the Raj* (London, 2000).

Steggles, Mary Ann and Richard Barnes, *British Sculpture in India: New Visions and Old Memories* (Norfolk, 2011).

Story, Alfred Thomas, *The Life and Work of Sir Joseph Noel Paton: Her Majesty's Limner for Scotland* (London, 1895).

Strachan, Hew, *Wellington's Legacy: The Reform of the British Army 1830–54* (Manchester, 1984).

Streets, Heather, *Martial Races: The Military, Race and Masculinity in British Imperial Culture 1857–1914* (Manchester, 2004).

Taylor, A. Cameron, *General Sir Alex Taylor G.C.B., R.E.: His Times, His Friends, and His Work Vol. 1* (London, 1913).

The Times, *The History of The Times: The Tradition Established, 1841–1884* (London, 1939).

Thomas, Julia, *Pictorial Victorians: The Inscription of Values in Word and Image* (Ohio, 2004).

Thum, Gregor and Maurus Reinkowski, *Helpless Imperialists: Imperial Failure, Fear, and Radicalization* (Göttingen, 2013).

Tickell, Alex, 'Scholarship Terrorists: The India House Hostel and the "Student Problem" in Edwardian London', in: R. Ahmed and S. Mukherjee (eds.), *South Asian Resistances in Britain, 1858–1947* (London, 2012), pp. 3–18.

Tickell, Alex, *Terrorism, Insurgency and Indian-English Literature, 1830–1947* (Oxford, 2012).

Tinker, Hugh, '1857 and 1957: The Mutiny and Modern India', *International Affairs* 34 (1958), pp. 57–65.

Trevelyan, George Otto, *Cawnpore* (London, 1866).

Trivedi, Dinesh Bihari, *Law and Order in Upper India: A Study of Oudh, 1856–1877* (New Delhi, 1990).

Trotter, Lionel James, *The Life of John Nicholson, Soldier and Administrator; Based on Private and Hitherto Unpublished Documents* (London, 1897).

Tulving, Endel and Zena Pearlstone, 'Availability versus Accessibility of Information in Memory Words', *Journal of Verbal Learning and Verbal Behaviour* 5 (1966), pp. 381–91.

Veer Van Der, Peter, *Imperial Encounters: Religion and Modernity in India and Britain* (Princeton, 2001).

Wagner, Kim, *The Great Fear of 1857: Rumours, Conspiracies and the Making of the Indian Uprising* (Oxford, 2010).

Wagner, Kim, '"Treading upon Fires": The "Mutiny"–Motif and Colonial Anxieties in British India', *Past and Present* 218 (2013), pp. 159–97.

Wagner, Kim, '"Calculated to Strike Terror": The Amritsar Massacre and the Spectre of Colonial Violence', *Past and Present* 233 (2016), pp. 185–225.

Wagner, Kim, *Amritsar 1919: An Empire of Fear and the Making of a Massacre* (London, 2019).

Ward, Andrew, *Our Bones Are Scattered: The Cawnpore Massacre and the Indian Mutiny* (New York, 1996).

Ward, Stuart (ed.), *British Culture and the End of Empire* (Manchester, 2001).

Williams, Gavin (ed.), *Hearing the Crimean War: Wartime Sound and the Unmaking of Sense* (Oxford, 2019).

Winter, Jay, *Sites of Memory, Sites of Mourning: The Great War in European Cultural History* (Cambridge, 1995).

Winter, Jay, 'Sites of Memory', in: S. Radstone and B. Schwarz (eds.), *Memory: Histories, Theories, Debates* (New York, 2010), pp. 312–24.

Woodham-Smith, Cecil, *The Reason Why* (London, 1955).

Wolpert, Andrew, *Remembering Defeat: Civil War and Civic Memory in Ancient Athens* (London, 2002).

Wolpert, Stanley A., *Tilak and Gokhale: Revolution and Reform in Making of Modern India* (Berkeley, 1967).

Woolner, Amy, *Thomas Woolner Sculptor and Poet, His Life in Letters Written* (New York, 1917).

Yadav, Kripal Chandra, *The Revolt of 1857 in Haryana* (Manohar, 1977).

Yalland, Zoe, *Traders and Nabobs: The British in Cawnpore 1765–1857* (Salisbury, 1987).

Yalland, Zoe, *Boxwallahs. The British in Cawnpore 1857–1901* (UK, 1994).

Young, James, 'The Counter-Monument: Memory against Itself in Germany Today', *Critical Inquiry* 18 (1992), pp. 267–96.

Young, James, *The Texture of Memory: Holocaust Memorials and Meaning* (New Haven, 1993).

Young, James, 'Memory/Monument', in: R. S. Nelson and R. Shiff (eds.), *Critical Terms for Art History* (Chicago, 2003), pp. 235–45.

Zavos, John, *The Emergence of Hindu Nationalism in India* (New Delhi, 2000).

Zerubavel, Eviata, *The Elephant in the Room: Silence and Denial in Everyday Life* (Oxford, 2006).

Zerubavel, Yael, *Recovered Roots: Collective Memory and the Making of Israeli National Tradition* (Chicago, 1997).

Index